San Francisco
AND THE BAY AREA

Barry Parr
Photography by Michael Yamashita

COMPASS AMERICAN GUIDES, INC.
Oakland, California

San Francisco and the Bay Area

Printing History
First Edition October 1990
Second Edition October 1991

Library of Congress Cataloging-in-Publication Data
Parr, Barry, 1955-
San Francisco and the Bay Area / Barry Parr : photography by
Michael Yamashita. — 2nd ed.
p.   cm.   —(Discover America)
Includes bibliographical references and index.
ISBN 1-878867-16-4 (pbk.) : $14.95
1. San Francisco (Calif.)—Description—Guide-books. 2. San Francisco Bay Area (Calif.)
—Description and travel—Guide books. I. Yamashita, Michael S.   II. Title.   III. Series
F869.S33P37 1992   91-33144 CIP
917.94'610453—dc20

Editor: Deke Castleman   Designer: David Hurst
Series Editor: Kit Duane   Map Design: Bob Race

First published in 1990 by Compass American Guides, Inc.
6051 Margarido Drive, Oakland, CA 94618, USA

ACKNOWLEDGEMENTS

Thanks are due to Shirley Fong-Torres for reading this manuscript with her experienced and encouraging eye, and for recommending restaurants and hotels for inclusion in the Backmatter. Grateful recognition also goes to proofreader Cynthia Vincent, to Peter Zimmerman for his careful line editing, and to Alvaro Gutierrez R. for assistance in tracking down photo opportunities. Kudos to designer David Hurst, and map designer Bob Race, for their creative, skillful, patient contributions to the appearance of this book, usually under trying circumstances. Thanks are also owed to Asha Johnson, whose invaluable advice on computers has facilitated my life on more than one occasion, to Brian Bardwell for assistance with the maps, Annie Hikido for her exacting standards in laying out the second edition, and to Li Suk Woon and the rest of the Hong Kong production staff. Last and not least, I salute Mike Yamashita, photographer *par excellence*, and Deke Castleman, my editor, whose articulate, friendly advice is invariably as witty as it is wise.

Unless otherwise stated below, all photography is by Michael Yamashita. The pictures on page 245 were photographed by Harold Parr. The photographs on pages 5, 14, 62 are used courtesy of Wells Fargo Bank; page 27 courtesy of California State Library; pages 15, 24, 42, 47 by permission of the Oakland Museum; pages 18, 32, 37, 41, 44, 49, 67, 184 courtesy of the San Francisco Library; and page 361 photograph by Ron Delany. "A Supermarket in California" by Allen Ginsberg from ALLEN GINSBERG COLLECTED POEMS 1947-1980, copyright 1955, © 1984 by Allen Ginsberg is reprinted by permission of Harper & Row, Publishers, Inc. "Home, Home, Home" by Lawrence Ferlinghetti, from ENDLESS LIFE: SELECTED POEMS, © 1981 by Lawrence Ferlinghetti, is reprinted by permission of New Directions Books.

*To my parents, Harold and Loraine,
who introduced me to my subject.*

C O N T E N T S

AUTHOR'S PREFACE

GUIDEBOOKS EMPHASIZE WHAT INTERESTS THEIR WRITERS. So it should be asked here, what interests the writer of this guide?

In brief, most everything. The morning's first cappuccino, and the evening's last espresso. Hash browns in a Hayward diner. Fog horns, lamenting, from Clement Street at night. The engine room of the liberty ship *Jeremiah O'Brien*, pounding under a full head of steam. Bagging a cheap Bierce or Sterling in a used-book store, and cracking it open on the N-Judah, a hundred-some-odd rattling feet beneath Buena Vista Park. Taking the kids to visit the crocs at the Academy of Sciences, or coaxing them down the murky steps of the rock tomb at the Egyptian Museum. Burritos and a Pacifico Clara at La Imperial, cushioned in the hearty clamor of a dinner time crowd. Cézanne, in silence, at the Legion of Honor. An aria hauntingly floating upon the glittering air of the War Memorial Opera House; or better yet, over the fast-disappearing tortellini at Rattos. The oily reek of the cable car barn, the whir of the cable pulleys, the frantic clang of bells. Starched tablecloths and blunt waiters at an old city grill.

Christmas shopping at Union Square. The salty tang on the air at the Hyde Street Pier. The warm lights of Sausalito, seen from the deck of the homeward ferry. The view from Diamond Heights. The ivy-covered stones and musty caves of the Buena Vista wine cellars. The softness of the path beneath enormous redwoods. A German beer at Schroeder's at noon, and at five, an Anchor Steam at Vesuvios. . . .

I could go on and on. In fact, I do.

Certainly if I had to organize these and all my other interests in order of preference, the book would run differently. Instead, I list them geographically, as befits a guidebook, starting with San Francisco, and proceeding on to day trips around the Bay Area. In the "Backmatter," you will find some names and addresses of a few recommended hotels, restaurants, bookstores, museums and tour companies; they are by no means the only good ones. And since I cannot know or even like everything, in "Practicalities" I recommended a few of the many wonderful books which cover ground that I have lightly tread.

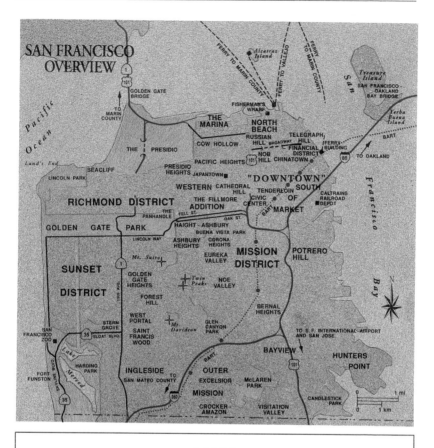

MAPS

INTRODUCTION

LIKE MANY GREAT CITIES, SAN FRANCISCO was built on a harbor. And like many hardscrabble, tinpot, boom-and-bust towns scattered through the Wild West, she was also slapped down in a rush on barren hills; worse yet, on hills stranded at the tip of a long, foggy peninsula.

To these two accidents of history San Francisco owes both her prosperity and her character.

It's hard to conceive of a worse place to build a *serious* city. Maybe not quite as ridiculous as Venice, sinking in the sea, or Timbuktu, stranded by a roving river in the sandy wastes. But those are has-beens, museum pieces forsaken by the type of supercharged entrepreneurs who built them. San Francisco, thank God, remains a dynamic, world-class city.

Still, as thoughtful San Franciscans sometimes admit, maybe the comparison to Venice is not all that far off. As wharves and factories decline and disappear, tourism becomes San Francisco's biggest growth industry. That's a hard lump to take for a city that was once the undisputed Queen of the West.

From her birth in the gold rush till the rise of other regional capitals at the turn of the century, San Francisco set the standards of American civilization west of the Mississippi. Culturally and economically, she stood at center stage of a vast sphere of influence reaching east to the Rockies, north to Alaska, and south and west to however far American ambitions might be carried by its traders and soldiers of fortune.

From Tombstone to the Klondike, when frontier capitalists sought to sink a mine or corner a market, they bankrolled it in San Francisco. When Hawaiian planters yearned for stateside pleasures, they donned their city hats and caught a ship to San Francisco. Along the Yukon, when miners craved news of the outside world, they'd part with gold for a Frisco paper. When the Modocs went to war and almost won, it was San Francisco who received the summons for help, and later, the beaten warriors themselves, ferried in chains to Alcatraz. From San Francisco sailed the fleets that seized the Philippines, and likewise, rolled the whiskey and oysters that kept times flush in Virginia City. And in return, whole mountains of silver ore and gold from a thousand godforsaken sagebrush towns were mined, crushed, refined, and shipped, as a matter of course, to San Francisco.

For better or worse, those times have passed. Much of what she was, she is no longer. But to her credit, San Francisco has weathered the loss of stature gracefully. Even now her citizens lay plans to recapture a starring role in the coming Pacific Rim century.

Say what you will about the new wealth and influence of upstart Los Angeles (and most northern Californians can contrive a few choice epithets), San Francisco remains a city of extraordinary presence. Small she may be, but she can part a path through throngs of larger cities with the cast of her eye alone. In her time, she has drunk champagne from a slipper and gone barefoot, dined on both the gristle and the tenderloin, embraced the noblest ideals of humankind, and packed more red-eyed mornings, tragedy, laughter, and waywardness than many a town three and four times her age.

"There are just three big cities in the United States that are *story* cities," observed the novelist, Frank Norris. "New York, of course, New Orleans, and best of the lot, San Francisco."

And what great stories they are. Just *look* at the company she's kept—bohemians, frontiersmen, wanderers, merchants, poets, prostitutes, big spenders, bridge

A tent "city" sprang up on Telegraph Hill during the gold rush.

San Francisco sporting goods, ca. 1850.

builders, lovers, lunatics, bankers, sailors, bums, rapscallions . . . . Ask any one of them, "What is San Francisco like?" and each would describe a place unlike any other.

To the ancient Ohlones, she was a cold, foggy shore on the fringe of paradise. To the conquistadores, grinding northward with cross and sword, she was the dire end of banishment, a wilderness of salvageable souls.

To enterprising Yankees, San Francisco will always be the instant city, miraculously begat on barren hills by hordes from every nation: the city of tents and mud, of gold and Comstock silver, alternately burning and rising, each time more stately, to the Grand Finale of 1906 when, from utter destruction, she triumphed phoenix-like from the ashes. This is the city of nabobs in gilded mansions, of cable cars and grand hotels, of gamblers and dance hall girls and the big, bad Barbary Coast; of Mark Twain swapping jokes at the Exchange Saloon, of six-shooters and sawdust-covered floors; of Clark Gable grinning, cigar in teeth, and Jeanette MacDonald belting out her song as the city burns around her.

And then there is the real city of rusty plumbing and moldy closets: the working stiff, the unions, the firetrap slums, the shipyards and train yards, the great strikes and greater civil engineering projects, the steel bridges, the WPA murals in

Coit Tower. This is the city of the Mooney trial, greasy-spoon lunch counters, crowded steam vents, and Salvation Army bands playing street corners south of Market.

For every mother's son and daughter, San Francisco is a gathering of immigrants, each with their separate festivals and foods, and each sampling freely from their neighbors—Chinatown, Russian Richmond, Little Italy, Hunters Point, Little Osaka, and the Mexican, German, Irish, and Samoan settlements of the sprawling Mission District. It's a feast of exotic smells and flavors, of cappuccino in small cafés, sourdough French bread, local wine, Dungeness crab, fortune cookies, chop suey, pasta, cioppino, and Joe's Special. Where else can you dine on Ukranian *golubtzy* to the sound of foghorns, or pick the remnants of Mongolian lamb from your teeth to the accompaniment of an Oktoberfest accordion band?

To the sailor Frisco is a favored port of call, a town of honky-tonks, tattoo parlors, topless joints, Anchor Steam Beer, and monumental Saturday night drunks; a city of blurred Monday mornings, slowly clearing; of sea gulls, white caps, and uniforms, a crisp flag whipping in a clean wind.

Then there's Sam Spade's turf. Hard-boiled, tender at the core. Fedora pulled low, cigarette on lip, dame on elbow. Al Capone doing hard time on The Rock. Crack dealers menacing the Projects. She can be one tough babe.

Yet, always over the next hill lies romantic San Francisco, that "cool, gray city of love;" where couples haunt the stairways, gazing out over a blue bay, flecked with white, gracefully trimmed with gossamer bridges . . . .

Then it's 6 a.m. and the bridges are jammed with commuters bound for Wall Street West—corporate HQ, bankers' clubs, bustling clerks, martini lunches, rising steel towers, migraine headaches. Duck left, and you're in the West Coast bastion of progressive idealism: the city of John Muir, the Sierra Club, the Gay Rights Movement, Free Speech, holistic health, and raised consciousness; but also the radical chic, and the cults and movements that continue to repel a fascinated Middle America. The United Nations was born in San Francisco; so were Jonestown and the Symbionese Liberation Army.

Nor let us forget the pipe-dream of Bohemia, where every generation finds and loses a new Latin Quarter. Gone are the artists and their cage birds from the shacks of Telegraph Hill; gone the poets from Papa Coppa's; faded the beatniks, with their wine and jazz; and gone, too, the flower children from a street called Love. Only their stories, and the Grateful Dead, live on . . . .

More than an accumulation of wood, steel, glass, and brick, San Francisco is a collection of people and their stories. Some are new. Some have been told and embellished for generations. Some are ugly. Some are stranger than fiction. Let the historians dicker which is which; to the traveler who seeks to know San Francisco, they are all of interest.

"California Dreamers" embodied in an Oakland Museum exhibit.

SAN FRANCISCO'S STORY

SAN FRANCISCO SITS WITH REASONABLE STABILITY on the southern shore of the Golden Gate, surrounded on three sides by seawater. To the west is the Pacific Ocean, perennially chilled by strong Alaskan currents, even on the hottest days, and torn by rough seas murderous to swimmers, and all too often inhospitable to ships. To the east is San Francisco Bay, deep, protected and so surpassing a harbor that it has been called by many the finest in the world. The two are joined by the Golden Gate, a narrow passage three miles long and a mile wide (4.8 x 1.6 km), which cuts San Francisco off from the northern part of the state, and is the largest gap in the Coast Ranges for a thousand miles.

The famous hills of San Francisco and the Bay Area are part of these Coast Ranges, which run north and south along almost the entire California coast. Their formidable barrier shields the inland valleys from the fogs and winds that plague San Francisco, making a summer hothouse of the interior. East of the Coast Ranges sprawls the fertile Central Valley, the nation's largest fruit and vegetable garden, and east of that, the longest block of granite in the world, the Sierra Nevada range. The rivers of the Sierra Nevada, cherished now for their precious water as they once were for their gold, pour down into the Central Valley, gathering into the Sacramento and San Joaquin rivers. Flowing from the north and south, respectively, these two rivers join in the delta east of Carquinez Straits, where they enter San Francisco Bay and are carried off by strong currents through the Golden Gate. In millennia past, these rivers gouged out the Gate and emptied into the sea some distance beyond. When the oceans rose at the end of the last Ice Age, the canyon and the valley behind were flooded, creating the inland bay of San Francisco.

Of the forces that shaped San Francisco, and which shape her still, the one most likely to concern residents and visitors in any given lifetime is the process of tectonic movement, better known as earthquakes. California's longest and most famous earthquake fault, the San Andreas, runs 650 miles (1,046 km) up the coast of California, slipping into the sea just south of San Francisco, and emerging on land again to the north, at Point Reyes. The plate to the west of the San Andreas moves north at an average speed of two inches (five cm) per year. When pressure builds at a sticking point, and then suddenly breaks loose, the surrounding earth

Old San Francisco's dash and opulence were mirrored in the Palace Hotel.

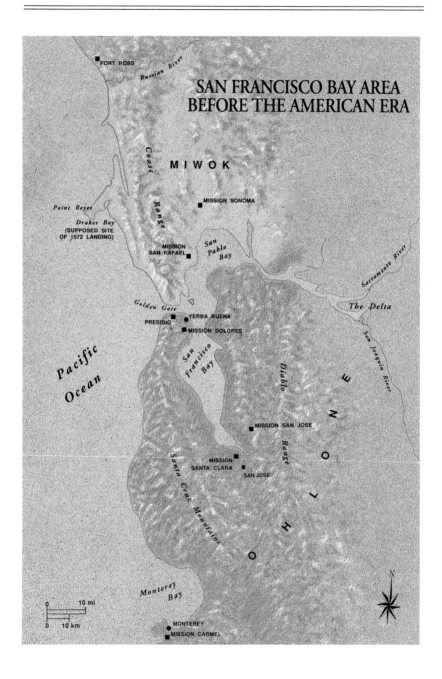

SAN FRANCISCO BAY AREA
BEFORE THE AMERICAN ERA

slips and shakes. Earthquakes are an unavoidable feature of the San Francisco Bay Area. The famous quake of 1906 was by no means the first—nor will the powerful shaker of 1989 be the last.

■ THE FIRST INHABITANTS

Unlike the desolate, windswept and inhospitable site of San Francisco itself, the Bay Area counties to the south, east, and north have always shown a natural hospitality to residents. When people first began crossing the Bering Straits from Asia some 20,000-36,000 years ago, the Bay Area was brimming with all the requirements of life. The gentle climate and rich patchwork of woodland, marsh, oak savannah, and upland habitats nurtured an abundance of seabirds, shellfish, ducks, antelope, deer, bear, elk, otter, fox, and rabbit, as well as edible grasses, roots and acorns. The region also supported a human population of about 10,000 people, who built some 30 or 40 permanent villages around the bay and south to Big Sur. The San Francisco Bay Area was the most densely populated region on the continent north of Mexico, but the site of San Francisco itself attracted few residents.

Based on language groupings, anthropologists identify the native people north of the Golden Gate as the Coast Miwok, while the dominant group throughout the rest of the Bay Area is known by the Spanish names of Ohlone, or Costanoan. In fact, each Ohlone sub-tribe considered itself independent and unique, separated from its neighbors by dialect and customs, despite regular trade and intermarriage. They shared a common dependence on shellfish, as is attested by the 450 gigantic piles of cast-off shells still found around the bay, most spectacularly at Coyote Hills in southern Alameda county. During summer they migrated inland to hunt game and collect acorns to make their mush and bread. Several thousand years of this stable cycle produced a gentle, musical, unwarlike culture that did not keep records of its own past. For an Ohlone to discuss the dead was taboo. Merely making mention of a dead relative in the Ohlone culture was an impropriety equal to cursing one in Western or Asian cultures. Perhaps that is why, after thousands of years on the shores of the bay, their annihilation passed so quietly.

Legends of California flittered about the taverns and libraries of Europe for years before anyone actually came for a look. Recent discoveries of ancient coins and stone anchors suggest that Chinese ships probably visited the California coast centuries before Columbus blundered into the Caribbean. The first *documented* visit by a foreigner to northern California, however, was made by the Portuguese explorer, João Cabrilho, who sailed up the coast in 1542, somehow missing the Golden Gate. Thirty-seven years later, in 1579, the English privateer Sir Francis Drake, while on an extended mission to harass the Spanish galleons and seize their treasures, made a landing somewhere in the Bay Area. Drake apparently also missed the narrow entrance to the Golden Gate in the fog. His chronicler's description of their anchorage leads most historians to place it at what is now called Drakes Bay, below Point Reyes. Pausing several weeks to repair his ships, Drake claimed the land for Queen Elizabeth I of England and christened it Nova Albion, inscribing his claim on a brass plate. The plate, or a convincing forgery, was found in 1933, and is now on display at the University of California in Berkeley.

■ THE HISPANICS

Another two hundred years passed before a European saw San Francisco Bay. While searching for Monterey Bay, glowingly described almost two centuries earlier by an earlier explorer, Sebastían Vizcaíno, a Spanish scouting party under the command of Gaspar de Portolá got the surprise of their lives when they stumbled on San Francisco Bay, in 1769, having overshot their true mark. Realizing that *this* was not Monterey Bay, the soldierly Portolá retraced his steps. The Spanish had invested too many hopes on Monterey to abandon it now. Only after they had established themselves there did they set out to colonize the magnificent harbor to the north.

That task was assigned to a determined soldier, Juan Bautista de Anza. With his lieutenant, Jose Moraga, a Franciscan priest named Francisco Palóu, and a party of 34 pioneer families, Anza set out on foot from Sonora, Mexico. After a grueling desert march, they arrived at the tip of the peninsula on June 27, 1776 (seven days before another landmark date on the opposite side of the continent). There they took possession for Spain by founding a fortress, the Presidio, on a strategic hill overlooking the Golden Gate, and a church a mile south on a small lake that they named in honor of Our Lady of Sorrows (Nuestra Señora de los Dolores). The adobe church that Father Palóu built on the site, the first of five missions around the bay, was dedicated to Saint Francis of Assisi. In time, the lake's name stuck as the popular name for Mission Dolores, while the great bay itself acquired the Mission's official name, San Francisco.

The Ohlones greeted the newcomers with amazement. Many believed them to be gods—a reason, perhaps, why they succumbed so readily to the new order. The Spanish in California were decidedly more interested in the native peoples *as subjects* than the English settlers on the Atlantic shore. Their stated purpose was to convert the natives to Christianity, to save their souls while teaching them enough farming, husbandry and industry to create a self-perpetuating rural society in California. The plan was disastrous. For people accustomed to the subtler pace of seasonal migrations, mission life was hellish. The natives lived in barracks, segregated by sex, and did forced labor. Many ran away, only to be caught, returned and punished by soldiers. New diseases decimated them. The death rate quickly surpassed the birth rate. Then, in 1821, Mexico broke away from Spain, and the new government secularized the missions. Order, harsh as it was, broke down. The missions decayed. Hopelessly lost from their old ways of life, the Ohlones starved in their homeland. Some drifted off to work the ranches, others to roam in homeless bands that were hunted down and killed. As a people, the Ohlone never recovered. Five thousand Indians, over half the population of the Bay Area before the Spanish arrived, lie buried in unmarked graves at Mission Dolores, Our Lady of Sorrows.

In the wake of sword and cross, Spanish (and later Mexican) civilian families, like Noé, Bernal, Moraga, and Vallejo, settled on vast government land grants, where they built cattle ranches and ruled as benevolent feudal lords. Like the Ohlones before them, the new *Californios* discovered that life in bounteous California could be very sweet indeed. Their ranches produced all that they needed, including an annual cash "crop" of hides, which they sold to passing ships for a good profit. Among the most ambitious of the rancho chieftains was a Swiss, Augustus Sutter, who built a fort to secure his vast empire near the spot where the American River empties into the Sacramento River—today the site of California's state capital, Sacramento.

Ironically, the hide trade destroyed their isolation by bringing foreign ships to San Francisco in slowly increasing numbers. The Western world was in an expansive mood. The Pacific was opening up, and San Francisco Bay made a splendid anchorage for a Pacific empire. Mexico lacked the power to enforce her claim. As early as 1812, the Russians established Fort Ross, ostensibly as a hunting station, 60 miles (100 km) north of San Francisco. French and English ships were investigating.

When the Yankee sailor-turned-writer Richard Henry Dana described his 1835 visit to the bay in *Two Years Before the Mast*, Americans pricked up their ears. Expansionists among them were particularly intrigued to learn that a small, mostly Yankee settlement was already established above a cove on the eastern side of the San Francisco peninsula.

■ THE YANKEES

American and English ships had long preferred Yerba Buena Cove to the traditional Spanish anchorage off the Presidio, because it was better sheltered. In the year of Dana's visit, an Anglo sailor named William Richardson built a house there, laying out a street and a village plaza. Being married to the Presidio *commandante's* daughter, Richardson settled with official blessing. Others followed, and the settlement became known as Yerba Buena.

Spanish armor.

With classic entrepreneurial spirit, Yerba Buena found a need and filled it, in this case, with a ship's chandler and a couple of grog shops. But it was enough. On the verge of the cataclysmic 1840s, the three sprigs on which San Francisco would bloom had sprouted. Each was separated by an hour's walk from the others. Two—the Mission Dolores and the Presidio—were fast declining, but the third, the wretched, flea-bitten, sand-blown, largely Yankee village of Yerba Buena, was preparing to take up the torch. Richardson's street, Calle de la Fundación (Foundation Street), would one day become Grant Avenue, and the dusty village plaza would become the even grubbier Portsmouth Plaza.

The American presence in California grew in the 1840s as increasing numbers of immigrants cut south from the Oregon Trail. The Mexican governor complained uselessly about the "hoards of Yankee emigrants whose progress we cannot arrest." America was expanding. "Manifest Destiny!" was the cry justifying westward migration, settlement, and war. In 1846, the United States annexed Texas and invaded Mexico. U.S. Senator Daniel Webster's dexterous tongue was claiming that San Francisco Bay alone was worth 10 Texases.

The climax came that same year. A party of bombastic Yankees in Sonoma, California, prodded on by a meddlesome American soldier of fortune named Captain John C. Frémont, raised a flag with a picture of a bear on it, and declared independence from Mexico. The California Republic lasted less than a month. On July 9, 1846, a party of American marines and sailors from the warship *Portsmouth*, under command of Captain John Montgomery, seized the plaza at Yerba Buena and ran the Stars and Stripes up a pole. The Presidio, staffed by 12 Mexican soldiers and a sergeant, surrendered peacefully. Yerba Buena, along with the entire state of California, was now American territory.

Big changes came quickly to Yerba Buena. Most propitiously, the citizens changed the town's name to San Francisco. Boosters argued that by taking the name of the famous bay, their town would grow famous by association and, more to the point, attract shipping away from any other bay-side ports. It was a shrewd move of enormous consequences. In keeping with their grand hopes, San Francisco's first elected administrator hired an Irish sailor, Jasper O'Farrell, to draw up a street plan for the town.

Even more ambitious plans were being laid by an enterprising newcomer named Sam Brannan, who had arrived at the head of a party of Mormons shortly after the American seizure. Some have called Brannan San Francisco's founding father. Others dismiss him as an opportunist or even a charlatan. Still, by hook or crook, Brannan managed to push to the head of nearly every scheme of improvement in San Francisco over the next booming decade. Brannan quickly broke with the Salt Lake church, and became San Francisco's leading booster. He delivered San Francisco's first English sermon, performed its first non-Catholic marriage, founded its first newspaper (*The California Star*), helped establish the first school, and built stores both in San Francisco and at Sutter's Fort. Yet Sam Brannan's greatest coup came in 1848, after Sutter's foreman, James Marshall, discovered gold in the American River. Fearful of the awful turmoil that the discovery would bring to his rancho, Sutter sought advice from Brannan, begging his confidence. Brannan offered solace. By most accounts, he then quickly bought up waterfront lots and placed orders to stock his stores in Sacramento and San Francisco with food, dry goods, and digging tools. The next week found him in San Francisco with a bottle of the glittering metal, shouting "Gold! Gold from the American River!"

As a lesson in history and shrewd business practices, let it not be forgotten that of the thousands of gold seekers who rushed into California in the ensuing madness, a few struck it rich. But it was Sam Brannan who became San Francisco's first millionaire.

SAILING WITH DANA

We sailed down this magnificent bay with a light wind, the tide, which was running out, carrying us at the rate of four or five knots. It was a fine day; the first of entire sunshine we had had for more than a month. We passed directly under the high cliff on which the presidio is built, and stood into the middle of the bay, from whence we could see small bays making up into the interior, large and beautifully wooded islands, and the mouths of several small rivers. If California ever becomes a prosperous country, this bay will be the center of its prosperity. The abundance of wood and water; the extreme fertility of its shores; the excellence of its climate, which is as near to being perfect as any in the world; and its facilities for navigation, affording the best anchoring grounds in the whole western coast of America,—all fit it for a place of great importance.

—Richard Henry Dana, from *Two Years Before the Mast*

■ THE GOLD RUSH

The California gold rush is arguably the most extraordinary event to ever befall an American city in peacetime. At the beginning of 1848, the year that gold was discovered, San Francisco was a backwater of some 800 souls. Within a few months, its population was approaching 25,000, and its postal service handling an estimated million letters a year. By 1852, despite having been practically burnt to the ground on six occasions, San Francisco was the fourth largest entrepôt in the United States. By 1860, 14 years after Montgomery had seized the sleepy village, it was a metropolis of 56,000, poised to underwrite a large portion of Union expenses in the Civil War.

In time, California's rich land and climate undoubtedly would have attracted floods of immigrants, but the gold rush telescoped a half century of growth into half a year. Within weeks, the news that had electrified California and Mexico was spreading like a shipboard plague to the Eastern seaboard, the Midwest, South America, Asia, Europe, and Australia. Within months, about 90,000 men (and a

Miners in 1852 wash the gold from their diggings in a "long tom."

very few women) struck out for California. (Another 150,000 would arrive before the rush ended in 1852.) Thousands of Americans commenced walking west, and thousands more set sail around Cape Horn or to the Isthmus of Panama. Packed ships sailed from Central and South America, the Sandwich Islands (Hawaii), China, and every seaport of Europe. The lucky ones who arrived in 1848 got first crack at the gold, but the bulk who arrived in 1849 earned the eternal sobriquet of *forty-niners*.

Most of those who came by ship landed in San Francisco, the first convenient anchorage within the Golden Gate. Other rival settlements on San Francisco Bay, particularly Benicia, were closer to the mines, but most of the argonauts were ignorant of California geography, and San Francisco *was* the famous name. On landing, many asked the way to the Mother Lode in the Sierra Nevada as though it was just up the street. Finding that a long overland journey still awaited them, they stopped to buy supplies and make plans. A tent city sprang up to house and serve them. As crews deserted to join the rush, abandoned ships were winched ashore (or the shore built out to them) for use as storehouses and hotels. Demand for nearly everything ran rampant, and supplies were perpetually being hoarded or liquidated by speculators. Prices for basic commodities (food, cots, picks, shovels) rocketed to heights that won't be seen again, if we're lucky, until well into the twenty-first century—yet they sold briskly enough in 1849.

Overnight, San Francisco became the most cosmopolitan city on Earth. Although Americans comprised about half the population from 1847 to 1860, the other half was a mixture of British subjects, with the Irish in the lead, and considerable minorities of Chinese, Hispanics, continental Europeans, and Hawaiians. Most of the Hispanics came from Mexico and Chile, while Germany, France, Switzerland, Poland, Sweden, Belgium, and Italy supplied most of the Continentals. In 1860, 10 percent of San Francisco was non-white, mostly Chinese.

The ratio between the sexes was downright alarming. In 1847, men outnumbered women two to one. Things worsened drastically by 1849, when the ratio jumped to ten to one. The relative lack of women remained a serious problem in San Francisco throughout most of the century, no doubt adding fire to the Barbary Coast, the city's notorious red-light district.

San Francisco's was a youthful population, liberally sprinkled with professionals and educated gentlemen. Most had come with every intention of returning home just as soon as they made their millions. For the majority, that day never came.

Benicia's old state capitol recalls its fleeting year of glory (1853-4).

Surface gold was picked clean by 1849, and the deeper placers, painstakingly washed through pans and cradles, wore thin by 1852. Gold mining was becoming a corporate enterprise, better suited to companies that could raise the capital to bore tunnels or invest in expensive hydraulic mining equipment. The independent forty-niner was an anachronism. A handful went home rich. Many more departed poor. Others fanned out through the West in search of another bonanza. Solvent or broke, thousands more made their way to San Francisco.

California gold played fickle with the forty-niners, but it had not eluded San Francisco. In 1853, some tents still crowded the hillsides, but a substantial city of wood and brick had taken root. Fires roared through the city regularly. Heinrich Schliemann, the German archaeologist, was roused from his Portsmouth Square Hotel bed by the huge fire of May 4, 1851, which burned a quarter of the city. He fled up Telegraph Hill in time to catch a "frightful but sublime view" of "the roaring of the storm, the cracking of the gunpowder, the cracking of the falling stonewalls, the cries of the people and the wonderful spectacle of an immense city burning . . . ." San Francisco rebuilt, only to burn again on November 9, 1852.

San Francisco rebuilt again. Aside from a permanent population well exceeding 30,000 people, the city now supported a lending library, scores of warehouses, theaters, eateries, hotels, brothels, a dozen newspapers, a handful of churches, and hundreds of saloons and gambling halls. New piers and landfill pushed out where Yerba Buena Cove once was, burying the old harbor along with the ships anchored therein. Forty square blocks of downtown were built on the landfill. Stockton Street, on the hill above, was the fashionable residential avenue. A new residential quarter reached south of Market to soon-to-be-fashionable Rincon Hill. Hispanic and Mediterranean settlers were already transforming Telegraph Hill and North Beach into a "Latin quarter." The Chinese had dispersed throughout the city, but their main settlement was forming along Sacramento Street. Another village of Chinese fishermen stood at the foot of Rincon Hill, in the shadow of today's Bay Bridge. Pacific Street, along the base of Telegraph Hill, was taking in some rough Australian characters, who called themselves the Sydney Ducks; in time, "Sydneytown" would reach full bloom as the notorious Barbary Coast.

A city full of frisky young gents can get a bit wild. Duels were fought in the crowded streets. Gangs of criminals robbed, extorted, and terrorized, sometimes setting fires and looting. The Chilean settlement on Telegraph Hill was a frequent target of hooligans like the Hounds, a gang of New Yorkers and Australians. The law was slow and the citizens impatient. In 1849, and again in 1851, Sam Brannan harangued the city's established community into taking justice into their own hands. The first incident ended with exile for six Hounds, but the mob settled for nothing less than lynching the second time around.

Vigilantism struck again in May 1856, after the righteous editor of the *Evening Bulletin*, James King of William, was gunned down by a shady city councilman who resented the *Bulletin's* charges of corruption. Thousands of citizens rallied around a new Committee of Vigilance, seizing the councilman, James Casey, and lynching him and a cohort, a gambler named Charles Cora. Taking up quarters in a sand-bagged building on Sacramento Street, nicknamed Fort Gunnybags, the committee set about striking terror in the criminal populace with torchlight parades and more lynchings. It finally disbanded on July 29, leaving its supporters and condemners both claiming victory, and the criminal element temporarily cowed.

Manic times breed eccentric characters, and San Francisco has bred more than a few from its earliest days. There was James Lick, the fabulous millionaire who was so tight that he wore cast-off clothes, until he repented toward the end of his life and gave his fortune away. Then there was William Walker, the adventurer who tried to make himself dictator of Nicaragua, only to die before a Honduran firing squad. And there was "Honest" Harry Meiggs, the beloved city booster who funded large and generous civic improvement schemes with borrowed cash, and skipped town hours before the bubble burst. The most fantastic eccentric of all, however, was Emperor Norton.

Joshua A. Norton came to San Francisco from London in 1849. He became a merchant, reinvested his profits in land, and prospered. In 1854, he set plans to corner the rice market, pouring all his resources into the scheme. Unfortunately for him, a rice ship sailed through the Golden Gate while he still held his hoard, and prices plummeted. Norton went bankrupt and disappeared. Then one day, several months later, he reappeared on Montgomery Street in military costume with epaulets, plumed hat and a cane. Stopping by the offices of the *San Francisco Bulletin*, he announced that he was henceforth to be known as Norton I, Emperor of the United States and Protector of Mexico.

Short, slight, bearded, with clear, fierce eyes and a proud mien, Emperor Norton set about seriously to rule his empire. San Francisco, tongue in cheek, decided to play along. A printer agreed to print the Emperor's currency, and merchants

agreed to honor it. The Emperor dined gratis wherever he pleased, and restaura-
teurs vied for the publicity of his patronage. It was said that no theater opened a
performance between 1855 and 1880 without reserving free first-night seats for
the Emperor and his faithful dogs, Lazarus and Bummer. Another seat was kept
for him in the Sacramento legislature, which he addressed in earnest on occasion.
When his uniform became ragged, he appeared before the Board of Supervisors,
who amended the city charter so that he would receive an allowance for as long as
he lived. In short, the city kept up its end of the madman's charade for almost 30
years, and he in turn never wore out his welcome. In fact, he took some pains to
govern conscientiously. His directive to erect a tree for children at Christmas on
Union Square is honored to this day. It was
said that he attended both Christian and
Jewish services to encourage religious harmony, and that he once diffused an anti-Chinese riot by standing at the front and recit-
ing the Lord's Prayer till the combat-
ants put down their fists and departed
in shame. When he died in 1880,
thousands from every quarter
of the city came to bury him
with all the pomp and dignity
befitting his rank.

Norton I, Emperor of the United States and Protector of Mexico.

■ BOOM TIMES, AND BUST

As the 1850s drew to an end, the spontaneous energy that animated gold rush San Francisco lost torque. The economy slowed, men drifted home or took up wage-paying jobs, and society began to stabilize. Californians worried over the recession, but also began to explore other golden opportunities that were awaiting them in farming, industry, and government corruption. By the late 1850s, San Francisco had weathered its first depression and was settling into a pattern of civic and commercial growth typical of most other American cities. Little did anyone expect that San Francisco was in for another big boom.

In 1859, some California drifters stumbled on a fabulous vein of silver in the desert mountains east of the Sierra Nevada. A new rush was on. Rough-and-tumble Virginia City sprang preposterously up on the steep, dry mountainside of Mount Davidson in Washoe, soon to be the new state of Nevada. Unlike the California gold rush of a decade earlier, the Comstock Lode, as it came to be known, was a game unsuited to stalwart independents. Capital, heavy equipment, engineers, and organized manpower were needed to run the expensive operation of extracting, crushing, and refining the ore. Experienced San Francisco mining companies responded with a speed and know-how that drove individual prospectors, literally, into the ground. San Francisco had a good return on investment. The Comstock Lode proved to be the world's richest silver deposit. The better part of two decades was needed to exhaust its bounty.

As Virginia City grew into a factory town, where shifts worked round the clock in grim conditions, San Francisco grew fabulously rich. In short time, a new breed of millionaire, the "Bonanza Kings," was staking out gilded mansions on Nob Hill and showering patronage on the plenteous new diversions that mushroomed up to serve them. But San Francisco's benefits did not stop at Nob Hill and luxurious French restaurants. Comstock silver stimulated general prosperity, creating jobs and optimism for the city at large. William C. Ralston, an early Comstock developer and partner in the Bank of California, lent his fortune and stature to many civic projects, including factories, mills, streets, theaters, office buildings, Golden Gate Park, and the largest, most princely hotel of its day, the Palace (see page 18). His contributions and boosterism inspired some to hail him as "the man who built San Francisco."

The extravagant tastes and wealth of Victorian San Francisco decorate the city's architecture. James Lick imported the Conservatory of Flowers (left), now in Golden Gate Park, for his private garden. The Archbishop's Mansion (interior, above) was built for the city's Catholic prelates.

These colorful times were fortunately well described to us by a host of San Francisco's writers. Bret Harte was among the first to receive national recognition for his heart-tugging stories of the gold rush. His cloying sentimentality, which proved popular in the East (and West), was counteracted by the misanthropic genius, Ambrose Bierce, whose *Devil's Dictionary* is a classic of American cynicism. They were backed by a host of lesser lights: South-Seas enthusiast Charles Stoddard and the eccentric frontier poet, Joaquin Miller, as well as the doyen of California poets and scribblers, Ina Coolbrith, loved by many, beloved by all. Most famous of all, and perhaps most characteristic of San Francisco despite the fact that he lived there for less than three years, was Mark Twain. His rambling, humorous, satirical voice *was* the voice of San Francisco's better half—tolerant and curious, appreciative of the finer things, debunking pomposity, comfortably American. Robert Louis Stevenson and Rudyard Kipling passed through town and left their marks, as did Oscar Wilde, in the 1880s. A new generation—George Sterling, Frank Norris, Gertrude Atherton, and Jack London—would rise before the century ended.

The 1860s in San Francisco was an era of robust new confidence. Californians rode out the Civil War in the Union camp with little sacrifice of life and, incidentally, profits intact. Now they were ready to take on the world. They were betting heavily on a new transcontinental railway that was pushing across the Sierra Nevada toward the East, financed by a Congress anxious to tie California (with its gold) and Nevada (with its silver) closer to the Union. Californians saw their isolation from the rest of the country as a barrier to development. It took a month to send a letter east by Panama steamer, and 20 to 24 days by Butterfield Stage. The Pony Express had done it in nine days to Saint Joseph, Missouri, but that enterprise went bankrupt after only 18 months, in 1861. The completion of the first transcontinental telegraph line improved communications, but Californians were betting that the railroad would bring a big boon to the state's economy.

The Central Pacific Railway was the pet project of an engineer named Theodore Judah, who personally surveyed the difficult route across the precipitous Sierra Nevada mountains. He sold his idea to four Sacramento businessmen, who found the government incentive of free land and cheap loans quite irresistible. The Big Four, as they came to be known, pushed the railroad into reality, joining up with the westward-bound Union Pacific at Promontory Point, Utah, in 1869. For their troubles, they reaped vast fortunes and created the most powerful political machine in California, the Southern Pacific Railway. They all built palaces on Nob Hill, where their names—Leland Stanford, Charles Crocker, Collis Huntington, and Mark Hopkins—are today enshrined in some of the finest hotels in San Francisco.

San Franciscans celebrated the transcontinental railroad's completion with characteristic abandon, ignoring the dire predictions of a remarkable economist, Henry George, who wrote in a San Francisco magazine that the railroad would enrich few and impoverish many. He claimed that completion of the line would flood California with cheap manufactured goods from the eastern States, ruining California's fledgling industrial base, while the ranks of the unemployed would swell with terminated railroad workers from all over the west. He was right.

Like everyone else, William Ralston had banked heavily on the transcontinental railway. But when the boom turned to bust, Ralston was caught overextended to the tune of five million dollars. With characteristic attention to smooth business form, he closed the doors of his bank, tendered his formal resignation, and drowned in San Francisco Bay.

The working classes chose another course. The unemployed rose in anger against the rich railroad men and, most tragically, against the thousands of Chinese workers who had been released from the railroad, and on whom they blamed the loss of American jobs. The depression of the 1870s heralded probably the most bleak era in San Francisco's history.

Nob Hill mansions embodied their masters' wealth, power, and ostentatiousness.

■ THE CHINESE

As the largest ethnic group in the city today, and one of the most influential since the beginning of the gold rush, the Chinese played an enormously important part in the opening of the West, California in particular. The first Chinese arrived in San Francisco in 1848, and by the following year there were about 300. They were welcomed with curiosity. Their merchants contributed to the material comfort of the rustic city, and American forty-niners readily learned to enjoy Chinese food and festivals.

The era of good feeling lasted only so long as easy gold. When the placers wore thin, laws were passed to restrict foreign competition, and sometimes enforced with violence. Even when forced to work only abandoned claims, most Chinese miners succeeded through persistent toil and lower expectations—after all, an ounce of gold went a lot further in China, where most intended to return, than it did in America. This determination to return to China encouraged few Cantonese

Though it has moved more than once and now occupies a modern building, the Kong Chow Temple is said by some to be the oldest Chinese temple in the United States.

miners to learn English or assimilate, which reinforced their segregation. Still, Mark Twain observed that most Chinese had qualities that made for valuable citizens, and that they were persecuted, quite simply, because they were different— different *and* successful.

Chinese laborers helped to build the dikes along the Sacramento River, and plant orchards and vineyards in the fertile California valleys. They pioneered California's fisheries, and were instrumental in developing textile manufacturing, leather-working, cigar-making, and other industries. They were highly valued in construction; in fact, San Francisco's first stone structure, the Parrott Building, was quarried in China and assembled by Chinese builders (who, incidentally, staged San Francisco's first labor strike). Their most celebrated job, however, was with the transcontinental railway, when 10,000 Chinese joined other teams in laying the tracks across the formidable Sierra Nevada range. The Chinese proved strong and brave rail men, who tackled dangerous jobs with fortitude, and set records for laying track. When the job was done and the workers released from contract, thousands drifted to San Francisco, raising the ranks of the unemployed.

The depression of the 1870s hit San Francisco hard. California factories found competition from the east coast too much to bear. Bankruptcies put hundreds out of work, sowing militancy among the unemployed. The disaffected seized the easiest scapegoat they could find: the Chinese. With encouragement from sand-lot fire-eaters, hooligans bullied them. Riotous mobs stormed Chinatown, both in San Francisco and other Western towns, destroying property, and all too often committing murder. Labor organizers used the power of the vote to push politicians to pass laws, like the Exclusion Act, to harass the Chinese, and ultimately to end Chinese immigration. The Chinese could not vote; the efforts of their organizations to fight these laws in court came to naught.

To understand what happened next, it helps to understand how Chinatown was organized.

Chinatown was, and in some respects still is, a village within a city. Partly in response to outside prejudice, but also out of inclination to live in a familiar society, Chinese emigrants during the nineteenth century built Chinatowns wherever they settled. There were many throughout the American West, but San Francisco's was the largest. In violent times its population swelled with refugees.

Most Chinese who came to America in the nineteenth century joined a *tong*, or social organization, based on their place of origin. A cross between a labor guild and an insurance company, tongs negotiated contracts for members, and provided protection and support in return for dues. Rivalry between different tongs, carried over from regional rivalries on the Chinese mainland, sometimes resulted in violence.

To control tong rivalry, Chinese merchants formed a federation of representatives of six of the largest tongs, called The Six Companies. (Membership later expanded to seven, but the name remained the same.) With occasional involvement by the Consul General of China, who had an office in San Francisco, the Six Companies managed Chinatown's public affairs, including its official relations with the outside community.

The Six Companies was a paternalistic organization. It took care of such matters as arbitrating disputes, issuing exit certificates to persons who could prove they had paid their debts, caring for the sick, and dispensing charity. Not all of their charity went to Chinatown. In *The Hatchet Men*, for instance, Richard Dillon notes that the Six Companies contributed $1,000 toward relief of victims of the Johnstown (Pennsylvania) flood, in 1889. The Six Companies' leadership also protested, unsuccessfully, against importing prostitutes from China. Unfortunately, their purpose was completely misunderstood by the non-Chinese public, who confused them with the fighting tongs, and charged them with violence and duplicity. Ironically, had the public backed the Six Companies, they probably could have prevented the era of Chinatown lawlessness called the tong wars.

The failure of the Six Companies to halt the tong wars was a direct result of anti-Chinese legislation—the Geary Act of 1892, which declared that all Chinese had to carry identity papers or face deportation. The Six Companies opposed the law by advising Chinese not to comply, while levying a small sum from members to hire lawyers to fight it in court. Although many of the best lawyers of the day insisted that the act was unconstitutional, it passed and was enforced. When the first Chinese were arrested for not carrying proper documentation, the Six Companies suffered a monumental loss of prestige. Underworld leaders moved fast to take advantage of the vacuum, strengthening individual tongs at the expense of the federation. Rival interests of different tongs quickly crossed, and rivalry quickly turned to violence.

Children were a rare sight in Chinatown until relatively recent years.

The tongs fought over control of gambling and prostitution—diversions quite understandably popular in the bachelor societies fossilized by the Exclusion Act. To supply the great demand for girls, they frequently resorted to kidnapping from China, but even girls who came by contract were as shamelessly exploited as the girls of the neighboring Barbary Coast. Extortion grew rampant, and the gangsters enforced their dictates with professional gunmen, known to police and later Hollywood films as highbinders, or hachetmen. The law-abiding majority of Chinatown, caught between an unsympathetic American public and lethal terrorism from within, suffered tremendously.

The tong wars were a reign of terror, and yet one that most non-Chinese followed only as a curiosity in the morning newspapers. It's only fair to note, however, that many non-Chinese rose to their defense. Many policemen genuinely served to protect the community, despite language barriers and widespread, often justified, mistrust of police. Working with English-speaking (and extremely brave, considering the risks) merchants, dedicated officers managed to bring some of the criminals to justice, but others were freed by corrupt lawyers and courts, returning to Chinatown swearing vengeance on their betrayers. Religious groups like the Methodists and the Presbyterians joined the fray.

Probably the most flamboyant crusader against the tong-controlled prostitution trade was a woman of splendidly ferocious character by the name of Donaldina Cameron. The spearhead of a Presbyterian mission force to rescue Chinese prostitutes, she swooped into her work with gargantuan energy. She was assisted in this war by a band of equally courageous (and even less well-known) agents and associates from Chinatown, who lived willingly under constant, deadly threat—for though gangsters were hesitant to harm a white woman (and to suffer the full force of U.S. law tumbling down on their heads), they worried considerably less about assassinating a fellow Chinese. It was said that Donaldina Cameron knew every rooftop and passageway of Chinatown, and was a veritable devil at hunting down hidden bagnios, which she physically stormed with the backup of her iron-hearted comrades and a police contingent. Even more importantly, she followed up on arrests with court battles. As her reputation grew, escaping prostitutes sought her refuge, often with the help of merchants or young lovers, who took grave risks, and sometimes paid with their lives. To this day, this extraordinary woman is still remembered as Lo Ma (Old Mother) in Chinatown.

Until toppled in 1911, the Manchu government forced all Chinese males to wear queues.

Donaldina Cameron helped drive the tongs into retreat, but two other phenomena really struck the killing blows. One was the 1906 earthquake, which initiated a complete rebuilding of Chinatown and the reestablishment of the Six Companies' prestige. The other, and most important, cause was the Americanization of the Chinese, which ended the hold that the tongs had over the community.

■ THE EARTHQUAKE AND FIRE

The years before 1906—especially the era of Mayor Eugene Schmitz and his grafting king-maker, Abe Ruef—were the most perniciously corrupt that the city ever knew. The Gilded Age, as it was known, pampered millionaires on Nob Hill while the labor movement boiled under pressure in the tenements south of Market. The middle classes built rows of wooden Victorians on hills far removed from the strife of Chinatown and the Barbary Coast, while confident downtown businesses expanded ever upward in daring new "skyscrapers." The port, bolstered by new business in the Philippines following the 1898 Spanish-American War, was booming. Ferries steamed between the new Ferry Building and the growing suburbs of Oakland and Marin County. Cable cars and streetcars linked distant neighborhoods of the city, pushing its boundaries to the Western Addition, the Mission District, and beyond. Theaters played to lively houses, and the higher-class red light district, the Tenderloin, waxed complacent under semi-official protection. In Golden Gate Park, the citizenry gathered in their Sunday best to stroll, picnic, and race fast coaches. San Francisco was *the* metropolis of the Pacific, the largest, finest, most powerful American city west of Chicago.

On the morning of April 18, 1906, San Francisco's 400,000 citizens were jolted awake by a quake now estimated at 8.25 on the Richter Scale. Chimneys crashed through roofs, gas and water mains broke all over town, and fissures opened in landfill streets. Surveying damage in the better residential districts, San Franciscans were relieved to see that the city had been spared calamity. Except for the flimsy tenements south of Market Street, the wooden Victorian neighborhoods had withstood the quake with only minor damage.

Downtown, however, received a worse shock. City Hall crumbled into rubble, a victim of the scams and shortcuts taken by scoundrelly politicians and their contractors. The Central Emergency Hospital also fell, burying doctors, nurses, and patients. Considering the severity of the quake, loss of life was small, yet devastating, in that one of the victims was Fire Chief Dennis Sullivan. More than any man in the city, Sullivan might have checked the disaster that followed.

Fifty-two fires broke out that morning. The fire department fought desperately, but with water mains broken and the fire chief dying, the flames spread unchecked. Racing through the tinderbox tenements south of Market, fire storms

engulfed the Palace Hotel, torched the skyscrapers, leaped over Market, and roared into the Financial District.

As thousands of refugees streamed to makeshift shelters in the parks and Presidio, others escaped by ferry to Oakland and Marin County. The army took over law and order in the city, with orders to kill looters on sight. Seven, in fact, were shot, one accidentally. Army dynamiters blasted through old neighborhoods in a clumsy attempt to clear firebreaks. By night, Oaklanders stared in horror at the burning city across the bay.

The flames burned for four days, destroying the downtown districts, Chinatown, North Beach, Russian Hill, Telegraph Hill, Nob Hill, and parts of the Mission District. It was finally contained at wide Van Ness by dynamiting the mansions along the eastern curb. The docks, protected by seawater sprayed by fireboats, survived, as did tiny pockets along the crests of Russian and Telegraph hills, and in the Barbary Coast. The Old Mint likewise survived to assume the role of the city's bank in the days ahead.

In all, 674 persons were listed as killed or missing. Three quarters of the city's residences and businesses burned, including almost the entire city center. More than half the city's population were homeless, with property loss estimated at $350 million. Nonetheless, San Franciscans remained remarkably upbeat. Survivors reported an almost holiday atmosphere in some tent cities. Relief funds poured in from around the country and many foreign countries. Japan sent the largest donation (a favor that San Francisco returned in the 1923 Tokyo quake).

Reconstruction started almost immediately. While government officials debated the merits of rebuilding on a newer, Paris-inspired street plan, merchants and homeowners went to work. Gutted buildings, like the Fairmont Hotel and the Merchants' Exchange, were quickly restored. Chinatown rose on its old site. South of Market districts started building vital new factories and warehouses. One after another, new theaters opened. Electric streetcars were installed, replacing cable car lines.

The citizens also took the opportunity to procure themselves a new government. Abe Ruef pleaded guilty to extortion, and was sentenced to 14 years in San Quentin Prison. Ex-Mayor Schmitz himself was awarded five years in exchange for 27 counts of graft and bribery; on appeal, however, his conviction was overturned. In 1912, with the city back on its feet, San Francisco found a mayor after its own heart in "Sunny Jim" Rolph. Mayor Rolph presided over construction of a brand

The fire of 1906 destroyed far more buildings than the earthquake.

new Civic Center and world's fair, the Panama Pacific International Exposition of 1915. Officially a celebration of the opening of the Panama Canal, the fair was San Francisco's boast to the world that it had recovered from 1906 with flying colors.

TWAIN MEETS HIS FIRST EARTHQUAKE

A month afterward I enjoyed my first earthquake. It was one which was long called the "great" earthquake, and is doubtless so distinguished till this day. It was just after noon, on a bright October day. I was coming down Third Street. The only objects in motion anywhere in sight in that thickly built and populous quarter, were a man in a buggy behind me, and a street car wending slowly up the cross street. Otherwise, all was solitude and a Sabbath stillness. As I turned the corner, around a frame house, there was a great rattle and jar, and it occurred to me that here was an item!—no doubt a fight in that house. Before I could turn and seek the door, there came a really terrific shock; the ground seemed to roll under me in waves, interrupted by a violent joggling up and down, and there was a heavy grinding noise as of brick houses rubbing together . . .

The "curiosities" of the earthquake were simply endless. Gentlemen and ladies who were sick, or were taking a siesta, or had dissipated till a late hour and were making up lost sleep, thronged into the public streets in all sorts of queer apparel, and some without any at all. One woman who had been washing a naked child, ran down the street holding it by the ankles as if it were a dressed turkey. Prominent citizens who were supposed to keep the Sabbath strictly, rushed out of saloons in their shirt-sleeves, with billiard cues in their hands. Dozens of men with necks swathed in napkins, rushed from barber-shops, lathered to the eyes or with one cheek clean shaved and the other still bearing a hairy stubble. . . . A lady sitting in her rocking and quaking parlor, saw the wall part at the ceiling, open and shut twice, like a mouth, and then drop the end of a brick on the floor like a tooth. She was a woman easily disgusted with foolishness, and she arose and went out of there. One lady who was coming down stairs was astonished to see a bronze Hercules lean forward on its pedestal as if to strike her with its club. They both reached the bottom of the flight at the same time—the woman insensible from the fright. . . .

—Mark Twain, description of the 1865 earthquake from *Roughing It*

The lofty esteem that old-time San Franciscans held for their fire fighters is eloquently illustrated in this splendid helmet of bygone days. San Francisco, which always has been and still is pre-dominantly a city of wood, burned to the ground on more than one occasion, despite the often heroic deeds of the fire depart-ment. Separate fire companies used to compete for the glory of being the first on the scene of a blaze, and San Franciscans followed the ex-ploits of their neighborhood companies in much the same way as modern citizens support their local sport teams.

The fire of 1906 burned so hot that it melted metal, fused dishes (left), and according to one story, actually incinerated a collection of diamonds stored in a South of Market safe.

■ GROWTH OF THE MODERN CITY

After its amazing recovery from the devastation of 1906 and its hugely successful party in 1915, San Francisco began to win acclaim as "the city that knows how." Few cities have ever deserved the "can-do" reputation more than San Francisco during the first half of the twentieth century. Girding itself with a new sea wall, it bore tunnels through its hills to run its new electric streetcars. New streets terraced up its steep hills, and whole tracts rose in the sandy wastes of the Richmond and Sunset districts. Stimulating the growth of new towns and farms in California, its banks led San Francisco to international stature as a financial center. Coit Tower and the Federal penitentiary on Alcatraz rose on their respective rocks in the 1930s. In 1934 the city, entirely with local funding, dammed the canyon of Hetch Hetchy, 150 miles (240 km) east in the Sierra Nevada, and linked it by aqueduct to the new reservoirs on the Peninsula. The following year, it commenced the first scheduled air service to the Orient, Pan Am's *China Clipper*.

Most amazingly, in the midst of the Great Depression, it confidently set out to build three of the biggest public works projects ever undertaken. The largest bridge in the world, the Oakland Bay Bridge, opened in 1936, followed five months later by the formidable link across the Golden Gate, then the planet's longest span. In 1939, the city completed construction of the largest man-made island in the world, Treasure Island, which was appropriated (before being turned over to the Navy) for a new World's Fair, the Golden Gate International Exposition.

When labor and capital were not working together to conquer San Francisco's natural barriers, they were often wrestling with the social barriers between them. Labor's demands for better pay and an eight-hour work day were justified, but its methods and influence were sometimes pernicious. The Workingman's Party, during the bitter years of the late nineteenth century, was a leading instigator of anti-Chinese protest. The Union Labor Party had put Schmitz in office. Still, they were no worse than the robber barons of the Gilded Age, who damned the public to make their millions.

Labor unrest continued into the new century. San Francisco restaurant workers, teamsters, and machinists went on strike in 1901, and railway workers followed in 1906. Laundry workers sought eight-hour days in 1907, and streetcar drivers walked off soon after. Tensions reached a climax on July 22, 1916, when Mayor Rolph organized a Preparedness Day Parade in anticipation of American entry

A vaulting triumph of human ingenuity: the Golden Gate Bridge.

into World War I. Many unionists blasted involvement in the war as a working-class burden and a diversion from domestic problems. In short, threats were made, and when a pipe bomb exploded along the parade route, killing 10 and injuring others, the unions were blamed. Two union militants, Tom Mooney and Warren Billings, were arrested, charged, and convicted—without sufficient evidence. For the next two decades they languished in prison, international symbols of labor's struggle, until the pair were released (and Mooney pardoned) in 1939.

The largest strike action in American history was the San Francisco longshoremen's walk-out of May 1930. When strike-breakers tried to force the lines, two people were killed and scores injured in the ensuing riots. The union fought back with a call for a general strike, which closed down the city for four days, inspiring solidarity among other Bay Area communities. It ended with the longshoremen winning their demands.

The Great Depression ended early in San Francisco, thanks in part to the injection of jobs and money by the bridge construction projects. World War II brought even greater growth—embittered, of course, by bloody losses in Europe and the Pacific—as local shipyards cranked up to battle speed. One and a half million troops embarked for the Pacific theater from San Francisco, and San Francisco watched anxiously as the Army built bunkers and batteries in anticipation of a Japanese invasion. Fortunately they were never needed. The big guns were obsolete before the war ended.

The war brought compounded tragedy to San Francisco's citizens of Japanese ancestry. Like other mainland issei, nisei, and sansei (first, second, and third generations of Japanese Americans), the San Francisco community was evacuated wholesale and imprisoned in camps. Despite the humiliation of their incarceration, more than 33,000 Japanese Americans (about a third of the total number detained) volunteered for military service. California's contingent, the 100th Battalion, had so many casualties in Europe that it was known as the Purple Heart Battalion. Joined with the Japanese-American 442nd Regiment from Hawaii, they fought through seven major campaigns, sustaining withering losses, and finished the war as the most heavily decorated regiment in American history. General "Vinegar Joe" Stilwell, who slogged through some of the most bitter fighting of World War II, bristled with feisty indignation when he spoke of the Japanese-American persecution and sacrifice: "They bought an awful hunk of America with their blood . . . you're damn right those nisei boys have a place in the American heart, now and forever. We cannot allow a single injustice to be done to the nisei without defeating the purpose for which we fought."

■ NOW WHAT?

The war brought great changes to San Francisco. The city's work force more than doubled as thousands of workers manned (and womanned) the wartime industries. Household economies and social patterns altered permanently as more women became breadwinners. The influx of new residents continued after the war ended. Suburban communities took the brunt of this new growth, unprecedented since the gold rush, as prosperous groups like the Italians (who were the dominant ethnic group in San Francisco for much of this century) and Irish started moving out in larger numbers.

The following decades also saw increased immigration from Asia and Latin America. A new atmosphere of tolerance had emerged from the war, fostered by American prosperity. Reformed immigration laws and overseas unrest, including the Chinese revolution of 1949, and the Korean and Vietnam wars, boosted the numbers of Asian immigrants. Many prospered. Chinese Americans replaced Italian Americans as San Francisco's largest ethnic group in the 1980s.

Not all ethnic groups realized their dreams. Thousands of African Americans from the South, arriving to work in the shipyards during World War II, settled in Hunters Point and the Western Addition. When the war ended and the yards closed or scaled down operations, many were unable to find work in the civil sector. Hunters Point and the Western Addition sank into localized depressions, deteriorating into slums. Though San Franciscans had learned to embrace Chinatown as a cultural (and tourist-industry) asset, they condemned these new inner-city ghettos as an embarrassing blight. During the 1950s and 1960s, clumsy government renovation efforts destroyed whole sectors of Victorian housing. Many of the poorly managed and inadequately policed government projects that replaced them would slide into drug-driven violence during the 1970s and 1980s. San Franciscans were shaken to realize that their city was not immune from what they considered Eastern "rust belt" urban problems.

Looking at it from the outside, however, San Francisco of the 1950s and 1960s seemed to offer an urbane, unspoiled, and exciting alternative to the problem-plagued cities of the American Northeast. The beatniks and hippies were only the most visible heralds of San Francisco's growing reputation as a haven from the established mores and constraints of Middle America. San Francisco's tolerance of alternative thinking appealed to the American gay community and other groups whose views on health, conservation, the arts, society, religion, and politics ran counter to the established grain. This mix of new ideas and people brought new dynamism to city life. Middle America, however, called it madness.

Changes do not come without turmoil. Since the 1960s, cults, fads, and weird events have spawned on San Francisco's Bay like caddis flies. One of the strangest episodes was the February 1974 kidnapping of Patty Hearst, a wealthy local newspaper publisher's daughter, by a radical group called the Symbionese Liberation Army (SLA). Patty soon announced that she had joined up with her abductors for the revolution, leading the FBI on a violent trail of robbery and fiery death to her capture in San Francisco more than a year later. An even more bizarre episode transpired in November 1978, when a transplanted San Francisco group called the People's Temple, led by Jim Jones, committed mass suicide in the jungles off Guyana. That same month, a city ex-Supervisor named Dan White, whose request for reinstatement had been rejected by Mayor George Moscone, assassinated the mayor and gay supervisor, Harvey Milk, right in City Hall.

The past decade has seen a rise in special-interest groups and single-issue politicians with no knack or desire for compromise, rendering the city's government incapable of clear consensus. Large-scale public works projects, like Yerba Buena Center and plans for the city's new ballpark, bogged down for years in political debate. While demonstrations, litigation, and ceaseless dickering continue to clog the city's arteries, thoughtful San Franciscans are wondering if "the city that knows how" has lost its know-how. Indeed, the port is dying. Industries are moving out. Even large corporations, complaining of high rents and anti-business attitudes in San Francisco, are retreating to the suburbs.

Still, for all the problems, one industry is stronger than ever: tourism. Despite the earthquake and highly visible problems of homelessness and litter, many neighborhoods have not looked so well for years. Decrepit Victorians in the Mission, Western Addition, and Haight-Ashbury are being transformed with paint and loving care to a new splendor. The arts are healthy, shopping districts are crowded, and restaurants have never been so diverse and busy. Perhaps most hopeful of all, a new generation of immigrants is setting down roots, revitalizing old neighborhoods, raising their children, and developing the skills and attitudes to fuel a new renaissance in the city by the bay.

The new Marriot Hotel appears to rise above Grant Avenue, the city's oldest street.

D O W N T O W N

SAN FRANCISCANS DIVIDE THEIR CITY INTO TWO ESTATES: the residential neighborhoods, and downtown. The two, according to common perception, are locked in eternal conflict. To local politicians, downtown interests serve big business, conservatives, and suburbanite commuters, while the neighborhoods represent liberal politics, the socially and environmentally conscious, and minority views. There's a good deal of truth in this, as there is in most grossly oversimplified generalizations.

Downtown is San Francisco's interface with the rest of the world. Every working day, some 225,000 people from the burbs (suburbs, exurbs) jam the bridges, trains, MUNI, BART, ferries, streets, and sidewalks—not to mention parking lots—in a Herculean effort to staff the offices and drive the wheels of international commerce. And needless to say, every evening finds them strangling the highways and skyways in a frantic rush to go home again.

To San Francisco's immeasurable benefit, people also *live* downtown. In the 1960s, when urbanologists warned that American city centers were dying, San Francisco initiated one of the country's first large urban renewal projects, the Golden Gateway. It succeeded. Hours after most commuters have abandoned the city for suburbia, downtown lights continue to blaze in all but the deepest chasms of the Financial District.

■ THE FINANCIAL DISTRICT

In a city renowned for spectacular entrances, there's none more exhilarating than the high road from Oakland across the Bay Bridge, when, rising from the water, San Francisco bursts into view, an urbane, stunning, civilized vision of hills and towers.

San Francisco's Financial District, a Pacific Rim dynamo and one of four ranking centers of American finance, was built to a compact, walkable scale. All the key financial touchstones—banks, brokers, exchanges, law offices, clubs, retailers, toney watering holes—are within ready walking distance from one another, nor do pedestrians have to contend with the city's infamously steep hills. The Financial

District rose on land filled in where Yerba Buena Cove once lapped at the feet of Rincon, Telegraph, Nob, and Russian hills. Hundreds of gold rush ships abandoned here in 1849 still lie at anchor today, beneath the streets and foundations of America's "Wall Street West."

As it always has, the Financial District occupies the north side of Market Street, with its most potent concentration at the intersection of Montgomery and California. Raked by honking horns and pounding jackhammers, the district shows up best during business hours, when frantic bike messengers in tribal regalia ride breakneck through the bustling streets, and the bistros and restaurants buzz with big-money deals.

On the bay at the foot of Market Street stands the **Ferry Building**, for many years the gateway to the city. Completed in 1903, it survived the 1906 holocaust through heroic effort of fire-boat crews, and went on to become the second busiest transport terminal in the world, after London's Charing Cross Railway Station. Up to 50 million passengers every year crossed the gangways of 170 daily ferries binding San Francisco to the American "mainland." All that ended with the opening of the Bay Bridge in 1937. Today, the Ferry Building is a shadow of its former preeminence. Its empty wings have been converted to offices, mostly of the World Trade Center. On the pier, a lifelike statue of Mahatma Gandhi, symbol of peaceful resistance and founder of the Indian state, is frozen in vigorous stride. A few high-speed ferries from Marin County now dock here. After the earthquake of October 1989, when the Bay Bridge span was severed for a month, emergency ferry service between the East Bay and San Francisco started up again. At press time, it continues tentatively.

From either side of the Ferry Building spreads further testimony to the past glories, and present languor, of San Francisco's port. The docks and wharves along Embarcadero, a wide road built atop a sea wall stretching six miles (10 km) from China Basin in the south to Fisherman's Wharf in the north, once roared and clanged with people and ships at work. Freighters, schooners, steamers, passenger liners, merchantmen, ferries, junks, square riggers, fishing boats, destroyers, and whaling barks have all, in their respective times, crowded these docks, where longshoremen and sailors labored hard and raised hell in the nearby saloons, chophouses, and flophouses. Virtually all are gone now, lost to Oakland's "mainland" port. Empty docks north of the Ferry Building are fast converting to more sedate usages, such as offices, restaurants, studios, and boutiques. One distinct improvement over all this upscale commercialization was the conversion of **Pier Seven**, the city's longest wharf, into a public promenade bedecked with genteel benches and lampposts, utilitarian fish-gutting sinks, and stirring views of bridge, bay, hill, tower, and a handsome old ferry, now condemned to serve time as a floating office. Between the Ferry Building and Bay Bridge the wharves have been razed, affording spectacular, if sadly quiet, views of bridge and harbor. Only south of the bridge, especially around Hunter's Point, does the Port of San Francisco still mean business.

From the Bay Bridge north to Broadway, the Embarcadero Freeway once vaulted overhead, blocking the sun, fencing off the Financial District from the bay, and swiping clean across the Ferry Building's face. The earthquake of 1989 tried its best to demolish it, and it stood in decrepitude for months while city officials

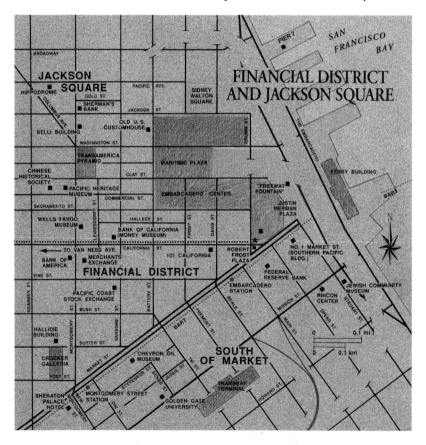

Financial District towers now dominate the old hills of San Francisco.

dickered whether to shore it up or finish knocking it down. The coup de grace came, finally, in 1991. A parody of this monstrosity, the **Villaincourt Fountain** now crouches in splendid isolation, surrounded by **Justin Herman Plaza**, looking for all the world like a jumble of massive freeway blocks regurgitating water. Like all controversial works of public art, it provokes strong passions of love and hate. Those who love it find it very dynamic and hugely inviting on hot days. Its designer, Mr. Villaincourt, gave San Francisco another example of his talents in 1987, when a musician from the rock group U2 vented his artistic expression with spray paint across the fountain. Hearing of the vandalism, Villaincourt caught a flight from Montreal to San Francisco in time to repay the group in kind across their concert stage.

Behind and above Justin Herman Plaza sprawls **Embarcadero Center**, an urbane oasis of landscaped walkways, bridges, patios, and courtyards linking four high-rise office buildings with 150 top-drawer shops, restaurants, and hotels catering to a largely corporate clientele. Pedestrian overpasses span north to **Maritime Plaza**, part of the Golden Gateway Redevelopment Project, an upmarket, high-rise, residential district built around open courts, fountains, and **Sydney Walton Park**, an islet of countryside in the midst of a city. The showpiece of this entire complex is the **Hyatt Regency Hotel**, with its spectacular atrium, dripping with vines from the open-sided corridors lofting 17 stories above. (The Guinness Museum of World Records claims this as the world's largest hotel lobby!) The nucleus of the atrium is a four-story sculptured ball by Charles Perry, set amidst a rippling creek and lush trees. A piano bar and weekly tea dancing keep the music flowing. Glass elevators glide silently up and down the walls and through the ceiling to the Equinox, a revolving cocktail lounge suspended in the midst of glittering towers. By night, views in all directions are enchanting.

Back on the street again, the California Street cable car begins its run to Van Ness Avenue from **Robert Frost Plaza**, where California intersects Market. Frost, the beloved New England poet, was in fact a native son of San Francisco. Though he moved away while still a boy, Frost never forgot the city of his childhood, and wrote fondly:

> *Such was life in the Golden Gate:*
> *Gold dusted all we drank and ate,*
> *And I was one of the children told,*
> *We all must eat our peck of gold.*

Gazing beyond passing cable cars as they climb up Nob Hill, you can spot the curving eaves of Chinatown. Those who bypass the cable car in favor of walking can explore the heart of the Financial District. Reminders of San Francisco's days as queen of the Wild West can still be found amidst the far more overwhelming symbols of the booming present. Along flag-bedecked California Street, the best monuments of post-modernist architecture blend sky-scraping power with touches of humanity. The round tower at **101 California**, designed by Philip Johnson and John Burgee, sports an Italianate plaza with flower-filled urns and a greenhouse lobby. **California Center**, a gargantuan building straddling handsome shopping arcades, houses the spectacular Mandarin Oriental Hotel in its crown—twin towers linked by sensational glass "skybridges," guaranteed to knock the toupee off anyone suffering from vertigo.

With all due respect to Wyatt Earp and Bat Masterson, it was California Street, and especially the blocks intersecting with Montgomery, that *really* won the West. Behind these mild-mannered facades whir the financial dynamos that powered the growth of mines, farms, towns, factories, and transport arteries of the emerging West, driving the frontier farther and farther east, till it finally died of exhaustion in the barren wilds of the Rocky Mountains.

The Bank of California, oldest banking corporation in the state, maintains its 1908 headquarters in the shadow of its present headquarters tower, at 400 California Street. This was the bank of William Ralston, who bankrolled one of the Comstock's greatest bonanzas. Its grand banking hall is guarded by a pair of fierce California mountain lions, carved by local sculptor Arthur Putnam. The basement vault lodges the **Museum of the Money of the American West**, a tidy little collection of gold nuggets, minting paraphernalia and mementos of the Comstock. Most intriguing are the pistols used in the notorious duel between California Chief Justice David S. Terry and U.S. Senator David Broderick. Judge Terry was a Southerner and supporter of slavery, Senator Broderick an ardent Union man. Neither got along politically or personally, and their bandied insults finally resulted in a challenge and acceptance. They met at Lake Merced on the morning of September 15, 1859, with seconds and a party of 80 witnesses. Judge Terry supplied the pistols. On the toss of a coin, he also won first choice. Such details might have stayed mere footnotes of history had not the gun presented to Senator Broderick misfired. Judge Terry immediately returned fire, and plugged Broderick in the chest. Broderick died a martyr, Terry was hissed as a villain, and pro-Union

sympathies soared in California. Take a close look at those pistols; 13 decades ago, there were many who'd have envied you the chance.

Headquarters of two other banks with starring roles in American history, Wells Fargo and Bank of America are also on California Street. The massive, 52-story Bank of America Building at California and Kearny was built in 1969 for what was then the largest bank in the world. With a workday population of more than 5,000 people, this building alone would make a sizable burg in many a state. After 3 p.m., when the top-floor Bankers Club transforms into the Carnelian Room, it offers some of the best views of the city open to the general public. On the plaza below, the large, hard, fist-like sculpture of black marble is known by financial district clerks as *The Banker's Heart*. (Its real name is *Transcendence*, by Masayuki Nagari.) To be fair, the father of the B of A was a warmhearted man. Born in San Jose of Italian immigrants, A.P. Giannini founded his bank, originally known as the Bank of Italy, to serve immigrants and people of small means who were shunted aside by less compassionate financial institutions. When the 1906 earthquake struck, Giannini personally rescued his bank's deposits ahead of the flames, hauling them hidden in orange crates to San Mateo. Before other banks' super-heated vaults could cool, Giannini was back in business, investing heavily in San Francisco. It proved a sound bet, as did later investments in California's fledgling farms and small towns. Giannini's most famous gamble was a preposterous bridge across the Golden Gate; and once again, he backed a winner. The modest **Bank of America History Room** on the mezzanine of the bank annex displays some vintage office machinery and historical photos.

Wells Fargo, a name that still calls up images of cracking whips and rattling coaches, keeps the vision alive in its **Wells Fargo History Room**, at 420 Montgomery. An original Wells Fargo stagecoach, route maps, postage stamps, weapons, and displays of Western paraphernalia crowd the two floors. Among the most interesting items are samples of Emperor Norton's currency, a half-completed coach box, which you may try for comfort as you listen to a passenger's recorded diary, and memorabilia of one Charles E. Bolton, alias Charles Boles, alias Black Bart. Bart was a dapper little fellow who, in the 1870s and 1880s, earned his living by highway robbery. His fame rests not only on his 28 stage holdups, but on the leaves of doggerel that he occasionally left behind with the pilfered strong boxes, signed "Black Bart, Po8."

A mural at Coit Tower recalls the drama and vitality of the old waterfront.

I rob the rich to feed the poor,
Which hardly is a sin;
A widow ne'er knocked at my door
But what I let her in.
So blame me not for what I've done,
I don't deserve your curses,
And if for any cause I'm hung,
Let it be for my verses.

Unfortunately for Bart and po8try lovers, he carelessly dropped a handkerchief at his final robbery. Special Detective Harry N. Morse traced it to a laundry on Bush Street, San Francisco, and was waiting there when Charles Bolton came to call. Engaging him in conversation about mining ventures, the detective invited Bolton back to his offices at Wells Fargo and Company, where he arrested him for highway robbery. Convicted, Bolton was given a remarkably light sentence of seven years at San Quentin State Penitentiary in Marin County. He served four years before being paroled for good behavior, and has never been heard from since. The big-hearted, two-fisted Wells Fargo museum is free, and keeps banking hours.

On the southeast corner of California and Montgomery stands the 1905 **Merchants Exchange**, one-time focal point of city trade, with a lookout tower once used to report ship arrivals to the floor below. Though it serves mixed uses now, the building's maritime connections are still remembered in the ship models and magnificent marine paintings by William Coulter in the

Black Bart.

Exchange Hall, now the First Interstate Bank. The building survived the 1906 quake but was gutted by the fire, and later restored to classic glory by Willis Polk. The current focus of trade in San Francisco is the **Pacific Coast Stock Exchange**, at the nearby corner of Pine and Sansome, the country's largest exchange outside New York. Visitors who enter the small front door can climb to the gallery to enjoy a bird's-eye view of frenzied brokers barking into phones and tearing out their hair on the floor below.

The cozy scale of old San Francisco still survives at the corner of Commercial and Leidesdorff streets. The forty-niners themselves might have felt at home among some of the facades on the low, brick rows staggering up Commercial Street toward Chinatown. The block between Kearny and Grant is one of the few remaining cobbled streets in San Francisco. The U.S. Subtreasury Building, at 608 Commercial, was erected in 1875 to accommodate the U.S. Mint. Inside the renovated shell, you can walk through the original brick vault, preserved as the **Pacific Heritage Museum**. Fine exhibits of Asian art are periodically rotated, and admission is free. (The Chinese Historical Society Museum, treated on page 115, is just up the street.)

The most distinctive landmark of San Francisco's new skyline, the **Transamerica Pyramid**, rises at the end of Leidesdorff. At 853 feet (260 m), it is the tallest building in the city. The 27th floor is open to the public, one of the few views from a downtown building that can be had without buying a drink or getting a job. On a warm day, to sit in the shade of the redwood grove growing on its eastern side is a delicious pleasure. When the fog blows in, parting at the needle like a silent, pale river round a monolithic rock, it's an almost zen-like experience.

The Pony Express once stopped across the street, at Montgomery and Merchant, where a plaque marks the end of the 1,966-mile (3,164-km) run from St. Joseph, Missouri. Yet it is the Pyramid's site itself that is most haunted by history, and most mourned by those who love San Francisco. The Montgomery Block, affectionately known as the Monkey Block by many generations of citizens, once stood here. Built in 1853 by the soon-to-be Civil War general, Henry Halleck, it was for decades the largest, sturdiest building west of the Mississippi, accommodating law offices, newspapers, and bars that contributed enormously to the culture and history of the city. Here it was that James Casey gunned down James King of William in 1855, activating the Second Vigilance Committee, which hanged Casey for his crime. It was here also that Mark Twain met the original

A Hyde Street cable car slices through a morning fog (overleaf).

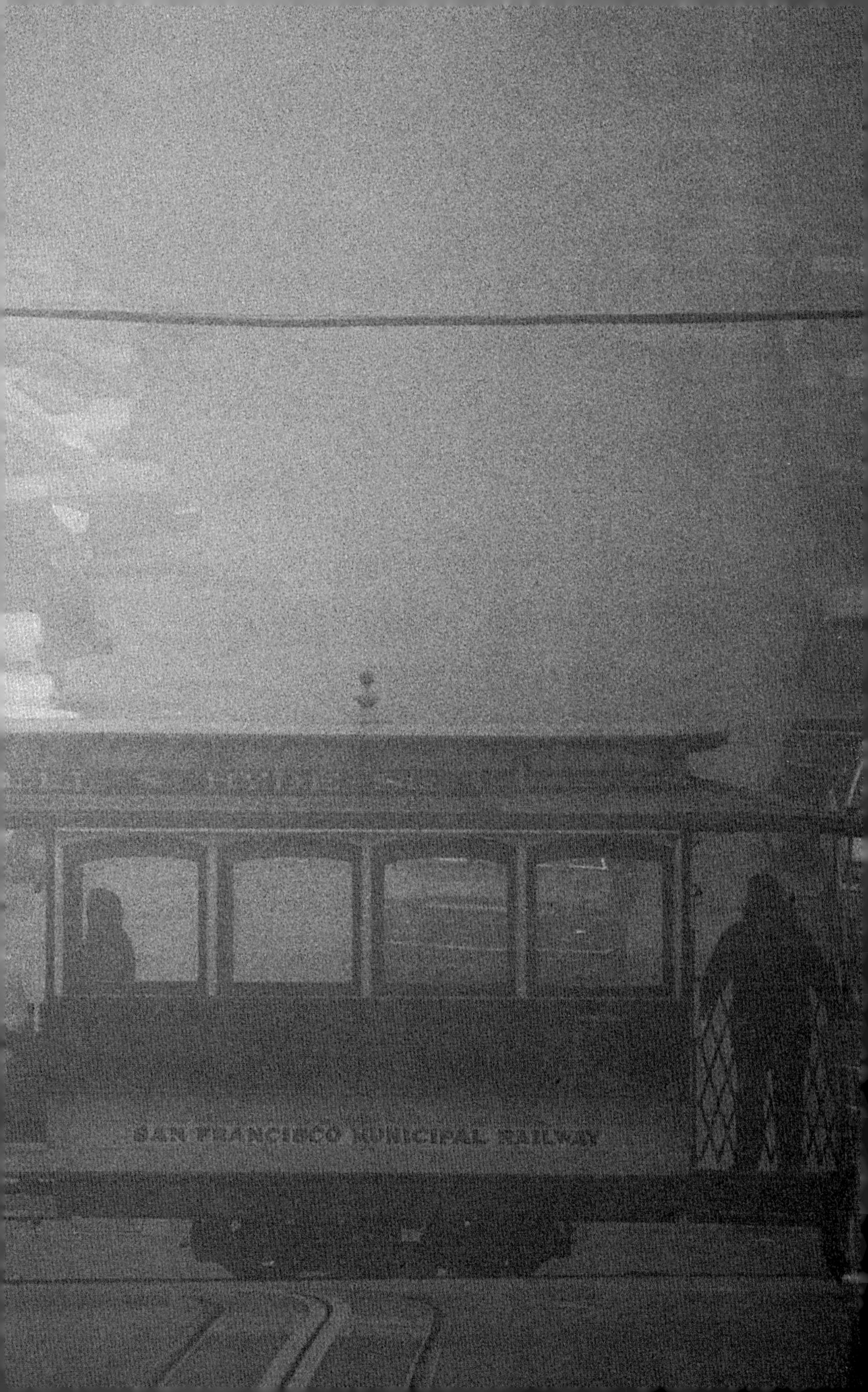
SAN FRANCISCO MUNICIPAL RAILWAY

Tom Sawyer, who owned a Turkish bath in the basement, and where he downed Pisco Punches in the Exchange Saloon while admiring the painting of Samson and Delilah above the bar (as did most male patrons, noted Twain). Twain kept rooms here; so did Ambrose Bierce, George Sterling, Frank Norris, Charlie Stoddard, Joaquin Miller, Gelett Burgess, and other writers. Dr. Sun Yat-sen also settled in for a spell to write the English version of the Chinese constitution while on world tour in quest of funds for the revolution. And at the turn of the century, Pappa Coppa's restaurant on this site was San Francisco's most frequented rendezvous off bohemian writers, poets, and artists, who decorated the walls with their works. Thus, through peace, revolution, rollicking nights, decadence, and stolidity, the Monkey Block nursed in classic San Francisco style as egalitarian an array of characters as ever graced a city. It survived the earthquake and, even more remarkably, the fire of 1906, but it could not survive the wrecker's ball, and fell for a parking lot in 1959.

■ JACKSON SQUARE

On to the Barbary Coast, alias the International Settlement, nowadays more properly called the Jackson Square Historical District, which is found across Washington Street north of the Pyramid. Once infamous as the most perverted hell-hole on Earth, San Francisco's Barbary Coast in its heyday set standards of wickedness and depravity that would have made Shanghai blush. At least that's the legend; whatever it was *really* like—and no doubt was a mean and dirty place—it couldn't *possibly* compare with the legend.

Spawned in the gold rush to cater to the lusts of a huge city of males drained of hope and with no passage home, the Barbary Coast coaxed the worst of mankind to do their worst, and the best to do no better. The Coast's main thoroughfare was Pacific Street, known to aficionados as "Terrific Pacific," a string of saloons, gambling dens, raunchy dance halls, and other attractions stretching some half a dozen blocks west from the waterfront. Choice sections of the Coast acquired their own sobriquets: Murderer's Corner, Battle Row, Devil's Acre, Dead Man's Alley. Brutality, prostitution, murder, drunkenness, and bestiality were commonplace. Vicious men lurched through torchlit streets, meeting casual death in grog shops with names like the Morgue, the Goat and Compass, Bull Run, and Devil's Kitchen.

Human beings were reduced to the lowest forms in performances of the grossest degradation. Hundreds of prostitutes worked the "cowyards" in narrow cribs stacked up to four stories high, or performed on stages with horses, pigs, and grizzly bears. One pathetic creature known as Oofty Goofty built a reputation by selling the privilege of beating him with a baseball bat across the backside, until the fighter John L. Sullivan crippled him with a pool cue for 50 cents. Another gent by the name of Dirty Tom McAlear made his living (and severely taxed his clients' imaginations) by eating anything that was plopped down before him, for pennies. Here also was sanctuary for the brutal gangs of hoodlums (a word said to have been coined in the Barbary Coast) who terrorized Chinatown. (Another Barbary Coast coinage was the word "Shanghaied," which described what happened to unsuspecting sailors who imbibed spiked drinks, called Mickey Finns. Mr. Mickey Finn himself, incidentally, was the Barbary Coast chemist who supplied the drugs.)

The Barbary Coast raged on for over six decades, eventually feeding on its own notoriety by catering to intrepid tourists and local slumming parties. Outraged preachers and newspaper editors called for divine punishment, or at the very least,

Old Barbary Coast inmates take a break from the action.

government action, to clean up the Coast. Not surprisingly, Heaven made the first move. In April of 1906, the day of reckoning came. The earth shook, buildings crumbled; fire storms swept through the Financial District, the mansions of Nob Hill, the tenements of Chinatown, North Beach, Russian Hill, and South of Market. Five hundred square blocks of San Francisco were incinerated. The streets, parks, Presidio, and transbay ferries swarmed with 250,000 refugees. But curiously, as the smoke and flames cleared, the very heart of the Barbary Coast was seen yet standing amidst the coals, miraculously spared. The party wasn't over! Not until 1917 did a government decree even attempt to bring the Coast to heel, and even then a smaller, tamer version called the International Settlement staggered on until mid-century.

Today, the Barbary Coast is well and truly dead, though fortunately, many of its buildings live on for our edification. It is now a thoroughly gentrified district of old brick structures quaintly renovated to quarter architects, antique sellers, and design studios, some of which cater only to professionals and are not welcoming of casual browsers (unless they be very well-padded, and in any event, possessing of an appointment). Even the old name has been turned out in favor of a peculiarly inappropriate euphemism, Jackson Square. You won't find a square here, but it is very worth your while to wander through the elegant, tree-lined streets, peering through windows and hunting down a few old landmarks. The Belli Building and its neighbors on the **700 block of Montgomery**, for instance, are curious relics of the 1850s, though sadly weakened in the Loma Prieta quake of 1989. At number 728, Bret Harte purportedly wrote "The Luck of Roaring Camp."

Around the corner on Jackson, the brick and cast-iron buildings at 451, 445, and 463 once housed **A. P. Hotaling's offices**, including his wholesale whiskey operation. This latter establishment occupies an esteemed position in the lore of the Barbary Coast, for its survival in the fire of 1906 inspired an immortal ode on cosmic justice:

> *If, as they say, God spanked the town for being over-frisky,*
> *Why did He burn the churches down and spare Hotaling's whiskey?*

Other points of interest include the bawdy **Hippodrome Theater**, now a showroom at 555 Pacific, but still preserving a resplendent facade in carved relief once considered very shocking indeed. (Arthur Putnam was the artist.) **Gold Street**, an alley that predates the Barbary Coast, appears little changed since the 1850s, though

San Francisco's financial towers now line both sides of Market Street.

most building interiors have been fortified against earthquakes. Its western end is marked by the **Bank of Lucas, Turner and Company**, 1853, better known today as the bank once managed (into bankruptcy) by William Tecumseh Sherman, who later went on to burn Atlanta in the Civil War. Stout's bookstore, required browsing for anyone with the faintest interest in architecture and design, now occupies part of the building. And while in the neighborhood, if you need a map—any map—try the Map House at 550 Jackson. Alternatively, walk two blocks east to the old Custom House at 555 Battery, where you'll find cartographers' paradise on the fifth floor, presided over by the **United States Geological Survey**.

Broadway and Kearny streets mark the edges of downtown San Francisco. To the north lies North Beach, to the west, Chinatown; both are covered in the next chapter. But downtown San Francisco expands on other fronts, so let us backtrack to Market Street. . . .

■ MARKET STREET

Market Street is San Francisco's main transport corridor, where BART and MUNI rush commuters in and out through tubes and tunnels, while buses, taxis, cars, bikes, and pedestrians vie for space above. When Jasper O'Farrell laid out the street plan in 1847, he envisioned Market as a grand thoroughfare cutting in a wide diagonal from the bay to the foot of Twin Peaks. But O'Farrell failed to foresee the havoc his plan would wreak on modern traffic. North of Market, he laid out small, human-scale city blocks in a grid aligned on a north-south axis. South of Market, he planned a much larger grid, better suited for vehicular traffic than pedestrians, and running roughly on a northwest-southeast axis. In consequence, every street intersecting Market hits at an awkward angle, and worse, the streets north of Market never meet the ones from the south, except by luck or some fancy driving. Instead of becoming a focal point for the Financial District, Market Street became the barrier to its southward expansion for the next 140 years. The barrier only now is being breached on a large scale, thanks to building height restrictions and spiraling real-estate prices north of Market.

Anyone uninitiated in the workings of the Financial District will want to stop by for an explanation at the **Federal Reserve Bank** at 100 Market, where they may study an interpretive display and film explaining its role as the "bankers' bank." Much more fun is the **Chevron Oil Museum** in the Standard Oil Building at 557-

75 Market, where you can try your hand at discovering oil reserves by computer, pitting your skills against the previous 665 participants.

An excellent travel book store, with an enormous selection of maps and books, is Rand McNally, at the corner of Second and Market.

A short block west, opposite the strategic intersection where Montgomery spills into Market, William Ralston built the Palace Hotel in 1873. With well over 700 rooms, it was the largest and most celebrated hostelry in the world at the time. Ralston had big plans for his little city. He furnished the hotel with little regard for reason or expense. Champagne and oysters were standard fare, and traveling royalty made it their home away from home. From the Crystal Roof Garden on the top floor, resident millionaires gazed down upon the carriages arriving in the Grand Court, seven stories below (see page 18). Oscar Wilde and Rudyard Kipling lodged at the Palace in the 1880s, and opera sensation Enrico Caruso got the snub of his career here on an April morning in 1906, when he was rudely awakened by a falling ceiling. The Palace burned in the fire that followed, and the heartily offended virtuoso left town swearing never to return.

A new Palace rose on the foundations of the old. Make a point to visit it, if only for a peek at the elegant **Garden Court**, inspired by the earlier Grand Court and one of the grandiose dining rooms in the city. The famous Maxfield Parrish painting of the Pied Piper of Hamelin in Maxwell's evokes strong memories of long-forgotten bedtime stories.

American Indian Contemporary Arts, on the second floor of 685 Market Street, exhibits crafts and art of the many native cultures of the United States. Hand-made Navajo blankets and jewelry, books, art, traditional clothing, taped music, and various other cultural treasures are sold in the gallery shop.

The **Crocker Galleria**, across Market Street and a half block west on Post, has an attractive arcade of gardens and shops under a barrel-vaulted roof. Framed at the northern end is the **Hallidie Building**, at 130 Sutter, reputed to be the world's first glass-curtain-walled building. (If glass-curtain walling fails to induce shivers up and down your spine, try thinking of it as the original glass-walled skyscraper.) When architect Willis Polk completed it in 1918, he was way ahead of his time. Polk, who left his mark throughout San Francisco, was a man devoted to perfection and indifferent to the petty interests of ordinary mortals. Once, when a New York corporate potentate seeking his services tried to praise his designs, the architect replied, "I would feel complimented if I thought you knew anything about art."

Heading home on BART, East Bay commuters enjoy a sunset over San Francisco (overleaf).

■ SOUTH OF MARKET

No area of San Francisco has changed so much and so fast as the South of Market district. Wealthy people began to flock to the up-and-coming residential enclave of Rincon Hill in the 1850s, but they just as rapidly left it when the new cable cars turned Nob Hill into the city's mansion district. As the rich took flight, middle-class, and later working-class, people moved in. The district became known as South o' the Slot, in reference to the cable car lines (which had slots for the cables) that ran up Market Street. In the 1906 fire, the blocks of cheap wooden houses burned so fast and hot that iron melted. The district was rebuilt with factories, warehouses, train yards, and businesses serving the port at China Basin. For the next 70 years, South of Market was known as Skid Road.

But now, what steel-and-marble vision is rising from the brick pile? The factories, train yards, and warehouses have closed or moved away. The sailors have mostly gone the way of the port. Even the drunks and other sad down-and-outers have mostly moved up to Fifth Street and beyond. In deference to New York's SoHo (South of Houston) district, Frisco trendies have rechristened South of Market as "SoMa." Like SoHo, SoMa's gentrifying vanguard were the painters, photographers, dancers, and sculptors who moved into the low-rent warehouses and abandoned factories, converting them into studios. On their heels came factory retail outlets for designer clothes, and then the fashionable nightspots and cafés. The decision to build a new convention hall, Moscone Center, as part of a larger redevelopment project called Yerba Buena Center, boosted land prices. Hotels and restaurants built to service conventioneers enhanced the area's residential appeal, encouraging a boom in upscale housing developments. Momentous land values in the traditional Financial District are pushing up new office towers in SoMa.

The writing is on the wall: the middle class is reclaiming South o' the Slot. Still, gentrification is spotty. The neighborhood character changes radically from one street to the next. Some blocks have a monolithic, even chilling, feel about them; but then, so often does the avant-garde. SoMa's nightlife conjures up brash and trendy overtones of punk, gay, leather, fifties, or new wave, appealing to a young and city-savvy crowd. Artists still cling on, though larger colonies of the starving variety are presently found in the Mission District and Bayview/Hunters Point. Factory retail outlets, which draw life from neighborhood decrepitude, are thriving, especially south of the James Lick Freeway. (These more southerly regions of SoMa will be treated on pages 240-241.)

Some of the most spectacular new architecture in town is going up South of Market, much of it incorporating existing buildings in the design, a salute to the quality and integrity of past architects. Two examples near Market Street are Number One Market Street and Rincon Center.

In **Number One Market Street**, architects Michael Paynor and Associates incorporated the 1917 Southern Pacific Building into their 1978 structure, which features a huge mosaic clock, an indoor plaza, and a cheerful fountain that curtains off a small plaza restaurant. Southern Pacific is the successor of the Central Pacific, builder of the first transcontinental railway, linking California to the East. The railroad also opened enormous tracts of California to farming and settlement, while acquiring vast landholdings and influence. By the latter third of the

---

Jack London Does So Ma

"*C*ome on,—I'll show you the real dirt," Brissenden said to him, one evening in January.

They had dined together in San Francisco, and were at the Ferry Building, returning to Oakland, when the whim came to him to show Martin the "real dirt." He turned and fled across the water-front, a meagre shadow in a flapping overcoat, with Martin straining to keep up with him. At a wholesale liquor store he bought two gallon-demijohns of old port, and with one in each hand boarded a Mission Street car, Martin at his heels burdened with several quart-bottles of whiskey.

If Ruth could see me now, was his thought, while he wondered as to what constituted the real dirt.

"Maybe nobody will be there," Brissenden said, when they dismounted and plunged off to the right into the heart of the working-class ghetto, south of Market Street. "In which case you'll miss what you've been looking for so long."

"And what the deuce is that?" Martin asked.

"Men, intelligent men, and not the gibbering nonentities I found you consorting with in that trader's den. You read the books and you found yourself all alone. Well, I'm going to show you tonight some other men who've read the books, so that you won't be lonely anymore."

PIPE DREAMS ON AN EMPTY STOMACH

... *My* feet tingled. I thought I was going to die the very next moment. But I didn't die, and walked four miles and picked up ten long butts and took them back to Marylou's hotel room and poured their tobacco in my old pipe and lit up. I was too young to know what had happened. In the window I smelled all the food of San Francisco. There were seafood places out there where the buns were hot, and the baskets were good enough to eat too; where the menus themselves were soft with food esculence as though dipped in hot broths and roasted dry and good enough to eat too. Just show me the bluefish spangle on a seafood menu and I'd eat it; let me smell the drawn butter and lobster claws. There were places where they specialized in thick red roast beef au jus, or roast chicken basted in wine. There were places where hamburgs sizzled on grills and the coffee was only a nickel. And oh, that pan-fried chowmein flavored air that blew into my room from Chinatown, vying with the spaghetti sauces of North Beach, the soft-shell crab of Fisherman's Wharf—nay, the ribs of Fillmore turning on spits! Throw in the Market Street chili beans, redhot, and french-fried potatoes of the Embarcadero wino night, and steamed clams from Sausalito across the bay, and that's my ah-dream of San Francisco. Add fog, hunger-making fog, and the throb of neons in the soft night, the clack of high-heeled beauties, white doves in a Chinese grocery window . . .

—Jack Kerouac, from *On The Road*

South of Market is well known for its clubs and nightlife

nineteenth century, railroad corporations had become the most powerful private institutions in the state. Frank Norris fiercely attacked their monopolistic rape of a Central Valley farming community in his novel, *The Octopus.* Behind is **Rincon Center**, incorporating a 1940 post office annex. Murals on the annex walls stirred bitter controversy when painted after World War II by Anton Refregiar, a Russian immigrant, because they showed the dirt under San Francisco's nails. A case in point is his rendition of Vigilante Days, depicting the assassination of James King of William by James Casey, while a menacing Vigilante Committee marches in the background and a man gets lynched. Other panels illustrate the anti-Chinese rabble-rousing, the transcontinental railway, the Mooney case, the 1906 earthquake, and an imaginary convocation of writers associated with San Francisco, including Mark Twain, Bret Harte, Jack London, Robert Louis Stevenson, and Ambrose Bierce. Through the modest annex door, the center bursts into a soaring atrium surrounded by little bistros and soothed by the patter of fountain water falling like rain from the lofty skylight.

The **Jewish Community Museum** at 121 Steuart Street provides a cultured venue for frequently changing exhibits on Jewish art and history. Recent exhibitions have dealt with such diverse themes as Jewish ghetto life in Italy from the fifteenth century, the plight of Ethiopian Jews in Israel, and political art inspired by the trial and 1953 execution of Julius and Ethel Rosenberg.

San Francisco's main commuter bus station, the Transbay Terminal, parks on Mission and First streets. One block west is **Golden Gate University**, a small urban campus with an emphasis on downtown San Francisco's two abiding passions, business and law. Their small but nifty bookstore huddles on Ecker, a side alley. While there, look up in the eaves of the building above tiny Ecker Square for a ceramic owl, placed there to keep pigeons from roosting. Nice try, guys.

One of San Francisco's most industrious collections of electronic miscellany, the **Telephone Pioneer Communications Museum**, occupies a jam-packed room just off the ornate lobby of the 1925 Pacific Tel and Tel headquarters building. Among the displays that relate the history, and hint at the future, of the telecommunications industry, are an old-style telephone booth, model satellite, San Francisco's first phone book, hands-on electronic displays, vintage switchboards, and other assorted telephone equipment dating back to the 1870s. One intriguing exhibit shows how beep baseball is played by the blind. Entrance to the museum, on the corner of Natoma and New Montgomery, is free.

Moscone Center, San Francisco's prime convention complex, occupies the entire block of Howard between Third, Fourth, and Folsom streets. It was the vanguard of the Yerba Buena development, an ambitious plan that (if all goes ahead) will one day incorporate offices, hotels, gardens, and a new home for the Museum of Modern Art. Named for San Francisco's assassinated mayor, George Moscone, the exhibit hall is an engineering curiosity well worth contemplating, if you happen to be there anyway. The arched roof supports are designed like a series of great, taut hunting bows, with the ends strung together by cables running under the floor. By tightening the cables, structural engineer T.Y. Lin was able to spring enough upward thrust to counter the enormous weight of the ground-level landscaping on the roof, without employing a single interior column. The result is a vast, open hall, one of the largest underground spaces in the world.

Across Fourth Street at number 250, the **Ansel Adams Center** hosts five galleries devoted to the art of photography. One gallery is permanently set aside for the work of the eminent photographer and San Francisco native, Ansel Adams, whose black-and-white landscapes of Yosemite and the American West are among the world's most widely recognized photographs. With a research library, bookstore, photography classes, and other programs, the center is an important fixture on the Bay Area art scene. Admission is free only on the first Tuesday of every month.

Lording over the corner of Fifth and Mission, the proud, classic revival, **old United States Mint** stands aloof from the other more pedestrian tenants of the block. Erected between 1869 and 1874 by the U.S. Treasury to stamp coinage from raw California gold and Nevada silver, The Granite Lady (as she is dubbed) minted some of the finest coins ever struck. Architect A.B. Mullet anchored the building on one of the few stone outcroppings within the old city boundaries; combined with her four-foot (1.22-m) granite walls and iron-shuttered windows, she was able to rebuff the earthquake and fire storm of 1906. Replaced in 1937 by the new San Francisco Mint on Market at Buchanan, The Granite Lady has now reopened as a free museum. On view are a stamp mill for crushing ore, huge assay scales, a $5 million pyramid of gold bullion, piles of gold coins, and an 1869 coin press on which visitors may stamp their own bronze medallions. At $1 a throw, it's the best souvenir in town. Basement vaults exude the musty smell of impregnability, and are still used to store a fortune in specie. A *must* visit for coin collectors is the numismatic shop run by the Treasury Department.

As you head west on Mission from the old mint, the transient, skid-row character that once pervaded much of the district south o' the slot still retains a footing. Sixth Street is a cross-Market extension of the seedy precinct known as the Tenderloin. Heading north on Fifth Street, however, you will soon find yourself at Market Street, and what is for many the very heart of San Francisco.

■ THE SHOPPING DISTRICT

Powell slams into Market at **Hallidie Plaza**, crossroads of the city. The lion's share of San Francisco's hotels are located nearby, as are many prominent theaters, restaurants, art galleries, shops, and department stores. The cable cars prelude their clanging journeys to Nob Hill, Chinatown, and Fisherman's Wharf with a clumsy, yet charming, pirouette on the **Powell Street turntable**. Here, the trajectories of callow executives from nearby office buildings collide with the paths of sheepish tourists, Tenderloin panhandlers, suburbanites with shopping bags, and park-bench prophets ruminating on the world's end. Meanwhile, information and maps can be gathered at the main **Convention and Visitors' Bureau** office downstairs near the Powell Street BART station.

San Francisco's downtown retail shopping district is the second largest in the country in terms of sales, and it whips number one, New York's Fifth Avenue, for compactness and convenience. Six major department stores are located in a five-block area, and some of the most elegant shingles in the world hang in the side streets. The district is well served by buses and the Powell Street station of BART and MUNI, and has more than 5,500 parking spaces for those shortsighted shoppers who insist on driving. And believe me, you might have to wait to get one of those spaces.

The 1988 opening of **San Francisco Centre** on the corner of Fifth and Market was hailed and booed as a beachhead of a middle-class campaign to retake a section of Market long given over to transients. San Francisco Centre is a vertical mall whose main tenant is the sumptuous, Seattle-based department store, Nordstrom. It boasts the world's first semi-spiral escalators, which wind mantra-like up the eight-story central well to a dome that opens to the sky on fine days. Next door, the venerable Emporium bustles under its own pink rotunda. Children love the Emporium's roof-top carnival and the colossal toy train megalopolis that takes over the top floor every Christmas.

Union Square, at the heart of the shopping district, was named for the pro-Union rallies held here during the Civil War, when there was a controversy whether California (and its gold) would throw in its lot with the North or South. Largely by the oratory of San Francisco preacher Thomas Starr King, the city went firmly pro-Union; and as San Francisco went, so went the state. Union Square is now the roof of the world's first underground multi-level parking garage. A column and statue commemorating Dewey's victory at Manila during the Spanish-American War gathers pigeons at center stage. Flower stands at its busy corners splash color through the streets.

On the west side of Union Square, the landmark Saint Francis Hotel was gutted in the fire of 1906. You can stroll through the elegant arcade, or rocket to the top of the new tower annex in spectacular, outside glass elevators. It was here that President Gerald Ford made his lucky escape from an assassin's bullet in 1975, and here also that Miles Archer, Sam Spade's partner in *The Maltese Falcon*, commenced the job that would shortly result in his murder on nearby **Burritt Street**, a site now marked by a plaque.

Sam Spade fans should also pay respects at John's Grill (63 Ellis Street), the shrine where Spade devoured a plate of chops, a spud, and sliced tomatoes. A Maltese Falcon Dining Room and den named for author Dashiell Hammett preserve photographs and memorabilia from the detective cult, including a replica of the infamous black bird itself. Next door is the back entrance to the handsome **Flood Building**, where Hammett's Continental Op gumshoe, and Hammett himself when he worked as a Pinkerton detective, kept their offices. And no, you won't find either on the directory board.

Fans of another detective can visit 221-B Baker Street, miraculously transported to the Sherlock Holmes Esquire Pub on the top floor of the Holiday Inn at Powell and Sutter.

Those rambling, many-storied meccas of the well-heeled shopper—Macy's, I. Magnin, Neiman-Marcus, and Saks Fifth Avenue—all have doors near Union Square. Perhaps their most popular commodity, especially during the Christmas season, is the festive atmosphere of big-city bustle, lights, rich scents, music, color, and a thousand other delights that even window-shoppers can afford. For just a bit more, give your feet a rest and your nostalgia a rush by taking tea under the grand glass dome that for decades surmounted the now-defunct City of Paris. (It now overspreads Neiman-Marcus, at the corner of Stockton and Geary.) And don't

miss the festive Yuletide decorations at F.A.O. Schwarz, the dazzling toy store at Stockton and O'Farrell. East of Union Square, framed by the four-block rectangle of Stockton, Geary, Kearny, and Sutter, are among the most unapologetically luxurious shopping streets in the country. Among the names here that bespeak exclusive tastes and wealth one may find Tiffany, Dunhill, Cartier, Gucci, Louis Vuitton, Laura Ashley, Bullock & Jones, Eddie Bauer, Wilkes Bashford, and Brooks Brothers, to name but a few. The lavish San Francisco institution at 250 Post Street, Gumps, has an old world feel that matches the rarity of its wares. Much of what they sell you will not find anywhere else, for Gumps specializes in one-of-a-kind treasures. Their jade collection is renowned the world round. Their furniture and decorations are works of art, and their works of art are, well, exceedingly expensive. Sally Stanford, San Francisco's favorite madame (and a woman of discriminating tastes), once referred to Gumps as "the Metropolitan Museum with cash registers. . . ." The magical extravagance of their autumn promotion, for which a score of buyers and artisans prepare all year, is legendary.

Maiden Lane, the petite darling of these blue-blooded streets, has a risqué past. She was once none other than notorious Morton Street, yet another of San Francisco's red-light districts. Frank Lloyd Wright designed the Circle Gallery Building at 140 Maiden Lane, a smaller version, but an obvious prototype, of his famed spiral interior in the Guggenheim Museum in New York. A small display of old cameras, including a spy model used in the Watergate break-in, is found at the free **Museum of Photography** on the second floor of the camera store at the corner of Kearny Street and Maiden Lane.

The San Francisco Bay Area is one of the premier centers of the antiquarian book trade. Although excellent bookstores can be found throughout the region, an uncommonly large host of antiquarian dealers keep shop within striking distance of Union Square. Unbeknownst to the casual walk-in trade, some of the finest are located on quiet upper floors, behind locked doors. These, for the most part, are the haunts of the serious book collector, the type who might be looking for a first edition Mark Twain, a signed John Muir, or a rare volume from the Italian Renaissance. (See "Backmatter" for some names and addresses.)

The Union Square area is also known for its galleries displaying the works of famous or established contemporary artists. Check the *Bay Area Gallery Guide*, published quarterly by the San Francisco Art Dealers' Association, and available free at member galleries.

San Francisco Centre shoppers ascend to Nordstrom's on spiral escalators.

■ THE THEATER DISTRICT

San Francisco's answer to Times Square, albeit a quiet answer, begins with **Lotta's Fountain** at the intersection of Geary, Kearny and Market, presented by the actress Lotta Crabtree, who got her start as a child dancer in California during the Gold Rush. Here San Francisco celebrated its most sentimental Christmas Eve, in 1910, when the Italian coloratura soprano, Luisa Tetrazzini, expressed her passionate gratitude to the city that "discovered" her five years earlier, by singing free to a crowd of thousands that filled the streets.

San Franciscans love and have always loved the theater and its troupers. During the gold rush, miners used to lob bags of gold dust on stage when young Lotta Crabtree danced, though rotten vegetables and worse were kept on hand for more critical judgment calls. The forty-niners were not really a brutish lot; in fact, gold rush San Franciscans were on average better educated than New Yorkers of their day. They enjoyed poetry, sat through Cantonese opera, and were passionately devoted to Shakespeare and grand opera, even in the most far-flung mining camps. San Francisco's first opera house opened to clamoring audiences as early as 1851. Though woolly and remote from European capitals, from the start it was pulling in stage companies from the grand opera and theater circuits, solely by the extraordinary enthusiasm of its audiences (and gate receipts). European superstars Lola Montez and Lillie Langtry forsook their royal lovers for San Francisco's adulation, and settled for a time in small California towns. As the great nineteenth-century actress, Helena Modjeska, used to say, "If they like you in San Francisco, you're all right."

Aside from Lotta Crabtree and Tetrazzini, San Francisco launched the careers of Adah Menken, Edwin Booth, and native son David Belasco. Ironically, San Francisco cannot claim discovery of her most influential daughter of the footlights, Isadora Duncan. Duncan's fortune and fame as the progenitor of modern dance were first recognized in New York and the capitals of Europe. Appropriately, Isadora's birthplace is the heart of San Francisco's theater district. The original building, at 501 Taylor Street, is gone, but a plaque marks the site.

The Bay Area supports a tremendous number and range of theaters and drama companies, so it seems a bit confining to pin the name "Theater District" on one small area. After all, several other nationally celebrated theater companies, like the

HOT ON THE BLACK BIRD'S TAIL

Spade went to the Geary Theatre, failed to see Cairo in the lobby, and posted himself on the curb in front, facing the theatre. The youth loitered with other loiterers before Marquard's restaurant below.

At ten minutes past eight Joel Cairo appeared, walking up Geary Street with his little mincing bobbing steps. Apparently he did not see Spade until the private detective touched his shoulder. He seemed moderately surprised for a moment, and then said: "Oh, yes, of course you saw the ticket."

"Uh-huh. I've got something I want to show you." Spade drew Cairo back towards the curb a little away from the other waiting theatre-goers. "The kid in the cap down by Marquard's."

Cairo murmured, "I'll see," and looked at his watch. He looked up Geary Street. He looked at the theatre-sign in front of him on which George Arliss was shown costumed as Shylock, and then his dark eyes crawled sidewise in their sockets until they were looking at the kid in the cap, at his cool pale face with curling lashes hiding lowered eyes.

"Who is he?" Spade asked.

Cairo smiled up at Spade. "I do not know him."

—Dashiell Hammett, from *The Maltese Falcon*

Berkeley Repertory, the Magic Theater, the Asian-American Theatre Company, and the Eureka Theatre, are in neighborhood districts. Still, if blue-haired theater matrons and jaded cabbies alike agree to call the half-dozen scattered blocks west of Union Square "The Theater District," who am I to argue? Scores of other Bay Area theaters present "Broadway" plays, musicals, and classic drama, but the Theater District offers them professionally produced, with larger budgets than are available to smaller neighborhood companies. Adding to the special theatrical atmosphere are the late-night cafés.

The doyen of the city's troupes is the American Conservatory Theater (ACT), a highly professional repertory company that tends to stick to the works of established dramatists, classic and contemporary, in its main productions. As a repertory, the company puts on several plays a season, rotating nightly. Works by Shakespeare, Shaw, Christopher Fry, and Tom Stoppard, among others, appear often, and the

SHOPPING DISTRICT
AND CIVIC CENTER

BUSH ST.

SUTTER ST.

POST ST.

GEARY ST.

O'FARRELL ST.

SERGEANT
JOHN MACAULAY
PARK

THE GREAT AMERICAN
MUSIC HALL

ELLIS ST.

SIERRA CLUB

FATHER
ALFRED
BOEDDEKER
PARK

EDDY ST.

CALIFORNIA
CULINARY
ACADEMY

TENDERLOIN

TURK ST.

FEDERAL
BUILDING

OPERA PLAZA

GOLDEN GATE   AVE.

STATE
BUILDING

SOCIETY OF
CALIFORNIA
PIONEERS

STATE
BUILDING

HIBERNIA
BANK BLDG.

McALLISTER ST.

VETERAN'S
MEMORIAL
BUILDING

MUSEUM OF
MODERN ART

UNITED
NATIONS
PLAZA

FULTON ST.

CIVIC

MAIN
LIBRARY

FEDERAL
BUILDING

CITY HALL

CENTER

OPERA HOUSE

ORPHEUM
THEATER

SAN FRANCISCO
BALLET SCHOOL

GROVE ST.

CIVIC CENTER
STATION

S.F.
PERFORMING
ARTS
LIBRARY &
MUSEUM

DAVIES
SYMPHONY
HALL

BOXING MUSEUM

POLICE MUSEUM

CIVIC
AUDITORIUM

HAYES ST.

FELL ST.

BART

PETER YORKE WAY

STARR KING WAY

GOUGH ST.

FRANKLIN ST.

VAN NESS   AVE.

POLK ST.

LARKIN ST.

HYDE ST.

LEAVENWORTH ST.

JONES ST.

8th ST.

9th ST.

101

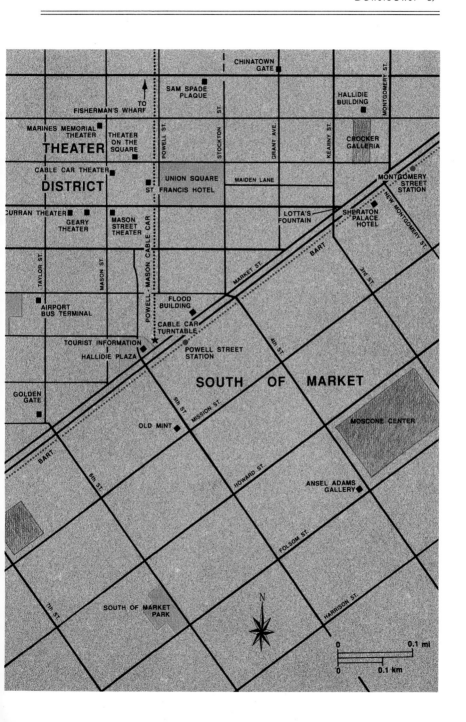

CHINATOWN GATE

SAM SPADE PLAQUE

TO FISHERMAN'S WHARF

HALLIDIE BUILDING

MONTGOMERY ST.

MARINES MEMORIAL THEATER

THEATER ON THE SQUARE

THEATER

POWELL ST

STOCKTON ST.

GRANT AVE.

KEARNY ST.

CROCKER GALLERIA

CABLE CAR THEATER

DISTRICT

ST. FRANCIS HOTEL

UNION SQUARE

MAIDEN LANE

MONTGOMERY STREET STATION

CURRAN THEATER

GEARY THEATER

MASON STREET THEATER

LOTTA'S FOUNTAIN

SHERATON PALACE HOTEL

NEW MONTGOMERY ST.

TAYLOR ST.

MASON ST.

POWELL - MASON CABLE CAR

MARKET ST.

BART

3rd ST.

AIRPORT BUS TERMINAL

FLOOD BUILDING

CABLE CAR TURNTABLE

TOURIST INFORMATION

HALLIDIE PLAZA

POWELL STREET STATION

SOUTH OF MARKET

4th ST.

GOLDEN GATE

5th ST.

MISSION ST.

OLD MINT

MOSCONE CENTER

BART

6th ST.

HOWARD ST.

ANSEL ADAMS GALLERY

FOLSOM ST.

7th ST.

SOUTH OF MARKET PARK

N

HARRISON ST.

0   0.1 mi

0   0.1 km

company has made an annual yuletide event of producing *A Christmas Carol.* Until its 1,300-seat Geary Theater (415 Geary Street) is overhauled from its thrashing in the Loma Prieta quake, the company continues to play other venues around town. ACT is much beloved by their public, so buy your tickets well in advance. Call the box office at (415) 749-2228.

Generalizations about most other Theater District venues are more difficult. For an up-to-date schedule of all performances, check the pink "Datebook" in the Sunday *Chronicle.* By and large, the Curran (445 Geary) offers Broadway drama road shows, while the 2,400-seat Golden Gate Theatre (25 Taylor) tends to specialize in Broadway musicals. The Cable Car Theatre (430 Mason), the Theatre on the Square (450 Post, upstairs from the Kensington Hotel), and the Marines Memorial Theater (609 Sutter) are known for their Off Broadway productions. The Plush Room Cabaret (940 Sutter, in the York Hotel) and Mason Street Theatre (340 Mason) host smaller plays and revues. Farther down in the Tenderloin, the Orpheum (1192 Market) struts and frets its hours upon the stage in its sadly benighted neighborhood. Farther west, the Great American Music Hall (859 O'Farrell) promises a very good time for ears, with music ranging from Grand Ol' Opry to New Age fusion.

The Theater District is also San Francisco's main hotel district, though the bright lights and the proximity of the transient Tenderloin neighborhood might encourage visitors unaccustomed to urban life to take lodging farther up Nob Hill, or to seek out an altogether quieter neighborhood.

Walking north from the Theater District, the steep rise of Nob Hill quickly becomes noticeable. The finer things in life come thick and fast here: hotels, shopping, restaurants, galleries, clubs. The ironically exclusive **Bohemian Club**, on the corner of Taylor and Post, was founded by people who would have laughed uproariously to see it now, a sanctuary for the likes of Richard Nixon, Henry Kissinger, Gerald Ford, and other powerful Establishment figures. In its early days, George Sterling, Jack London, Ina Coolbrith, Ambrose Bierce, John Muir, and Joaquin Miller were the *original* bohemians.

■ THE TENDERLOIN

The dreariest high-crime district in San Francisco is the Tenderloin. It is easy to stumble into because it lies between the downtown shopping district and the Civic Center, at the edge of the greatest concentration of hotels in the city. Its exact boundaries are fuzzy, but it is generally pinned down between Larkin, Mason, and O'Farrell streets, with a dogleg over Market and down Sixth Street toward Howard.

The Tenderloin, in case you wonder, is a kind of vigorous skid row and red-light district of porn shops, pimps, streetwalkers and massage parlor fronts. It attracts runaways and their exploiters, as well as drug dealers, drunks, transvestites and down-and-outers—not to mention stag businessmen and conventioneers. The Tenderloin has the highest rate of rape in the city, and ought to be avoided by unaccompanied females, even by day. Because of cheap rents, the Tenderloin also has the largest concentration of elderly poor people. Many live a life of fear, barricaded behind locked doors.

But all is not a tale of woe. The Tenderloin is in the midst of change. Within the past decade, Southeast Asian families have been quietly colonizing a large swatch of territory here, especially in the blocks along Ellis Street. Most of them are ethnic Chinese from Vietnam, Laos, and Cambodia, many of whom survived 40 years of warfare and unbelievable hardship to get here, and who do not flinch easily at the mere reputation of mean streets. Still, the sight of children playing amidst cars and derelicts is unsettling to parents and outsiders alike, and movements are afoot to build a children's park in this heavily concrete sector. Through such efforts, the Southeast Asian influence may yet transform the Tenderloin from a no-man's land to a thriving family community. Already, its markets and restaurants are attracting patrons from other neighborhoods, and even some tourists. Especially inviting are the small neighborhood cafés, mostly of the cheap and hearty Vietnamese type called *phö*, where a huge bowl of spiced soup, with a condiment of fresh bean sprouts, lemon, pepper and mint leaf, is the *pièce de résistance*.

The "City by the Bay" clambers over its trademark hills (overleaf).

■ CIVIC CENTER

No spectacle of civic architecture in the country is more grand than San Francisco's Civic Center; and yet, there is no more disgraceful display of failed humanity than the derelict army that seems permanently encamped on its plaza and perimeters.

City Hall's magnificent dome is a symbol of proportion and reason, a triumph of beauty and benevolent power. The sight of transients camping there is another symbol, an ambiguous one that says little for control and order, ideals, or compassion. Where to house them, of course, is a problem with no easy answers, but until a solution is found, a visit here will be a shocking experience.

Civic Center is a supreme example of the Beaux Arts style in America. Beaux Arts was a movement initiated by young American architects who had studied at the French Ecole des Beaux-Arts. Inspired by classical architecture and infused with the City Beautiful movement, the new school of civic planning called for formality in design, with wide boulevards, colonnades, parks, and plazas. Its ideas swept the country at the turn of the twentieth century. When enthused San Franciscans asked Chicago architect David Burnham to draft new plans for their city, he retreated to the top of Twin Peaks for two years of study and sketching. Published in 1905, his Burnham Plan called for a Paris-style revamp of San Francisco's streets, making use of the hills as great, park-like pedestals for monuments, with grand boulevards leading off from a magnificent Civic Center.

The 1906 earthquake wiped the slate clean, and seemed a God-given opportunity to institute the Burnham Plan. But San Franciscans were in a hurry to rebuild, and before the bureaucrats could rouse themselves, the city's commercial and residential sections were already rising on the old street grid. Fortunately, government sloth for once paid off at Civic Center, which was rebuilt more slowly on City Beautiful principles. Old City Hall had crumbled in the quake, a victim of government corruption that siphoned off construction funds and used substandard materials. Outraged San Franciscans mandated a new government, and a new Civic Center.

One of the first acts of Mayor "Sunny Jim" Rolph when elected in 1911, was to call for bids for a new city hall. The winning design came from the firm of Bakewell & Brown, two local boys who had submitted it with no serious expectation that San Francisco would choose such an extravagant plan.

Arthur Brown Jr., a graduate of the Beaux Arts school, was the designer. His old fraternity partner, John Bakewell Jr., ran the business end of the operation. They went on to build other great buildings, including Civic Center's War Memorial Opera House, Berkeley's city hall, several structures on the Stanford and Berkeley campuses, and Coit Tower; but **San Francisco City Hall** was both the cornerstone and capstone of Brown's long, distinguished career. The dome, modeled after Saint Peter's at the Vatican, rises three feet (one meter) higher above its floor than the nation's capitol. To stand below that ornate dome and flowing staircase inspires awe for the powers of Caesar. Henri Crenier's Renaissance-style sculptures over the Polk Street entrance represent the figures of San Francisco, California's Riches, Commerce, and Navigation. Watching over the Van Ness Avenue entrance are Labor, Industry, Truth, Learning, the Arts, and Wisdom. Long may they live!

United Nations Plaza, between Market Street and City Hall, commemorates the charter meeting of that august body, which took place in June 1945 at the War Memorial Opera House. A largely Asian-style farmers' market sets up on the plaza on Wednesdays and Sundays. Rich in color and vitality, the **Civic Center Market** is a cornucopia of fresh, hard-to-find Southeast Asian vegetables and processed foods.

San Francisco's **Main Library** fronts the plaza. Its third-floor San Francisco History Room and Archives keeps the city's historical volumes and photographs, displaying some memorabilia under glass. Closed on Sundays, Mondays, and Wednesday mornings, this little museum is infinitely more rewarding for delvers than browsers.

Two tiny, but pugnacious, exhibits occupy hallways of the Civic Auditorium (99 Grove Way). Boxing fans can cast an eye over the gloves, shoes, robes, and other mementos of great pugilists of old San Francisco and the Bay Area, housed in the modest **Boxing Museum**, on the third floor. The equally modest **Police Museum** on the fourth floor displays handcuffs, uniforms, badges, district maps, and historical photos of San Francisco's bygone police forces. Both museums are free and open on weekends, though first floor staff might grant you entry at other times if you ask nicely.

Aficionados of architecture should detour to see the 1892 **Hibernia Bank building** at the corner of Jones and McAllister. Architect Willis Polk (who did not design it) called it the most beautiful building in San Francisco—quite a compliment from an egoist with impeccable taste. The building is slated to become the new Tenderloin police station.

The **Society of California Pioneers museum** at 450 McAllister Street is a splendid, if tiny, shrine to California history. Its ground floor gallery displays some fine old California oil paintings, while the video theater in the basement gives a livelier version of the past.

Outside the Van Ness entrance to City Hall, an ornate iron gate joins the twin Veterans Memorial Building and the War Memorial Opera House. The **Museum of Modern Art** occupies the third and fourth floors of the Veterans Memorial Building (though talk of moving it to Yerba Buena Center may bear fruit if the latter ever gets built). Their permanent collection of works by American and European artists, sculptors, and film-makers, includes paintings by Picasso, Matisse, Dali, and Monet. Lack of room prevents more than a minute percentage from being shown at any given time. The museum bookshop is said to be the largest retailer of art books (not to mention posters, cards, catalogs, artistic toys, and T-shirts) on the Pacific Coast. The museum also sports an art library and artsy café. Admission fees are moderate.

The ultimate place to see and be seen in San Francisco is at the opera during its September to December season. Dressed to the nines, San Francisco's glitterati

Intermission at Davies Symphony Hall draws crowds to the windows (above). City Hall's rotunda has watched over seven decades of progress and turmoil (left).

arrive in limousines on opening night, tailed by paparazzi and society editors. Devoted fans of more modest means jam the standing-room-only section when stars, like Pavarotti, come to shake the rafters. The lavish costumes and settings are awe-inspiring; all in all, the San Francisco opera is among the world's most critically acclaimed. Those who just can't get enough may retire after the performance for supper at Max's Opera Café in Opera Plaza (601 Van Ness), where the waiters and waitresses are said to occasionally break into arias in the evening. The San Francisco Opera Shop (199 Grove) sells opera glasses, books, and recordings, not to mention espresso at an intimate coffee bar well aired with the house music. To inquire about a night at the opera, telephone (415) 864-3330.

Like its opera, San Francisco's ballet and symphony are internationally distinguished. One of the nation's oldest dance companies, the **San Francisco Ballet** performs in the War Memorial Opera House when it is not on the road, and favors a classical repertoire. The **San Francisco Symphony** keeps house at Louise M. Davies Hall, built in 1981 on the corner of Van Ness and Grove. The symphony season runs from September through May. Davies Hall is equipped with the largest concert hall organ in North America, built by the Ruffatti brothers of Padua, Italy. Its 9,235 pipes are played with the help of a sophisticated computer. For ballet tickets, phone (415) 621-3838; for the symphony, (415) 431-5400.

A mandatory side-trip for aficionados of local theater, opera, dance, and music is the **San Francisco Performing Arts Library and Museum**, one block west of Davies Hall, at the corner of Grove and Gough streets. A wealth of trappings of the footlit stage—theater posters, playbills, newspaper clippings, and some 4,000 books on the performing arts from the gold rush to the present—invest the archives and gallery walls with the smell of greasepaint, the roar of crowds.

The culinary arts are also well represented in the Civic Center area, thanks in large part to the city's premier training ground for chefs, the **California Culinary Academy** (625 Polk). In their 16-month course on classical French, Italian, and nouvelle cuisines, students run a gauntlet of pastries, wines, appetizers, salads, dressings, canapés, decorative meats, entrées, terrines, garnishes, cut vegetables, soups, and desserts, while learning the economies and etiquette of kitchen and restaurant. The best part is, you can taste the fruits of their labors. Besides operating a retail bakery and small café, the academy serves lunch and dinner at set times on weekdays in a glass-enclosed hall, permitting diners to watch the ongoing work in the kitchens, and in the basement Academy Grill. Service is excellent and prices are extremely reasonable. Reservations are recommended and dining hours are short, so call (415) 771-3500 before going.

Headquarters of the **Sierra Club**, the international environmentalist organization founded by John Muir to preserve and foster appreciation of California's Sierra Nevada range, stands one block north at 730 Polk Street. Its street-level store sells books on travel, nature, and conservation.

GOING HOME

*W*here are they going
all these brave intrepid animals
Fur and flesh
in steel cabinets
on wheels
high-tailing it
Four PM Friday freeway
over the hidden land
San Francisco's burning
with the late sun
in a million windows
The four-wheeled animals
are leaving it to burn
They're escaping
almost flying
home to the nest
home to the warm caves
in the hidden hills & valleys
home to daddy home to mama
home to the little wonders
home to the pot plants behind the garage
The cars the painted cabinets
streak for home home home
THRU TRAFFIC MERGE LEFT
home to the hidden turning
the hidden yearning
home to San Jose
home to Santa Cruz & Monterey
home to Hamilton Avenue
home to the Safeway the safest way
YIELD
LEFT LANE MUST TURN LEFT . . .
—Lawrence Ferlinghetti,
from "Home Home Home,"
Landscapes of Living & Dying

NABOBS, SOJOURNERS, BOHEMIANS

THE LOW HILLS RISING UP BEHIND DOWNTOWN San Francisco are no Rocky Mountains, but they are a formidable barrier nonetheless. The principal civic, financial, and commercial functions of San Francisco cluster on the flat lands around the foot of these hills, where bureaucrats and capitalists (and their esteemed clients) can tread the course of least resistance. But climb any hill out of downtown San Francisco, and you turn your back on the world of big business and big government.

Nob Hill, Telegraph Hill and Russian Hill, with their attendant communities of North Beach and Chinatown, were among San Francisco's earliest residential areas, nurturing a succession of outcast communities, eccentrics, and escapists, not to mention plenty of just ordinary family folk. Within five minutes' walk of the hard-nosed towers of Montgomery Street, you can buy a Chinese pear or hear Puccini sung on a jukebox. Within 10 minutes, you can watch a game of bocce or pay respects to Kuan Kung, god of war and literature. Within 15, the all-seeing Top of the Mark can be your throne, or if you prefer, a wooden step beneath dangling fuchsias on Telegraph Hill. And all around you, tens of thousands of local residents and passers-by are playing out their lives in neighborhood bistros, schools, markets, churches, temples, restaurants, clubs, newspapers, hospitals, and funeral parlors, while cable cars rattle and clang through the boisterous streets.

Cynics lament that some of these neighborhoods have become mere symbols of what they used to be. Yes, commercialism has made gross inroads at Fisherman's Wharf. Beatniks and nabobs, for the most part, have gone the way of cheap rents and unregulated monopolies, and even the Italians of Little Italy are growing thin on the ground. Yet, as long as red wine, green tea, Napier Lane, gelato, dim sum, fettuccine, and City Lights Bookstore survive, these most San Franciscan of San Francisco's old neighborhoods will continue to salve the soul and feed the senses.

The "Italian Cathedral" rises over the rooftops of North Beach.

■ NOB HILL

San Franciscans like to say that the *Nob* of Nob Hill is a contraction of *nabob*, meaning a Moghul prince. This etymology is dubious, but it has poetic license. Some of America's favorite nabobs, who ripped their fabulous fortunes from the silver mines and railroad rights-of-way of the American West, built their mansions on the gilded crown of Nob Hill.

Hemmed in on the south by Union Square, the Theater District, and the Tenderloin, on the west by busy Polk Gulch, and on the east by teeming Chinatown, Nob Hill stands aloof from the tumultuous city. Today, however, it's not so exclusive as when Robert Louis Stevenson called it "the hill of palaces." The dapper doormen at the grand hotels cater to a newer, more transient breed of mini-nabob. But the ghosts of the old Big Four and the Bonanza Kings live on, not only in Nob Hill's place names, but in its rarified air of understated wealth (not that there was anything understated about the hill's colossal Victorian prosperity). Today's

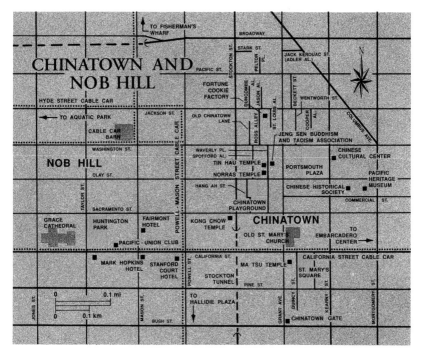

Elegant Nob Hill drops steeply toward the bustling theater district.

fortunes are more restrained, more evenly spread. The palaces have shrunk to town houses, penthouses, and hotel suites. The corps of servants that once bowed to one master and mistress now pamper hordes of splurging tourists.

The invention of the cable car in 1873 sealed Nob Hill's fate as a suitable aerie for Victorian millionaires. It was said that Leland Stanford built the California Street line for his wife's convenience, laying the tracks right past their door at the corner of Powell and California. Today, you can eyeball those tracks clear down the California Street canyon of the Financial District, past Ralston's and Gianinni's and the Wells Fargo banks, to the imposing Southern Pacific Building on Market Street. Southern Pacific, of course, is the reincarnation of the Central Pacific, the company founded by Stanford and the other Big Four (Hopkins, Crocker, and Huntington) to build the first transcontinental railway. The Big Four reaped obscene fortunes and power from the arrangement. In time, their empire straddled much of the American West, rolling over all who got in its way.

The ultimate triumph of Stanford's life, however, eluded him. He and his wife had a son, whom they doted on. Leland Stanford Jr. was raised in the lap of Nob Hill, a privileged quarter of chiming clocks and scurrying servants, where rare and wondrous toys for the lad arrived from around the world. The best of everything was lavished upon him, and he grew up showing great talents in several disciplines, particularly archaeology. But sadly, in his sixteenth year, while on a European tour with the family, the boy died, plunging his parents into sorrow unswayed by all the money in the world. They returned to San Francisco and channeled their grief into building a memorial to perpetuate his name for the benefit of other sons and daughters of California. That monument is Stanford University.

Like all the other wooden palaces on Nob Hill, the great Stanford mansion burned in the 1906 fire. The massive granite wall that once surrounded it still partially encloses the present structure, the Stanford Court Hotel. It is, in the best tradition of nabobbery, one of the finest hotels in the world. Stanford's cable cars still come trundling up from the lowlands, pausing briefly outside his vanished front door. The Powell-Mason and Powell-Hyde street lines, climbing up Powell from Market, cross the California Street line at this same corner.

Mark Hopkins, the Big Four's number two man, built his mansion next door to Stanford's, at the top of California Street. Today, the Mark Hopkins Hotel (1 Nob

Hill) rises on the site, capped by the city's most famous view-bar, the **Top of the Mark.** You can see for miles from every window, the celebrated view (though maybe not the venue) that inspired the city's signature song, immortalized by Tony Bennett: "*I Left My Heart in San Francisco.*"

Another elegant landmark of after-hours San Francisco rises across the street. Named for Comstock millionaire James Fair, the Fairmont Hotel was built by his daughter atop the foundation of the Fair mansion, and is a grand survivor of the quake of 1906, though it was gutted in the fire. The stately marble lobby in its day has greeted many a blue-blood. The **Fairmont Crown,** reached by a heart-grabbing ride in a glass elevator up the outside of the hotel's modern tower, is San Francisco's loftiest watering hole. The Tonga Room offers dancing by a South Sea lagoon, complete with a tropical thunderstorm.

Across the street from the Fairmont stands the solid brownstone **Flood mansion.** The only Nob Hill mansion to survive the fire of 1906, Bonanza King James Flood's one-time residence (1000 California Street) is now the exclusive Pacific-Union Club. It's called the P-U in local parlance. Don't even bother to knock.

Alone among his partners, Charles Crocker lacks the posthumous honor of having his name grace a Nob Hill hotel. Instead, his old mansion made way for San Francisco's supreme Protestant house of God, **Grace Cathedral.** Gazing at the towers and spire of that high-minded edifice, it is difficult to envision this as the scene of San Francisco's most grotesque example of filthy-rich rascality. There was a time when Charlie Crocker owned *most* of that block and wanted it *all.* That elusive corner lot, however, was owned by a Chinese undertaker named Nicholas Yung, who declined to sell for anything less than a price too high for Crocker's pride to bear. In retaliation, Crocker built a 40-foot (12-m) "spite fence" around Yung's property, enclosing the house on three sides. San Franciscans were outraged by this symbol of oppression. Even Dennis Kearney, voice of the Workingman's Party and infamous for his anti-Chinese rhetoric, marched his men up Nob Hill in protest, exhorting them to tear down the fence and lynch Crocker. They did neither, nor did Crocker or Yung budge from their positions. Historian Randolph Delehanty notes that both men died with the stalemate unresolved, leaving their heirs to settle the matter. The Yung estate eventually was sold to the Crocker estate, and all passed quietly to the Episcopal Diocese after the 1906 earthquake rendered the property untenable for worldly use.

Flags atop Nob Hill's grand hotels recall the banners of a princely estate (overleaf).

No matter how lovely Grace Cathedral looks—and it is a beaut, inspired by Notre Dame in Paris—one can never escape the nagging fact that it is made of reinforced concrete. Why that should detract from the *idea* of religious beauty is not hard to understand. The great cathedrals of Europe, built block by block over decades, sometimes centuries, physically embody their builders' inspired, personal devotion. A cathedral erected in compliance with a building code established to protect worshippers from earthquakes and other acts of God just does not epitomize the same fervor of piety. Still, Grace is a lovely cathedral, from the doors (cast from Lorenzo Ghiberti's *Gates of Paradise*, from the Cathedral Baptistry in Florence) to the great rose window (built in Chartres in 1970). Most beautiful of all is the flood of music that pours out during the choral evensongs, and when the pipe organ or carillon is played, especially in the Christmas season. Phone (415) 776-6611 for the choral calendar.

Collis P. Huntington, last of the Big Four, once owned the site of Huntington Park, across the street. Huntington bought the land from the widow of Southern Pacific's lawyer, David Colton—which is odd, since the Big Four had accused Colton of embezzlement and sued for a piece of his estate. This lawsuit was the sensation of its age, an unfolding drama of graft and bribery among the rich and famous, which titillated a fascinated public for eight years and scandalized Congress into a flurry of reform laws directed against the robber barons. Today the grand house is gone. Huntington Park is a quiet, sedate place with a charming little fountain, much beloved by elderly Chinese ladies who do their morning *tai chi* above the ashes of the Big Four's mansions. Those who wish to further contemplate this great American saga in an atmosphere evocative of the era may retire across California Street to The Big Four, a splendid restaurant in the posh Huntington Hotel.

The California Street cable car line drops down the west side of Nob Hill five blocks farther to Van Ness Avenue. This valley is known as **Polk Gulch**, after Polk Street, which runs north from City Hall to Aquatic Park, parallel to Van Ness. Polk Street was the setting of McTeague's dentistry office in Frank Norris's *McTeague*. It was also one of the earliest established gay neighborhoods of the city, but has since been eclipsed by Castro Street. Polk Street south of California has gone a bit seedy of late, but the northern stretch remains a vigorous commercial and residential area with an increasing Chinese influence. Of the many interesting shops and restaurants along here are the Tibet Shop (1807 Polk) and Fields Book Store (1419 Polk).

■ CABLE CAR BARN

If you have never seen the Cable Car Barn, the Powell Street cable car lines offer a more interesting descent of Nob Hill. The Barn, on the corner of Mason and Washington, is the powerhouse of the entire cable car system. The cable car was invented by cable engineer Andrew Hallidie and first tested successfully on Clay Street in 1873. Hallidie's inspiration, the story goes, came after watching a horse-drawn streetcar slip down one of San Francisco's steep streets, dragging the horses behind. Hallidie set about to devise a mechanical system that would pull cars up the steep hills and around the city's many 90-degree turns. He succeeded, and though devilishly complex, the cable car is a work of genius.

A cable car has no engine. The kinetic energy is all in the cable, a continuous loop of steel constantly moving at 9.5 miles per hour (15.5 kph) throughout the maze of pulleys under the streets, from the beginning of a line to the end. When the cable car operators (two to a car—a gripman and a conductor/brakeman) want to move, the gripman forces his "grip" into the slot in the street wherein rides the cable, and grasps it tightly. The cable then pulls the car up the hill. At corners and terraces, where the cable passes over a pulley, the gripman must release the grip to

The cable car barn hums as its powerful wheels pull the cables.

allow the car to coast over the pulley. The brakeman receives his workout on the descent of the city's steep hills, a real test of nerve and machine, particularly on the Hyde Street grade of Russian Hill.

The engines that drive the cables are housed in the Cable Car Barn. This building hums with power. On the mezzanine floor, you can look down upon the powerful 14-foot (4.3-m) wheels that turn the cables, and inspect the old cable cars on display. Be sure to descend to a basement window to see how the cable feeds around corners under the street. You can buy souvenirs and books explaining the operation in much greater detail from the mezzanine shop. The museum is free, and is open daily.

Before turning up Clay Street for Russian Hill, the cable car conductors shout, "Chinatown!" Stockton, the main shopping street for Chinatown residents, is only one block down.

■ CHINATOWN

Chinatown is a clash of five senses, a crush of humanity, a blur of ambrosial steams and flavors, a cacophony of clattering pots and market cries, the grim whir of sewing machines behind windowless walls, an odor of dried fungus.

Rudyard Kipling called it "a ward of the city of Canton," setting a theme for later tour guides, who prefer to compare Chinatown to Hong Kong. Which is nonsense. In fact, it's a little like comparing Grover's Corners to the City of London.

Chinatown is a distinctively American hybrid of a Cantonese market town— *Cantonese* inasmuch as most of its residents are ethnically Cantonese, and *American* inasmuch as fortune cookies, Chinese New Year parades, dragon-wrapped lampposts, Miss Chinatown contests, Chinatown tourist kitsch, some of the best apple pie in the city, and much more, are distinctively American phenomena. And that's just scratching the surface.

Chinatown's founders were mainly from two classes. City merchants, mostly from Guangzhou (Canton City), were few in number, but they rose to prominence in the community by virtue of their wealth, polish, and ability to speak English. The vast majority of early Chinese immigrants, however, were rural males, laborers largely from Toishan County, whose local dialect is quite distinct from that of Guangzhou. Most of these were sojourners, that is, men who intended to return

Waverly, "the street of painted balconies," is now noted for its temples.

Tai chi, an ancient Chinese form of exercise, is performed in controlled slow motion, rigidly disciplined, painstakingly methodical. Some have called it "Chinese shadow boxing," an inadequate description, for the movements only vaguely resemble the more crudely martial Western form of boxing. If performed diligently over one's lifetime, tai chi is said to keep the muscles and cardiovascular system toned and healthy. Every morning brings devotees, many of them elderly, to the open spaces around Chinatown, particularly Portsmouth Plaza, Huntington Park, and Washington Square, where teachers lead them through the graceful moves.

Children are the most vital ingredient of Chinatown's future.

to China after making their fortune—as indeed many did, bringing back new ideas that hastened the downfall of the Qing Dynasty. Few learned English, which contributed to their isolation in America. They banded together in clubs, or *tongs*, based on their surname or county of origin. The word "tong" has a negative connotation in English today, but in Chinese it means only "association." Most "tongs," or associations, in Chinatown were and are perfectly benign social clubs. The tong was the principal political and social force of old Chinatown, most benevolently in the form of a confederation of tongs called the Six Companies; but least so in the form of the fighting tongs of the late nineteenth century.

This peculiarly masculine, working-class society was mummified by the Exclusion Act of 1882. Instead of developing into a family-oriented neighborhood, San Francisco Chinatown remained for years a stunted frontier settlement in the midst of a city, where flourished all the vices comforting to lonely men—drugs, gambling, prostitution, and the corruption and violence associated with the control of same. Ironically, the *real* opium dens, slave girls, and highbinders that inspired sinister Hollywood movies about Chinatown were themselves kept in business largely by the American Exclusion laws. (In a double twist of irony, Chinatown's unique character also inspired stereotypes in the *Chinese* cinema: a stock character of Hong Kong movies and anecdotes up until the 1960s was "Uncle from Gold Mountain"—an aging, rich, spendthrift, good-hearted oaf on the lookout for a young wife.)

Today's Chinatown is a whole different world. Since immigration laws were relaxed in the 1960s, the influx of immigrant families from Hong Kong, China, Taiwan, and Southeast Asia have rejuvenated it. Crusty old Toishan bachelors and Cantonese merchants still hold their own, but they are part of a far richer tapestry of lanky peasants and Taiwanese tycoons, fry cooks and spoiled-brat starlets, sober-sided professionals and shell-shocked refugees, sophisticates and factory workers, aunties with their daily shopping and, most precious to a once-stagnant community, children.

Most of this new "community" no longer lives in Chinatown. The prosperous, the educated, and the ambitious move on to the suburbs. Non-English-speaking immigrants and the elderly poor, for the most part, stay behind. Life for them can be hard. Chinatown is the most densely populated neighborhood in the States outside of Harlem. Housing is poor. Sweatshops exploit immigrants ignorant of American labor laws. For those who move away, however, the grimmer realities of Chinatown fade behind a kind of spiritual, or perhaps visceral, symbol.

Here, suburbanites can and do regularly repair to eat Chinese food, read Chinese newspapers, shop for Chinese groceries, browse through the Chinese library and bookstores, go to a Chinese movie, and, in short, retouch some aspect of their (or their forebears') heritage.

Not all of Chinatown's "suburbs" are distant. The nucleus of Chinatown remains the 24-block area bounded by Kearny, Bush, Powell, and Broadway, but the contiguous community now incorporates the less hectic streets of North Beach, Telegraph Hill, Russian Hill, and Nob Hill. Stockton Street is the main Chinese thorough-

Chinatown lamppost.

Portsmouth Square is the living room of many Chinatown elderly, (top). The Li Po (bottom), a Chinatown watering hole for many years, was named for China's most famous poet.

fare, while Grant is the mecca of tourists. The streets in between—Pacific, Jackson, Washington, Clay, Sacramento, and the alleys that connect them—best retain the atmosphere of old Chinatown.

The only way to tour Chinatown is on foot. The streets are too congested for comfortable driving, and finding a parking space is like winning the lottery. Even the parking garage under Portsmouth Square often has a line of cars *waiting just to get in the door.* You may have better luck parking beneath the Holiday Inn across the street, or under Saint Mary's Square. Visitors might well consider joining one of the walking tours that go "behind the scenes" in Chinatown, such as the Wok Wiz or Chinese Cultural Center tours (see "Backmatter").

Chinatown, for most visitors, begins at the **Chinatown Gate** on Grant at Bush. It is an ornate, touristy version of the ceremonial gate that you might find in Chinese villages, inscribed with the village name and the gate's benefactor—in this case, the Chinatown Chamber of Commerce.

Outside the gate, **Grant Avenue** is one of San Francisco's swankiest shopping streets (described in the previous chapter). Within the gate, the two blocks to California Street are the tidiest of Chinatown, attracting classier shops selling silks, gems, embroidered linens and blouses, antiques, furniture, and art goods. You can find some nice things, but in regard to the prices, bear in mind that Grant Avenue caters especially to tourists.

The corner of California and Grant is one of the city's most photographed scenes, embracing cable cars, pagoda-roofed buildings and **Old Saint Mary's Church.** Looking down through the Financial District, you can see the Bay Bridge above Market Street. The cable car runs up California to the top of Nob Hill, intersecting Grant about mid-slope. Old Saint Mary's was San Francisco's Catholic cathedral from 1853 to 1891. Its famous brick tower bears a clock and inscription, "Son, Observe the time and fly from evil." Though gutted by flames in 1906, its sturdy foundation (imported from China) and walls (imported from the East Coast) survived. Emperor Norton, while waving at a passing cable car, collapsed and died here in 1880.

Old Saint Mary's is not the only temple on this corner. Two floors up at 562 Grant Avenue you will find the **Ma-Tsu Temple of the United States of America.** This modern temple combines shrines to Buddha and the popular gods Tin Hau (Queen of Heaven), Kuan Kung, Kwun Yum, and an earth god. Courteous visitors are welcome.

A half block down from California, **Saint Mary's Square** basks quietly amongst taller buildings. Saint Mary's restful mood is enhanced by Benjiamano Bufano's peaceful statue of Sun Yat-sen, founder of the Republic of China. A native of Guangdong (Canton) Province, but educated in Hawaii and Hong Kong, Sun sought to overthrow the Qing Dynasty. Under explicit sentence of death in his own country, he traveled around the world drumming up money for the revolution. During his stay in San Francisco, he founded a newspaper and wrote the English version of China's constitution in the Montgomery Block, a short stroll down from Saint Mary's Square, but now demolished. He also made many trips to Chinese communities around the state. Through their generous contributions, Californians were thus instrumental in founding the Republic of China.

Chinatown grows more frenetic in the six-block walk along Grant between California and Broadway. Here you will find many of Chinatown's big restaurants and tourist knickknack shops, but also others that offer more curious browsing, such as the Chinatown Kite Shop (717 Grant), the Wok Shop (804 Grant), and the Ten Ren Tea Company (949 Grant). A uniquely Chinese-American creation, the cave-like Li Po Bar (916 Grant) is named after China's most famous poet, a wildly romantic warrior and wine-loving courtier, who drowned while drunkenly embracing the reflection of the moon in a river. The last block of Grant before it hits Broadway is the business heart of old Chinatown, now eclipsed by Stockton Street. For decades, the old fish markets on this block peddled fish and crabs live from foaming tanks, but the tanks are now being replaced by displays on ice.

Be sure to detour down Commercial Street, a narrow, partially cobbled lane that contains the only museum in the country devoted exclusively to Chinese-American history. The **Chinese Historical Society** attempts to trace and preserve a record of the myriad Chinese contributions to the growth of America, and especially California, where Chinese played key roles in agriculture, fishing, mining, industry, and civil engineering, not to mention the arts, science, military, and service industries. Among the historical treasures in the society's collection are a tiger fork from the Weaverville "tong war," a papier-mâché dragon's head, old photographs, gold rush paraphernalia, and the old, handwritten Chinatown telephone book. The museum, at 650 Commercial Street, is open Wednesday through Sunday afternoons. It's free, but donations are appreciated. (The Pacific Heritage Museum at 608 Commercial Street is noted on page 63.)

The block of Grant between Washington and Clay was the original street of Yankee San Francisco. Back when the waves of Yerba Buena Cove still lapped at what is now Montgomery Street, Grant Avenue (then called *Calle de la Fundación,* or Foundation Street) was laid out by an English sea captain and his Mexican wife. Their village plaza, just down the hill, proved very useful for corralling the horses and livestock of visiting vaqueros, as well as the occasional goat. After American Marines raised the flag there in 1846, claiming California for the Union, they rechristened it after their ship, the USS *Portsmouth.*

Young Portsmouth Square (*Square* changed back to *Plaza* in 1927) was the heart of gold rush San Francisco, hosting a motley array of civic assemblages, town meetings, celebrations, duels, and lynchings, as well as the city's first school, bookstore, and newspaper, and the finest hotels of the gold rush era. As landfill pushed the waterfront farther east, however, the business district moved with it, and Portsmouth Square lost its luster. Union Square, and later Civic Center, assumed its public duties. Today, though rather ill-kempt and sprinkled with panhandlers, **Portsmouth Plaza** serves as a much-needed backyard for densely packed Chinatown.

When Robert Louis Stevenson lived in San Francisco (1879-1880), he liked to sit in Portsmouth Square to watch the tide of humanity roll by. A **monument to Stevenson** stands at the northwest corner of the plaza today—a model of the *Hispaniola* from *Treasure Island,* with some lines from his "Christmas Sermon."

The tide of humanity that so fascinated Stevenson still flows through Portsmouth Plaza. At dawn, novices and old hands assemble here for *tai chi,* an ancient Chinese exercise that resembles a slow-motion ballet. In the afternoons, the plaza fills with scores of men playing checkers, cards, *go,* and other games. Many are single, elderly, boarding-house tenants who have no other family. Having come of age during or just after the Exclusion Act, which restricted Chinese immigration between 1882 and 1943, they were unable to find wives from the male-dominated Chinatown community, and fell into lifelong habits of bachelorhood. Portsmouth Plaza is both their living room and social club.

The **Chinese Cultural Center** occupies the third floor of the Chinatown Holiday Inn, across the footbridge from Portsmouth Plaza. The lectures, seminars, and exhibitions of works by Chinese-American artists and writers are geared more for community than tourists, but the center does have a small gift shop. It also sponsors walking tours, including a culinary tour with lunch.

The blocks across Kearny Street from Portsmouth Plaza are still called Manilatown by old-timers. Although the expansion of Chinatown has tended to blur the ethnic lines, a number of Filipinos still live in the residential hotels, and a handful of small cafés serve home-style Philippine specialties.

Self-sufficient Chinatown stocks traditional herbs and produce.

Backtracking to Grant, head uphill along the steep lateral lanes of Chinatown: Pacific, Jackson, Washington, Clay, and Sacramento. Keep your eyes open for **herbalist shops**, windows cluttered with medicinal and aphrodisiac potions, ginseng roots, fungus, elk horn, and occasional oddities like snake wine. The old-fashioned herbalist shops are most atmospheric, jammed with chests of Chinese roots and herbs. Many herbalists are scattered through Chinatown, but Washington seems particularly rich in them. Try Tin Cheung Co. at 849 Washington, Superior at 839 Washington, or Tai Fung Wo at 857 Washington Street.

Ross Alley is the shadiest-looking thoroughfare in Chinatown. Its history lives up to its appearance, but today its most sinister aspect is the whine of hidden sewing machines in the garment factories. Visitors are welcome in the tiny fortune cookie factory at 52 Ross to see the cookie machine in action. You can, of course, buy fortune cookies here, including some "French" *adult* fortune cookies, which read like they were written by naughty 10-year-olds.

Waverly Place, between Washington and Sacramento, is called the "street of painted balconies" for reasons obvious to anyone who looks up. During the tong war era, Waverly was known as the toughest street in Chinatown. With three temples, Waverly is also a religious center of sorts. Respectful passers-by are entirely welcome to visit any of the temples, though photography is not encouraged. A small contribution in the donation boxes is always helpful for maintenance. Chances are that no one will speak English in the temples, but the caretakers are usually friendly.

The **Jeng Sen Buddhism and Taoism Association** (146 Waverly) provides a good introduction to the tolerant Chinese religion, which embraces many gods and diverse notions. The caretakers will give you a printed explanation of Taoism and Buddhism, in English. The Jeng Sen temple is open most weekdays.

Across the street at 123 Waverly, a long climb up to the fourth floor, the **Tin Hau Temple** is the most atmospheric of Chinatown's temples, hung with lanterns and smokey from incense and the fires of burnt offerings. The main altar is dedicated to Tin Hau, Queen of Heaven and protector of seafarers and sojourners, but the temple also accommodates shrines to other gods. It dates from 1852.

The Buddhist Association of America oversees the **Norras Temple** at 109 Waverly. From the street, you can often hear the saffron-robed monks chanting and striking bells, while the drums of kung fu clubs practicing lion dancing resound from elsewhere in the building.

Sacramento Street, once Chinatown's main stem, is still known by the name that signifies "Chinatown" to overseas Chinese—*Tang Yahn Gai,* literally "Tang People's Street." (The Tang Dynasty is considered the most brilliant era of Chinese history, hence the Cantonese fondness for referring to themselves as Tang people.) Between Waverly and Hang Ah streets is one of the outstanding children's playgrounds of San Francisco, with a maze of climbing ladders and slides, and plenty of sand. On the block above Stockton, the clinker-brick Donaldina Cameron House (920 Sacramento), named after the Chinatown crusader, replaced the earlier mission that burned in 1906.

Broad Stockton Street is the main market street for Chinatown residents. Its southern end enters Chinatown by way of the Stockton Tunnel, connecting with the Union Square shopping district at its other end. At the Chinatown end of the tunnel, on the corner of Stockton and Sacramento above the post office, the **Kong Chow Temple** (855 Stockton Street) looks out over Chinatown and the Financial District from the top floor. Though the building itself is entirely modern, some say this is the oldest Chinese temple in the country. Its carved, gilded altars and furnishings are venerable and magnificent. The main shrine honors the god Kuan Kung, a fierce, yet noble, poetry-reading general during the Three Kingdoms era (220-280 A.D.), who was deified after being captured and executed. Kuan Kung is now the patron god of warriors and literature, much beloved by persons in professions requiring courage and fighting skill, including both police and criminals.

Nearby, at 843 Stockton Street, stands the modern headquarters of the Six Companies, the patriarchal government body of old Chinatown. Now called the Chinese Consolidated Benevolent Association, its influence these days is considerably more token than toothy. The Taiwan flags advertise its political orientation.

Unlike the dingy alleys down the hill, Stockton Street's appeal is not historic, but immediate. No more crowded street exists in San Francisco than the stretch of Stockton between Sacramento and Broadway on a Saturday afternoon. Pedestrians throng the sidewalks outside markets crammed with fresh fish, bok choy, cabbages, mangos, bitter melon, apples, oranges, roast ducks, pressed ducks, barbecued pork, dry goods, oils, sweets, and shoppers shouting orders to the quick-fingered meat choppers. Curbside, hawkers haggle over live chickens and ducks from the backs of flatbed trucks, while vats of squirming fish and crabs are hoisted down to aproned butchers.

Beyond Broadway, Chinatown presses along Stockton into traditionally Italian North Beach, clear to Columbus Avenue. Chinatown's largest supplier of books on

Dim sum can be a boisterous, zestful, noisy experience (overleaf).

China is East Wind Books, in the basement of 1435 Stockton Street. Their English-language store is around the corner, at 633 Vallejo. This neighborhood used to be (and to a lesser degree still is) the city rendezvous of the Basques brought to the United States on contract to tend sheep in the high deserts of the Great Basin. The Obrero Hotel and Restaurant, upstairs near the corner of Stockton and Pacific, is a longtime lodging house for Basques. The Obrero now caters to the general public, but still serves Basque food, family-style, with set menus nightly. Pension rooms are clean and cheap—a real find for the budget traveler or diner who appreciates a simple, homey, friendly setting. Another long-time local Basque restaurant is Des Alpes, around the corner at 732 Broadway.

Speaking of food, no visit to Chinatown should neglect the stomach. Chinese is the emperor of world cuisines, and Cantonese is China's own undisputed king—though American palates seem to prefer the spicier northern styles of cooking, which explains the recent proliferation of Hunan, Sichuan, and Mandarin restaurants in the city. Chinatown's new immigrants are also opening restaurants serving Vietnamese food, as well as the Hakka and Chaozhou variations of the Cantonese. Still, Chinatown's main culinary focus remains traditional Cantonese food, with its two outstanding offerings of dim sum and seafood.

Dim sum are light refreshments—little dumplings of shrimp, pork, and scores of other fillings, light pastries, and minced meats—served traditionally from passing carts or trays, with tea. Aside from a few organs that might make the uninitiated queasy—a bit of tripe, a duck's foot, a piece of pig's intestine—dim sum is invariably a happy revelation. Dim sum is traditionally served for breakfast or lunch. Most popular to Western tastes are the wrapped shrimp (*ha gow*), wrapped pork with shrimp (*siu mai*), rice pasta stuffed with meat or shrimp (*cheung fun*), and roast pork buns (*char siu bao*). Most dim sum restaurants are noisy affairs where the varieties of dishes are belted out in piercing tenors and sopranos by the passing serving ladies. If you can't get into the rumbustious spirit of these clamoring, packed-out restaurants, where the maitre d's patrol with walkie-talkies and you may have to order by hunt-and-point methods, then please stick to the more genteel northern-style restaurants. But if you like great food in a truly hang-loose setting, then by all means come prepared for an invigorating experience. The Tung Fong (808 Pacific), the Miriwa (728 Pacific), and New Asia (722 Pacific) are but three of the larger Chinatown "teahouses" serving dim sum. The Hang Ah, on the alley of the same name that runs between Clay and Sacramento, is popular among non-locals for its quaint decor (basement setting, uneven floor levels) and quieter atmosphere. It's fair to note, however, that the world's most demanding dim sum gastronomes, Hong Kong expatriates, contend that the best dim sum is found *away* from Chinatown at large Hong Kong satellite restaurants, such as North Sea Village in Sausalito, the Hong Kong Flower Lounge in Millbrae and the Richmond District, Yank Sing and Harbor Village in the Financial District, and East Ocean in Emeryville. (See "Backmatter" for addresses.)

Seafood dishes are readily available in most Chinatown restaurants. You can get good seafood at the big, fancy restaurants catering to tourists and special Chinese banquets, or you can pay less for a meal just as good in a modest, casual setting catering to locals. Most of the big, expensive restaurants congregate along Grant Avenue. Washington and Jackson streets are packed with crowded, tiny restaurants, some downstairs, some up. These are not tourist places, and if you don't mind homey cooking and service, they offer some of San Francisco's best dining bargains. Kam Lok, an unobtrusive dive at 834 Washington Street, and Ocean Garden (735 Jackson) are excellent choices.

The Chinatown equivalent of the American diner is the noodle and *juk* shop. They keep late hours and serve quick short-order meals like fried or soup noodles, rice plates and *juk* (rice porridge).

■ NORTH BEACH

The beach has long been buried by landfill, but its potent name still carries meaning beyond mere geographical reference. On a local level, North Beach represents the focus of the ethnic Italians, a place of trattoria, cappuccino, aromatic delicatessens, and music. On a national level, North Beach means *Bohemia*, or more specifically, *beatnik*. Between the Italians and bohemians, North Beach has been christened San Francisco's Latin Quarter. The reputation is increasingly hard to keep up.

North Beach fills the floor of the valley that hangs between Russian and Telegraph hills. Columbus Street cuts a wide diagonal right down the middle, and is the main road between downtown San Francisco and Fisherman's Wharf. The northern edge of North Beach, which once pushed almost to Fisherman's Wharf (itself a long-time Italian stronghold) is now obliterated by the hotels and gift shops that cover the waterfront. The southern boundary, traditionally, is Broadway.

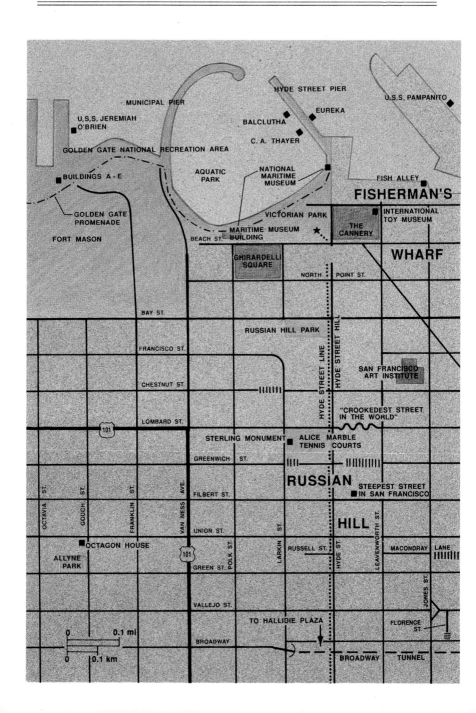

MUNICIPAL PIER

HYDE STREET PIER

U.S.S. PAMPANITO

U.S.S. JEREMIAH O'BRIEN

EUREKA

BALCLUTHA

C. A. THAYER

GOLDEN GATE NATIONAL RECREATION AREA

AQUATIC PARK

NATIONAL MARITIME MUSEUM

FISH ALLEY

BUILDINGS A - E

FISHERMAN'S

GOLDEN GATE PROMENADE

FORT MASON

VICTORIAN PARK

MARITIME MUSEUM BUILDING

BEACH ST.

THE CANNERY

INTERNATIONAL TOY MUSEUM

WHARF

GHIRARDELLI SQUARE

NORTH POINT ST.

BAY ST.

RUSSIAN HILL PARK

FRANCISCO ST.

HYDE STREET LINE

HYDE STREET HILL

CHESTNUT ST.

SAN FRANCISCO ART INSTITUTE

LOMBARD ST.

"CROOKEDEST STREET IN THE WORLD"

101

STERLING MONUMENT

ALICE MARBLE TENNIS COURTS

GREENWICH ST.

OCTAVIA ST.

GOUGH ST.

FRANKLIN ST.

VAN NESS AVE.

FILBERT ST.

RUSSIAN

STEEPEST STREET IN SAN FRANCISCO

HILL

LEAVENWORTH ST.

UNION ST.

OCTAGON HOUSE

101

POLK ST.

LARKIN ST.

RUSSELL ST.

HYDE ST.

MACONDRAY LANE

ALLYNE PARK

GREEN ST.

JONES ST.

VALLEJO ST.

TO HALLIDIE PLAZA

FLORENCE ST.

0   0.1 mi

BROADWAY

0   0.1 km

BROADWAY   TUNNEL

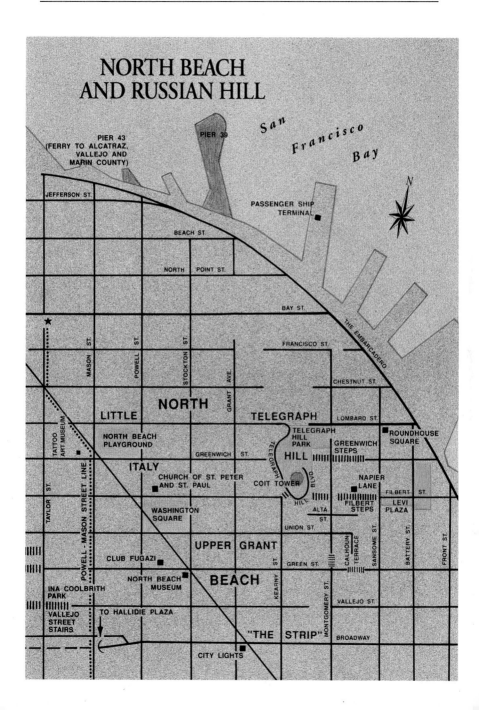

NORTH BEACH
AND RUSSIAN HILL

San
Francisco
Bay

PIER 43
(FERRY TO ALCATRAZ,
VALLEJO AND
MARIN COUNTY)

PIER 39

N

JEFFERSON ST.

PASSENGER SHIP
TERMINAL

BEACH ST.

NORTH POINT ST.

BAY ST.

THE EMBARCADERO

FRANCISCO ST.

MASON ST.

POWELL ST.

STOCKTON ST.

GRANT AVE.

CHESTNUT ST.

NORTH

LITTLE

TELEGRAPH

LOMBARD ST.

TATTOO
ART MUSEUM

NORTH BEACH
PLAYGROUND

TELEGRAPH
HILL
PARK

GREENWICH
STEPS

ROUNDHOUSE
SQUARE

GREENWICH ST.

HILL

ITALY

CHURCH OF ST. PETER
AND ST. PAUL

COIT TOWER

NAPIER
LANE

FILBERT ST.

TAYLOR ST.

POWELL - MASON STREET LINE

TELEGRAPH

HILL

FILBERT
STEPS

LEVI
PLAZA

WASHINGTON
SQUARE

ALTA
ST.

UNION ST.

UPPER GRANT

CALHOUN
TERRACE

SANSOME ST.

BATTERY ST.

FRONT ST.

GREEN ST.

CLUB FUGAZI

NORTH BEACH
MUSEUM

BEACH

KEARNY ST.

MONTGOMERY ST.

INA COOLBRITH
PARK

VALLEJO ST.

VALLEJO
STREET
STAIRS

TO HALLIDIE PLAZA

"THE STRIP"

BROADWAY

CITY LIGHTS

Broadway was long known as the Marco Polo Zone because it marked where Chinatown ended and Little Italy began. This is no longer the case. Chinatown now pushes far into North Beach, and the predominant ethnic group in North Beach today is Chinese. A lot of old-time Italians bitterly grumble about this, and no doubt the weakening Italian influence is disheartening to those who love the fascinating distinction between these two wonderful neighborhoods. Sad it may be, but an ethnic community cannot be preserved as a museum. Neighborhoods change. Before North Beach was Italian, it was Irish. Before the Irish came, it was Chilean. (The old church of Nuestra Señora de Guadalupe at 908 Broadway still recalls its Hispanic parishioners.) And for that matter, before Fisherman's Wharf was Italian, it was *Chinese.*

Though Italians were early immigrants to San Francisco, the Italian community of North Beach took root relatively late in the nineteenth century, filling out after the turn of the century during the heyday of immigration from Italy. By 1940, they were the predominant foreign-born group in the city. Their families prospered, their children grew up as Americans, and they moved to the suburbs, selling the family homes and businesses. The heyday of Chinese immigration, on the other hand, came much later in the century, during the 1970s and 1980s (though, of course, the 1850s and 1860s were also boom decades of Chinese immigration). The old boundaries of Chinatown were rendered inadequate. Paralleling the Italians, the Chinese also prospered, supplanting them as the largest foreign-born group in the city. And like the Italians, the Americanized generations have moved out of the old neighborhood center. As a community of first-generation immigrants in the late twentieth century, Little Italy simply cannot match the vitality of Chinatown.

But let us not sing a dirge for Little Italy. North Beach is still a colorful focus of the Italian-American community. The annual Columbus Day Parade in October is the biggest celebration of the year here. Italian teams still gather at the bocce grounds at North Beach playground. Best of all, the gustatory pleasures are fully celebrated in North Beach. Its many Italian restaurants, coffee houses, bakeries, pasta makers, gelato stores, and other establishments make it one of the supremely stimulating neighborhoods of San Francisco.

The Financial District, Chinatown, Telegraph Hill, Jackson Square, and North Beach all chafe against one another at **Broadway**, a strip of clubs and sleazy porno joints, barkers, late-night rowdies, and more than a few perfectly decent establishments. Starting with the infamous Barbary Coast, one block south on Pacific, this area has been a major center of the city's nightlife since the gold rush. In the fifties and sixties, comedy and folk clubs like the Purple Onion and the hungry i (both around the corner from Broadway, under new ownership) booked such upstarts as the Smothers Brothers, Dick Gregory, Mort Sahl, Barbra Streisand, Bill Cosby, Lenny Bruce, and Phyllis Diller. Then, in 1964, Carol Doda danced topless at the Condor, revolutionizing The Strip, as it was and is still known. Two years later, The Strip went bottomless, starting a new craze. Strip joints opened up and down, and one place even raised a platform on a pole outside, where go-go dancers shimmied and wiggled for passing cars. The Strip was well on the way to becoming obnoxious. Locals tend to avoid it in favor of Columbus, though new restaurants now opening may make it more attractive. Ah, but some traditions never die: Finocchio's (506 Broadway) has been having fun in drag, mostly for tourists, throughout the past half century.

A pretentious bronze plaque on the wall of the Condor, at the corner of Columbus and Broadway, credits The Strip as the birthplace of the world's first topless and bottomless stage shows. These claims must be viewed with skepticism. Even without accounting for the grosser perversities of the Barbary Coast, one block and a hundred years south, surely the honor of hosting the first topless dance must belong to Babylon or Gomorrah, to name but two possible precedents.

San Francisco's most famous bookstore is Lawrence Ferlinghetti's **City Lights Bookstore**, at 261 Columbus, on the corner of Jack Kerouac Street (which until recently was known as Adler Alley). City Lights was the first all-paperback bookstore in the country; but more than that, it was and is the literary meeting place of North Beach. Its odd-shaped, rambling rooms and basement, poetry room, and literary programs are an inspiration to small-press writers and poets and people who get a charge from ideas that run against the grain.

City Lights is forever associated with the watershed event of the Beat Generation. In 1956, Ferlinghetti published *Howl*, Allen Ginsberg's raging eulogy for an alienated generation. Ginsberg had written it in one weekend in San Francisco, and two weeks later read it to a wildly enthusiastic crowd at the Six Gallery in the Marina District. After publication, local police brought charges of obscenity against Ginsberg, Ferlinghetti, and City Lights' manager Shigeyoshi Murao. The long court battle was followed by acquittal, with the judge ruling that an author "should be real in treating his subject and be allowed to express his thoughts and ideas in his own words."

Unfortunately for North Beach, the publicity turned unwanted national attention on the new Bohemia. The alienated generation that congregated in its coffee houses and clubs were called the Beat Generation, a phrase coined by Jack Kerouac in his romantic portrayal of a manic subculture, *On the Road.* New York may have spawned them, but North Beach became their most identifiable symbol. With handy, cheap Chinese and Italian food and wine, and an urbane indifference to eccentric manner and dress, North Beach nurtured the beats, and they in turn cultivated its café society and folksy clubs. The beats (or *beatniks*, as San Francisco columnist Herb Caen called them) rejected established mores as absurd, and sought fulfillment (or extinction of conventional behavior and thought) in spontaneous self-expression—free-style poetry, prose, music, art, endless talk, and obsessive hungering for new sensations.

The public loved the caricature of the beatnik: ragged and dirty, angry but cool, libertine, digging everything, lost in a haze of cheap wine, marijuana, and be-bop music. Before long, tour buses were crawling through the streets of North Beach. To make a long story short, as North Beach became a tourist attraction, the things that *real* bohemians thrive on—cheap rent, cheap eats, and cheap drink—disappeared. The beats, for the most part, went straight or moved on—many of them to the Haight-Ashbury.

Though North Beach today is harder on the pocketbook, fortunately it's still good for the soul. It remains a haunt of café society, where locals and visitors still cultivate that fine old European habit of frequenting coffee houses and bistros, listening to music, chatting, or just sitting and watching the other patrons. The best spots are patronized by neighborhood Italians and a few bohemian-like characters, lovers of conversation, scowlers into morning newspapers, thumbers of noses at establishment values, sketch artists, scribblers of poetry and other hacks, not to mention haughty young fashion plates of independent means. Plunk down your four bits and join the club.

Vesuvio's is exactly such a place. Across the alley from City Lights, on Jack Kerouac Street, it has been serving Bohemians and other folks since 1949. It's a quirky bar, full of curiosities and interesting people. The Welsh poet Dylan Thomas, on his literary tours, relished his visits there. Across Columbus Avenue, Spec's and Tosca are two other atmospheric watering holes, the former a bar chock-full of curios and the latter a coffee house.

Molinari's deli is a paradise for lovers of Italian salamis and salads.

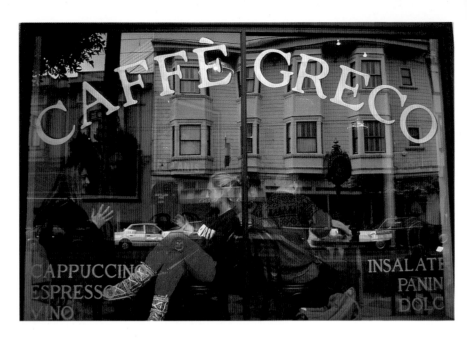

From grinder (above) to café (top), coffee is a mainstay of North Beach life.

Old Bohemians still repair to City Lights Bookstore (top) and Vesuvio's (above).

The heart of Beatnikdom used to be upper Grant, between Broadway and Filbert. Almost all the old haunts are gone, but Caffè Trieste still battens down the corner of Vallejo at Grant, where it opened in 1956, making it the oldest coffee house on the West Coast. It stays open late. The juke box plays Italian folk music and opera. On Saturdays at 1 p.m., the family owners sing opera for their patrons, always drawing a large crowd. While on Grant, if you need anything for the Italian kitchen—food mills, pasta makers, apple corers, ravioli rolling pins, tomato seed removers—don't miss Figone Hardware (1351 Grant), an old-fashioned neighborhood institution that also stocks plumbing pipe, shovels, seeds, electrical fixtures, building supplies, paint, etc. Whatever Figone lacks, you can find at the incense-smitten Schlock Shop (1418 Grant), purveyor of everything and nothing in particular, including a funky selection of hats, from sailor to raccoon. Iacopi Meats (1460 Grant) is the oldest butcher shop in San Francisco, and the place to buy *prosciutto* (Italian ham) and *pancetta* (a kind of rolled bacon), both cured on the sawdust-covered premises.

The four blocks of Columbus between Broadway and Filbert, and their lively side streets, are the busiest of Little Italy. By night, their window-side tables glow with warm light and jovial company. By day, the lunchtime crowds and shoppers fill the sidewalks. Columbus Avenue hosts the city's largest collection of cafés: Caffè Puccini, Café Stella, Caffè Greco, and Café Roma, to name but four on the 400 block, plus the venerable Bohemian Cigar Store (Columbus at Union), purveyor of espresso and good cheer, as well as tobacco. A forest of cheeses and sausages and other Italian treats at Molinari's (373 Columbus) enraptures with the smell alone. For another whiff of heaven, tootle round the corner to Vallejo and Stockton, where Victoria Bakery's basement ovens turn out breads, cakes, and cookies from several regions of Italy, including festival and wedding treats. Caferata Ravioli Factory (700 Columbus) has a small restaurant in tow for those who can't wait until they get home to try the tortellini, ravioli, and other specialities.

Take a short detour to 1435 Stockton to see the small **North Beach Museum**, on the upstairs level of a bank. You can readily get a feel for the appearances of North Beach, old and new, from the photos and artifacts. The museum keeps banker's hours, and is free. Nearby, Cavalli & Company (1441 Stockton) sells Italian books, magazines, and recordings. Across the street, the U.S. Restaurant fills out the triangular corner of Stockton and Columbus. It is famous for its hearty portions of good, solid, reasonably priced Italian and American breakfasts, lunches, and dinners.

Club Fugazi (678 Green) has been running Beach Blanket Babylon so long now that it has become a San Francisco institution. The cabaret-style show is famous for its outlandish, gigantic hats and outrageous songs. Reservations are necessary; phone the box office at (415) 421-4222.

Washington Square is the heart of North Beach. Here, mostly elderly Chinese and Italians gather on (usually separate) park benches to talk about the Old Country. Backed by the spectacular **Saints Peter and Paul Catholic Church**, the "Italian Cathedral" of San Francisco, the square really does exude a Mediterranean ambience. As the church was being built in 1922, Cecil B. DeMille showed up to film the construction for a scene in *The Ten Commandments*. A good place to soak it all in is Malvina's, an old North Beach café now in newer quarters on Stockton at Union. It opens early for the first cup of the day, with pastries and breads at the ready. Kitty-corner is one of the city's oldest restaurants, Fior D'Italia, which has been run by the same family for over a century.

The old statue of Ben Franklin in the middle of the park stands above a time capsule. It expired recently, giving up a hoard of nineteenth-century temperance tracts. (The statue's patron, a crusading teetotaler named Dr. Cogswell, intended this as a water fountain; note the defunct fountain heads around the base.) The capsule was promptly refilled with a poem by Ferlinghetti, a recording of the Hoodoo Rhythm Devils, a pair of Levi's, and a bottle of wine. Next opening: 2079.

Another statue in Washington Square is a sentimental monument to San Francisco's once-beloved firemen, donated by the eccentric Lillie Hitchcock Coit. The scene shows two fire fighters with a rescued child. One fireman stands with an outstretched hand, which passers-by contrive to keep filled with all manner of objects, usually beverage containers. Once upon a time, fire fighters were the dashing heros to every child of San Francisco, and to none more so than Lillie Coit. As a child trapped in a house afire, she never forgot the thrill of the clanging engines, and the strong, fearless fireman who climbed up to rescue her. Throughout her life, whenever she heard the bells and horses, she would drop any business (even a wedding) and chase after them, cheering them on. She was a wealthy woman, and before her death she donated the money to build Coit Tower on the top of Telegraph Hill, one of San Francisco's most cherished monuments, and easily visible on Telegraph

A city of stunning vistas, San Francisco changes from every hill top (overleaf).

Hill, above. Look closely; legend claims that it was designed to resemble a fire nozzle, but don't believe it.

A quiet statue of a drinking man stands in the small iron-fenced triangle of park at the southwest corner of Washington Square, on the west side of Columbus Avenue. The sculptor was Melvin Cummings, a professor at the precursor of the San Francisco Art Institute on Russian Hill. The model is said to be the same that Rodin used for *Saint John the Baptist* (which you may see in the Palace of Fine Arts).

One of the victims of the Loma Prieta quake was a small South of Market museum devoted to the art of tattooing. SoMa's loss was North Beach's gain: **Lyle Tuttle's Tattoo Art Museum** has opened again at 837 Columbus Avenue. I've never heard anyone refute its claim as the world's foremost museum of its type, a collection of printed articles, designs, and tattooing paraphernalia. On the old premises, Tuttle used to tattoo customers within view of his gallery patrons. At his new establishment, however, if you want to take a tattoo home, you've got to go upstairs.

■ RUSSIAN HILL

Telegraph and Russian hills both were cultivating reputations as bohemian neighborhoods long before North Beach received the call. Of these, Russian Hill was the earlier. Today, it is a retreat of the elite, but its stairways and vistas are open to all. Russian Hill takes its name not from any large Slavic presence, but from the belief that visiting Russian ship crews down from Sitka to hunt sea otter used to bury their dead here.

Movie producers love Russian Hill. It has what many believe to be the most classic San Franciscan vistas: stunning backgrounds of white hill and blue bay, with foreground settings of old bay-windowed houses and suddenly plunging streets, just perfect for dramatic car chases.

To reach Russian Hill, you can ride the Powell-Hyde cable car; in fact, you *ought* to ride it at least once in your life. But neither should you miss the chance to walk around Russian Hill, one of the rarer pleasures of the city. A spectacular walking route from North Beach climbs steeply up **Vallejo Street**; so steeply, in fact, that the road gives way to stairs beyond Mason Street. The city falls away as you rise, opening up Hollywood backdrops of bridges, bay, Coit Tower, and the downtown high-risers. Puffing up to Ina Coolbrith Park, at Taylor, you can well understand why Russian Hill was long neglected by the worthies of the community, but greatly appreciated by poor souls with fine tastes. Naturally, it became something of a writers' colony.

Ina Coolbrith Park is named after one of San Francisco's most undersung poets and literary inspirations. She was the first American child to enter California in a wagon train, crossing over Beckwourth Pass in a saddle shared with the trailblazing mountain man, Jim Beckwourth. After an unhappy marriage to a businessman in the hamlet of Los Angeles, she relocated to San Francisco, where she made her home on Russian Hill, wrote poetry, and helped to edit the *Overland Monthly*. More than one local scribbler was reputed to have fallen in love with her, including Mark Twain, Bret Harte (who reportedly offered to divorce his wife for her), Charlie Stoddard (who threatened suicide if she didn't marry him), and bitter Ambrose Bierce (who ordinarily hated women, at least intellectually). She never did remarry, however, but invited all to join her literary circle at her house on Russian Hill. She corresponded with European and East Coast poets, and became a librarian both for the Bohemian Club and the Oakland Free Library. It was in that latter capacity that she met 12-year-old Jack London, and set him on a course of reading that defined his formal education. In 1919, she became California's first Poet Laureate.

Cross Taylor Street and continue up the Vallejo Street stairs to the southern "summit" of twin-peaked Russian Hill. This small warren of lanes at the top, now quite exclusive, was once home to an eclectic array of creative types, including Bierce, Gelett Burgess, Frank Norris, and Willis Polk, who built his own house at the top of the stairs (1013 Vallejo). Don Herron notes a tradition that Burgess was inspired by the sight of a cow grazing on Russian Hill to pen his best-known rhyme:

> *I never saw a purple cow*
> *I never hope to see one,*
> *But I can tell you anyhow,*
> *I'd rather see than be one.*

Tiny, pretty **Florence Street** leads off to the south, halting at a small staircase where you should stop to admire the downtown view, including a romantic broadside of Grace Cathedral. Step on down to Broadway. This is not the Broadway of big lights and dancing mammaries. *That* Broadway was channeled by tunnel under Russian

Hill to Polk Gulch in the early 1950s. *This* Broadway is the *old* route that climbed over the hill. You can see why they built the tunnel: At this point, Broadway slips so suddenly from underfoot that some thoughtful city planner has built a wall across it to stop cars from going over. Ina Coolbrith's last Russian Hill house (her earlier abode burned in 1906) stands at 1067 Broadway.

If you still haven't ridden your Russian Hill cable car, a good place to catch one is two blocks west on Hyde Street. It's also a promising spot for lunch or an ice cream.

The second summit of Russian Hill rises six blocks farther north along the Powell-Hyde cable car line. En route, you will pass Russell Street; Jack Kerouac lived at number 29 while writing *On the Road* in 1952. Neil Cassady (inspiration for Dean Moriarty) and his wife, Carolyn, lived downstairs. (See Don Herron's *The Literary World of San Francisco* for other Kerouac sites.)

Another romantic detour wends east on Green Street, past the 1857 Fusier Octagon House (1067 Green) and an old firehouse (1088 Green) where the owner allegedly keeps the fire pole in fine working order; neither are open to the public, unfortunately. **Macondray Lane**, a half block north on Jones, is a rare piece of real estate. Turn east, and follow it through a wood, past cottage doors, over uneven paving stones, and down rickety wooden steps to rejoin the city on Taylor Street. You'll feel like you've walked a country mile. But no country you can name.

Heading north on Hyde again, you pass the **Filbert Street hill** on the right. If you're on a cable car, you won't see it; you have to dismount and walk to the brink. Actually, to call Filbert a "hill" is like calling Beethoven's Fifth a snappy tune. At 31.5 degrees, it's the steepest driveable grade in San Francisco. Be warned; if you take it Steve McQueen-style, barreling over the crest and screeching into a right turn up Leavenworth, your car's going to need a fresh set of shocks and a new transmission when you get out of the hospital. Take it easy, and you can do it *twice*.

The second summit of Russian Hill is a park on the corner of Greenwich and Hyde. Poetry lovers (if indeed such creatures still exist) should walk up the Greenwich steps past the Alice Marble tennis courts, to the secluded **George Sterling Glade**. This spot was treasured by Sterling, San Francisco's King of Bohemia, Ambrose Bierce's disciple, Jack London's best friend, a founding member of Carmel's artist colony, a poet called the finest of his age by many of his contemporaries, but also an alcoholic, and finally, in 1926, a suicide. A small monument in the park is inscribed with one of his San Francisco poems:

The city's firemen are still known as San Francisco's Finest.

Tho the dark be cold and blind
Yet her sea fog's touch is kind
And her mightier caress
Is joy and the pain thereof;
And great is thy tenderness
O cool, grey City of Love!

Sterling died in the Bohemian Club, leaving behind some half-burned snatches of poetry that have since become legends in the cult of Sterling, which appeals to literate romantics, occultists, and counterculture figures, as well as to lovers of intensely beautiful language and imagery. In his day, Sterling was known for (among other things) his sense of horror and demonic imagery, a quality no doubt encouraged by the macabre Bierce. Sterling's most famous lines in this vein, inscribed on the wall of the now-demolished Papa Coppa's restaurant on Montgomery Street, read *"The blue-eyed vampire, sated at her feast, Smiles bloodily against the leprous moon."* Strange, sad, and beautiful character, George Sterling; deserves to be better known.

Another literary touchstone stands on the northwest corner of Lombard and Hyde: Mrs. Robert Louis Stevenson's house. The writer died before Willis Polk built it. The crowds of tourists outside are probably not here to admire it, however. They are more interested in flagging down the Hyde Street cable car or snapping pictures in front of San Francisco's two most famous streets.

"The crookedest street in the world" is the block of Lombard between Hyde and Leavenworth. You can walk down, enjoying its views, gardens, red cobblestones, and the little mid-block terrace called Montclair. But hey, you really ought to enjoy it the way God and Karl Malden intended you to, at the wheel of a sedan, grinding fenders on every turn.

Back at the top of Lombard and Hyde, after gazing at the Bay Bridge and Coit Tower, do something that almost no tourist ever does: cross the hill to see the view on the other side of Russian Hill—the Marina district, the Presidio, and the Golden Gate Bridge. The most famous view, however, is straight north, down Hyde Street and over the tall masts on the wharves, toward Alcatraz and beyond. If you had a nickel for every time a photographer shot a cable car with this backdrop, you could probably retire to Russian Hill. The steep stretch of the Hyde Street grade, between Francisco and Bay streets, registers 21.3 degrees.

QUOTATIONS FROM BITTER BIERCE

Discriminate: *v.i.* To note the particulars in which one person or thing is, if possible, more objectionable than another.

Happiness: *n.* An agreeable sensation arising from the contemplating the misery of another.

History: *n.* An account, mostly false, of events mostly unimportant, which are brought about by rulers, mostly knaves, and soldiers, mostly fools.

Love: *n.* A temporary insanity curable by marriage.

November: *n.* The eleventh twelfth of a weariness.

Piracy: *n.* Commerce without its folly-swaddles, just as God made it.

Quill: *n.* An implement of torture yielded by a goose and commonly wielded by an ass.

Rash: *adj.* Insensible to the value of our advice.

Rear: *n.* In American military matters, that exposed part of the Army that is closest to Congress.

Riot: *n.* A popular entertainment given to the military by innocent bystanders.

Saint: *n.* A dead sinner, revised and edited.

—Ambrose Bierce, from *The Devil's Dictionary.*

Most visitors will want to continue down Hyde to Fisherman's Wharf, but if you wish to explore Russian Hill a little further, you will be rewarded for your efforts. Those who strike west on Francisco, around the terrace to Chestnut, will be within whistling distance of one of Russian Hill's nicest surprises. The **San Francisco Art Institute** (800 Chestnut Street), established in 1871, is the oldest art school in the western U.S. It's an eccentric building, very conducive to artistic temperaments. The entrance brings to mind a medieval Italian monastery, with courtyard, cloisters, tiled fountain, and bell tower; the overgrown vacant lot across the street adds to the effect. It's somewhat of a letdown to know it was built of reinforced concrete (in 1926, by the same outfit that did City Hall and Coit Tower —Bakewell and Brown). The fact that it's concrete doesn't seem to bother the ghost who lives in the tower, however.

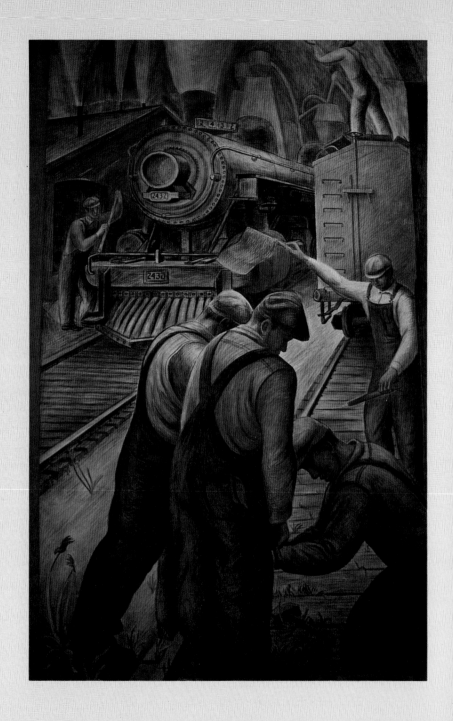

The small cafeteria in back is one of the few places in residential Russian Hill where you can enjoy a cup of coffee with a view over Fisherman's Wharf. The modernistic backside of the school also contains some small galleries, artists' workshops, an art supply store (with a good stock of handmade papers), and a rooftop theater in the shape of a ship's stern, great for reading on sunny days. Saving the best for last, before you leave, visit the **Diego Rivera Gallery**, to the left of the main entrance on Chestnut. One wall is illuminated with a massive fresco of working men (and a woman), painted by Rivera in 1931. Rivera's work, celebrating the power, color, and epic saga of people who toil, had great influence on San Francisco Depression-era artists, as you can see when you visit the more famous (because more public) murals in Coit Tower on Telegraph Hill.

■ TELEGRAPH HILL

Telegraph Hill was named for the semaphore installed at its crest in 1850 to notify downtown merchants of ship arrivals. As anyone who stands on the top today can attest, its sight lines still reach through the harbor and out the Golden Gate.

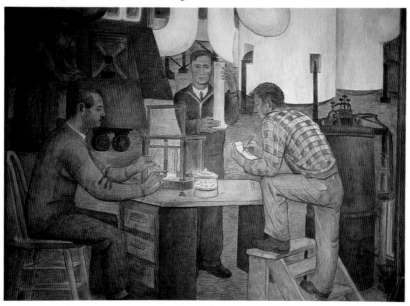

The nobility of work is the overriding theme of Coit Tower's murals.

Telegraph Hill rises from Broadway in the south so abruptly that residents just half a block up Kearny and Montgomery streets look down on Broadway neon and rooftops. The rise on the west side from North Beach is likewise steep, but neither can match the cliffs of the east side, falling sharply away to the old wharf and warehouse district. These cliffs are largely man-made. Quarries blasted away at the hillside, mostly for landfill and sea walls, until 1914. In earlier days, ships' crews quarried the rock for ballast. As they took on goods in other ports, they left the ballast as paving stones. Thus, the east slope of Telegraph Hill today spreads halfway around the world.

The hill has always been a neighborhood of immigrants. During the gold rush, Chileans were among the largest groups to settle on there. As San Francisco settled down, the Irish moved up in droves, followed by smaller numbers of Italians, Spanish, Mexicans, Portuguese, Scandinavians, Germans, Chinese, and even some Yankees. After the earthquake of 1906, when the Irish departed for the Mission District, the Italians filled the vacuum, making Telegraph a distinctly Italian hill until recent years. Today, the Chinese have probably surpassed the Italians as the major ethnic group, especially on the North Beach side.

Eastern Telegraph Hill's relative remoteness from the rest of the city in the 1890s made it, like Russian Hill of an earlier era, an attractive district for bohemians, artists, and theatrical people. Even the humblest shacks offered spectacular views. Wine and rent were cheap. The Muses flourished. Charles Stoddard, a writer who spent his youth on Telegraph Hill, described this wonderful Bohemia in his book, *In the Footprints of the Padres*. "The cottages were indeed nestlike: they were so small, so compact, so cozy, so overrun with vines and flowering foliage. Usually of one story, or of a story-and-a-half at most, they clung to the hillside facing the water, and looked out upon its noble expanse from tiny balconies as delicate and dainty as toys. . . . They loomed above their front yards while their backyards lorded it over their roofs. . . . They were usually approached by ascending or descending stairways, or by airy bridges that spanned little gullies where ran rivulets in the winter season. There were parrots on perches at the doorways of those cottages, and songbirds in cages that were hidden away in the vines. There were pet poodles there. I think that there were more lap dogs than watch dogs in that early California."

By the 1940s, the artists were gone. The crest and eastern side of Telegraph had become chic—and so it remains today. It was, in many ways, San Francisco's first gentrified neighborhood, and the artists have been on the run ever since.

To drive on Telegraph Hill requires patience. Between Broadway and Bay Street, nine wide blocks to the north, there are no through roads. Parking is horrendous. If you drive to **Coit Tower** (up Lombard from North Beach), expect to wait. And wait and wait. It's better to walk, though the steep climb from Washington Square is not for sissies. Filbert and Greenwich streets, densely packed with houses, give way to stairs and greenery at Telegraph Hill Boulevard, which hooks around from Lombard to Pioneer Park and Coit Tower, on the summit. A statue of Columbus, erected in 1957, stands in the middle of the parking circle, gazing off toward the ex-federal penitentiary on Alcatraz.

Coit Tower was built as a monument to San Francisco's Volunteer Fire Department with money left by Lillie Hitchcock Coit. The firm of Arthur Brown drew up plans for a cylindrical observation tower on the top of Telegraph Hill. Work started early in 1933; by October of the same year, the tower was finished. Though only 180 feet (55 m) tall, Coit Tower gets a 284-foot (87-m) boost from Telegraph Hill. From the top, the Bay Area spreads out gloriously in every direction. There are coin-operated telescopes for closer looks. You can pick out landmark after landmark: Mount Diablo on the eastern horizon, the Claremont Resort in the Oakland hills, the Campanile at Berkeley, the Richmond Bridge, Alcatraz, Sausalito and Mount Tamalpais in Marin County, the Golden Gate Bridge, the Presidio, Fisherman's Wharf, wiggly Lombard Street, the rooftops of Nob Hill and Chinatown, Grace Cathedral, Twin Peaks, the downtown towers, the Bay Bridge. . . .

Back in the tower lobby, take a closer look at the murals on the walls. Commissioned during the Great Depression by the Civil Works Administration, the frescoes were painted by a team of 25 local artists. The murals present an incredibly vigorous picture of California life during the 1930s, a gallery of characters and scenes embracing crowded city streets, rich agricultural valleys, the mineral-rich mountains, libraries, ranch and farm hands, engineers, machinery, working animals, and a lunch counter, bank, department store, and press room. For subjects, the artists painted their friends and supervisors, and even Coit Tower's watchman. Their themes celebrate the richness of California's resources and people, the dignity and brotherhood of honest labor (as well as its exploitation), economic injustice, and political anger. The paintings are spiked with signs of militancy—a clenched fist, ominous newspaper headlines, the idle rich gazing at the tattered poor, a robbery in progress in the crowd at the corner of Market and Montgomery—portents of a revolution that many expected and even yearned for in 1934. The controversy over these powerful images delayed their unveiling, and smouldered for years afterward.

Coit tower is open daily. There's a small gift shop in the lobby. You'll have to buy a ticket to ride the elevator to the top.

If you have time for but one walk in San Francisco, turn your dogs loose on the eastern flank of Telegraph Hill. The steep **Greenwich and Filbert steps** nurture some of the most sylvan cityscapes in the country, most of it unapproachable by automobile. Both stairs start on the east side of Coit Tower: Greenwich Street stairs descend from the parking circle, while the Filbert Street stairs descend just a little farther down the road, where Telegraph Hill Boulevard swerves right. Whether Greenwich or Filbert makes the nicer walk is a moot point. Walk down one and up the other, and you will know the best of both.

Brick-paved Greenwich meanders down through thick foliage to emerge near a cliff on the dead-end of Montgomery Street, where perches a crenelated old wooden restaurant, Julius' Castle. Until they "widened" the street, there used to be a turntable here for automobiles. Glance over the edge before bearing right to the second stretch of Greenwich stairs, marked by a street sign, but otherwise looking like private steps to the side yard of the building. Dropping past old houses and small urban pastures of dog fennel, nasturtium, and fenced garden flowers, the Greenwich stairway lands on Sansome Street, at the eastern foot of Telegraph Hill. Turn south to meet the Filbert steps.

Filbert is the more formally landscaped stairway, a charming companion of roses, fuchsias, lilies, ivy, and other garden flowers and trees. Like Greenwich, the public steps are continuously met by private paths and stairs and picket gates that lead off to houses, coddled in flower pots and foliage, some old, some not. Just above Montgomery, near a romantic, rambling restaurant called The Shadows, there are some small terraces with benches. From here, you can study the handsome art deco apartment house at 1360 Montgomery, on the corner of Filbert.

Below Montgomery, the Filbert steps turn to wood—rickety wood, with the nails sticking out. Unpainted and enchantingly cushioned in baby tears and ferns, it leads down to the rarest of San Francisco's country lanes, Napier. Last of the city's wood plank streets, **Napier Lane** seems to be heavily populated by beautiful cats. By all means, clomp to the end of the lane and back for a look at the old houses, which survived the fire of 1906, but for the sake of the residents and their precious atmosphere, let us strangers keep our grosser presence fleeting. Below Napier Lane, the Filbert steps drop down to Sansome Street on a new concrete stairway.

Bohemian heir to North Beach of the fifties was Haight Street of the sixties and seventies.

Whether you walk Greenwich or Filbert, take some time to explore **Montgomery Street** before descending to Sansome. This was the street where heroic Italians made a last stand to rescue their little homes from the great fire of 1906. In desperation, according to the story, they broke out casks of red wine and doused their houses with vino, cooling and saving them from the flames. It's a pity the tactic didn't work with developers. Still, a handful of these wine-baptized houses *reportedly* survives. A likely candidate is 9 Upper Calhoun Terrace, which dates from 1854. Other nineteenth century survivors can be spotted by walkers. If you like heights, take a look at the views from **Upper Calhoun Terrace** and the end of **Alta Street**. People with vertigo can't live on Telegraph Hill.

The stretch of flat ground between Telegraph Hill and the Embarcadero wharves is covered landfill once given over to brick warehouses and train tracks. The industries have long since moved, and today many of the warehouses have been beautifully remodeled into designer studios, condos, restaurants, and offices, at least one with rooftop tennis courts. Even the old roundhouse engine shed for the San Francisco North Belt Railway, at the corner of Sansome and Lombard, has been converted to an attractive office called (somewhat contradictorily) Roundhouse Square. Antique furniture showrooms operate from large basements on Battery and Green streets. They make for fascinating browsing, though who actually *buys* all those gargantuan wooden beds and deconsecrated church pulpits is a mystery.

Levi's Plaza, between Sansome and Battery streets at Filbert, is the corporate headquarters of Levi Strauss, manufacturer of blue jeans. During the gold rush, Levi Strauss came to San Francisco, where he no doubt met a good number of men with holes in their britches. He set about to invent some sturdier pants using rivet-studded tent canvas. Levi's blue jeans not only tickled forty-niners' fancies, but were destined to become perhaps the greatest fashion statement of the latter half of the twentieth century. Like fortune cookies, steam beer, and cable cars, blue jeans rank as a San Francisco original.

Even without its historical context, the Levi Strauss headquarters should be seen for its admirable design. The staggered lines of the building, set against the staggered housing on Telegraph Hill, enhances the view, while its brick facade echoes the surrounding warehouse walls. Bookstores, bakeries, restaurants, and a café on the plaza have turned an erstwhile industrial zone into a stimulating and pleasant place to relax. But best of all is the splashing fountain in Levi Plaza, built of Sierra granite, inviting you to climb through it, as you might with a real mountain stream. Across

Battery Street, this mountain "creek" flows through a grassy, boulder-studded "meadow" designed by landscape architect Lawrence Halprin. How much more civilized a corporate statement than a mammoth steel tower!

■ FISHERMAN'S WHARF

Before the Virgin Mary's name was ever invoked to bless San Francisco's fishing fleet, Tin Hau looked after her fishermen. The Chinese pioneered the business at Fisherman's Wharf. The Genoese came soon after, pushing out the Chinese, and in turn were edged aside by the Sicilians. The harbor of Fisherman's Wharf was known as an Italian lake for much of its life, and the daily sailings out and back of the fleet were a colorful sight in old San Francisco.

With over-fishing and pollution, San Francisco Bay fisheries grew slack after World War II. Though you can still find boats and fishermen at the wharf, the big money-earner today is tourism fueled by the romantic scenery and fresh seafood. Unfortunately, a proliferation of souvenir and schlock shops have washed up in their wake. But don't be scared away. There is a lot to see and do at Fisherman's Wharf, even if the hucksterism turns you off. It's good to know, too, that the city of San Francisco is seeking ways to revitalize the industry with new facilities, and perhaps even a Tokyo-style fish market.

Pier 39 is one of the newer tourist attractions at Fisherman's Wharf. T-shirts,, leather, posters, cookies, and souvenirs form a substantial part of the merchandise sold on the pier, refurbished to look like a quaint fishing village. Views are nice, and children may enjoy the two-story merry-go-round, but the most popular attraction is the seasonal colony of sea lions who come to bask on the boat docks. For folks who like their history lively and colorful, the San Francisco Experience, a multimedia production, spices up the Frisco story with fog machines and other props.

Between Pier 39 and Pier 45, you can hire three-wheeled pedicabs for tours to Chinatown or along the wharf to Aquatic Park. You can also take helicopter rides and boat tours from here (see "Backmatter"). The most fascinating tour of all goes to **Alcatraz**, once the most notorious federal penitentiary in the country, but now administered as part of the Golden Gate National Recreation Area. Known as "The Rock," Alcatraz was built to cage the toughest of the tough. Famous guests have included such superstars of crime as Machine Gun Kelly, Al Capone, Alvin

A SUPERMARKET IN CALIFORNIA

*W*hat thoughts I have of you tonight, Walt Whitman, for I walked down the sidestreets under the trees with a headache self-conscious looking at the full moon.

In my hungry fatigue, and shopping for images, I went into the neon fruit supermarket, dreaming of your enumerations!

What peaches and what penumbras! Whole families shopping at night! Aisles full of husbands! Wives in the avocados, babies in the tomatoes!—and you, Garcia Lorca, what were you doing down by the watermelons?

I saw you, Walt Whitman, childless, lonely old grubber, poking among the meats in the refrigerator and eyeing the grocery boys.

I heard you asking questions of each: Who killed the pork chops? What price bananas? Are you my Angel?

I wandered in and out of the brilliant stacks of cans following you, and followed in my imagination by the store detective.

We strode down the open corridors together in our solitary fancy tasting artichokes, possessing every frozen delicacy, and never passing the cashier.

Where are we going, Walt Whitman? The doors close in an hour. Which way does your beard point tonight?

(I touch your book and dream of our odyssey in the supermarket and feel absurd.)

Will we walk all night through solitary streets? The trees add shade to shade, lights out in the houses, we'll both be lonely.

Will we stroll dreaming of the lost America of love past blue automobiles in driveways, home to our silent cottage?

Ah, dear father, graybeard, lonely old courage-teacher, what America did you have when Charon quit poling his ferry and you got out on a smoking bank and stood watching the boat disappear on the black waters of Lethe?

—Allen Ginsberg, "A Supermarket in California"

"Creepy" Carpis, and Robert Stroud, the Birdman of Alcatraz who, in fact, did all his bird research at Leavenworth before being sent to Alcatraz for a prison murder. What did The Rock have that Sing Sing didn't? Aside from its terrible reputation, a tough and mostly silent regimen, and a tantalizing view of civilization at its most hedonistic, probably not much. True, Alcatraz was surrounded by a frigid bay, raked by powerful currents. On the other hand, it had good food and warm showers—the better, it was said, to keep prisoners too soft to escape.

After a scenic ferry ride from the wharf, contemporary visitors are loosed on The Rock to explore on their own. Climbing up the grim hill through the sally port, most people head straight for the large cell block on the top of the island. There, they wander quietly through the hospital ward (where the crazed Birdman spent much of his time), cafeteria, recreation yard, and solitary confinement in "D" block, where bullet holes in the wall testify to the bloody prison uprising in 1946. Most sobering of all is to stand among the tiers of empty cell blocks and imagine what life was like here. The rangers (whose ranks are sometimes bolstered by ex-prisoners and guards who served time here) have many stories to tell of life on The Rock.

The undisputed king of the San Francisco catch is Dungeness crab.

One of the most mysterious stories involves Frank Morris (portrayed by Clint Eastwood in *Escape from Alcatraz*) and the Anglin brothers. After digging through the ventilation shafts in their cells, they prepared for their escapes by fashioning lifelike decoy masks from plaster and hair gathered from the barbershop. On the appointed night, they tucked the dummies into their beds, and escaped to the roof. Having manufactured a raft from raincoats, they inflated it with an accordion, and shoved off the island in the dark. They were never seen again. Officially, they are presumed dead—drowned and swept by currents through the Golden Gate. But who knows for sure? Still, their extraordinary getaway hastened the prison's closure a year later, in 1963. You can see a dummy setup in main cell block (jocularly called Broadway), but the real masks are in the Maritime Museum archives at Aquatic Park (see below).

If you haven't had enough of The Rock by the time you leave, buy some books in the store near the Alcatraz pier. Incidentally, you'll need to make reservations during summer and on weekends for this popular tour. Prices are not cheap; but it's worth it. Phone (415) 556-0560 for information.

The dismal prison on Alcatraz now hosts only tourists.

Back on the mainland, another interesting tour is found at Pier 45. Anyone who has ever wondered about life aboard a World War II submarine should see the **USS** *Pampanito.* This fighting submarine sank six Japanese ships and damaged four others during the war, narrowly escaping destruction on two occasions. She participated in the tragic raid that sank the *Kachidoki Maru* and *Rakuyo Maru,* which were carrying British and Australian POWs, though she managed to rescue 73. Keep in mind, as you squeeze through the tight passages, that this ship carried a complement of 10 officers and 70 enlisted men. The *Pampanito* gives new meaning to the word *claustrophobia.* It's open daily for self-guided tours.

The success of the famous Italian seafood restaurants of Fisherman's Wharf—Scoma's, Castaglione's, Alioto's, Sabella's, and others—demonstrates the relativep profitability of *cooking* fish over *catching* them. In the hubbub of tourists and smelly crab pots cluttering the walks in front you can still find live and cooked shrimp and crabs for sale. Unfortunately, the shellfish have to share the stalls with trinkets, postcards, and such an unseaworthy snack as chicken. To try the local specialty, Dungeness crab, come between mid-November and June; the peak of the season is around December.

The real Fisherman's Wharf still harbors many fishing boats (above). Once a fruit-canning plant, the Cannery is now a fancy mall (left).

If you want to see, hear, and smell the *real* **Fisherman's Wharf**, go behind the restaurants to the boat harbor, where wheeling gulls and barking sea lions try to bum free meals from the fish handlers. Walk out along the shore-facing side of Pier 45 to see the working boats. Many today are owned by Vietnamese and Korean fishermen. In the hours before dawn, trucks and packers crowd the narrow wharf at Fish Alley, on the harbor side of Jefferson Street between Jones and Hyde. During the day, it's a quiet place to watch the boats.

Jefferson Street and its intersecting byways are easily the most popular tourist destination in San Francisco—and they look it. If you came to San Francisco to buy a T-shirt, this is the place to do it. Among the spots competing for your attention are the **Wax Museum at Fisherman's Wharf** (145 Jefferson) and the **Lazer Maze** (107 Jefferson), where (mostly) kids try to zap some 50 life-size "robots" with "lazer" guns before getting zapped themselves. In the breathless spirit of the old cartoon series, the **Ripley's Believe It or Not Museum** (175 Jefferson) regales visitors with its two-headed calf, a wax figure of the man with two pupils in each eyeball, humorous tombstone inscriptions, and many other such curiosities. The **Guinness Museum of World Records** (235 Jefferson) enshrines such marvels as the world's smallest printed book; an energetic statue of "Wheelie King" Doug Domokos riding 145 miles (242 km) on the back wheel of his motorcycle; a model of the 62 pancakes that a certain gent devoured in six minutes 58 seconds for a world record; and an admittedly *astounding* video of the "fastest draw in the world," in action. All these places are real crowd pleasers.

The Cannery, at 2801 Leavenworth, was one of the country's first brick factory buildings to be converted into a shopping mall. This old fruit-canning factory now entices browsers with dozens of restaurants, clothing boutiques, galleries, and specialty shops selling such eclectic items as collector dolls, candles, designer fishing gear, and Native American arts and crafts. The **San Francisco International Toy Museum** is located on the second floor. For a fee, you may view—and play with—a rotating collection of fine and historic toys. The **Museum of the History of San Francisco**, opened in July of 1991, promises to fulfill a long-awaited dream of gathering the city's rich and far-flung historical collections together under one roof. So far, only small, rotating collections can be exhibited at one time in the small, third-floor hall. This is the seed of a great museum rather than a venue likely to fire up enthusiasm among the unconverted; but it's still very exciting to lovers of San Francisco. The Cannery also hosts a comedy club and a cooking school.

Less fun, but still intriguing, is the small collection of glass eyes, spectacles, sur-
gical instruments, and assorted eye patches at the nearby **Museum of Ophthalmology** (555 Beach) in the lobby of the American Academy of Ophthalmology.
Admission is free.

West on Beach Street, at the corner of Hyde, the Buena Vista Café is famous
among tourists and locals for its convivial atmosphere and its claim of having introduced Irish Coffee to America. Irish Coffee, of course, is still on the menu.

Victorian Park, across the street, is end of the line for the Powell-Hyde cable
car. Along the Beach Street sidewalk, especially on weekends, crowds of street artisans gather to sell jewelry and knickknacks, and to perform magic, mime, music,
and dance. It can be a very festive atmosphere—in limited doses.

The most sophisticated and attractive of the Fisherman's Wharf shopping centers is **Ghirardelli Square**. Most of its red-brick factory buildings, erected between
1900 and 1916, were part of the Ghirardelli chocolate factory. The Ghirardelli
sign on the roof is a local landmark. The maze of passages, warm buildings, and
sunny plazas are delightful for walking or sitting. The highly browsable shops display an array of crafts, foods, clothing, jewelry, books and toys, though some of
the specialties are hard to classify. The Nature Company sells wonderful things
like crystals and birdcalls, not to mention nature books and prints, telescopes, di-
nosaur-bone excavation kits, plant presses, time-zone clocks, natural science experiments, and recordings of evening storms passing over Big Sur. The Sharper Image
is harder to pin down, with rare toys for grown-ups, like globes that hover on a
column of air, and crystal balls that flash with darting lightning bolts. The Ghirardelli Chocolate Manufactory, on the plaza below the Clock Tower, sells the famous chocolate, although it is now manufactured in the East Bay. You can mull
over the old chocolate-making machines while waiting for a sundae.

Across Beach Street from Ghirardelli Square, at the foot of Polk Street, the **San
Francisco National Maritime Museum** building sits like an ocean liner run
aground in **Aquatic Park**. Its halls are filled with ship models, nautical instruments, and old photographs and paintings that recount the spirited maritime history of San Francisco Bay. Maps, charts, books, and archives are stored in the J.
Porter Shaw nautical library at Fort Mason, a short walk to the west. Nautical
books and cards are also sold at the Maritime Store on Hyde Street Pier.

The pride and joy of the Maritime Museum is its collection of vintage ships
from the Pacific and San Francisco trade, most of which are docked at **Hyde Street**

Pier. Children especially love the ships. The admission fee to enter this outdoor museum is worth every penny.

The *Balclutha* is the flagship of the museum, a magnificent, three-masted Cape Horn veteran launched in 1887. The *Balclutha* used to make two round trips yearly between the British Isles and San Francisco, trading coal and whiskey for California wheat. Later she worked in the Alaskan fish-packing trade, spending winters in San Francisco Bay. Walk the decks and explore the cabins and hold, where displays from the packing business and other seagoing paraphernalia lie about in colorful clutter.

The handsome paddle wheeler *Eureka* was originally launched as a train ferry in the 1890s, and then ferried autos and people between her present berth and the North Bay from 1922 to 1941. The magazine store (for display purposes only) on the upper deck has some interesting period magazines.

The *C.A. Thayer*, another three-masted sailing ship, used to sail in the lumber trade along the Pacific coast. She retired in 1950. The tiny *Alma*, a lumber scow from the North Bay, is too small to allow landlubbers. The *Eppleton Hall*, a British paddle-wheel harbor tug, is closed while awaiting restoration. Other vessels under care of the Maritime Museum are scattered at other berths. The *Wampama*, a steam schooner from the Pacific coast trade, is now at dock in Sausalito undergoing refurbishment. The submarine *Pampanito* (already mentioned) is at Pier 45 on the other side of Fisherman's Wharf. The *Jeremiah O'Brien*, a World War II liberty ship, is docked at nearby Fort Mason.

Aquatic Park is popular among a certain kind of swimmer who is immune to cold water. The rest of us can enjoy the stirring maritime scenery on the usually brisk walk along curving Municipal Pier. The steeples, towers, masts, and crowded hillsides, the white sails on the bay, the Golden Gate Bridge, and the great, gray *Jeremiah O'Brien* at Fort Mason fill the eyes, as the robust sea air fills the lungs. If you're in a mood for more of the same, turn west toward Fort Mason.

Full of fun in the water, sea lions can become real pests on the wharves.

THE CULTIVATED QUARTER

THE NORTHWESTERN CORNER OF SAN FRANCISCO encompasses some of the city's most opulent, poised, and cultivated neighborhoods. Sure, there are decrepit sections, too, but over all, the hard realities of urban life are less apparent there than in any other quarter. San Franciscans treat this section rather like their own backyard—jamming favored shopping and supping precincts, like Union, Clement, and Fillmore streets; puttering around the museums; retreating to the cultivated solitudes of Golden Gate and Lincoln parks. This is San Francisco's most romantic quarter, a bright collage of noisy markets and thundering seacoasts, Old Masters in silent rooms, spiked cannons, and overgrown gardens, haunted by cypresses and foghorn music.

■ GOLDEN GATE NATIONAL RECREATION AREA

What other major American city comes boxed in a national park? Embracing San Francisco's northern and western shores, Golden Gate National Recreation Area (GGNRA) links a number of abandoned military properties in San Francisco with extensive tracts of the Marin Headlands, a semi-wilderness across the Golden Gate Bridge. With more than 68 square miles (176 sq km), the GGNRA is already bigger than the city itself. And when the United States government goes through with plans to decommission the Presidio, that, too, will revert to parkland.

Park headquarters for the GGNRA is Fort Mason, command post for the U.S. Army in the West from the 1860s through the 1880s, and a major military depot during America's Pacific wars. Fort Mason still retains its warlike mien, but the old quarters, warehouses, and docks are now given over to the fruits of peace. One of San Francisco's most important cultural centers, Fort Mason today shelters a host of museums, theaters, galleries, and nonprofit institutions promoting culture and conservation. A free monthly newspaper, *Fort Mason Center*, keeps track of events. Another quarterly publication, *The Park*, promotes the GGNRA's activities. For up-to-the-minute news, maps, and information, go to the headquarters building one block in from the Franklin Street Gate, or call (415) 556-0560.

Then make your way across the Great Meadow and down the steps toward the bay-side wharves. From these piers, where fishermen now try their luck, one and a

St. Ignatius is thought by many to be the city's most beautiful church.

half million U.S. soldiers embarked for the Pacific theater during World War II. A reminder of those grim days, the SS *Jeremiah O'Brien* anchors at Pier 3. The last Liberty Ship still in regular operation, the *Jeremiah O'Brien* carried grain, arms, and cargo in both the Atlantic and Pacific during World War II. Visitors always have free run of the ship, but by all means *do* try to see it when the steam's up and crew's aboard, when you can climb to the chart rooms for a chat with the captain, or crank round the gun turrets under orders of the gunnery mate. The descent to the stifling engine room, skirting pounding pistons and scalding pipes, is a spectacle of well-crafted and cared-for machinery. Wander about the engine room, inspecting the gauges and boilers, pumps and pistons; squeeze down the narrow screw shaft passage to the ship's stern. Crew members bend over backward to demonstrate how it all works, even to the point of reversing the engine upon request—truly the highlight of any mechanic's visit to San Francisco. But you don't have to be a mechanic to appreciate such power and dynamism. Kids love it. The *Jeremiah O'Brien* opens daily, and the admission fee is moderate. Original Liberty Ship crews fire up the engines on the third weekend of every month (except December), and periodically take her out for a run on the bay or the Sacramento River.

The converted warehouses are a smorgasbord of curious sights, lively arts, and noble causes. The tiny **San Francisco Craft and Folk Art Museum** (Building A) exhibits and sells handmade crafts from around the world. Next door, the Marin Zen Center runs Green's, a phenomenally popular vegetarian restaurant with splendid views of bobbing yachts and the Golden Gate Bridge. If you don't have reservations, you can still buy something from their bakery. The J. Porter Shaw Library (Building E) preserves an extensive collection of maritime charts and books.

The **Mexican Museum** (Building D) displays the arts and culture of Mexico and Mexican Americans; a moderate admission fee is charged. Their adjacent shop (no admission charge) sells a variety of Mexican handicrafts and has a free map of Mission District walking tours. Contemporary Italian and Italian-American artists display their works at the **Museo Italo Americano** in Building C, while across the hall, the **African-American Historical & Cultural Society** maintains a library, gallery space, and exhibits of African arts. Its museum of African-American history and culture honors some of San Francisco's early pioneers, among them William Alexander Leidesdorff. A Virgin Island sea captain, Leidesdorff sailed his ship, the

Julia Ann, into San Francisco Bay in 1841. He liked the place, and stayed. Before his death at 38, he built a fortune in the shipping business, opened San Francisco's first hotel, and served as city treasurer, American vice consul of Yerba Buena, and administrator of the first American public school in California. His warehouses stood on the present site of Leidesdorff Street, in the Financial District. Leidesdorff is buried under the floor of Mission Dolores.

Some of San Francisco's premier experimental theaters are at Fort Mason. The intimate, avant-garde Magic Theater (Building D) has premiered the works of Pulitzer Prize-winning playwright Sam Shepard. Young Performers Theater (Building C) is both an acting school and playhouse for children, the perfect place to introduce your kids to the magical world of live theater. (Its counterpart in the art world, the Children's Art Center, is on the ground floor.) The Cowell Theater (Pier 2) and Life on the Water Theater (Building B) also host dramatic productions.

The **Golden Gate Promenade**, a scenic 3.5-mile (5.6-km) pathway along San Francisco's north shore from Aquatic Park to the Golden Gate Bridge, crosses Fort Mason. Linking San Francisco's urban core with its wilder hinterlands, the Promenade traverses rocky coast, driftwood beach, historic army land, and exclusive city enclaves, ending at Fort Point, in the shadow of the Golden Gate Bridge. From there, hikers can strike south on the 9.1-mile (14.6-km) Coastal Trail to Baker Beach, Lincoln Park, the Cliff House, Ocean Beach, and Fort Funston, or north across the Golden Gate Bridge on backpack trips to the Marin Headlands, Muir Woods, Mount Tamalpais, and Point Reyes National Seashore. Fishermen take their pick of favored spots along the way, and everyone enjoys the stupendous views of city, bay, and the rust-colored Golden Gate Bridge.

■ THE MARINA

Beyond the west gate of Fort Mason, Golden Gate Promenade sweeps past Gas Light Cove yacht harbor, named for the handsome Victorian public utilities building that stands on the corner of Buchanan and North Point. This is the Marina District, a flat, tidy, pastel neighborhood of wide, swept sidewalks, smacking of respectability. Because it was built on landfill, notoriously unstable in a tremor, the Marina was one of the two city districts hardest hit in the 1989 earthquake (the

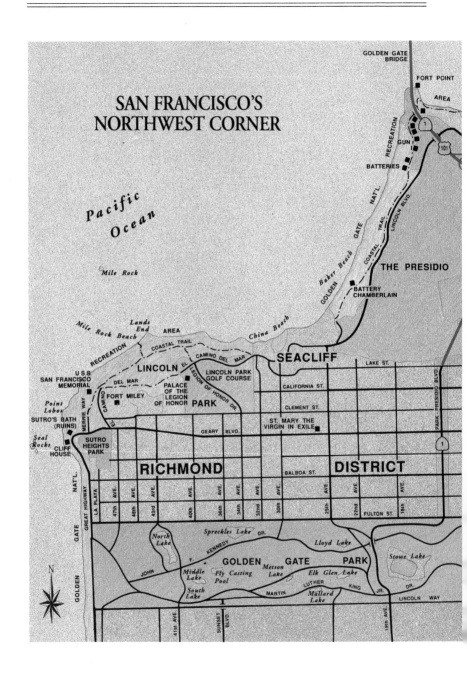

SAN FRANCISCO'S
NORTHWEST CORNER

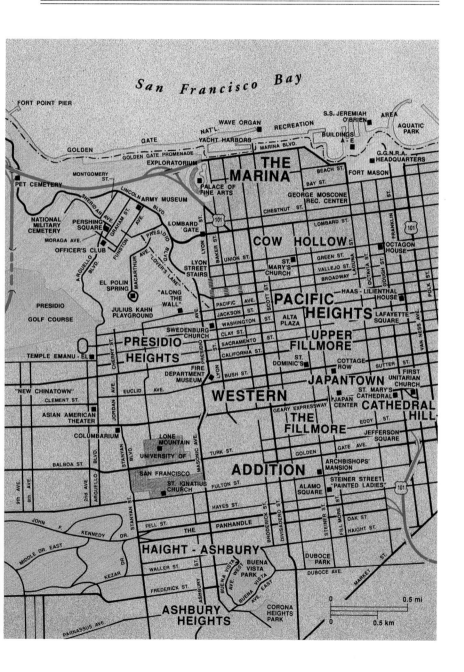

other being South of Market). Only minutes after the quake, pictures of collapsed Marina District housing and a fire were flashing across the country, and indeed the world, inadvertently leading many to believe that flames were engulfing the entire city. In fact, most of the scenes of greatest residential damage in San Francisco were shot in the Marina. Though the district's particular vulnerability in the next quake no doubt worries most residents, life has returned to normal here.

Chestnut, the Marina's main shopping street, was long considered exactly that—a chestnut—until the trendy commercialization of nearby Union Street taught Marina residents to cherish its neighborly virtues. Chestnut's quiet mix of delis, restaurants, cafés, and boutiques, with a homey bookstore and magic shop thrown in, still caters to a mostly local clientele.

In contrast, Marina Green is the promenade *par excellence* for the chic set, who come from miles around to walk their dogs or tend their boats moored at the adjacent St. Francis and Golden Gate yacht clubs. The Green also rates high among kite fliers for the unobstructed winds that blow fine and fresh from the Golden Gate. Views are superb.

At the west end of Marina Green, walkers can continue west on the Golden Gate Promenade to Fort Point, or they can turn east to the end of the West Harbor jetty to see the world's most peculiar musical instrument. Frankly, the **wave organ** resembles no Wurlitzer you've ever seen. What it looks like most, in fact, is a jumbled rostrum of broken tombstones strangulated by pipes crawling up from the sea bed. Waves striking the submerged ends of the pipes force air out through the other ends, moaning and gurgling, a true sea ditty if ever there was one. Stone mason George Gonzalez and assistant director of the Exploratorium, Peter Richards, designed the wave organ to play loudest at high tides.

If you turn south at Marina Green, walking one block on Baker Street, you will come to the **Palace of Fine Arts**, San Francisco's last vestige of its most glorious fair. The Panama-Pacific International Exhibition of 1915 officially marked the opening of the Panama Canal, but most San Franciscans knew it was really a monumental coming-out party for a city risen from the ashes of 1906. Its splendor was, by most accounts, unmatched by any world's fair before or since. Local poet Edwin Markham, admittedly fond of rhetorical hyperbole, deemed it "the greatest revelation of beauty that has ever been seen on earth," but even the sobersided *New York World* swore it was so "indescribably beautiful" that "it gives you a choky feeling in

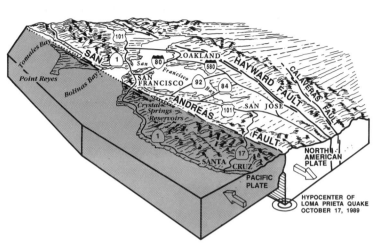

EARTHQUAKE!

5.04 P.M., OCTOBER 17: THE SAN FRANCISCO GIANTS vs. the Oakland Athletics in the second game of the 1989 "Bay Bridge" World Series. Just as the teams are warming up, Candlestick Park begins to tremble. The lights go out, the fans cheer. They're uneasy, but no one at Candlestick realizes, in those first few moments, that this is the largest temblor to hit the Bay Area since 1906.

Within 15.24 seconds, more than 60 people are killed, most crushed by falling concrete on the Nimitz Freeway in Oakland. A 50-foot section of the road bed drops out of the Bay Bridge, 3,757 people sustain injuries, houses slip their foundations, and electricity fails. Hardest hit are the Monterey Bay towns of Watsonville and Santa Cruz, the double-deck Cypress Street section of West Oakland's Nimitz Freeway, and San Francisco's Marina and South of Market districts, both built on landfill.

The Loma Prieta Earthquake, as scientists later dub it (after its epicenter near Loma Prieta peak in the Santa Cruz Mountains), registers 7.1 on the Richter Scale, a considerable shake, but certainly not the worst that can occur. The far more powerful quake of 1906 is estimated to have hit 8.3. No one knows when or where the next big one will strike, but many scientists believe the Hayward Fault to be a likely candidate. It's only a matter of time.

Lincoln Park sports arguably the world's most spectacular golf course (overleaf).

your throat as you look at it." Visitors delighted in the fairyland of brilliant electrical lighting, the Tower of Jewels, a five-acre working model of the Panama Canal, the "palaces" of Education, Horticulture, and Industry, and the fair's lovely centerpiece, the Palace of Fine Arts, designed by Bernard Maybeck as a colonnaded mock-Roman ruin built beside a reflecting pool. (A complete model of the Panama-Pacific fair, incidentally, is displayed at the Presidio Army Museum.)

When the fair closed and the buildings were dismantled, San Franciscans could not bear to raze the Palace of Fine Arts, sparing it for a half century's slow decay until a Marina resident generously donated the funds to rebuild it in 1962. A monumental salute to art for art's sake, the Palace of Fine Arts still rises enchantingly from its sylvan duck pond, a fantastic rotunda transported from a romanticized classic age. Sculptured maidens atop the colonnades weep piteously, filling the palace with a melancholy air of mystery.

Immediately behind the rotunda, at 3601 Lyon Street, stands the **Exploratorium**, dubbed the finest science museum in the country by *Scientific American*. Even people who find science a bore are engrossed by the Exploratorium, and no one has more fun than kids—older kids, that is. The Exploratorium was founded by Frank Oppenheimer (brother of A-bomb inventor J. Robert Oppenheimer) to encourage people to explore the wonders of physics and the human senses. Visitors do not merely learn how things work; they actually take hold of the more than 400 hands-on displays and experiments and *make* them work. You can custom design a bubble, engineer a water spout, create fog or St. Elmo's fire in a vacuum, step into an optical illusion, or crawl through the sound- and light-proof **Tactile Dome** to test your reaction to an environment free from most sensation. Other experiments explain the behavior of light, color, motion, sound, plant and animal behavior, and electricity. There are also classes, a film program, and a marvelous store stocking scientific toys, maps, books, and experiments. Opening hours change throughout the year, so phone (415) 563-7337 for the latest. The Tactile Dome requires reservations. Admission is not cheap, but is still a bargain for an experience that could be the highlight of a child's visit to San Francisco.

■ THE PRESIDIO

The main gate of the Presidio stands ajar on Lyon Street at Lombard, three blocks south of the Exploratorium. The Presidio was founded by the Spanish in 1776 to guard the entrance of San Francisco Bay. The Americans inherited the Presidio from Mexico when they annexed California, and turned it over to the U.S. Sixth Army, making it the longest-serving military base in the United States. Now, after more than two centuries, it is slated for closing. By law it will eventually revert to ownership by the GGNRA, but for the present, it is still the operating headquarters of the U.S. Sixth Army, and a base eminently well-suited for an officer and a gentleman.

Though riddled with military housing, the 1,446-acre (585-ha) Presidio contains the largest tract of forest in the city, as well as the Presidio Army Museum, a National Cemetery, beautiful walking paths, rows of nineteenth-century officers' houses and barracks, and El Polin Spring, revered by the Ohlone and the Spanish for its fertility-inducing properties. Fort Point and the gun batteries above Baker Beach, once part of the reservation, are now administered by the GGNRA. A car is handy here, though serious walkers and history buffs can obtain a map of a seven-mile (12-kilometer) history trail from the Army Museum, where it begins.

The tragic heroine of San Francisco's most famous love story, was born and raised on the Presidio. In 1806, when Concepcion Arguello was 15 years old, a seasoned Russian diplomat, Nikolai Rezanof, arrived in San Francisco Bay seeking aid for the starving Russian colony at Sitka, Alaska. As *comandante* of the Presidio, Concepcion's father entertained him with the best Hispanic hospitality, despite well-justified suspicions of Russian intentions. Completely green in the ways of the politic world, Concepcion fell in love with the Russian, who in turn proposed marriage. Before sailing through the Golden Gate with his hard-won supplies, he reminded her that since he was Russian Orthodox and she a Roman Catholic, he would have to get permission from both the czar and the pope. The journey, he noted, would take years, but Concepcion said she would wait.

Rezanof never returned. In time, Concepcion retired to a Dominican convent, disavowing all connection with the world, and burying her sorrow beneath decades of silence and daily ritual. Then one day came bittersweet news: her fiancé had not abandoned her. He had frozen to death in the snows of Siberia some 40 years before, en route to petition the czar. Concepcion died in the convent, and is buried in Benicia, where strangers still strew her grave with flowers.

The heart of the Presidio is Pershing Square, where the flag is raised at 6 a.m. (7:30 on weekends) and lowered at 5 p.m., to the cannon's roar. General John Pershing, the first commander of American troops in Europe during World War I, served at the Presidio for several years prior to departing for Mexico in pursuit of Pancho Villa, in 1916. General Pershing suffered a personal calamity here in 1915, when fire destroyed his house, killing his wife and three daughters.

The Officers' Club on Moraga Avenue, at the southern end of Pershing Square, incorporates some of the adobe walls of the Spanish-era fort, but the oldest complete building on the Presidio is the handsome Old Station Hospital, now the **Presidio Army Museum.** Built in 1863 on the corner of what is now Funston and Lincoln, it is surrounded by spiked artillery and mothballed missiles. There is no entry fee. The tone of the museum is conciliatory rather than militaristic, befitting campaigns now faded into history. Uniforms, dioramas, wartime propaganda, old photographs, weapons, tools once a daily part of army life, and other military trappings are displayed with a hint of nostalgia for the raw and brutal nineteenth century, when the army was a vital symbol of American order in the frontier West. Portraits of Native American statesmen and warriors hang on the walls, exuding an air of proud defiance and desperation.

The base commissary, now run by Burger King, has the best Golden Gate Bridge views of any restaurant, for the money. It's open to the public on the north side of Lincoln Boulevard, a short walk west of the Army Museum.

The **National Military Cemetery,** where American war veterans are buried, lies farther west on Lincoln Boulevard. Less dramatic than the cemeteries of Normandy or Gettysburg, where every stone marks a life cut down on the field, the National Military Cemetery is nonetheless a compelling spot to reflect on the generations and individuals that bore the brunt of sacrifice in America's wars. The flag here is never lowered. Among the more famous gravestones you may find the names of the Indian scout, Two Bits, and Union Civil War spy Pauline Cushman Fryer, an actress by profession.

Judging by the burgeoning number of new markers at the **pet cemetery** on Crissy Field Avenue, civilians have apparently usurped this graveyard once reserved for four-legged military personnel. Behind the white picket fence lies many a beastly hero:

——❧——
Trouble 1956-1965
He was no trouble
——❧——

——❧——
'Skipper'
Best damn dog we ever had
——❧——

——❧——
Here lie our
beloved rats
-Chocolate-
-Candy-
——❧——

As guardian of the sea approaches to San Francisco Bay, the Presidio hosts several abandoned artillery emplacements, some dating back to the nineteenth century. Its Pacific-facing ridge once bristled with the guns of batteries Marcus Miller, Godfrey, Dynamite, Crosby, and Chamberlain. This formidable pack, now defanged, are linked along the Coastal Trail, which runs south from the Golden Gate Bridge. The 1906-vintage **Battery Chamberlain** still contains a 95,000-pound (43-MT) disappearing gun carriage, designed to avoid incoming shells by ducking behind reinforced concrete walls. The mechanism still works. Rangers offer weekend tours.

Military animals and pets are laid to rest in the Presidio pet cemetery.

Baker Beach, below, like most north coast beaches, is dangerous for swimming. It does offer fishing and panoramic views, while the planted forests of Monterey pine and cypress provide shelter from the wind for picnickers. Drivers can park on Bowley Street.

Hikers bound for Land's End and points south on the Coastal Trail, incidentally, can cut across Lobos Creek on the southern end of Baker Beach, and climb to the gate at the end of 25th Avenue North, in Seacliff. Striking south along any street, the hiker soon meets El Camino Del Mar; turn left (west) and continue up the hill to rejoin the Coastal Trail in Lincoln Park. You can get a map from Fort Mason, Fort Point, or the Cliff House.

■ FORT POINT

The most spectacular fortress on the California coast is Fort Point, crouching with spine-tingling drama beneath the southern arch of the Golden Gate Bridge. You do not find too many Civil War-era forts west of Vicksburg, but Fort Point is the genuine article, built between 1853 and 1861 to guard the entrance of San Francisco Bay from marauders. Planted a mere 10 feet (three m) above the water, and exposed to rough winds that sometimes whip the sea over the approach road, Fort Point is one of San Francisco's most exhilarating surprises.

Fort Winfield Scott, as it is officially known, once bristled with 126 cannon, but never fired a shot in anger; just as well, too, because it was obsolete almost before it was completed. Of similar design to historic Fort Sumter, Fort Point's brick walls were likewise rendered vulnerable to the new rifled-bore artillery barrels (which put a spin on fired shells) and heavier munitions developed in the Civil War.

Visitors enter through great, studded doors to a sally port, where defenders firing through gun embrasures could pick off storming parties before they breached the next door. The massive walls are built around a courtyard, where three tiers rise up on vaulting arches to a barbette roof. On the ground floor, southeast corner, the powder room is arranged much as it used to be, encased behind 15-foot thick (4.6-m) walls. The extraordinary vaulting brickwork is a rarity in San Francisco, where the abundance of good timber encouraged wood-frame housing. Amazingly, Fort Point survived the 1906 quake with flying colors.

Living quarters occupied the east side, with officers on the second floor and enlisted men on the third, 70 to each barracks. Among their regular duties, the men were under orders to wash their feet twice a week, and to take a bath once a month. Their quarters now contain a small but interesting museum, with pictures, uniforms, and weapons. All in all, Fort Point must have been a cold, bleak, and very boring assignment.

Casemates overlooking the Golden Gate mark the business end of operations, presenting four tiers of formidable firepower to any enemy ship that got within a three-mile (five-km) range. Climbing to the rooftop barbette, where rotating guns could fire over the parapets at moving ships, visitors are usually blasted with cold Pacific winds. It's worth every goose bump for the spectacular views of bridge, bay, rocks, and the craziest clique of wind surfers you've ever seen. Watching them skirt and dart about the hulking, frigid, green Pacific waves in the shadow of the gargantuan bridge piers makes for one of the most riveting and dramatic cityscapes in the world.

Entrance to the fort is free to the public daily. Regular tours are given by docents dressed in Civil War garb, but you can wander about at will. Cannon-loading demonstrations are given daily. Check the bookstore for the schedule, information, and a terrific array of historical publications.

One of San Francisco's best public piers lies a short walk back toward Fisherman's Wharf from Fort Point, just beyond the park service office. With splendid views of the city and the Golden Gate, the L-shaped pier almost always hosts a score or two of busy sport crabbers and fishermen. Watching them haul in their catch can be lots of fun, especially for kids.

■ THE GOLDEN GATE

The skylines of New York, Paris, and Hong Kong are potent symbols of earthly power and order, but San Francisco at the Golden Gate is radiant beyond compare. The Golden Gate Bridge is arguably the Earth's most harmonious mastery of nature by mankind. What other structure radiates such majesty, such complexity of character? Viewed from any angle, or comprehended statistically, the bridge is marvelous both to rational minds and romantic ones, a symbol of serene grace in the midst of roiling clouds and open sea, a beacon of vaulting triumph, reason,

The Golden Gate Bridge is the perfect collaboration of man and nature (overleaf).

beauty, and mathematical truth, and yet, a brooding mystery, a haunting presence, a siren song of suicides.

The view from Fort Point is awesome, from Lincoln Park, majestic, and from the Marin Headlands, almost unbelievably sublime. From the Berkeley Hills it is seen tenuously stretched, as if faintly threading a continental rift; looking up from below, it is overpoweringly vast. To motor across on a sunny day is to consort with elegance; to walk it on a windy one is pure exhilaration—or terror, if you fear heights. From the deck of a ship approaching from a long Pacific crossing, it can move a wandering native soul to tears, or cheers.

Like most complex personalities, the Golden Gate Bridge is easier to appreciate when you know its history. Three miles long and one mile wide (5 x 1.6 kilometers), the Golden Gate is the largest gap in the Coast Ranges for many miles, and yet it was completely missed by Cabrilho, Drake, and other European explorers over the centuries. How could anything so big and important have been overlooked for so long? Perhaps it was foggy; but it's also true that from a distance at sea, the narrow gate appears solidly plugged by the Berkeley Hills behind it. Once discovered by Europeans, however, the excellent bay behind it attracted envious scouts from many nations. When Washington finally sprang for it in 1846, some congressmen were calling it the greatest natural asset of the Far West.

An asset, yes; but no candy-asset. The tidal surge through the gate sucks out a volume of water equal to 14 times the flow of the Mississippi at speeds up to 60 miles (97 km) per hour. The currents have carved a deep canyon beneath the Gate. Wracked by storms and fogs, the rocky shores outside the Gate have claimed their share of shipwrecks. Against such extraordinary odds, bridging it was unthinkable to all but madmen and poets.

Appropriately enough, Emperor Norton was one of the first to propose it. He was followed up by a poet named Joseph Strauss, who also happened to be an engineer. Strauss drew up plans and built models that showed it could be done. Yet even as the physical problems were solved, an unsympathetic public still scorned the idea of defacing such a magnificent work of nature. Over 2,000 lawsuits were filed to stop the bridge. Sixty years ago, it was still possible to win such a number of suits in a lifetime. Bonds were passed in 1930 by Bay Area voters who were willing to give it a try. (Construction fees of $35 million were paid off by bridge tolls in 1971.)

Actual work started in 1933. Eleven workmen were killed during construction, and storms once wrecked access piers, but the bridge was completed and opened in May 1937. When financier A.P. Giannini of the Bank of America asked how long it would last, Strauss replied "forever" if cared for properly. More levelheaded engineers say it's good for 200 years—which portends a bonanza year for scrap dealers in 2137.

The sheer size of the bridge is astonishing, especially if you walk out on it, as everyone should. Its art-deco towers rise 746 feet (227 m) above the water, about as high as a 48-story building. If you include the underwater portion, the tallest tower is almost as high as the Transamerica Pyramid. When it was built, its towers were the highest west of Manhattan, and the 4,200-foot (1,280-m) main span was the longest in the world; it has now been surpassed on both accounts. The bridge can sway 27.5 feet (8.3 m) from east to west in a wind (or earthquake). It takes four years to paint the bridge, an ongoing job to prevent it from rusting.

You can park on either side of the bridge and walk across. On the San Francisco side, be sure to see the section of cut bridge cable displayed in the gardens near the parking lot. The cables contain enough wire to encircle the earth three times at the equator. The statue of Joseph Strauss, nearby, honors the tiny man who proved it could be built. Though Strauss was the force behind the bridge, he has too long received sole credit as *the* bridge builder. In fact, his assistant, Clifford Paine, deserves much of the credit for the engineering feat.

Climb the steps to the Roundhouse store, where you can stamp a penny with an image of the Bridge for 50 cents, or choose from a wide assortment of other mementos; no other American structure, save perhaps the Statue of Liberty, has inspired more schlock. Those who fancy flirting with their own immortality can have a brick inscribed with their name and a message, which then is used to pave the concourse.

The walk across the bridge is about two miles (three km), one way. At 246 feet (75 m) above the sea, it is like walking a catwalk around the top of a 16-story building. Looking down on Fort Point and on ships passing under the Bridge, or looking up the precarious cable walkways, spotting dangling painters at work, a person with respect for heights can feel giddy. The Bay gives scant cushion for anyone falling from such heights, but amazingly, a handful of attempted suicides has survived the jump. The number of those who have not has reached 900.

■ COW HOLLOW

The Marina District is walled in on the south by the rather abrupt rise of Pacific Heights. The trough at the foot of Pacific Heights, now engraved by Union Street, was once known as Cow Hollow for the score or so of dairy farms that operated here in the nineteenth century. Alas, the pastures, richly watered by springs, disappeared with the advance of progress. In 1891, the last of Cow Hollow's namesakes was sent, kicking and mooing, into exile.

After six decades as a stodgy residential neighborhood, **Union Street** in the fifties underwent a second rejuvenation. With a paint job to the gingerbread and wrought ironwork, old Victorian houses were transformed into boutiques, coffee houses, restaurants, and fine shops. Soon, Union Street was enjoying a reputation among cognoscenti as a chic shopping district. Word spread, and by the seventies, outlanders and tourists were arriving in droves to hobnob on Union Street, driving much of the chic set over the hill to Upper Fillmore.

Truly, one of San Francisco's hallmark pleasures is the eight-block stroll down Union between Van Ness and Steiner, poking through the courtyards, shops, and bookstores, idling in the cafés, chatting in the bars, expounding in the galleries, supping in the nosheries, and, in general, completely indulging one's lounger's instincts. There's something for everyone, from Heffalump's wonderful toy store (1694 Union) to a water bar serving over 30 varieties of bottled H_2O from Europe and Asia —not to mention all the other purveyors of crystals, pies, herbs, futons, masks, African jewelry, paper products, Afghan rugs, lingerie, bath potions, tribal art, down comforters, French pastry, ceramic cows,

Many Cow Hollow Victorians have been converted to charming commercial use.

Union Street is one of the city's best for walking, shopping, and supping.

and metaphysical books. The fernier Union Street watering holes cater to a singles crowd.

The **Octagon House**, at the corner of Union and Gough, is an architectural curiosity, built in 1861 with the idea that an octagonal shape allows maximum sunlight into a house. You won't have a chance to test that theory because the original interior has been altered. The house is now the only colonial museum west of Texas, and displays the decorative furnishings of the Colonial and Federal periods. A small donation permits you to wander among the antique tables and chairs, and to inspect the prize collection of autographs by the signers of the Declaration of Independence. The Octagon House is open to the public during afternoons of the second and fourth Thursdays, and the second Sunday, of every month.

Redwood-sheltered **Allyne Park**, next door behind the white picket fence, is San Francisco's most charming city park. Let yourself in at one of the gates. It has the feel of somebody's backyard.

Another local oasis is the churchyard of **St. Mary's Episcopal** (2301 Union), where one of Cow Hollow's springs still flows up to water long vanished pastures. The spring, hidden from the street by a hedge and lych-gate, endows the rustic scene with the peace and solitude of an English country churchyard.

Accommodations are available on Union Street in bed-and-breakfast houses, where the comfy flowers-and-sherry ambience matches the neighborhood character. For those who want to soak up one of San Francisco's most charming neighborhoods, if you have the budget, consider lodging in Cow Hollow.

■ PACIFIC HEIGHTS

The western end of Union Street halts at the Presidio wall, where **Lyon Street** bounds southward and upward to Pacific Heights. Here dwell San Francisco's bluest-bloods. It is by no means a small neighborhood. Pacific Heights commandeers the crest of a long, high ridge rising in the east from Van Ness Avenue and rolling 14 blocks west to the Presidio's eastern wall. On the north side, overlooking the Bay, the mansions and apartments march down terraces as far as Green Street. On the south side, overlooking Hayes Valley and Twin Peaks, the streets drop more gradually to California Street. Presidio Heights, an even more exclusive enclave, takes up the torch at the Presidio wall, and runs several blocks farther.

The best way to get a feel for the Heights is to walk, enjoying the splendid architectural wealth of Gothic door-knockers, mansard roofs, fairy-tale turrets, gables, statuary, Tudor facing, wrought iron fences, topiary, burnished lamps, carved doors, and clinging ivy. Bay vistas are the best that money can buy. By night, some half-opened curtain might treat you to a fleeting glimpse of a fine old library or a roaring fire, which you may, if you wish, enjoy vicariously. The Christmas holidays herald a special profusion of lights and decorations.

Where to walk? If not quite aimlessly, let it at least be wherever fancy takes you. Certainly Lyon Street above Union is a good place to start. As you climb its landscaped steps, magnificent views open up over the Marina District to the Bay, the Palace of Fine Arts floating like a magic castle in the foreground. At intersecting streets, like Broadway and Vallejo, avenues of mansions march solidly east. Finally, cresting the top, look west down Pacific at one of the city's most romantic views: the partially red-brick street plunges steeply down into a secluded kingdom known as Presidio Heights, whose rich hinterland embraces the parallel blocks of Jackson, Washington and Clay. This particular stretch of Pacific between Lyon and Spruce is known as "along the wall," in deference to the low stone Presidio wall that separates civilians from warriors. "Along the wall" means old money and cultivated tastes. Governesses gather with their little charges at Julius Kahn Playground, beyond the wall at Spruce Street. Surrounding cypress woods, rolling across the Presidio hills, absorb the fog and hush the footfalls of passers-by.

A few blocks west along the Presidio wall, Presidio Terrace nurses a clutch of palatial mansions on a circular drive, in the shadow of **Temple Emanu-El.** Inspired by the grandiose dome of Santa Sophia in old Constantinople, this landmark synagogue was built by Arthur Brown, whose other works include City Hall and Coit Tower. The temple is open to the public during the afternoon from Monday to Friday. Enter at the corner of Arguello and Lake.

A humbler, but still genteel, architectural statement is made by the **Church of New Jerusalem,** better known as the Swedenborg Church, at 2107 Lyon, between Jackson and Washington. Designed and assembled with loving care by architects and artists of the American Craftsman Movement in 1894, the church and its garden show the careful attention to detail and beauty that characterized much of Renaissance or classical Japanese workmanship. Yet, the tiny church is distinctively Californian. Its carved wooden beams, wood-burning fireplace, stained glass windows, and even its chairs handcrafted of hardwood and woven tule bulrush exude the cozy, yet reverent, atmosphere of a California forest. No wonder it's San Francisco's most popular wedding chapel.

The farther east you go in Pacific Heights, the more the old mansions have given way to apartment houses. Clusters of fine old Victorians still stand between the monoliths, hidden like Russian Easter eggs in the nooks of a garden wall. Many of these remaining mansions have become too expensive to maintain as dwellings, and have been transformed into schools, nonprofit foundations, and even hotels.

The **Haas-Lilienthal House** at 2007 Franklin Street is one of the eccentric wooden Victorians that typifies old San Francisco. Owned and operated as a museum by the Foundation for San Francisco's Architectural Heritage, the house was built in 1886 with the jaunty bay windows, luxuriant ornamentation, fanciful gables, and Queen Anne-style circular tower so characteristic of the exuberant Victorian era. The rooms are still furnished with many of the Haas and Lilienthal family heirlooms. Foundation guides lead tours on Wednesdays and Sundays. A moderate donation is requested at the door; phone (415) 441-3004.

Lodging in a Victorian is an ideal way to get to the heart of San Francisco. The Sherman House, a historical landmark at 2160 Green Street, pampers guests with luxurious period rooms, secluded gardens, French dining, and a spectacular three-story music room once graced by the great Caruso himself. The eccentric Mansion Hotel (2220 Sacramento) features a huge collection of Beniamino Bufano statues, a plush Victorian dining room (open to the public), and a disembodied head that sings at night for guests in the parlor, where thine host might also be prevailed upon to play his musical saw. Not everyone's cup of tea, perhaps, but unique.

Two of San Francisco's prettiest hilltop parks are in Pacific Heights, surrounded by handsome architecture and elegant views. **Lafayette Park** is a delightful garden, flowery and well-wooded, smelling of pine and eucalyptus. **Alta Plaza**, on the other hand, rises in vigorously symmetrical terraces like a great, green Mayan pyramid—an oddly forceful monument in an otherwise well-groomed, genteel neighborhood.

Denizens of Pacific Heights, one surmises, repair to Sacramento Street between Spruce and Lyon, and to Upper Fillmore, between California and Jackson, to do their shopping. With an emphasis on chic boutiques, antiques, fine gifts, and children's outfits, **Sacramento Street** is one of the more refined shopping streets in the city. Youngsters love Bookfriends (3610 Sacramento), a rambling bookstore, where the *Goodnight Moon* room recreates the setting of the Margaret Wise Brown classic.

After leveling Nob Hill's mansions, the fire of 1906 was halted at Van Ness Avenue.

While Sacramento enjoys its quiet evenings, the lights of **Upper Fillmore**, seven blocks east, sparkle long into the night. Catering to a stable, well-to-do, and largely youthful clientele, urbane Upper Fillmore is the epitome of contemporary American trendiness, the domain of sushi and designer foods, luxury services, nail salons, import groceries, hot tubs, dessert boutiques, cafés, and rich young things with mannequin faces. The popular Clay Cinema, on Fillmore near Clay Street, shows art and international films. If Proust were alive and living in San Francisco, no doubt his Swann would have felt at home on Upper Fillmore.

■ WESTERN ADDITION

Ironically, until recently Fillmore was known as one of San Francisco's poorer streets. Even now, Fillmore below Geary remains depressed, a characteristic of much of the Western Addition, which has known more than its share of downs and ups. Its greatest up was that it survived the 1906 earthquake and fire, leaving intact the city's largest Victorian neighborhood. But its greatest down, as a neighborhood,

Wealthy Pacific Heights, beyond Van Ness, remained unscathed.

was the deterioration of those same Victorians through neglect, and then demolition as part of desperate redevelopment schemes.

The district acquired its name in the 1870s, when a spate of building to the east of Van Ness Avenue affixed a *western addition* to the old city core. Probably its most famous resident was a woman named Mary Ellen Pleasant, once better known as Mammy Pleasant, who lived in a house owned by Thomas Bell near the corner of Bush and Octavia. (The house is gone, but six venerable eucalyptus trees that she planted still grow in front, where a memorial plaque has been placed by the African-American Cultural Society.) Few figures in San Francisco history have inspired more mystery. Her notoriety followed hard on the death of her employer, Thomas Bell, who was killed in a fall from his third-floor balcony. Some claimed that he was pushed by Mary Pleasant, but no one ever claimed it in court or to her face. Nonetheless, rumors circulated until her death, and after, that she was a procuress, a murderess, and a witch. Modern accounts don't dispel the mystery, but are more likely to credit her as a consummate businesswoman, an ardent abolitionist, and a commanding, fearless person who demanded and received respect. The daughter of a black mother and Cherokee father, Mary Pleasant arrived in San Francisco during the gold rush. She opened a successful boarding house (which some say was a discreet bordello), and used her personal fortune to help finance the western terminus of the Underground Railway. Her San Francisco home was a sanctuary for runaway slaves. When John Brown was seized at Harper's Ferry, Maryland, a conspiratorial note signed with her initials was found on his person, but she escaped before any investigation could be mounted. Her interest in the plight of African Americans did not end with the Civil War. In 1865, she sued a San Francisco streetcar company over rude treatment to black riders, and won.

Of the many ethnic groups that have settled the Western Addition, among the most prominent were the Jewish community, which congregated here during the first third of the twentieth century, the Japanese, who built "Little Osaka" around Post Street, and African Americans, whose community centered along Fillmore. Little Osaka was uprooted during World War II by Japanese-American internment, though many returned after the war. Conversely, the African-American community grew rapidly during the war as workers arrived from the South to build ships. When war jobs died out and unemployed black workers were passed over by private-sector companies, the neighborhood fell on hard times. The old

Victorians deteriorated into slummy firetraps, and were replaced with ugly urban renewal projects.

Today, the Western Addition is undergoing rampant gentrification of its remaining Victorian enclaves. Modern city planners, wiser from their earlier mistakes, are designing with much more attention to aesthetics and social use. Still, many of the government housing projects of the Western Addition are plagued by high crime rates, especially in the blocks south of Geary.

One of San Francisco's most charming Victorian streets is **Cottage Row**, between Sutter and Bush, a half block east from Fillmore. Like Macondray Lane on Russian Hill, Cottage Row is another of those little country lanes so improbably spirited to the midst of the metropolis. While there, walk the extra block to Marcus Books (1712 Fillmore, between Sutter and Post) for a large selection of works by black authors and about African-American history and culture.

One block west of Fillmore, on the corner of Bush and Steiner, stands one of San Francisco's most popular religious shrines. Catholic pilgrims, many from Latin America, search out **St. Dominic's Church** to pay their respects to the statue of St. Jude, patron saint of lost causes.

Fillmore marks the western edge of Nihonmachi, or **Japantown**, a compact neighborhood loosely rounded by Geary, Octavia, and Pine. For persons completely unfamiliar with Oriental cultures, the comparison between Japantown and Chinatown could serve to show that China and Japan are as different as, say, Italy and Denmark. Of course, Japantown does not attempt to be a faithful recreation of "the old country." Like Little Italy, it is a distinctively American hybrid, but harboring a treasury of details that can evoke a sense of Japan, much as a bonsai may evoke a whole forest, or a bite of *sfrappole* can bring back memories of old Bologna. Keep your senses primed as you walk through the district, and you may find such cultural touchstones in the hardware stores, the family-owned markets and bakeries, the Zen and Konko missions, and the comfortable, human scale of the streets and architecture. The one-block, open-air **Buchanan Mall**, between Post and Sutter, is the most self-consciously old-style Japanese street. Paved with riverine cobbles and lined by Japanese restaurants and shops, it is a comfortable, pleasant place to stroll or sit.

A more ambitious vision of modern Japan stands beyond Post Street. Japan Center is a three-block concrete mall, hemmed in by Fillmore, Geary, and Laguna, which many find ugly and impersonal. The interior, however, can be inviting, and

Traditional costume, dancing, and a barrel of sake spice up a Japantown festival.

certainly provides some fascinating cultural insights. Among the Japanese goods and provisions available are futons, cooking utensils, arts and crafts, clothing, furniture (including items specially designed for small apartment living), antiques, fine paper products, pearls, tourist knickknacks, and a wide selection of Japanese books, videos, cassettes, and compact discs. The center also contains about 30 restaurants, from coffee shops to sushi bars, noodle houses to formal Japanese restaurants, some with *tatami* rooms. Visitors are fascinated by Isobune, where the sushi boats float by on a miniature river, and by the table-side chefs at Benihana's, who put on skilled knife demonstrations while preparing meals. Casual Sapporo-ya, which makes its own noodles on an antique ramen machine, is popular for snacks. The adjacent Miyako Hotel, while blending Japanese trappings (like kimono-clad waitresses) with Western comforts (such as chairs), also offers some genuine Japanese-style rooms with tatami floors and Japanese baths.

Japantown's sometimes sleepy facade belies its cultural vigor. Language and cultural classes, including such arts as cooking and flower arrangement, are advertised on the Japan Center community bulletin board. Seasonal festivals bring dancers, drummers, artists, and craftspeople from around the Bay Area. The Kokusai Theater (1746 Post) devotes itself to Japanese-language films. The AMC Kabuki 8 Theaters, on the other hand, do not: anchoring the Fillmore end of Japan Center, they offer classic and contemporary films from all countries.

Downstairs, the Kabuki Hot Spring bath house mollifies the soul as it cleanses the body—or rather, *after* cleansing the body. The idea in a Japanese bath is to lather, scrub, and rinse yourself *thoroughly* before getting into the hot bath to soak. The Kabuki has a traditional communal bath, as well as sauna and steam rooms, and is open to men and women on different days. As gentle New Age music soothes away stress, you can relax under an after-bath shiatsu (finger-pressure) massage. (And yes, sir, I mean a *real* massage.) The works aren't cheap, but you will come out feeling like a new person. Kabuki Hot Spring is located at 1750 Geary Boulevard, on the ground floor of Japan Center.

From Japantown, you can walk two blocks up Geary (east) to the top of Cathedral Hill, named for St. Mary's Cathedral, an unabashedly modern edifice rising at the corner of Geary and Gough. However peculiar the exterior, the vast interior is astounding, even in this atrium-jaded city. Built in 1971, it speaks boldly of an age of faith bolstered by the worldly powers of science and engineering. Enormous compound arches lift the cross-shaped dome 190 feet (58 m) above the floor, opening the walls to expansive views out over the city. The majestic Ruffati organ explodes from the depths on an enormous concrete pedestal like a throne rising up t⌐ glory. If you like your cathedrals exuberant, you'll love St. Mary's.

The **First Unitarian Church** across the street is a much more staid, though handsome, stone structure dating from 1889. First Unitarian was the church of Thomas Starr King, the preacher who is credited with swaying California to the Union side in the Civil War. So enamored was California of this service that Thomas Starr King is one of the two statues that represent the state in the Hall of Fame in Washington. (The other is Father Junipero Serra.) King died before the war ended, in 1864. His tomb is outside the southeastern corner of the church.

Making your way west again, preferably by car or public transport (because of healthy distances), you can visit three far-flung outposts of the Western Addition. The **Museum of Russian Culture**, at 2450 Sutter Street, keeps a large collection of icons, artifacts, and memorabilia of the Bay Area's scattered Russian community. This small, quiet repository of art and books welcomes researchers, and is open Saturdays or by appointment. Call (415) 921-7631.

Firehouse buffs will want to visit the **Fire Department Museum**, at 655 Presidio Avenue, where they can obtain a list of 26 vintage firehouses that still survive around the city, all of them retired from service. The museum captures the real veneration that San Franciscans have traditionally shown for their fire companies—not a strange phenomenon in a city of wood. Separate fire companies used to compete for the honors of extinguishing blazes, and their paraphernalia here reflects those glory days. The collection includes an 1850 hose cart, an 1897 steam fire engine, hats, axes, and extinguishers. The museum is annexed to a real firehouse, where a splendid old hook and ladder truck is parked.

South of Geary, **Alamo Square** anchors down another gentrifying section of the Western Addition. Many old Victorians line the park, including the famous row along Steiner Street so often pictured in books of the city. The old Imperial Russian Consulate still stands at 1198 Fulton; and the Archbishops' Mansion on the corner of Fulton and Steiner, once the official home of local Catholic prelates, has now been converted into one of the most palatial bed-and-breakfast inns in the country. Guests may sip sherry in the lap of Edwardian luxury, or play a few bars on Noel Coward's piano.

From the southwestern corner of Alamo Square, you can see the enchanting towers of St. Ignatius church and the forested slopes of Buena Vista Park and Mount Sutro. Though still a bit frayed in places, the neighborhood surrounding Alamo Square is one of San Francisco's most breathtaking. Look north across the valley for another view of Alta Plaza's Mayan symmetry. Some say it's a landing platform for spacecraft.

■ THE RICHMOND DISTRICT

The name of Lone Mountain has struck a chord of terror in more than one generation of San Francisco children. That's because it stood for years at dead center of the city's necropolis, surrounded in all directions by acres of bone yards.

Where have all the graveyards gone? Gone to Colma, every one; at least the ones that they could find. Richmond District gardeners have been surprised more than once while planting their petunias.

In a city as small as San Francisco, the enormous cemetery plots were needed for the living, and so in 1914, Mayor Sunny Jim Rolph ordered all persons owning or claiming lots in the cemeteries to move their occupants to Colma, a city just south of San Francisco devoted to caring for the dead. Unclaimed bodies were buried in mass graves in Colma, and the stones were used, in part, to pave the city's sea walls. You can still see some on the jetty at the wave organ.

Today, Lone Mountain is crowned by a tower that is part of University of San Francisco. Founded by the Jesuits in 1855, USF is the oldest university in San Francisco, though it moved three times before settling on its present spectacular hilltop. Their campus contains the most majestic church in the city, St. Ignatius. Its handsome dome and campanile, and its 210-foot (66-m) twin spires, spectacularly lit at night, ennoble more than one city vista.

Only one remnant of Lone Mountain's cemeteries remains today—the **Columbarium**. Once surrounded by the Odd Fellows cemetery, it is now engulfed by buildings, and approached from the appropriately dead-end Loraine Street. The Columbarium is a splendid neoclassical rotunda filled with urns and memorial niches. Capped with a copper roof and decorated with precious vases and a Tiffany window, the four-story building keeps the cremated remains of some 6,000 people, many of them pioneer families. If you bring a companion, you can

St. Mary's Cathedral is a spectacular new rendition of an ancient architectural form.

test the building's marvelous acoustics on any of the upper floors. Standing on one side, you should be able to hold a quiet conversation with someone hidden around the opposite side. The Columbarium is open to the public on mornings from Tuesday through Saturday.

Clearing the cemeteries made way for San Francisco's Richmond District, by far a worthy trade-off. This western third of San Francisco, combined with the Sunset District south of Golden Gate Park, is known collectively as "the Avenues," because most of the streets running north and south are numbered avenues. At one time the Richmond was called the Outer Lands, and even the Great Sand Waste, for the obvious reason that it *was* a wasteland of shifting sand dunes and a few scraggly knolls. The land was opened for settlement largely through the efforts of a Prussian named Adolf Sutro, sometimes called the Father of the Richmond, who owned a good stretch of the Outer Lands. Sutro had made his fortune in the Comstock, and retired to a mansion across from the Cliff House, which he also owned. Next door he erected the largest bath house in the world, Sutro Baths, and connected it to the city with a steam railway. Thus, he built both the inducement and the means for people to go to the Richmond.

Today, the Richmond is a solidly middle-class neighborhood of great ethnic diversity happily sandwiched between the Presidio and Lincoln Park on the north, and Golden Gate Park on the south. The Russians were among the first major ethnic groups in the outer Richmond, when some 10,000 White Russians arrived in the years after the 1917 Revolution. Their passage to America was eased by the tireless lobbying of an extraordinary priest, known as John the Barefoot, who was to become San Francisco's first Russian Orthodox bishop. Like the Italians of North Beach, the Russian community has mostly aged or moved to the suburbs, but many still return for services at **Saint Mary the Virgin in Exile**, particularly for the colorful Russian Orthodox Easter services. The gold, onion-domed church on Geary between 26th and 27th avenues opens for Mass in the morning, when visitors *may* be allowed to view its enormous chandeliers, icons and relics. John the Barefoot is buried beneath the floor.

Like the Russians themselves, the restaurants and tea rooms that used to be a part of slavic Richmond have dwindled. One notable exception is Russian Renaissance, a restaurant at 5241 Geary. The icon-like murals that cover the walls and ceiling with scenes from Russian folklore and history took artist Serge Smernoff 14 years to complete. You can still find Russian newspapers in the stores, and a

St. Mary the Virgin in Exile is the religious center of Russian life in the Richmond.

scattering of onion-domed buildings in the side streets. The 1990s are witnessing a resurgence of Russian immigration to San Francisco. Whether they will revitalize the Russian flavor of this part of the Richmond remains to be seen.

Many elderly Russians still congregate on the playground benches of **Mountain Lake Park**, a pretty spot on the Presidio's border near Park Presidio Boulevard. Anza camped here when he came to found the Presidio, in 1776. Thousands of refugees followed suit on the nearby golf course in 1906. Kids and adults alike will love the playground's large swings and rolling-pin slides.

The most prominent ethnic group in the Richmond nowadays is Chinese. The stretch of the Avenues between Arguello Boulevard and Park Presidio, especially along Clement Street, is known as **New Chinatown**, which lacks both the tourist glitz and squalor of Grant Avenue's Chinatown, while its markets and restaurants can beat it for quality and convenience.

Attracted by the strong Asian American presence in the Richmond, the Asian American Theater has settled into a new home on Arguello at the corner of Clement. One of the premier small theaters in the country, it has produced works by Tony-Award-winning playwright David Henry Hwang and other local artists.

The Richmond's restaurants attract more locals than tourists. The long stretch of Clement and Geary in the Richmond has long been known as San Francisco's premier restaurant row, celebrated for its great culinary diversity and quality. Nowadays the restaurants are more plentiful than ever, but the Richmond's once exceptional diversity now decidedly emphasizes East Asian cuisines. Chinese offerings are the most prolific, with *dim sum* and seafood (Cantonese), Mandarin, Shanghai, Hunan, Sichuan, Chaozhou, Hakka, and vegetarian. Vietnamese, Italian, French, Mexican, Japanese, Thai, American, and Korean are amply represented, but you can also find such rarer cuisines as Cambodian, Russian, Moroccan, Peruvian, Spanish, Danish, Laotian, Armenian, Indonesian, Singaporian, and Burmese—not to mention all the ubiquitous cafés, delis, dessert and ice cream parlors, and Irish pubs. You can idle away the hours between meals and late into the evenings at bookstores like Green Apple and Albatross II, or at night spots like the Holy City Zoo Comedy Club (408 Clement), where Robin Williams got an early boost, or the Last Day Saloon, next door.

All in all, the Richmond is nothing spectacular in the Disneyland sense of the word; but with good food, good drink, good books, and entertaining company, it is one of the most comfortable and stimulating neighborhoods in the city. And as if that weren't enough, it is well placed for escaping to the parks.

■ LINCOLN PARK AND LAND'S END

Seacliff, an exclusive neighborhood of stirring sea views, is incomparably coddled between the Presidio and Lincoln Park. The Coastal Trail from the Presidio passes through the streets of the neighborhood. You can hook into it on the east side at Baker Beach, at the end of 25th Avenue north, and on the west side near where El Camino del Mar meets Lincoln Park.

In Seacliff, devotees of Ansel Adams can take a small detour to the house at 129 24th Avenue, where he grew up. In those days, this was out in the sticks. The house is not open to the public.

Another detour takes you to **China Beach**, named for the Chinese fishermen who used to camp here in earlier days. China Beach is an exception to the no-swimming rule of thumb at San Francisco beaches. The water is safe enough here, though never warm. The beach has changing rooms, showers, restrooms, and a lifeguard station.

San Francisco's most rugged stretch of seacoast is Land's End, west of Seacliff. Until closed by landslides, El Camino del Mar once ran through here to the Cliff House. Sutro's railway also passed through. Nowadays, both road and rail rights-of-way are footpaths administered by the GGNRA and Lincoln Park. Between the two parks, San Francisco enjoys both its wildest landscapes and its most rarefied vision of civilization, the Legion of Honor.

Few museums in all the world have a setting as magnificent as the **California Palace of the Legion of Honor**. Approached by car through Lincoln Park Golf Course from 34th Avenue and Clement, the Legion rises handsomely from its Lincoln Park hilltop like a classical French palace, fronted with colonnades, a triumphal arch, and heroic equestrian bronzes of El Cid and Joan of Arc. One of five original castings of Rodin's famous statue, *The Thinker*, cogitates in the courtyard, while another Rodin, *The Shades*, commands a noble view over the Golden Gate. A shockingly incongruous sculpture by George Segal, *The Holocaust*, clings half-hidden behind a corner of the balustrade. Its emaciated corpses and barbed wire shriek out with shameless effrontery amidst the Legion's perfect setting—which, of course, is precisely the point.

Founded by Alma de Bretteville Spreckels, the French-born wife of a local sugar baron, the Legion was dedicated to American soldiers fallen in France during World War I. Marshals Joffre and Foch both attended the opening in 1924, each marking the occasion by planting a cypress on the Legion's southern side. For years devoted exclusively to the display of French Art, the Legion of Honor has recently absorbed the European collection from the M.H. de Young Museum, across town, giving it a much broader scope. Francophiles may grumble, as indeed they do, but the Legion still exudes a staunchly Gallic air.

Surveying eight centuries of European art, the permanent collection contains works by El Greco, Rembrandt, Rubens, Van Dyke, Van Cleve, Renoir, Seurat, Cézanne, Degas, Boucher, Monet, Manet, Courbet, Cellini, and Rodin, who alone accounts for more than 70 sculptures. One of the most impressive pieces is an 11-foot high (3.3-m) bronze wine vase by Gustave Doré, depicting cherubs and vermin in drunken revel. Of special note are the period rooms, particularly the somber Medieval Spanish room with the Mudejar ceiling, and the painted, paneled room from the house of the Mayor of Turin (both of which were moved from the de Young Museum, and not yet installed at press time). The **Achenbach Foundation for Graphic Arts**, downstairs, cares for the largest collection of graphic prints in the western United States, including a splendid selection of Japanese woodblock prints.

The Thinker *is one of several works by Rodin at the Legion of Honor.*

Aside from the collections and exhibitions, the Legion of Honor organizes regular docent tours and hundreds of film, lecture, painting, and music programs, including weekly pipe organ concerts in the Rodin Gallery. Its Florence Gould Theater, one of the most intimate venues in town, hosts regular programs of chamber music, jazz and dance, as well as demonstrations of historical musical styles and instruments.

It charges a moderate admission price, waived on the first Wednesday of every month, and the first Saturday from 10 a.m. to noon. A small shop at the entrance offers a nice array of cards and books. On the lower floor, Café Chanticleer is a cheery setting for a light lunch.

Outside again, if you like the Legion's facade, stroll around back for another perspective. En route, take note of the black engraved stone on the north side of El Camino del Mar. It is a monument to the *Kanrin Maru*, the first Japanese ship to arrive in San Francisco Bay bearing emissaries to America. Its American counterpart sailed simultaneously in the other direction. The year was 1860.

Behind that monument, a hard-to-find path cuts down the edge of the golf course to the **Coastal Trail**, which leads between the Golden Gate Bridge and the Cliff House via Land's End. (You'll find a second path to the west, at the end of the parking lot.) There are no roads here. Stay on the paths; the cliffs crumble easily, and someone falls or is swept away by freak waves nearly every year. The seas off Land's End are shipwreck waters. On foggy days, the sound of the horns and the smell of fog and the sea produce the kind of atmosphere that make Byronic hearts swoon with sweet melancholy. On clear days, the vistas sweep from Seacliff past the Presidio and the Golden Gate Bridge to rugged Point Bonita Lighthouse, in Marin County, the north channel's outside gatepost. In the foreground, Mile Rock Lighthouse blinks its lonely vigil through rough seas and calm. A spur off the Coastal Trail winds down to tiny Mile Rock Beach, a favorite of stalwart sunbathers.

As the Coastal Trail rounds **Point Lobos**, skirting thick, matted tunnels of cypress, it feeds into Merrie Way, near the Cliff House. Stairs lead uphill at this point to the bridge of the **USS *San Francisco***, overlooking the sea at El Camino del Mar. Torn by shells, the piece of ship now stands as a memorial to 107 crew and officers killed in the 1942 Battle of Guadalcanal. The wooden observation house on the hill behind is the old Marine Exchange Lookout. Built to watch for ships entering the Golden Gate, it would announce the news to the more centrally located Telegraph Hill by semaphore. On the hill above the lookout, military buffs can explore Fort Miley's abandoned gun emplacements, built to greet less friendly ships.

Hikers can return to the Legion of Honor by the trail at the northerly dead-end of El Camino del Mar; otherwise a right turn on Point Lobos Avenue takes you to the Cliff House.

■ THE PACIFIC SHORE

The **Cliff House** was one of the city's first tourist attractions. Mark Twain described a visit here in the 1860s, when it was already garnering a reputation as a fast place for fast people. When Sutro bought it in the 1880s, he stopped the hanky-panky and started to run it as a family resort. After the old Cliff House burned in 1894, Sutro erected a wondrous wooden castle on the site, bolstering business with a huge bathhouse next door. Unfortunately for lovers of the Gothic, the building burned in 1907. Be sure to see its picture in the lobby of the contemporary Cliff House, which dates from 1908.

Still a tourist shrine, Cliff House bars and restaurants mix warm repast with stirring views of sea stacks and rugged breakers. The GGNRA runs a visitor center downstairs, with a view over Sutro's Baths. On the patio outside, visitors can step inside a large camera, the Camera Obscura, for views of landscape, seascape, and fellow tourists. Barking sea lions play just off shore on **Seal Rocks**. Their ghostly roars take on added drama in fog or murk of darkness. On clear days, Point Reyes stands out clearly in the north, protected as far as you can see by state and national parklands. By night, the towns of Muir Beach, Stinson Beach, and Bolinas glow small and bright amidst the black hills and sea. Thirty-two miles (53 km) to the west, you can sometimes pick out San Francisco's farthest outpost, the Farallon Islands, a rugged sanctuary for birds and sea lions. During the gold rush, enterprising businessmen used to collect murre eggs from there to sell for breakfast in the city.

The gulf between the Farallon Islands and the Golden Gate is part of the Red Triangle, a somewhat lurid name for a patch of ocean that the Great White Shark calls home. Recorded attacks on humans here are not overly common; but then, neither are swimmers.

The Cliff House also shelters the **Musée Méchanique**, a collection of coin-operated mechanical games and devices, the kind that used to be found in penny arcades around the civilized world. Plunk your quarters down to play the vintage pinball machines, mechanical fortune teller, miniature carnival, automated band instruments, and more. Admission is free, but bring plenty of pocket change for the machines.

The ruins in the rocks north of the Cliff House are **Sutro's Baths**, a Victorian pleasure palace opened in 1896. Its six salt baths and hundreds of dressing rooms had room for 24,000 swimmers under a soaring glass dome. An aerial cable car, the Sky Tram, once ran from the Cliff House to the rocks beyond, where visitors could view the crashing seas from a tunnel cut clear through the rocks. The baths

A FOGGY EXCURSION

*F*rom the moment we left the stable, almost, the fog was so thick that we could scarcely see fifty yards behind or before, or overhead; and for a while, as we approached the Cliff House, we could not see the horse at all, and were obliged to steer by his ears, which stood up dimly out of the dense white mist that enveloped him. But for those friendly beacons, we must have been cast away and lost.

—Mark Twain's description of an early morning jaunt to the Cliff House, in *The Golden Era*, July 3, 1864.

This most spectacular version of the Cliff House burned in 1907.

burned in 1966, and the tram was dismantled soon after. You can still walk to the tunnel, and clear through the now-exposed opening above the rocks. Watch out for holes in the floor of the cave, where the surf pounds and gurgles through subterranean passages at high tide.

Sutro lived on an estate high on the hill across the road from the Cliff House. The house was torn down after his death, and his estate turned into **Sutro Heights Park.** Old walls and feral gardens lend a romantic air of ruin to the grounds. Views from high ground here reach to Ocean Beach, the Richmond and Sunset districts, Golden Gate Park, Fort Funston, and beyond, a tremendous study in perspective—all the streets, the park boundaries and the beach itself intersect at 90-degree angles.

The waters off **Ocean Beach**, running four miles (6.5 km) to San Francisco's border and beyond, are not very hospitable. Chill winds usually render sunbathing uncomfortable, while severe undertow makes swimming perilous, not to mention illegal. Ocean Beach still pulls the crowds in on the hottest days, however, and almost always provides a magnificent backdrop for seashore strolls or horseback rides.

Now a hole in the ground, Sutro's was once the world's largest bathhouse.

Ocean Beach is pretty to look at, but a menace to swimmers.

■ GOLDEN GATE PARK

Like the Golden Gate Bridge, Golden Gate Park was built despite a litany of nay-sayers who insisted that it couldn't be done. With 1,017 acres (412 ha), it is probably the largest cultivated park in the United States, if not the world.

In league with the Hanging Gardens of Babylon, Golden Gate Park is a work of art on a heroic scale, where lakes, forests, glades, waterfalls, streams, hills, and even the earth itself have been designed by human hands. Yet, what mankind nurtured, Mother Nature has now good-naturedly adopted as her own. A more botanically vibrant piece of ground would be difficult to find in any temperate clime.

When plans for a park first started tickling the fancy of boosters like William Ralston, the likeliest pieces of real estate near the center of town were already taken. Instead, the city acquired an oblong piece of the Great Sand Wastes, three miles long and a half-mile wide (4.8 by .8 km), at its closest point about three miles (five km) from downtown. It was the largest sand desert on the California coast. Such folly no doubt caused many a guffaw in the saloons and press-rooms of Montgomery Street. Even Frederick Law Olmsted, the landscape designer who built New York's 840-acre (340-ha) Central Park, threw up his hands in disgust at the site, which he thought incapable of supporting trees. He graciously admitted his mistake later.

In 1871, the contract for designing Golden Gate Park went to an engineer named William Hammand Hall, who had already surveyed the Outside Lands for the federal government. Hall went straight to work. First, he had to secure the blowing sand. He did this by sowing barley, then lupine on top of that, and grass on top of the lupine. With a mat of grass established, he planted trees. At the same time, he started constructing a wall on Ocean Beach to stop the dunes from blowing inland. He proceeded to grade, build roads, lay water pipe, and plant thousands of trees in the eastern section of the park, which had more promising soil than the coastal side. He also built the Panhandle, a long strip of park designed as an elegant carriage entry.

Hall's work was soon appreciated by San Franciscans, who started flocking to the young park for picnics and carriage races. But though San Franciscans loved the new park, government corruption and political shenanigans were eating at the park budget. After repeated attacks and trumped-up charges of extravagance and corruption, Hall resigned in disgust, in 1876. Funds were slashed, and Golden Gate Park drifted into a decade of decline. Plants and roads were neglected, crime and corruption flourished. Finally, in desperate straits, the government called Hall back again.

Hall took the job on condition that he could appoint his own successor, a man capable of pressing on with the park's construction while fending off the rascally politicians. His appointment, a Scotsman named John McLaren, took over as Superintendent in 1890 and served for the next 53 years. Fondly known as "Uncle John" by his staff and generations of grateful San Franciscans, McLaren was not only a master gardener who personally planted thousands of trees, but a canny handler of people.

McLaren believed that parks should be natural, beautiful settings where people can retreat from such urban trappings as buildings, statues, and roads. Under McLaren's trusteeship, Golden Gate Park blossomed into the masterpiece of landscape gardening that it is today. He brought in exotic plants from around the world and earned international fame for his extraordinary abilities to make them flourish. Against the pressures of developers he fought like a terrier, outplaying politicians at their own games. Once, for instance, when plans were hatched to bisect the park with another road, McLaren deftly nominated a plot in the planners' path for a police academy. The Police Department rushed to McLaren's support, and the road stopped dead in its tracks. The academy, of course, had to be built, but in due course it was reabsorbed back into the park as the Senior Center, as it stands today, at 37th Avenue.

McLaren eventually outlived all opponents, escorting his park beyond their reach into the middle of the twentieth century. Until he expired, still Superintendent, at the age of 93, his staunch loyalty to the Vegetable Kingdom never wavered. When asked what he wanted for his 90th birthday, the Superintendent demanded without hesitation a load of manure to spread around his park. He was joking, of course; McLaren had already been commandeering the city's manure supply for years.

The genius of Hall's plan and McLaren's implementation was that they are so well hidden. The land and woods appear so naturally lovely that it seems impossible to be by human design. Yet, nothing is by chance. Strategic pockets of fuchsias, camelias, roses, tulips, dahlias, cherry, magnolia, and other bright-blooming

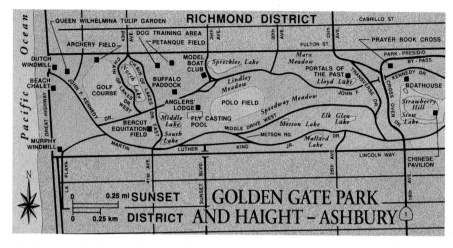

shrubs were placed to lend spectacular color to every season. The roads and walk-ways were laid out meanderingly, not only to discourage speeding, but to preserve the sense of exquisite seclusion. Even the prevailing winds have been checked and deflected by careful grading and planting. Golden Gate Park is a treasure; and yet more like a treasure hunt, for exploring it is quite as good as finding what you seek. The park never overwhelms. Rather it rewards quietly, with layer on layer of unlimited discovery for the visitor who can spend a lifetime or two getting at the heart of its mystery.

Golden Gate Park accommodates an amazing number of special activities with-out any one encroaching on another. Of course, all major sports—tennis, baseball, soccer, football, polo, golf, bicycle racing, handball, jogging, basketball, horseback riding lessons, hiking, skating, archery, rowing, and lounging in the shade—are amply represented, but more obscure special interests are also royally cared for. Lawn bowlers have their lawns, fly fishermen their special casting pool, horseshoe pitchers their own elaborate grounds, card-players their designated shelter. There is a field for playing *petanque*, a French species of lawn bowling. Children have three special playgrounds. Model yacht sailors have their own lake. Even dogs have four grounds set aside for their training and other personal needs.

Cultural activities are equally well planned: There are art museums, an aquari-um, planetarium, museum of natural history and science, band shell, botanical garden, merry-go-round, and clubhouses for anglers, golfers, beach-goers, model boat sailors, and senior citizens.

All this is put together in a setting of unrivaled botanical wealth. The richness and complexity of the park's special gardens are mind-boggling. Surely, the only way to do Golden Gate Park justice is to get a good map and follow your own interests. Any tour of the park should begin at **McLaren Lodge**, on the eastern edge of the park near the corner of Stanyan and Fell. In the days when park-keepers resided in the parks, Uncle John lived here. Now park headquarters, it supplies maps and information; call (415) 666-7201.

There are many good ways to tour the park. A car is not the best of them, save perhaps on a rainy day. With 27 miles (43 km) of footpaths and 7.5 miles (12 km) of equestrian trails, walking and horseback riding are pure joy. Many roads in Golden Gate Park are closed to motor traffic on Sundays from 8 a.m. to dusk, providing a perfect place for bicyclists and skaters. (With up to 20,000 skaters on the roads on a sunny Sunday, walkers may prefer to deal with the cars.) You can rent bikes and skates from outlets on the edge of the park.

The most magical spot in the park for youngsters is **Children's Playground**, the oldest public playground in the United States. Generations of San Franciscans have filled their imaginations in this enchanted sand-garden of swings and slides and make-believe fortresses. Younger kids especially love the carousel, a nine-teenth-century Greek temple where storybook horses, cats, pigs, and other beasts prance to the music of a stirring band organ. Fittingly, adults are not allowed on the playground unless accompanied by children.

The oldest and most stately building in the park is the **Conservatory of Flowers**, imported from Europe and assembled in 1878. A jungle of orchids, ferns, water lilies, tropical flowers, and even some sporadic birds thrive in the humid atmo-sphere. A small entrance fee is charged. The gardens around the Conservatory are particularly lush. Paths lead through thickets of oak, blooming flowers, and a primeval glade of giant ferns. The nearby John McLaren Rhododendron Dell is enchanting in bloom. A small statue of Uncle John himself—a man who hated statues—poses in front, as if picking a pine cone from a tree. Children of the sixties may want to detour north across the park boundary to see the Airplane House at 2400 Fulton Street, where the Jefferson Airplane held court.

Most visitors to Golden Gate Park congregate in the area around the **Music Concourse**, at the heart of the park's busy eastern half. The Concourse was site of the California Midwinter Fair of 1894, a grand affair despite McLaren's teeth-grinding. Bands play free on Sundays in the ornate band shell known as the Spreckels Music Temple.

Fronting the Concourse on the south is San Francisco's oldest science museum, the **California Academy of Sciences**. With natural displays of African and North American animals, an aquarium and planetarium, and tens of thousands of reptiles, mounted plants, insects, minerals, and fossils all under one roof, the Academy has long been the Bay Area's most popular science museum.

Inside the main entrance, Herbst Portico, a wonderful store stocks science and natural history books, art, and thoughtful games that attract parents and children alike. To one side is the **African Hall**, where leopards, lions, monkeys, antelope, a large gorilla, and other animals stare from landscaped dioramas. Sit near the zebras and giraffes at an African watering hole through a simulated cycle of day and night, surrounded by the sounds of unseen insects, birds, and roaring lions.

The spectacular **Wild California Hall** centers on a huge diorama of Farallon Island cliffs, complete with churning surf, screeching gulls and enormous sea elephants. Other displays of California flora and fauna feature grizzly bears, condors, oak woodlands, salt marshes, and dioramas of kelp and seawater magnified 50 times to show plankton, shrimp, beetles, and flies the size of your Uncle Herman's hunting dog.

Continue through the mineral and fossil galleries to **Steinhart Aquarium**, where 14,000 fish, crabs, turtles, dolphins, penguins, sea horses, eels, an octopus, and other specimens swim in lushly appointed tanks. Docents at the tide pool tank invite you to touch the starfish, sea urchins, anemones, and other animals. Walking up the spiral ramp to the **Fish Roundabout**, you will be completely surrounded by a doughnut-shaped tank filled with shoals of sharks, bass, snapper, rays, and yellowtail. **The Swamp**, an alligator pit bordered by the snake and lizard terrariums, always attracts a lot of attention.

A good introduction to comparative human cultures for youngsters is the **Wattis Hall of Man**, where dioramas highlight traditional lifestyles of Polynesian, Melanesian, Native American, Asian, and other peoples.

The galleries of earth and space sciences display model dinosaur skeletons, a piece of moon rock, a large revolving globe, a scale for measuring comparative weights on the earth and its moon, and the hypnotic **Foucault Pendulum**, which slowly marks the earth's rotation. The most dynamic display is the **earthquake platform**, which demonstrates how earthquakes of differing magnitudes feel, working up to the big one of 1906.

The star projector of **Morrison Planetarium**, which was built in Germany before the Second World War, ranks as one of the most well-crafted instruments of its kind. If you have never been to a planetarium, you will be impressed by the realism of the Morrison's night skies, glowing with stars of differing magnitudes and hues. Even if you are already familiar with planetarium shows, the high technical quality of the Morrison, with its regular program changes, makes repeat visits always interesting. Tickets are reasonable, though hard to get on weekends. Kids younger than six are not encouraged, but will be admitted with a special pass.

Imagine lights and patterns pulsating across the sky to Pink Floyd or William Tell's Overture—it's the **Laserium**, a computerized krypton-gas laser synchronized d to music, and played across the planetarium's ceiling. Music and patterns are always different, but the organizers preserve a choice between classical and modern. Call (415) 750-7140 for show times and reservations.

The newest exhibit, **Life Through Time**, traces the history of evolution with models of prehistoric animals roaming through ancient habitats.

The Academy is large and varied, so make a day of it. It has a nice cafeteria in case you get hungry, and a fun little youth center with docents on hand to help kids get enthused about science and the natural world. The Academy opens daily. An admission fee is charged at the door, and the Planetarium and Laserium cost extra. Entrance to the museum is free on the first Wednesday of every month, but you still have to pay for the Laserium and Planetarium. Phone (415) 750-7145 for recorded information.

The **M.H. de Young Memorial Museum** and the Asian Art Museum share a building across the concourse from the Academy of Sciences. Horse-drawn carriages line up on the curb for excursions around the park. The museums' forecourt contains the sculptor Earl Cummings' *Pool of Enchantment*—a young Indian boy piping to a pair of mountain lions.

The de Young offers a broad survey of American and British art, with a smattering of Mediterranean, Oceanic, African, and pre-Columbian American artifacts. Special galleries highlight Western landscapes, American furniture of the Federal Period, still life, sculpture, and British decorative arts. Among the American artists featured are George Caitland, Frederic Remington, Albert Bierstadt, Thomas Moran, Charles Russell, Thomas Eakins, Grant Wood, John Singleton Copley, Benjamin West, James Whistler, Rembrandt Peale, John Singer Sargent, and silversmith Paul Revere. The modern period is largely left to the Museum of Modern Art, at Civic Center.

The **Asian Art Museum** houses the largest gathering of Asian art outside of Asia, a collection so vast (and a display area so small) that only 10 per cent of it can be shown at one time.

The arts of China occupy the ground floor, dazzling the eye against the lush, emerald backdrop of the Japanese tea garden. The collection draws from over 5,000 ceramic and lacquer articles, scrolls, sculptures, and other objects dating from as far back as the Zhou and Shang dynasties (1400-1000 B.C.). Among the rarer items are scores of exquisitely translucent white ceramics, and other pieces of florescent blues and greens; the oldest known Chinese sculpture of Buddha inscribed with a date (equivalent to A.D. 338); Tang Dynasty (A.D. 618-907) earthenware animals; and a seventeenth-century bowl and pedestal decorated with dangling rings that was carved for a Qing Emperor from a single piece of white jade. The rest of the jade collection, ranging over 30 centuries, is no less astounding.

Upstairs, collections from Japan, India, Korea, Nepal, Burma, Kampuchea, and other countries include Khmer stone carvings, Indian gods and goddesses, a sixteenth-century suit of samurai armor, *netsuke* (small, carved pieces of wood and ivory), and an amazingly petite nineteenth-century wooden palanquin from Japan, decorated with red and black lacquer and gold leaf.

A single fee provides entry to both the Asian Art and de Young museums. Docent tours of special galleries run regularly through the day. A small but bursting shop sells art books, cards and prints from both the Western and Asian collections. Café de Young offers light refreshments, sandwiches and hot meals either indoors or in the Oakes Garden, surrounded by camelias and classical statuary. For information, phone the Asian Art Museum at (415) 668-8921, and the de Young at (415) 750-3659.

To best sense the Japanese Tea Garden's subtle spell, avoid the crowds.

The **Japanese Tea Garden** has been one of San Francisco's most enduring attractions since the 1894 Midwinter Fair. When the fair ended, the park commission hired a full-time gardener, Makota Hagiwara, to tend the gardens and operate the tea concession. The Japanese Tea Garden flourished under the Hagiwara family's care until politicians, goaded by anti-Japanese sentiments, forced their removal at the turn of the century. McLaren, who valued good gardening more than bad politics, asked them back, and the family kept the garden until they were interned during World War II. A plaque honoring the Hagiwara family stands by the main gate.

The garden's carefully tended paths and shrubbery, ornamental gates and lanterns, and pools swarming with gold and black carp are delightful, provided you can visit early on a weekday morning, or on a rainy day. During weekends, the garden is almost too crowded to appreciate, with tourists clamoring to be photographed on the famous steep-arched bridge, or in front of *Amazarashi-no-hotoke-Buddha*, alias the *Buddha who Sits through Sun and Rain without Shelter*. Cast in Japan in 1790, he is probably the largest bronze ever exported from Asia. The cherry trees bloom in April, a special sight.

You can enter the Japanese Tea Garden daily for a small entry fee, waived on the first Wednesday of the month. (If the crowding is too much, go see the Asian gardens at nearby Strybing Arboretum instead.) A small souvenir shop and pavilion serving green tea and cookies stand in the garden. San Francisco's most famous culinary invention originated here in 1909—the fortune cookie. Although Makota Hagiwara was the first to make them, the fortune cookie was popularized by Chinatown restaurants as a *Chinese* "tradition." In fact, you do not find fortune cookies at all in China.

A very special English garden grows across the Concourse, beyond the Academy of Sciences. The **Shakespeare Garden** contains only flowers and plants mentioned in Shakespeare's works. In case you forget your lines, the relevant ones are cast in bronze on the garden wall. A rare bust of the Bard himself is kept in a box under lock and key, a copy of a cast made in 1814 from a stone bust in Stratford-Upon-Avon, which was itself hewn by Garrett Jansen upon Shakespeare's death. Being only thrice removed from the actual face of Shakespeare, it is thus reputed to be one of the most realistic likenesses. If you want to see it, ask first at McLaren Lodge.

Golden Gate Park's most concentrated collection of rare and exotic plants grows in **Strybing Arboretum** and Botanical Gardens. In addition to representative species and gardens from Australia, New Zealand, Africa, Asia, and the Americas, several gardens maintain special themes, including the New World Cloud Forest, and the succulent, dwarf, Biblical, and California gardens. Medical and culinary herbs grow in the Garden of Fragrance, designed for the blind to appreciate through touch and smell. Plants are labeled in Braille. The Asian Garden, built around the simple Moon-Viewing Pavilion, is lovely and quiet even when the Japanese Tea Garden is overrun with tourists. Nearby, a small stream winds through a grove of stately California redwood trees. Look for the rare Dawn Redwood from China, the only species of redwood that grows outside of California and southern Oregon. You can buy wildflower seeds, cards and books on nature and horticulture at a small store near the main entrance, or peruse some of the 12,000 volumes on plants at the Helen Crocker Russell Library, housed in the adjacent County Fair Building. (The San Francisco County fair is really a flower show.)

Encircling 428-foot high (130-m) Strawberry Hill, **Stow Lake** is the park's largest lake, and a favorite for rowers, who rent their boats at the northwest corner of the lake. A circumnavigation of Strawberry Hill Island takes in its two bridges, Huntington Falls, and the Chinese pavilion. A gift from the city of Taipei, the pavilion was shipped in 6,000 pieces and assembled on the island. Less fortunate was a Spanish Cistercian monastery, dismantled and imported by William Randolph Hearst, and abandoned after fire burned the crates it was packed in. The overgrown stones are still piled east of Stow Lake.

Prayer Book Cross, a copy of a Celtic cross from the British isle of Iona, stands on a hill above Rainbow Falls, a McLaren-made creek inspired by a California mountain stream. The creek flows into **Lloyd Lake**, in which is reflected San Francisco's sentimental monument to the 1906 earthquake—**Portals of the Past**. The portals were all that was left standing of a Nob Hill mansion after the fires were quelled.

The western half of Golden Gate Park is far quieter than the busy eastern half. Here, during the week, a stroller on Speedway, Marx, and Lindley meadows, or along the Chain of Lakes, meets few passers-by. Holding down the westernmost corners of the park are two windmills from Holland, installed at the turn of the century to irrigate the park. It has been said that the southern one, the Murphy

The great outdoors for many San Franciscans is Golden Gate Park.

Windmill, is the largest of its kind in the world, though it is in want of renovation. The northern **Dutch Windmill** has been restored to working order. The Queen Wilhelmina Tulip Garden blooms in spring at its foot.

■ A CORNER OF THE SUNSET

Something about Golden Gate Park makes a person hungry. Of course, you can eat in the museums or pack a picnic, but two commercial districts are also handy to the park's eastern end. Everyone has heard of Haight Street, of course, but the other little neighborhood just beyond the **Ninth Avenue gate** is a local secret.

Most people think of the Sunset District as boring—a nice place to live, but you wouldn't want to visit there. Some of Golden Gate Park's magic seems to have rubbed off on its northeastern corner, however, where Irving and Judah cross Ninth Avenue. Just a 10-minute walk from the Music Concourse, this homey little neighborhood offers several excellent restaurants, bakeries, bistros, and shops. Come for a hearty breakfast, pop in for lunch, or browse through the bookstores till midnight. In case you are heading back downtown, the N-Judah MUNI streetcar runs right through the neighborhood. But what's the rush? If you want a place to read or talk, try the Owl and Monkey coffeehouse (1336 Ninth Avenue).

On the thickly wooded slopes of Mt. Sutro, the gargantuan University of California (UCSF) Medical Center sets the serious mood of Parnassus Avenue. One of the last cobbled streets in the City, Edgewood Avenue, climbs up UCFS's eastern boundary, ending in a eucalyptus forest. Walkers can reach it via **Farnsworth steps**, enjoying a grand view over the Richmond District and the red, steep roofs of the Haight-Ashbury. Walking east on Parnassus, you'll soon hit **Stanyan Street**, a fair and friendly prospect of thriving little shops on the verge of the neighborhood known to San Franciscans as the Haight, and to everyone else as Haight-Ashbury.

■ THE HAIGHT-ASHBURY

Like North Beach, Nob Hill, and the Barbary Coast, Haight-Ashbury is a name that transcends mere geographical designation. A mishmash of images comes to mind when one hears it: pop Zen, black-light posters, incense, flowers, purple velvet, buckskin, proffered joints, tambourines, Victoriana, long hair, psychedelia, acid rock, free love, peace signs, cosmic harmony, and bongos in the park. No one can ever forget Haight-Ashbury in the sixties, even those who never saw it. The 1967 Summer of Love lasted a scant three months, but it defined the city for the generation who came of age at that time, and it still generates its own pervasive mythology. Some 200,000 young people came to San Francisco that year, drawn by an enchanting vision of freedom and social harmony.

Haight-Ashbury started life as a solid family neighborhood along Haight Street, a commercial center for the new Golden Gate Park. Large, rambling, wooden houses sprouted on its cross streets, named for city supervisors Stanyan, Cole, Clayton, Shrader, and Ashbury. The wide, green **Panhandle**, designed as a carriage entry to Golden Gate Park, was lined by Victorian rows of Queen Anne towers and gables that lent a kind of Parisian grandeur to a city otherwise choked by dense housing. After the streetcar tunnel under Buena Vista Park was completed in 1928, however, middle-class citizenry started departing for the suburbs in the Sunset, and the bypassed Haight-Ashbury began its long, slow decline in fortune. By the early 1960s, it was a run-down district of cheap rents in subdivided Victorians. Still, the almost exotic beauty of its architecture and grand planning remained.

Almost completely surrounded by parks, and haunted throughout by decaying stateliness, the Haight-Ashbury seemed a lyrical, almost magical setting to the generations raised in insulated suburbs and small towns. Seeking to shed the restraints of Establishment, they came to indulge their senses through communal living, drugs, music, free love, and outright fantasy, to *live* their protest against materialism, the war in Vietnam, racial strife, social inequality, and parental control. The *San Francisco Examiner* called them "hippies." Decked out in scruffy clothes and long hair, they were not, of course, an exclusively San Franciscan phenomenon, but "Hashbury" (as it was called in the press) became their most celebrated mecca. The music industry spread the gospel. Local rock groups like Jefferson Airplane and the Grateful Dead played free around the Haight and Golden Gate Park, and scores of other stars were made in the nearby Fillmore West and Winterland auditoriums by rock impresario Bill Graham. Psychedelic concert posters from the Haight appeared on bedroom walls across the country, and across the Atlantic. Songs like Eric Burdon's "San Francisco Nights" inspired many to come and experience the "street called Love" for themselves. (And taking a cue from the Scott MacKenzie ode, many really *did* wear flowers in their hair.)

By autumn, the Summer of Love was already changing. Tourist buses and media exposure soured the novelty. Thousands of curious wanna-be flower children swelled the Haight population, straining the resources, easy prey for streetwise manipulators. Drugs and pushers took their toll. The war in Vietnam blazed on, intruding on the celebration of life. Many true believers left the district for communes and small towns. The Haight lurched toward decrepitude and violence.

Like much of Victorian San Francisco, the Haight-Ashbury today is gentrifying. It's hardly surprising. Few neighborhoods harbor such beautiful houses, and none can match its bosky parkland "backyard." Many of the pre-sixties businesses—like the bike rental outlets—are prospering. New bars and restaurants along Haight cater to a politically aware *and* financially secure clientele—a contradiction of terms in the old Hashbury. The head shops have closed, but you can still have your mind expanded at places like Bones of our Ancestors (622 Shrader), which sells crystals, and Forma (1715 Haight), where you can buy a Mexican altar to the

Hairdo Voodoo, where residents of the Haight can get their hair done.

dead. Aging Aquarians may glean a feel of the past at Pipe Dreams (1376 Haight; see picture on page 147), where water pipes and Grateful Dead paraphernalia are sold. The Anarchist Collective Bookstore holds vigil across the street.

The Haight is not geared for tourists. You will not find here a community of quaint, aging hippies. Many residents bitterly resent the Haight's gentrification. A store on Haight, for instance, was torched in 1988 to block its opening, because it was part of a national chain. Runaways and skinheads, still attracted by the sixties myth, gravitate there. Drugs are rampant. Scores of street people congregate on the edge of Golden Gate Park, at the head of Haight. Love no longer is the answer.

Six blocks down Haight from Golden Gate Park, a forest of twisting, matted trees rises abruptly, like some fantastically overgrown Tuscan hillside. When seen from below, or from a distance, **Buena Vista Park** presents one of the wildest, most enchanting aspects of San Francisco. Climbing up the steep paths into the park is less exalting, except for the views, if you can find the holes through the trees. From the middle of the hill, where the pitched roofs of Ashbury Heights tumble down toward the Panhandle, look north across the marble-white city and the parks' green rectangles, beyond the church towers of St. Ignatius to the bridge-spiked headlands of the Golden Gate, as exotic as Istanbul, more beautiful than Paris. You can almost understand how such an enchanting place might inspire tangerine dreams of a New Jerusalem.

■ ASHBURY HEIGHTS

Now you are climbing into real hill country, where winding streets finally start to shake the standard San Francisco grid. Submerged under an aging but respectable neighborhood, the little peak of **Mt. Olympus** still nurtures a curious pedestal, where Sutro once erected a statue of the goddess of liberty, the *Triumph of Light*. Sadly, the lady was vandalized and carted off years ago, and even the views are blocked by buildings.

Like Mt. Olympus, **Corona Heights** is a purely local curiosity, an ugly red hill gouged out by brick-making operations in the last century. Excellent views from the Heights bore straight down Market Street, and south to Eureka Valley. Avoid the cliffs on the eastern edge. Below the park on Museum Way is a nifty little museum for city kids to learn how Mother Nature runs her show. The **Josephine Randall Junior Museum** keeps a menagerie of snakes, owls, raccoons, lambs, goats and other animals for youngsters to touch and care for. Summer classes and simple displays make science fun for kids.

Leaving Ashbury Heights by the back door, you can descend toward Market Street and the Mission District via **Vulcan Stairs**, one of the more exotic city walks. Departing from Levant Street, Vulcan enters another country, where quiet, almost *rural* houses peer out from behind small gardens of dangling fuchsias, stalks, pines, roses, daisies, succulents, and fennel. In summer, plump blackberries and plums hang ripe for the picking—I mean by the residents, of course. The views fall dramatically from craggy Corona Heights down to Eureka Valley, where rainbow flags festoon the Victorians with a air of fantasy; and indeed, it is something of a brave new world.

THE UNDISCOVERED HALF

SAN FRANCISCO'S SOUTHERN HALF IS LEFT PRETTY MUCH to those who live there. Every day, to be sure, a few tourist buses can be found parked in front of Mission Dolores or inching around the heights of Twin Peaks. But of these, how many of their passengers stop to smell the *flores* along thriving 24th Street, or sidle down the secluded stairways that hang from the city's highest slopes? Almost none.

The tourist industry's neglect of the southern neighborhoods is, for better or worse, a situation that will probably reverse itself in time. It just so happens that the gentrification of San Francisco's "quaint" neighborhoods started at Telegraph Hill, working its way across the city by slow degrees. The Upper Fillmore, South of Market, Western Addition, and Haight-Ashbury, each in their turn, have braced against the tide of higher rents and wealthier tenants that followed their "discovery," washing up a flotsam of boutiques and restaurants, and a reputation among the trendy as a fashionable "new" neighborhood.

For now, fortunately, most of San Francisco's southern half simply does not appeal to the sight- and action-oriented tourist. The southern half contains the city's most desolate industrial zones, its largest stretches of residential poverty, and its greatest concentration of neighborhoods just bland enough to discourage exploration. But it's also true that you will find a lot of what has already been celebrated in the northern half, mercifully unprettified by three decades of rampant tourism. For the traveler who appreciates vibrant cultures and cuisines, enchanting cityscapes, neighborly folks, and a good cup of coffee in a cultivated setting, the southern half deserves to be discovered.

■ THE MISSION DISTRICT

The most *naturally* hospitable spot in San Francisco is the Mission District. Like the Spanish clerics who followed them, the local Ohlone tribe (they called themselves the Ramaytush) chose this broad, sheltered valley to build their largest settlement. The mercantile Americans shifted the focus of settlement to the harbor at Yerba Buena Cove, now the Financial District, leaving the Mission Valley largely undeveloped until the 1860s. The district became one of San Francisco's first suburbs. By the early part of this century, a preponderance of Irish immigrants in this neighborhood even gave it a distinctive accent, called "Mish," which was said to sound something like Brooklynese. The greater portion of the Mission District was spared destruction in the 1906 fire, and today retains some of San Francisco's finest examples of Victorian architecture.

Ironically, the predominant ethnic flavor of the Mission today is once again Hispanic. Since the 1960s, increased immigration from Mexico, Central America, and South America has made this San Francisco's largest Latin American neighborhood. Spanish alternates freely with English in the shops and on the streets. About half the residents are Hispanic; of these, roughly half trace their roots to Mexico and the rest to other Latin countries, including El Salvador, Panama, Nicaragua, Colombia, Peru, and Guatemala.

The Mission District is San Francisco's most visually colorful district—culturally vibrant, yet down at the heel. Twin Peaks block the Pacific fogs, making it the brightest and warmest neighborhood in the city. Its low rooflines and wide streets seem to catch the sun. Crowds of people fill the streets in a way that never happens in the Sunset or Marina: shy country folk, fast-talking businessmen, panhandlers, dancers, artists, mothers with babies, muscle-bound teenagers, aging revolutionaries, the walking wounded. Market fruits and vegetables, pounding music, and deep, rich aromas of cooking food spill out onto sidewalks. Higher up, brilliant murals ignite the walls in monumental tribute to families, community, work, the harvest, political strife, and dreamier, fanciful themes. You can tour these colorful murals, a major Mexican art form, by picking up a free walker's map from the Mexican Museum at Fort Mason and at Precita Eyes Mural Arts Center, 534 Precita Avenue, just south of Army Street in the Mission District.

The largest public festival of the Mission District is Cinco de Mayo—the *Fifth of May*. Often called Mexican Independence Day, it celebrates the victory of Mexican troops under command of General Zaragoza over the French invasion forces of Napoleon III, in 1862. Highlight of the festivities is a parade through the Mission. Another colorful festival, the Day of the Dead, culminates on November 2 with a nighttime candlelight parade of skeletal celebrants. It might be called a Latino version of Halloween, but more macabre, though with a streak of graveyard humor, and religious roots intact. Local bakeries and crafts shops prepare for the festival days beforehand with eerie (or gaudily devotional) altars, skull candies, and bone-shaped breads called *calaveras*.

The Pan-American character of the Mission is enshrined in its restaurants. Mexican sets the tone, but you can also find authentic Argentine, Nicaraguan, Brazilian,

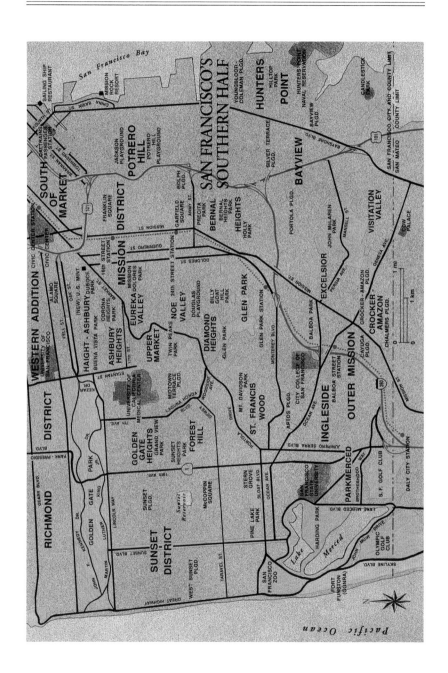

Cuban, Puerto Rican, Salvadoran, Peruvian, and other Latin American kitchens, many of them intimate, hearty, and cheap neighborhood establishments where expatriates gather to eat and socialize. Outlanders are very welcome, too, but in some of the cozier places be understanding of house politics, or avoid the subject altogether. Among refugees from war and persecution—and there are many in the Mission District—politics is a very personal and emotional subject.

The Mission is the likeliest candidate for San Francisco's reigning bohemian district, a perfect example of how alternative intellectual strains prosper best amidst cheap eats and rents, *not* quaintness. Bohemia isn't tidy; but that doesn't mean it can't comfortably entertain its guests. One wonderfully homey coffeehouse is Café Macondo, owned by a Colombian lady, on 16th street between Guerrero and Valencia. No tourists here. The comfy chairs and tables, chess board, and quiet company are delightful.

The continued presence of ungentrified industry also helps retain the Mission's character. If you want to see how Levi's famous britches are made, take a tour of the Levi Strauss factory (at 250 Valencia, near Market Street) on Wednesday mornings at 10:30 a.m. Reservations are a must; call (415) 565-9159 on Tuesdays. **Mission Dolores** stands at the corner of 16th and Dolores streets, as it has since before the streets existed. Built in 1791, it's the oldest standing building in San Francisco. It was the sixth mission to be founded in California, on orders from Father Serra, whom California honors with a statue in Washington's Hall of Fame (the other statue being Thomas Starr King). Father Serra was beatified by the Catholic Church in September 1988, and may yet become California's first Roman Catholic saint.

Visitors are charged a small fee to enter the walled mission compound to see the church, a small museum, gift shop, and the beautiful graveyard. The walls were built of brick made from sun-dried mud and manure, called adobe. Though not the strongest material, Mission Dolores survived the 1906 earthquake, while the American-era basilica next door, crumbled. On rare hot days, Mission Dolores exudes a musty coolness. Its beautiful painted ceilings are based on original Ohlone designs done with vegetable dyes. The bells, altars and statues were carried from Mexico by mule.

The peaceful, overgrown cemetery, watched over by a brooding statue of Father Serra, has many a tale to tell. (One of them is not, as fans of Hitchcock's *Vertigo* might wish, the whereabouts of Kim Novak's double.) A number of mostly Hispanic, Italian, and Irish pioneers is buried here and in the church, including

William Leidesdorff, the Noé Family, Don Luis Antonio Arguello, first Mexican governor of California, and San Francisco's first mayor, Don Francisco de Haro. It was said that De Haro died of lingering heartbreak after Kit Carson, while in the service of Captain John C. Frémont, shot his twin sons during a poor excuse for a revolutionary skirmish.

Another poignant story is buried with Charles Cora, who was hanged by vigilantes in 1856. His wife of one day, Arabella, lies at his side. The couple were married at the prompting of the priest who had come to deliver last rites before Cora's execution. Arabella had played an unintentional part in Cora's downfall. As Cora's mistress, she was snubbed one evening at the opera by U.S. Marshal William Richardson. Cora and the lawman exchanged words over the incident, which escalated to a fight, during which the gambler shot the marshal dead. By all accounts, including the one accepted by the jury, Marshal Richardson was the aggressor and the homicide justified. The vigilantes did not accept the jury's verdict, however, and the fruits of their justice lie here for all to see. Aside from Cora, two other victims of vigilante justice, James Casey and James "Yankee" Sullivan, are also buried here.

Unlike Mission Dolores, which survived the 1906 earthquake, the adjacent basilica was destroyed and rebuilt.

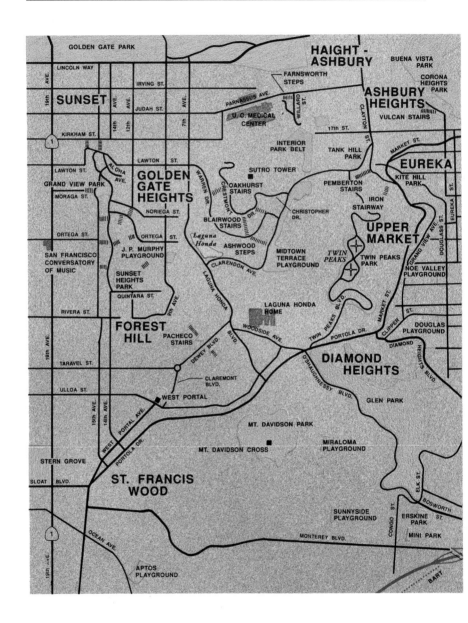

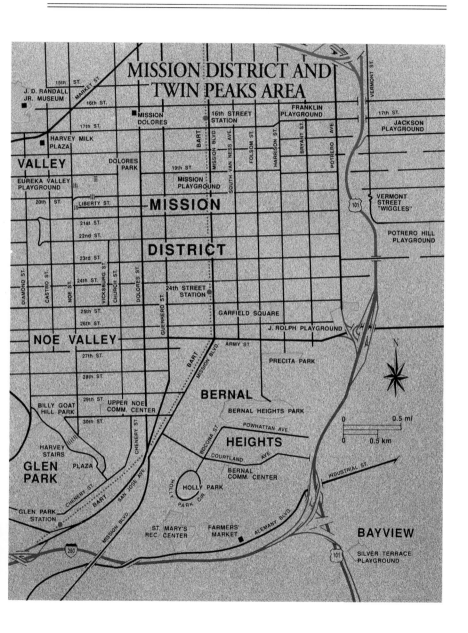

Colorful murals adorn many a wall in the Mission District.

The most tragic tale of Our Lady of Sorrows is also the one least known. In this quiet churchyard, about 5,000 Ohlone men, women, and children are buried in unmarked graves; the large rock grotto in the middle of the cemetery is their memorial. Most died of measles in the early 1800s. The remainder died of other causes. In 1850, when California's first U.S. Indian agent came here to take a census, he found only one Native American left, a man named Pedro Alcantara, who spoke of his love for a missing son, and said that he was the last of his tribe.

Lively, low-rent Mission Street is the district's main thoroughfare, but the stretch of **24th Street** between Mission and Potrero has a more neighborly Latin ambiance. Restaurants and piñata-hung family grocery stores cater to the local community. This is the place to go for such Latino specialties as *nopales* (cactus leaves), fresh and dried chilies, *paletas* (frozen fruit-juice bars), Mexican cheeses, tropical American fruits (including a wide variety of bananas and plantains), and ready-made burritos, tamales, tacos, and pies. If your nose leads you to the corner of Alabama and 24th, stop in for cake, cookies, *churros* (twisted, fried-dough snacks), or pastries at La Victoria, a wonderful Mexican bakery. The **Galeria de la Raza**, on the corner of Bryant, exhibits the works of Hispanic artists, and is a good place to find the often bizarre altars for the Day of the Dead. Next door, Studio 54 sells traditional and contemporary art, books and handicrafts.

The southern edge of Mission Valley is marked by the rise of **Bernal Heights**. It is, in fact, one of the homelier hills of the city—but homely doesn't mean we don't love it, for its character is endearingly San Franciscan. One story says that Bernal Heights was settled by a clever ruse in 1876, when developers triggered a miniature gold rush (and raised land prices) by lacing the summit with gold. Bernal Heights has an almost rural feel in places. Take Franconia Street, for instance, as it rambles around the side of the hill, angling in and out in ways that genteel city streets are taught not to do, and even going so far as to turn to gravel around the middle. Plunked down on the heights are big, fiercely independent, hillbilly houses that sit askew, with land around them. Some were built after the earthquake of 1906 with timbers salvaged from wreckage. Long considered a bit of a bumpkin, Bernal Heights has been able to preserve its comfortable and affordable lifestyle up to now. But alas, in the San Francisco scheme of things, yesterday's rustic neighborhood is today's quaint victim of gentrification—and tomorrow's exclusive district. Residents of Bernal Heights are worrying that the secret may be out.

On the southern side of Bernal Heights, near where Highway 280 meets the James Lick Freeway (Highway 101), you will find the granddaddy of fresh produce markets in the city, the **San Francisco Farmer's Market.** California farmers come to sell their excess fruits and vegetables, including some varieties that you won't find in the supermarket. It's open Tuesday through Friday from 8:30 a.m. to 5 p.m., and Saturday from 6 a.m. to 6 p.m. Come early on Saturday for the widest selection. You will find the market at 100 Alemany Boulevard.

■ EUREKA VALLEY

The slope of Twin Peaks rises abruptly to the west of Mission Valley. In the best San Franciscan tradition, its hillside streets below Market were built on a right-angle grid, so that they appear on a map to be as flat as Mission Street. Don't be fooled. Noe and Eureka valleys are two of the hilliest neighborhoods in the city. This natural barrier to easy public access has kept them remote from major transport arteries, and therefore quiet, stable, middle class and Victorian in appearance, though not in character. Still, Noe Valley and Eureka Valley are very different from one another, and the latter, particularly, is unique.

To call Eureka Valley the city's largest gay neighborhood is true, but inadequate, for its standing in the Gay Rights Movement is of international scope. Although other cities may have greater numbers of gay men, in no other major city do they openly comprise such a large percentage of the population, enjoying such social freedom and political clout. The exact population of gay men and women in San Francisco is wildly disputed (and impossible to count), but 100,000 is a commonly quoted figure that *seems* reasonable.

The main commercial street of Eureka Valley is **Castro Street,** which prompts most people to refer to the neighborhood now as The Castro. Harvey Milk Plaza, at the corner of Market and Castro, is named for San Francisco's first openly gay supervisor, who was assassinated with Mayor George Moscone by a disgruntled ex-supervisor, Dan White, on November 28, 1978. When White was convicted the following May of an incredibly lesser offense (voluntary manslaughter by reason of "diminished capacity"), thousands of protesters besieged Civic Center in riotous anger. Every June, the annual Gay Freedom Day parade marches from Castro Street to City Hall, scene of the murders.

The Castro has a strong sense of community. All goods and services necessary for a happy and fulfilling urban life are locally available, so that it can be a world unto itself for those who wish it. Bars, greeting-card shops, restaurants, cafés, furniture stores, hair salons, delis, bookstores, and scores of other shops cater to a predominantly gay clientele. The Castro Theater, a vintage neighborhood cinema showing classic films, pulls in patrons from well beyond the neighborhood. The neighborhood hosts a street fair in August and the city's most fantastic Halloween party on October 31, when shopkeepers and customers alike dress in costume for the day.

Actually, you may see some bizarre costumes on Castro Street on any day of the year. Don't let that intimidate you. Eureka Valley can be very civil and hospitable to visitors who don't react obnoxiously. It is a beautifully maintained neighborhood, stylish in that a good deal of money and effort go toward cultivating a distinctive ambiance. Along Castro, Victorian parody vies with avant-garde to set the tone. Many shop signs pun cleverly. Beyond the commercial district, pitched-roof Victorians leapfrog up the hillsides, brilliantly decorated and wrapped in well-tended gardens. Even the cats lounging in the sunny windows seem placed there by design.

■ NOE VALLEY

If you climb up Castro Street to the ridge above, a long, steep haul, you will crest the hill near 22nd Street before dropping into Noe Valley. This dividing ridge between Noe and Eureka valleys—where 21st, Hill and Liberty cross Collingwood, Castro, Noe, and Sanchez—is one of the prettiest residential enclaves in the City. Quiet, attractive streets and stairs lead to views that tourists seldom see.

Noe Valley is the Switzerland of San Francisco. Hilly, clean, prosperous and stable, it cherishes its lofty seclusion high above the teeming flatlands. Overhead, the barren summits of Twin Peaks, with their bone-chilling winds, will put you in mind of the Alps—on a foggy day, of course, and better yet, with a nip or two of brandy. Even the steep-pitched Victorian rooftops seem to be eternally awaiting snow, which never comes. Its residents are loyal to their community. They do not maintain a standing army, but they do have a neighborhood library on Jersey Street, where lectures, films, seminars, local art shows, and publications keep everyone abreast of community affairs. A free neighborhood newspaper, the *Noe*

The Castro Theater is celebrated for its classic films.

Valley Voice, is published in a wooden church built in 1888 at 1021 Sanchez Street.

Noe Valley's stretch of **24th Street** contains all the conveniences of big city life with the scale and character of a small town's Main Street. There seems to be a heavy concentration of coffee houses and dessert parlors along here, rating high points from people with time on their hands and change in their pockets. One of the best mystery bookstores around is on the corner of Diamond and 24th. The neighborhood boasts several good restaurants, some clothing boutiques, toy stores, and even an old-fashioned neighborhood grocery or two, where you will probably find the proprietor sitting at the counter watching the ball game on TV.

Cornice art.

■ TWIN PEAKS

As you climb toward Upper Market and Diamond Heights, the City spreads out like a child's counterpane, with toy houses stacked in the tucks and ridges, their roofs of black, gray, red, blue, and green. Romantics say that San Francisco has seven hills. Nit-pickers, in fact, have counted a total of 43. The most famous ones—Russian, Nob, and Telegraph—are midgets compared to the range of hills that rise in the geographic center of the city. Of these, Twin Peaks, Mount Sutro, and Mount Davidson all top 900 feet (275 m).

When Daniel Burnham required a View of Views from which to make his master plan for San Francisco, he retreated for two years to the top of **Twin Peaks**. Burnham and his plan have long blown town, but Twin Peaks and its view are still there, more magnificent than ever—the night expanse of lights was never so magnificent in Burnham's day. Twin Peaks Boulevard encircles both peaks near their summits, with parking.

Wooded Mount Sutro is the platform for San Francisco's tallest structure, a much-hated (because very obtrusive) radio antenna called Sutro Tower. Red-striped and gigantic, it's visible from all over the Bay Area.

Mount Davidson is the highest hill in the city. Thick woods obstruct the views afforded from naked Twin Peaks. Paths from the surrounding neighborhood wind to the top, where a huge cross stands, visible from miles around. At 103 feet (31 m) tall, it just might be the largest cross in the New World. Every Easter, thousands of people gather here for sunrise services. The cross also attracts its share of detractors, who demand that it be dismantled because it stands on public land in violation of the constitutional separation of church and state. Legalistically, they may have a case; let's just hope nobody tells them where the City and County of San Francisco gets its name.

Between Mount Davidson and Twin Peaks, a wilder aspect of pre-Yankee San Francisco still survives in **Glen Canyon Park**. Once part of a Spanish cattle ranch, the rugged canyon is now a day camp and playground for local kids.

The neighborhoods on the slopes of these peaks are newer than most in the flatlands, and their streets were built to follow the contours of the hill, not a surveyor's grids. Were it not for their spectacular views, many of these neighborhoods would be rather plain. Some of the terraces are linked by stairways. Partly overgrown Pemberton stairway is the best in the Upper Market area. Wooded Mount Sutro supports Oakhurst Lane, the longest, highest stairway in the city, as well as the Ashwood, Blairwood, and Glenhaven stairs. One of the least-known stairway walks is Harry Street, a ramshackle affair that clambers between Beacon and Laidley streets, on Glen Park's eastern edge, with a bird's-eye view of Noe Valley. San Francisco's most elegant stairway sweeps up from near Dewey Boulevard into sheltered Forest Hills, an affluent enclave on the western slopes of Twin Peaks. Adah Bakalinsky's *Stairway Walks in San Francisco* is an excellent guide for searching out these and other hidden steps.

In a city of outstanding views, some shock even natives, mainly because they have not been snapped to death by photographers. **Sunset Heights** is one example. Fantastically situated on high, steep, exposed hills west of Mount Sutro, the area offers surprise views around almost every corner, with steep stairways connecting different levels. Looking west, the cross-hatched Richmond and Sunset districts resemble an unfolded map, on which you can pick out Seal Rocks, the Farallon Islands, Golden Gate Park, Point Reyes, and other landmarks. Climb the stairway to the lofty knob of **Grand View Park** for the best views.

■ WEST PORTAL

Saint Francis Wood is yet another of San Francisco's moneyed neighborhoods. Frederick Law Olmsted, who designed New York's Central Park, helped John Galen Howard lay out these urbane streets, with their fountains and gateways, in 1912.

West Portal, next door, is its main shopping street. West Portal refers to the western entrance of the 2.25-mile (3.6-km) streetcar tunnel under Twin Peaks. The tunnel opened in 1917. Until the Market Street section was put underground in the 1970s, the tunnel's eastern portal was on Market Street at Castro. Nowadays, when you ride the K-Ingleside, L-Taraval, or M-Ocean View streetcars from downtown, your first glimpse of sunlight is at West Portal.

There is something vaguely romantic about West Portal. Imagine sitting in a restaurant overlooking the street at dusk, perhaps with streaks of rain on the window, watching the streetcars come and go. Commuters returning from downtown rush off to do their grocery shopping, while others scurry aboard for the ride back—perhaps for an evening at the theater. All the hallmarks of San Francisco chic are here, the tidy shops and ethnic restaurants. Despite its cosmopolitan airs,

West Portal most resembles some nondescript Central European streetcar suburb. It's a great place for a romantic rendezvous, not least because it provides an expedient getaway should that prove necessary.

■ THE SUNSET DISTRICT AND POINTS SOUTH

From a stranger's standpoint (as mentioned already on page 216), the northeastern corner of the Sunset, where Ninth Avenue crosses Judah and Irving, is the most interesting section of the district.

Otherwise, the Sunset is an overwhelmingly orderly, middle-class residential area sandwiched between the peaks and Ocean Beach. The summer fog here is relentless. San Franciscans from other neighborhoods occasionally find their way out here for a foreign film at the Surf (Irving at 46th), a Sunday concert in Stern Grove or a recital at the San Francisco Conservatory of Music (1201 Ortega). But on the whole, the Sunset keeps pretty much to itself. Though little commercial pockets dot the landscape, the most steadfastly commercial streets are 19th Avenue and Taraval.

Once upon a time in what is now **Stern Grove**, there was a roadhouse of ill repute called the Trocadero Inn. It achieved its greatest notoriety as the place where Abe Ruef, the corrupt political boss of Mayor Schmitz's regime, was captured after a gunfight with police. For better or for worse, the Troc has long since been rehabilitated.

The main gate of the **San Francisco Zoo** is on Sloat Boulevard, a stone's throw or two from Ocean Beach. Though not ranked as one of the best American zoos, recent renovations have upgraded some of the older cages to animal habitats. The gorillas' new home gives them room to roam, rocks and trees to climb, and a thick window through which they may safely observe the *homo sapiens* at close range. Silkworms, tarantulas, black widows, termites, beetles, crickets, scorpions, and other vermin dwell in the Insect Zoo, where you can also observe bees at work in a living hive, without getting stung. The Children's Zoo lets kids feed and touch barnyard animals. In the Kresge Nocturnal Gallery, visitors can study a bush baby, slow loris, and other nocturnal animals in their natural settings. The Phoebe Hearst Discovery Hall uses computers to stimulate questions and answers about primates. Other zoo attractions are Wolf Woods, Koala Crossing, the Lion House, Monkey Island, Musk Ox Meadow, and a host of rhinos, elephants, hippos, tigers, giraffes, zebras, bears, penguins, and other birds and beasts. A roaring good show is feeding time in the Lion House, daily at 2 p.m., except Monday. The zoo operates guided tours, snack bars, a gift shop, a popular playground, and a magnificent carousel, built in 1921 by William Dentzel. The admission charge is moderate.

The last of the exposed sand wastes that once overspread the Richmond and Sunset districts survives today at **Fort Funston**. Now part of the GGNRA, this old military property on San Francisco's southernmost coast was once used for trial beachhead landings by the army. Today, its barren, windy cliffs are popular for hang gliding.

Lake Merced is another natural area that has miraculously survived the city's expansion. Now protected as a park, San Francisco's largest lake provides a natural habitat for wildlife, as well as recreation for fishermen, boaters, joggers, golfers, and birdwatchers. Bring your own (non-motorized) boat, or rent one from the Boat House on Harding Road.

San Francisco State University's modern campus stands on the eastern shore of Lake Merced. One of the most academically acclaimed schools in the state university system, the school is home to the Sutro Library (480 Winston Drive), inherited from the Sutro estate, and one of the West's earliest and largest collections of books. Another intellectual property of note on campus is the American Poetry Archives, the world's largest videotaped collection of poets reading their works or being interviewed. The archives is open to the public in room 117 of the Humanities Building; phone in advance: (415) 338-1056.

Beyond the University is the suburban neighborhood of **Ingleside**. Ingleside's greatest claim to fame is that it has the world's second-largest sundial—or is it the third? Sundial worshippers can make the pilgrimage to Entrada Court to genuflect before the 26-foot high (eight-meter) device.

■ THE BORDER NEIGHBORHOODS

The residential districts along San Francisco's southern border—Hunter's Point, Visitacion Valley, Bayview, Ocean View and the Outer Mission—are *terra incognita* to most San Franciscans who do not live there. That's not to say that they aren't interesting, so long as you realize that they are working class or poor residential neighborhoods that do not cater to tourism.

The Excelsior and Crocker-Amazon neighborhoods, lumped together with the **Outer Mission**, are down-home cosmopolitan places. The residents trace their roots in roughly equal numbers to Asia, Africa, Europe, and the Americas. Unlike the prosperous, international Richmond District, the Excelsior is the poor-man's polyglot, vibrant in a colloquial, unflamboyant way. Sure, it needs a little "softening up" before it's ready to entertain visitors. In the meantime, local residents take it for granted and enjoy the lower rents.

Sandwiched between the Excelsior and Visitacion Valley, **McLaren Park** preserves a large hill from development. Most of the park has been left alone as natural, uncultivated grassland. The views are unique. Look south across Visitacion Valley to Mount San Bruno; the hulking Cow Palace, an all-purpose auditorium, dominates the valley from the Daly City side of the city line. Look north, and the towers of San Francisco rise like an Emerald City behind the grid of the Bayview District, tossed over its hills like a checkered quilt.

Bayview-Hunters Point has strong name recognition among San Franciscans, almost none of it favorable. Outsiders don't come here much, except en route to Candlestick Park to see the Giants or Forty-Niners play, or to the Cow Palace for rodeos, rock concerts, and stock shows. During World War II, Hunters Point was the largest shipyard on the West Coast, attracting large numbers of out-of-state workers, who settled in makeshift housing beyond the docks. Hunters Point became, and remains, the largest predominantly African-American district in the city. Since the war, the speed and quality of urban renewal has not been universally inspiring, though many of Bayview's hills and old houses, punctuated by wooden church steeples, retain distinctively San Franciscan qualities admired by visitors to other districts. Unfortunately, Bayview-Hunters Point is ravaged by high unemployment, drugs, and violence. Parts are heavily industrialized, and many residential neighborhoods are extremely depressed.

■ POTRERO HILL

Long a quiet backwater in the midst of the city, **Potrero Hill** is one of the latest districts to feel the winds of gentrification. So far, the southern half of the hill, closest to Hunters Point, remains in the lee, but the northern half is very much a community like Noe Valley, with a quiet, pleasant shopping street along 20th. Potrero Hill even has its own library (on 20th) and newspaper, *The Potrero View*.

The little-known vista from Grand View Park encompasses the Sunset District, Golden Gate Park, and the distant Richmond district.

Views to the west over the Mission, and north toward downtown, are inspiring. Vermont Street from McKinley Square squiggles down the hill like a miniature Lombard, but without the tourists. The Anchor Brewing Company produces its famous Steam Beer at 1705 Mariposa Street.

Eastern Potrero Hill drops down to the docks, a working mixture of old brick warehouses and modern cranes. If you like the sight of oceangoing ships and wharves, go to Mission Rock Resort, next to the public pier on the southern end of China Basin Road. The back deck has tables and benches with fascinating views across Central Basin to huge ships draining their bilge at the docks. The resort serves food and drink, and kids are welcome around back.

■ OUTER SOUTH OF MARKET

The SoMa district between Market Street and the James Lick Freeway, an area being colonized by the Financial District, was introduced on pages 74-80. South of the James Lick, however, other colonizers are at work. On the flatlands north of Potrero Hill, plans are afoot to gentrify the once rough-and-ready dock and train yard area of China Basin into a residential neighborhood called Mission Bay. Already the wharves at the mouth of China Basin, on the north side, have been gussied up into a harbor fit for private pleasure craft. The **Sailing Ship Restaurant** at Pier 42 is an actual sailing vessel, once called the *Ellen*. After service on the southern oceans at the turn of the century, she was drafted for troop and supply transport during World War I, and followed that with a stint of smuggling during Prohibition. Bought by Columbia Studios to star in *Mutiny on the Bounty*, she was later sold to a San Franciscan restaurateur. Winched ashore, she now sits high and dry, with food and drink for all hands.

Many of the fine old brick warehouses built throughout this area are being converted into **designer showroom centers** and **factory outlets**. Banana Republic, Van Heusen, C.P. Shades, Esprit, New York Cosmetic & Fragrance, Gunne Sax, Grodin's, Jeanne-Marc and many others sell factory second, out-of-season, or irregular silks, leather, cosmetics, dancewear, teddy bears, sportswear, children's clothing, jewelry, bridal wear, and other discount items. The greatest cluster of factory outlets for discount, name-brand apparel is centered in the blocks bounded by Second, Bryant, Fourth, and Townsend streets. Get a map from any of the stores, or phone for one at (415) 896-0988 or (415) 648-9240. This publication lists over 40 outlets in alphabetical order, with descriptions of goods sold, addresses, and opening hours.

In the midst of this decayed industrial zone, **South Park** is a quirky remnant of the district's brief fling as San Francisco's pedigreed residential district. Built in 1856 on a plan inspired by London's Berkeley Square, the oval park was fenced and surrounded by mansions, whose owners kept the keys to the gate. With the invention of cable cars, the rich departed South Park for Nob Hill, abandoning it to poorer families, factories, warehouses and sailor hotels. It bottomed out as a skid row when construction of the Bay Bridge leveled Rincon Hill for its western anchorage. South Park remained depressed until quite recently, when artists and designers discovered that its abandoned warehouses made great studios.

Now, a wealthier class is once again returning to South Park. The sidewalk tables of the new South Park Café add a touch of class to the oval. Other eateries are springing up to cater to shoppers and a growing population of office types who work in the neighborhood. Still raw enough to keep suburbanites at bay, South Park is poised for takeoff.

Jack London was born in 1876 around the corner from South Park, at 615 Third Street. The house burned in the fire of 1906, but the approximate site is marked by a plaque.

The **Cartoon Art Museum** (665 Third) devotes itself to the preservation and study of a vigorous American art form. In addition to its rotating displays, this small museum keeps permanent collections of comic books, editorial cartoons, comic strips, animation, advertising, greeting card art, and more. A recent exhibit showed often humorous self-portraits of famous cartoonists, such as Reg Smythe (Andy Capp), Mort Walker (Beetle Bailey, Hi and Lois), Bill Griffith (Zippy the Pinhead), Hank Ketcham (Dennis the Menace), Chic Young (Blondie), Al Capp (Li'l Abner), and Dave Berg (from *Mad Magazine*). Open Thursday and Friday afternoons and on Saturday, the museum charges a small entrance fee.

■ THE BAY BRIDGE

Bay Area residents love their bridges. The span across the Golden Gate inspires a virtual cult following, who garland it with all manner of glorious praise. Fans of the **San Francisco-Oakland Bay Bridge** don't have much truck for that kind of hogwash. And why should they?

The Bay Bridge is a big ol' hairy-chested roustabout span that does the work of two Golden Gate bridges. Five lanes wide, two decks deep, it joins causeway, truss, cantilever, tunnel, and double suspension spans to make the largest high-level steel bridge on Earth. About 2.25 billion vehicles crossed it during its first half-century of work. Today, the rate is about 250,000 *daily*. When it was completed in 1936, there was none bigger. How big? In length, about 8.25 miles (13.3 km), of which 4.25 miles (6.8 km) are over water. The tunnel bored through Yerba Buena Island was the world's widest when built. The massive center anchorage, which anchors the ends of the two suspension spans in the middle of the bay, alone is bigger than the Great Pyramid at Giza and deeper than any other pier in the world. The bridge was designed by Charles Purcell, who called it a tribute to the intelligence

The Bay Bridge receives less attention and more traffic than the Golden Gate, but is a beauty in its own right, by night . . .

of the American workingman. When you consider that the Bay Bridge and the Golden Gate Bridge were built *simultaneously*, who can fail to marvel at the vigor and confidence of the San Franciscans of yore!

The earthquake of 1989 severed the bridge where the cantilever section and the Oakland approach ramp join, knocking out 50-foot (17-m) sections of both decks. Fortunately, neither section dropped into the water, but the crossing was closed for one month of repairs. While engineers rejoined the sections, road crews completely resurfaced the decks, a job that normally takes two years to do.

The Bay Bridge is not open to pedestrians. Drivers can exit the bridge midway at **Yerba Buena Island** to see the classic view of the suspension span marching into San Francisco. There is no designated overlook on Yerba Buena, but you can park along the road to the top of the island. To get there, take the Treasure Island exit, and turn right immediately before reaching the short causeway to Treasure Island Naval Base. If you go too far, the military guard at the gate can redirect you.

While on the summit of Yerba Buena, stop in at the **Coast Guard Vessel Traffic Service** to see how ships are monitored by radar as they move through the bay and upriver as far as Stockton and Sacramento. Visitors are admitted any hour of the day or night; just ring the doorbell.

. . .or day.

Yet another Depression-era superlative: When it was completed in 1937, **Treasure Island** was the largest man-made island in the world. It was originally intended as the site of San Francisco's first airport, but only Pan Am's *China Clipper* flights to Asia and the Pacific ever flew from here. Instead, the city gave Treasure Island to the U.S. Navy in exchange for the site of the present airport. It's impossible to miss the magnificent view across the water to the Financial District from Treasure Island.

Visit the **Navy, Marine Corps, Coast Guard Museum** on the Navy Base after signing in at the front gate. The museum occupies the *China Clipper* terminal building. On permanent exhibit are mementos of the Golden Gate International Exposition, a world's fair held here in 1939 and 1940 to celebrate completion of the bridges. Uniforms, weapons, nautical instruments, paintings, murals, a lighthouse lens, and other treasures help illustrate the history of the maritime services. You can buy pictures of naval ships from a large selection at the counter. The museum is open daily, and it won't cost you one red cent.

Symbol of the 1939 Worlds Fair, Pacifica *(above) shared the spotlight with the new China Clipper (top).*

THE EAST BAY

LOOK EAST FROM THE TOWERS OF SAN FRANCISCO'S Financial District, beyond the fuming streets and the great Bay Bridge, and you'll see a place where lions still roam wild.

Lions? In the East Bay?

Indeed. *Mountain* lions. But rare is the San Franciscan who will ever see one. When slipping off for a day in the country, San Franciscans prefer to head north to glamorous Marin, or south to the coastline of San Mateo. The East Bay hills are considered little more than a backdrop for dazzling city views. And that suits the mountain lions just fine, thank you.

To the original San Franciscans, the Ohlone Indians, the ranges to the east were far more than just another pretty vista; they were the origins of life itself. In bygone ages when the rest of the world was drowned in sea water, so they believed, the highest peak, Mount Diablo, was an island, home of Coyote, creator of mankind. For thousands of years, the Ohlones drew life from the ranges, an existence beautifully described by Malcolm Margolin in *The Ohlone Way.* In annual journeys to the interior valleys and slopes, they gathered acorns, seeds, and wild game from the bursting, natural storehouses of native oak and riparian woodlands. Hailed as the year's happiest season, these cyclical migrations moved from the bay to favorite camps, past rocks and glens and woods revered by the Ohlone, perhaps as we might cherish a Taj Mahal or Westminster Abbey.

The eighteenth century, however, abruptly ended this way of life. The Spanish arrived at San Francisco Bay, overawing the Ohlone with European technology and confining them on harsh mission farms, where they died by the thousands of European diseases. Those who escaped were hunted down and punished. Within one generation, their villages, their ancient traditions, and most of their people had been extinguished. The hills, oaks, and sacred places may live on, but no one can ever know them as intimately as the Ohlone once did.

The East Bay comprises Alameda and Contra Costa counties. Oakland and Berkeley are the two most obvious destinations for travelers, but scores of other (deservedly) less well-known towns and suburbs have some very exciting things to see, depending on the traveler's special interests. Among these are John Muir's house in Martinez, the Livermore wineries, playwright Eugene O'Neill's house, and the wilder reaches of the East Bay parklands.

A ship heads under the Bay Bridge toward the busy Port of Oakland.

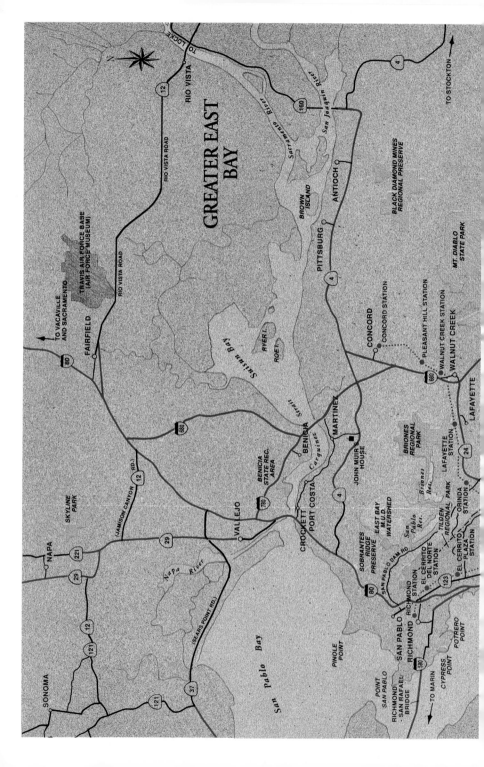

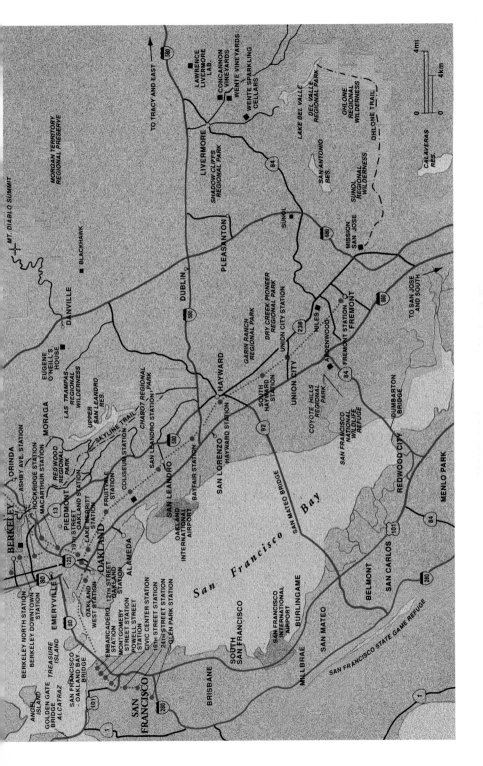

■ OAKLAND OVERVIEW

The eastern end of the Bay Bridge drops down to Oakland, passing docks and train yards, and merges into one of the biggest, busiest freeway interchanges in the country. It's not very pretty, but it is very appropriate. Oakland means business.

Oakland is the butt of a lot of San Francisco jokes. One wag points out that when you cross the Bay Bridge into San Francisco, you have to pay a dollar toll; but to go to Oakland doesn't cost a plugged nickel. And of course, there is that famous, oft-quoted line by Gertrude Stein about Oakland, where she lived as a child: "There is no there there."

It's a pity that Oakland must be forever stigmatized by a noted writer's second most quoted line (the first being, of course, her immortal "A rose is a rose is a rose"). As Don Herron points out in his *Literary World of San Francisco*, however, if you put the quote in context, it doesn't seem so barbed. What Stein actually wrote was "what was the use of my having come from Oakland it was not natural to have come from there yes write about it if I like or anything if I like but not there, there is no there there." Heavy stuff, but down-to-earth Oaklanders prefer one of Hemingway's least famous quotes: "A stone is a stone is a *stein*."

Oakland is a great city. Yes, it has grave drug problems, high crime rates, ghettos, and poverty. But it's also true that very few of Oakland's finer qualities ever find their way into print. Oakland is a city of great character and gumption. Its museum is one of the best in the West. The regional parks in Oakland Hills are second to none. Oakland's skyline, from the shores of Lake Merritt, is postcard pretty. The downtown district is booming, friendly and readily accessible from BART. Café society and the arts are flourishing.

Another thing about Oakland: its movers and shakers come from across a spectrum of ethnic Greeks, Portuguese, blacks, Italians, Mexicans, Vietnamese, Lebanese, Chinese, Koreans, and other peoples who make up the city. African Americans comprise Oakland's largest ethnic community, from which the mayor, police chief, museum director, and publisher of the largest newspaper all hail.

The best thing about Oakland, and the thing that really worries San Franciscans, is that Oakland is laying foundations for a great future. Oakland's port, manufacturing base, railways, BART service, professional sports facilities, *and* weather are superior to San Francisco's. The downtown area is fast developing into a potent, if much smaller, rival to San Francisco, both in finance and retailing. Potential for tourism is growing apace, with a distinct advantage that most of the sights that appeal to tourists are close to BART stations.

■ DOWNTOWN OAKLAND

Visitors can make a day of exploring downtown Oakland. You can walk around Lake Merritt, taking in Chinatown, the public markets, Victorian Row, the Oakland Museum, a few good bookstores, coffee, and shopping, and still have time for dinner at the estuary. Three BART stations serve the area: Oakland City Center/ 12th Street, 19th Street, and Lake Merritt.

Long blighted by crime and neglect, downtown Oakland snapped out of the doldrums a few years back. The focus of Oakland's Civic Center ought to be City Hall, at the intersection of Broadway, 14th Street, and San Pablo Avenue, across from the flat-iron Broadway Building, and above BART's Oakland City Center station. It is upstaged, however, by the new **John B. Williams Plaza**, a lively forum of fountains and Victorian inspired modern architecture. Across Broadway, bustling DeLauer Newsstand (1310 Broadway), an institution reeking of cigars and imported newspapers, keeps its finger on the pulse of the world, 24 hours a day.

Oakland's main business and retail district follows **Broadway** some seven blocks north to Grand Avenue, poking more tentatively east and west down the side streets. The streets have an open, human-scale feel, more like a big town than a city. Their small shops and lunch counters remind old-timers of the thirties. Most evocative of that era is the 1931-vintage **Paramount Theater** (2025 Broadway), built in the best tradition of the great movie palaces of Hollywood's heyday. Restored to its original beauty, the Paramount is one of the supreme examples of art-deco design in the country. It is now a theater for live performances, but you can tour the building only for a look at the historic interior (designed by Timothy Pflueger, who also did the towers of the San Francisco-Oakland Bay Bridge) on the first and third Saturdays of every month.

The **Tribune Tower** on 13th and Franklin, a landmark since 1923, houses the editorial offices of the city's largest newspaper, the *Oakland Tribune*. Around the corner at 274 14th Street, Holmes Books is Oakland's cathedral for book worshippers, having occupied these same three floors since the original Holmes fled San

Lake Merritt is the brilliant centerpiece of downtown Oakland (overleaf).

Francisco after the 1906 earthquake. Its sizable California history room attracts pilgrims from around the state. Less well known, but deserving of greater fame, are the Gull Book Gallery, a consortium of dealers, and Bibliomania, near the corner of San Pablo and 15th.

Back at Civic Center again, head west on Broadway. Within two blocks on the left-hand (south) side of the street, you come to the outskirts of Oakland's Chinatown. On the right, having passed Oakland's splendid new Hyatt Regency Hotel and Oakland Convention Center, you will find yourself at **Victorian Row.**

Built between the 1860s and 1880s, these two square blocks of solid wood and brick buildings, many still under renovation, are the most splendid and evocative of Oakland's old-time districts. Recently opened is the 1913-vintage Washington Inn (495 10th Street), a cozy retreat to a more elegant decade, though just across the street from the modern Convention Center. A short stroll away, a new Ethiopian restaurant and the Pacific Coast Brewing Company pub help liven up the evenings.

But don't think the Victorian Row neighborhood is strictly genteel. Anyone who misses or never knew the adventure and fun of market shopping should see what else is happening here. Before supermarkets, Oaklanders used to flock to the large food bazaars of this district, where they could buy from the stalls brimming with fresh fish, fruits, vegetables, meats, bakery goods, and delicatessen goods. Like the public markets of Europe and Asia, Oakland's markets were a bustling hub of stalls, where fish and vegetable mongers cried out their bargains to passing shoppers, and hawkers carved off samples of cheese or salami to help customers make up their minds. After a lapse of some years, Oakland's great public markets are back again. The **Outdoor Market** spills over the cross streets of Ninth and Washington every Friday from 8:30 a.m. to 1:30 p.m., marshalling a bazaar of fresh fruits and vegetables, handicrafts, entertainments, and other delicacies, including a delicious, locally made lemon butter.

Meanwhile, the **Housewives Market** is thriving one kitty-corner block farther, on the corner of Clay and Ninth. The Housewives is a United Nations of markets, where butchers, bakers, and cooks with traditions hailing from around the world meet to mingle and sell their foods, cooked, preserved, and fresh: Portuguese sausages, Filipino fish heads, Korean pickled cabbage, Asian pig snouts, Mexican tamales, Middle Eastern breads, dried goods from Asia, French and English cheeses, down-home barbecued ribs, and ever so much more. You can eat here, or shop for a different ethnic feast every meal for a week.

Another marvelous international grocer is **Ratto's**, at 821 Washington. A new century has dawned since Ratto's was founded, bringing with it several wars, new waves of immigrants, and countless changes brought by new technology; but despite heavy damage in the 1989 earthquake, it's *still* 1897 in Ratto's. The old wooden floors and shelves stacked with sacks and bottles and racks of foods from around the globe exude an aroma that's one third salami and two-thirds indescribable. The list of stock is mind-boggling: Irish porridge, sun-dried tomatoes, Russian mustard, Brazilian soda pop, sushi rice, horehound candy, olive oils from six different countries, escargot, Hungarian peppers, Ethiopian *berbere*, hickory mist, Haitian vanilla, bonbons, curries, Chilean mushrooms, raspberry vinegar, hummus, Thai chilis, juniper berries, Indian chutneys, cooking chocolate, Australian ginger, Kenyan coffees, truffles, coconut, Turkish dried apricots, European garlic, Maine lobsters, Indonesian satay, Cajun sauces, goose fat from France, and scores of cheeses and pastas from Italy. To the side of the grocery section, Ratto's runs a cafeteria. Friday nights bring glorious Pasta Opera, when visiting virtuosos serenade guests with arias as they dine on pasta and vino. You'll need reservations; call (510) 832-6503.

Even more restaurants and markets await across Broadway from Victorian Row in **Oakland Chinatown**. Founded in the 1870s, this neighborhood is today enjoying an unprecedented renaissance sparked by immigration, investment, and new construction. Compared to San Francisco's Chinatown, Oakland's is more open and homey, nor does it engage in the business of selling tourist schlock. It also feels more cosmopolitan, attracting many Koreans, Filipinos, Vietnamese, Cambodians, Laotians, Burmese and Thais, though in fact many of these are *ethnic* Chinese.

The heart of Chinatown is the blocks bounded by Broadway, 8th, 11th, and Harrison, but a large concentration of Chinese Americans have settled all the way to Lake Merritt, and beyond. The Oakland Chinatown Chamber of Commerce publishes a handy brochure map listing the names and addresses of Chinatown businesses, which you can pick up at the Hyatt Regency on Broadway. But it's just as enjoyable to wander through the district without a map, skirting the crates of vegetables that spill onto the sidewalk, eyeing the produce and fish, dodging the deliverymen's dollies, sampling the dim sum or Vietnamese noodles. Jade Villa (800 Broadway) is a much-appreciated alternative to the San Francisco *dim sum* scene.

■ THE ESTUARY

From Victorian Row and Chinatown, Broadway continues south under the Nimitz Freeway (Interstate 880) seven blocks more to Jack London Square, on the Estuary. A short detour west at Fifth Street to Clay brings you to **Bret Harte Boardwalk**, a short row of refurbished Victorians named for the writer of sentimental gold rush stories, who lived in his uncle's house across the street, now demolished.

Another detour one block east at Third Street runs into the **Oakland wholesale produce market**, at its most bustling in the hours before dawn, when the streets are jammed with trucks, loading and unloading. Though by no means a tourist "sight," there is something undeniably engrossing in the old wooden buildings, broad sidewalks roofed in corrugated metal, stacks of crated fruits and vegetables, and the happy commotion of people at work. For those who need an eye-opener, or just breakfast, repair to one of the hole-in-the-wall diners.

Jack London Square, named for Oakland's most famous writer, never was much of a square. Nowadays, it's so thoroughly altered that the city is trying to encourage people to refer to it by a new name, **Jack London Waterfront**. The splendid public plaza, with stores and restaurants, is far less rampantly commercialized than San Francisco's Fisherman's Wharf. The ships on the estuary, and the yachts tied up at the waterfront, make a pretty enough picture from window-side seats of the seafood restaurants. Though the estuary air still carries a provocative tang, and Oakland's hard-working container harbor is visible westward up the channel, Jack London wouldn't know the place.

Although born in San Francisco, Jack London was raised in Oakland, where he was coached in his reading at the Oakland Free Library by the librarian, Ina Coolbrith. Several of the houses where London lived still stand in Oakland (which you can find with the help of Don Herron's aforementioned guide), but it is the waterfront that he is most powerfully associated with. It was along here that he docked his boat, the *Razzle Dazzle*, which carried him on night raids of rivals' oyster beds. So adept was he at this dangerous game that he earned the title "Prince of the Oyster Pirates." It was here, also, that he drank in the bars and met many of the characters who would later appear in his novels.

One authentic London hangout still stands by the wharf, a saloon called **Heinold's First and Last Chance**. London supposedly bought the *Razzle Dazzle* here when he was 16 years old. Still open for business, Heinold's is a curious shack half sunken below present street level. Nearby stands the cabin where London lived during the Klondike gold rush of 1897-98. Rediscovered in Yukon Territory in 1960, it was spirited back to its present site overlooking the Oakland Estuary. Continuing south along the waterfront, you come to a new development of wooden arcade shops and restaurants called **Jack London Village**. It is something like Pier 39 in San Francisco, though neither so crowded nor so blatantly exploitative of tourism. Views from the restaurants over the estuary to Alameda's thickly sparred and masted waterfront are engrossing, or romantic, depending on the company.

■ LAKE MERRITT

Only a short stroll east from the heart of Chinatown, the Lake Merritt BART Station hides underneath Madison Park, between Eighth and Ninth streets. The **Oakland Museum** is only one block north of the station. Devoted to California's culture and history, both natural and human, it is one of the West's most important, fun, and handsome museums. Rising in irregular steps around a central garden court, the building seems to have been inspired by the Hanging Gardens of Babylon. Each level is devoted to a different subject.

On the ground floor, a museum store shares space with the natural science wing, where you can take an imaginary cross-country walk across California's different ecological zones: Pacific shore, coastal foothills, Central Valley, Sierra foothills, Sierra Nevada range, and finally, the high deserts of the Great Basin. Displays of representative terrain, plants, and animals from every zone give a brilliant introduction to California's geography and ecology.

The second-floor history section is designed to show how *real* people *really* lived in California, from prehistoric times to the present. Pride and joy of this gallery is the gleaming, red, horse-drawn fire engine, but the homier, everyday objects and dioramas are more personally evocative of our ancestors and their times.

The top floor art gallery focuses on painters and photographers with California connections, including Albert Bierstadt, Eadweard Muybridge, Dorothea Lange, and Imogen Cunningham. The landscapes of Yosemite and gold rush San Francisco are especially spectacular.

Galleries for temporary exhibits round out the top floor. The museum's cafeteria spills onto the outdoor terraces on the second floor, overlooking the gardens. Entrance is free. There's a parking garage in the basement.

The chief architect of downtown Oakland's exquisite setting is **Lake Merritt**, a saltwater rendezvous of migrating birds, which became the first state game refuge in America in 1870. A few years ago, newspapers were reporting that the lake, connected by channel to the Oakland Estuary, had become a living refuge for thousands of foreign sea creatures, which had arrived here as unwitting passengers aboard oceangoing ships docking in Oakland's inner harbor. Whether any truth rests therein is debatable, but it's nice to speculate that some strange species of octopus dwells beneath those beautiful blue waters. Surrounded by a paved three-mile (4.8 km) path for pedestrians and cyclists, Lake Merritt is a brilliant foil for the offices and apartments that ring its shore.

Lovely **Lakeside Park**, with its small aviary and science center, shades the northern shore under green woods and gardens. Youngsters love to visit **Children's Fairyland**, where they can play among scenes from nursery rhymes and stories. You can rent a boat from one of two boat houses (north and west sides), or take a ride on toy miniature paddle-wheel boats that run on weekends. On rainy days, you may prefer a tour of the century-old **Camron-Stanford House** (1418 Lakeside Drive), furnished in the rich Victorian style; call (510) 836-1976 for details.

The Oakland Museum, the state's best for history, is strong on Californiana.

Grand Avenue, sweeping across the edge of Lakeside Park and up toward the hills, is a pretty commercial district designed, in a more leisurely era, for strolling. Elegant lampposts, tidy lawns, warm-windowed restaurants, drugstores, soda fountains, and the Egypto-art-deco Grand Lake Theater give the street the urbane, slightly formal feel of a Hollywood back lot set. If you follow Grand Avenue up to the Piedmont city line, two-thirds of a mile (one km) from the lake, turn off on Jean Street to the Rose Garden, Oakland's most romantic venue for elegant outdoor weddings. The surrounding neighborhoods of large, single-family dwellings, ensconced in their gardens and tree-lined streets, are to Oakland what Pacific Heights is to San Francisco (though Piedmont is a separate city).

■ ROCKRIDGE

For those who can't get enough espresso in San Francisco, Oakland has cultivated yet another marathon coffeehouse gauntlet along College Avenue in the Rockridge area. Actually, given Oakland's superior weather and the sidewalk tables

An Oakland version of "Rocky" works out on shore of Lake Merritt.

along the street, many hedonists would argue that it is an improvement over anything San Francisco has to offer. Strung for some two miles (three km) between
the California College of Arts and Crafts, on the corner of Broadway in Oakland,
and the University of California in Berkeley, College Avenue attracts a slightly off-
beat, mellow crowd of all races and walks of life, including many college students
and yuppies. Besides coffee, College Avenue also nurtures bookstores, ethnic
restaurants, a host of children's clothing stores, and interesting specialty shops.
Parking is increasingly tough, so come by BART; College passes right under BART's
Rockridge Station.

Just before the Berkeley city line, Claremont Avenue angles off College toward
the hills and the palatial **Claremont Resort**. Completed in 1914, it remains the
most picturesque hotel in the Bay Area. An enchanting vision of wooden towers,
chimneys and gables, the Claremont is so vast that you can easily see it with the
naked eye from San Francisco. With a cavalier ambiance reminiscent of the carefree Roaring Twenties (the exterior more so than the remodeled interior), the
Claremont seems happily lost in a world where tea is served on the tennis courts,
and people still dress for dinner—not because of tradition, but for the fun of pre-
tending that they are part of the tradition. Even the casually dressed drop by the
Terrace Lounge for smashing views out over the lowlands and the Bay.

The **Judah L. Magnes Memorial Museum** occupies a four-story brick mansion
at 2911 Russell Street, just over the Berkeley line. Lectures, film shows, the Blu-
menthal Library, a museum shop, and special exhibitions supplement a collection
of historical artifacts pertaining to Jewish history, from classical times to contemporary. Among the items kept in this third-largest Jewish museum of the Western
Hemisphere are paintings by Marc Chagall and Max Liebermann, antiquities from
Jewish communities in India and Turkey, ceremonial art treasures from Europe,
and a singed Torah scroll rescued from a synagogue torched by Nazis in Germany.
The museum is open daily from Sunday through Thursday.

■ THE UNIVERSITY AT BERKELEY

Berkeley—you either love it or hate it. There is no middle ground, save perhaps a
love-hate relationship.

Intellectually, Berkeley is the most exciting city in the West, jammed with scholars
from around the world, new ideas and discoveries, Nobel laureates, books, classic

cinemas, and seekers of revolution, social freedom, or just a soapbox. There's also a wealthy, liberal Berkeley, crusaders in quest of a gastronomic holy grail, a new breed of Medici whose generous patronage fuels a renaissance of bakers, paper-makers, organic farmers, espresso-pourers, micro-brewers, and other inspired artisans. And then there's revolutionary Berkeley, a socialistic town with a People's Park and a history of determining its own foreign policy, where even the food has to be politically correct. Lacking the capacity for looking beyond Berkeley's admittedly spectacular lunatic fringe, Middle America has christened it *Berserkley*.

When the University of California at Berkeley was founded in 1868, it was called the Athens of the Pacific. The campus grew to be one of the largest and most beautiful anywhere, with a faculty and alumni who have, quite literally, changed the way the world thinks. To list all its contributions to science and the humanities is a task too daunting for these pages, but probably the two most momentous events were the development of nuclear science, and the protest movements of the sixties.

You can reach the campus easily from the Berkeley BART station, on Shattuck Avenue, the city's main business district. The foot of the campus, at University Gate, is a two-block walk up toward the hills. You can also take the free shuttle bus (called Humphry Go-BART) from the corner of Shattuck and Berkeley Way to Mining Circle near the top of the main campus. Check the map and transport information before leaving the BART station.

Though downtown Berkeley has a life of its own, it is overshadowed by the nearby campus. Downtown's busy restaurants, stores, and entertainments attract shoals of students and faculty day and night. The Berkeley Repertory Theater, one of the finest dramatic companies in the state, performs at 2025 Addison Street.

The Berkeley campus was laid out along twin branches of Strawberry Creek by Frederick Law Olmsted. A montage of architectural styles graces the campus, from log cabin to Greek revival, Gothic to high-tech. Glens and garden-like settings abound between the buildings. The eucalyptus trees to the right of the West Entrance at the end of University Avenue are reputed to be the tallest in the world. The forks of Strawberry Creek meet in the grove before being swallowed up under the pavements of downtown Berkeley. Before taking another step, get yourself a free campus map at the entrance kiosk.

Many points of interest await on campus, and no ideal order for seeing them. You are free to walk through the buildings, and eat in the dining commons.

Doe Library is the central depository of books on campus, supplemented by several department libraries and the large Moffitt Undergraduate Library. The collected papers of Mark Twain are kept upstairs in the Doe. Perhaps the most interesting library for visitors is the adjacent **Bancroft Library**, which maintains the university's rare book collection and a small museum of Californiana, including gold rush paintings and the brass plate supposedly left by Sir Francis Drake during his sixteenth century visit to California. The consensus nowadays is that it's a fake.

Sather Tower, better known as **the Campanile** because of its likeness to the *campanile* (bell-tower) of Saint Mark's Cathedral in Venice, is Berkeley's most famous landmark. Visitors can ride the elevator 200 feet (61 m) to the top for a superlative view of downtown Oakland, San Francisco, Marin County, and straight out the Golden Gate to the Farallon Islands. Though the tower strikes the hours automatically, a bell-ringer ascends to play the carillon at noon and before 8 a.m. during semester. You can hear it all over campus, and though it is interesting to watch the carillonneur at work, you'll have to cover your ears or suffer being (one hopes only temporarily) deafened. There is a small charge to ascend.

Though modest in size and aspect, Le Conte Hall has burned a trajectory across the history of science for its role as Berkeley's venerable physics department.

Between students and street life, Berkeley is never dull.

Berkeley's reputation as a leader in physics was already established before Ernest Lawrence won the Nobel Prize in 1939 for inventing a machine called a cyclotron, which he built on the hill above campus. Experiments in the cyclotron by Glenn Seaborg and other scientists resulted in the discovery of plutonium in 1941. Berkeley scientists went on to explore new frontiers of nuclear physics, building the bevatron, and discovering 13 synthetic elements (including Berkelium and Californium), the antiproton and antineutron, and carbon 14 (one of the keys to understanding radiocarbon dating and photosynthesis). The most notorious off-spring of this brave new world, however, came in 1941 when, realizing that war was imminent, the U.S. government approached Lawrence with a secret project. A team of scientists, including Edward Teller (who later developed the hydrogen bomb), met under the direction of J. Robert Oppenheimer in Le Conte Hall, where they roughed out the first plans for a new type of bomb. The project soon moved to New Mexico for development and testing, and the results fell on Hiroshima and Nagasaki in 1945.

The Earth Sciences Building contains a small, but interesting, **Paleontology Museum**, with a working seismograph and fossils (or model skeletons) of prehistoric animals, including a Tyrannosaurus skull and the skeletons of a saber-toothed tiger, Parasaurolophus, and a hulking prehistoric ancestor of the hippopotamus, called Palaeoparadoxia.

One of the most handsome buildings on campus is Hearst Mining Building, built in 1907 and entered through an impressive rotunda. Its mineral displays and pictures of western mining operations give the place an atmosphere of old-time California before it was flooded with quiche-eaters. A nice touch is the mine tunnel in the hill beside the building, no doubt used for engineering demonstrations.

The **Lowie Museum of Anthropology** occupies a ground-floor corner of Kroeber Hall. Exhibits change regularly, but the permanent collection features thousands of artifacts of Native American, European, Asian, African, and Pacific cultures, including a sarcophagus of a wealthy Etruscan lady, and the weapons and tools made by Ishi, the last California Indian to come into contact with whites. Ishi walked into Oroville, California, from his mountain home in 1911. Anthropologist A.L. Kroeber invited Ishi to live at the Museum of Anthropology in San Francisco, now the site of the U.C. Medical Center, where Ishi taught him firsthand about the Yana language, handicrafts, music, and customs.

Wurster Hall, the College of Environmental Design across the courtyard, is a splendid example of where the Brutalist movement in architecture gets its name.

The 8,500-seat Greek Theater above the main campus on Gayley Road was designed after the theater at Epidaurus, Greece. California Memorial Stadium is the Berkeley venue of the fiercely contested annual Big Game between the Berkeley and Stanford football teams. On the knoll beyond, the building that resembles a Scottish castle is Bowles Hall, a fraternity.

Foreign and American students share the residence hall called International House, or I-House, on Piedmont at the top of Bancroft Way. Its friendly little café is open to the public. Frat Row extends south on Piedmont.

The **University Art Museum** at 2626 Bancroft Way is a concrete sculpture of open galleries dovetailing into a central hall. The museum has works from Asian and Western artists, a sculpture gallery, and cafeteria. The **Pacific Film Archives**, with a door around the corner on Durant, screens celluloid obscurities and classics nightly, and provides screening rooms for film researchers. The museum charges a small admissions fee.

The liveliest part of the university is **Sproul Plaza**, just outside **Sather Gate**. Activists and leafleteers are thick on the ground here, a Berkeley tradition since 1964. That was the year that students challenged university regulations controlling public speech on campus. The Free Speech Movement gained momentum, culminating in a sit-in at Sproul Hall and the largest mass arrest in California's history.. The movement spread throughout the country and to campuses around the world. Throughout the Vietnam War, Sproul Plaza was a forum for anti-war protests, some of which were met with tear gas and the National Guard. Ludwick's Fountain, near the Student Union, honors Ludwick Von Schwaranburg, a dog whose passion for cleanliness led to a life-long habit of bathing here daily, which clearly impressed both students and regents.

The **Botanical Gardens** and the **Lawrence Hall of Science** are both reached by ascending Stadium Rim Road, which starts on Gayley between the Greek Theater and the stadium. At the junction behind the stadium, North Canyon climbs up to the Botanical Garden and its small parking lot. At this point, North Canyon changes to Centennial Drive and climbs in another steep spurt to Lawrence Hall of Science. You *can* walk, but it's so long and steep that you're better off driving or riding the shuttle from Mining Circle, in front of Hearst Mining Building.

Berkeley's peerless botanical gardens shelter more than 7,500 species from around the world, arranged in thematic gardens linked by paths. Californian, Asian, African, European, South American, and other sections are used for scientific research, but are also beautiful just for walking. A small botanical bookstore and information center stands at the gate.

The Lawrence Hall of Science, like the Exploratorium in San Francisco, inspires people, especially children, with the wonder and excitement of science. Using holograms, computers, lasers, telescopes, a planetarium, laboratories, and other resources, visitors can reach an understanding of such difficult concepts as evolution, prehistoric human migration, atomic theory, random selection, biological engineering and the history of science, while having fun. Traveling exhibits and science fairs are set up regularly, including the ever-popular displays of enormous (though not quite life-size) mechanical dinosaurs, called Dynomation. A magnificent array of books, experiments, and scientific toys is sold in the lobby store. The Hall of Science charges a moderate admission fee, and is open daily. By night, incidentally, the view of the city lights from the parking lot is astounding.

■ BERKELEY TOWN

Sproul Plaza feeds into **Telegraph Avenue** on the south side of campus, where the streams of humanity flow with almost Gangetic fecundity. Here, undergraduates rub karmas with anarchists, musicians, crafts-sellers, prophets, lunatics, booksellers, revolutionaries, artists, missionaries, sorority girls, runaways, pushers, professors, and assorted riffraff. For big-city people accustomed to running a gauntlet of street people, Telegraph Avenue holds no terrors. For more timid souls, it is a chance to turn one's thoughts to the woof and warp of the human condition.

Nirvana of book lovers, the south side packs in more booksellers per acre than any other corner of the Bay Area—and probably the country, west of the Appalachians. Among the book emporia on Bancroft, University Press Books stocks publications of university presses from around the world, while the tiny Map Center sells travel and wilderness handbooks from the back of an alley. Three blocks up Telegraph, beyond Haste Street, Berkeley opens up its big guns. Cody's not only sells books; it fosters literacy with coffee and regular readings by local and visiting authors. Moe's is reputed to be the largest used book store in the Bay Area. Shambhala deals in metaphysics, Eastern religions and Asian medicine. Shakespeare and Company anchors down the corner across the street. At least five more major booksellers and buyers flesh out the neighborhood, and business is always booming during term. And if book-hunting makes you a bit peckish, or if you want a cozy place to read your latest purchases, you'll be happy to know that coffee houses absolutely *thrive* in this neighborhood.

Sather Gate (top) and an Egyptian motif from Berkeley's Life Sciences Building.

Berkeley's most potent symbol of radicalism is **People's Park**, which sits a half block up from Telegraph, on a rectangle of land bounded by Haste, Bowditch, and Dwight. Although owned by the university, the land was seized for a park in 1969 by a coalition of hippies, activists, and radical students. Attempts by the university to retake the land sparked rioting, in which one man was killed, another blinded, and scores injured by county sheriff buckshot. The property has sat in limbo ever since, and though it is a vibrant symbol to radicals, in reality it is little more than a vacant lot where pushers and vagrants congregate.

When students talk about Northside, they are referring to the first block of Euclid, a mellower street than Telegraph, but blessed with its own eateries, bookstore, and cinema.

The rolling residential hills of North Berkeley shelter an enchanting neighborhood of tree-lined lanes, rambling old houses, English gardens, leafy stairways and hidden parks. Tenured faculty have traditionally sought homes here. Especially pleasant are the **Berkeley Rose Garden**, falling on terraces from Euclid, a half mile (.8 km) up from campus, and the jumble of boulders that climbers use for training on Indian Rock Road. (An excellent guide to some of these unique houses, streets, and stairways, as well as to the rest of the city, is Don Pitcher's *Berkeley Inside/Out*.)

North Berkeley is famous for its food. Upper Shattuck Avenue, between Virginia and Rose, has been christened in the press as "**Gourmet Ghetto**," a reputation initiated by Chez Panisse, celebrated as an innovator of what is now known as California cuisine. Scores of other kitchens dedicated to creative French-inspired cookery—or to unreconstructed ethnic cuisines—have sprung up along Solano and University avenues, upper Shattuck, the up-and-coming Fourth Street (at the foot of University), and the aforementioned College Avenue, turning them into the reigning restaurant rows of the East Bay. Many of the retail shops on these streets, likewise, deal in the unusual and the exquisite. On Fourth Street, for instance, you can while away the time waiting for a table at Bette's Oceanview Café or the Fourth Street Grill by browsing for handmade paper, designer garden tools, stained glass, or crystal-growing kits.

The neighboring town of Emeryville has also made its mark on the East Bay culinary scene with its new **Emeryville Public Market**. Prepared foods from a patchwork of cultures make this lively, easy-going venue perfect for a casual lunch or dinner. Stay awhile to visit Diesel Books, the boutique brewery, and the produce market.

■ THE EAST BAY PARKLANDS

The East Bay ranges, of which the Oakland and Berkeley hills form the vanguard, mark the eastern rampart of one of the most spectacular, diverse, and extensive urban greenbelts in the country. Most San Franciscans are probably unaware of this. So richly endowed is the Bay Area with beautiful parks that most would surely give the East Bay hills a distant fourth in a beauty contest with the hill parks of Marin County, the Santa Cruz Mountains, and the Peninsula.

Still, it is impressive to know that the East Bay Regional Park system, with 63,000 acres (25,500 ha) spread through 46 parks, crossed and linked by a thousand miles of trails, is the second largest urban park system in the United States, after Chicago's Cook County Forest Preserve. The range of things to do here confounds the inveterate city dweller. You can hike, fish, watch birds, climb rocks, or practice archery. You can go sailing, picnicking, swimming, golfing, shooting, camping, biking, canoeing, or backpacking. You can tour a mine, ride a miniature steam train, study fossils, or watch a blacksmith pound a red-hot horseshoe into shape. And no matter what you do, you can still be back in San Francisco, refreshed in body and soul, in time for dinner.

But the best thing about the parks is that they provide an escape from the harried pace of civilization. Their pungent, creaking forests of gum invite wanderers to leave the city far behind, to experience the simple insect hum of summer in the hills, the drone of bees, a blue jay's raucous cry, the rustle of a fox creeping through fat tule bulrushes, the splash of spring water pumped cold from the earth, the clang of a hiker's gate closing on empty fields. Such soothing airs and fancy scents, tranquility, and sensual rejuvenation would cost a pretty penny in the city; out in the East Bay parklands, it goes for nothing.

The park district office supplies brochures from their headquarters at 11500 Skyline Boulevard, in Oakland; call (510) 531-9300. Maps, brochures, and further information on lectures and park-sponsored nature and history programs are also available at ranger stations in the individual parks.

The bulwark of the East Bay Regional Park District is the string of parks along the crest of the Oakland and Berkeley hills. **Tilden**, on the hill behind the University of California at Berkeley, has something for everyone. The local model railroad club has set up a miniature steam train yard in the park, where weekend engineers are happy to take small passengers on a chug around the park. Everyone is always welcome on the granddaddy of the tiny locomotives, The Little Train. For

The peerless view toward San Francisco from the Lawrence Hall of Science (overleaf).

youngsters, there are pony rides, a children's farm, and a vintage merry-go-round with a jaunty honky-tonk music box. Tilden's extensive botanic garden compresses the world into a few acres, while swimmers and sunbathers can escape the summer's heat at Lake Anza. Best of all, Tilden is a great place to hook into the huge trail system of the East Bay hills, with shorter strolls to neighboring Wildcat Canyon Regional Park, and much more serious treks to Redwood, Chabot, and Briones regional parks, and points beyond. Efforts are underway to connect all the major East Bay parks by a trail that loops completely around San Francisco Bay.

The **Skyline National Trail**, connecting Wildcat Canyon north of Berkeley with Anthony Chabot Regional Park, some 30 miles (50 kilometers) to the south, is already several years old. Along the way, it passes through Tilden, Sibley Volcanic, Huckleberry, and Redwood regional parks. Following the crest of the Oakland hills, hikers climb to spectacular vistas of sparkling blue water, the Golden Gate, and the bay cities. By night, their vast street grids and distant towers glow with the most fantastic light show this side of Las Vegas. Turning east, a completely different vision of rugged hills rolls away, green in winter, gold in summer. Drivers, too, can enjoy that view from Skyline Boulevard, on Tilden's edge.

The stretches of trail through the forests of **Redwood Regional Park** are perhaps the East Bay's most enchanting. Standing among these noble second-growth redwoods, it is hard to imagine the awesome monsters that lived here until only last century. They were logged for timber to build the cities below. At least one rotted stump, now marked by a ring of its second-growth offspring, hints of a vanished behemoth that may have been larger than any tree now known to mankind. Another famous giant of the last century, the Blossom Rock Tree, was so huge that ships entering the Golden Gate some 18 miles west (30 km) used it as a navigation marker.

At the southern end of the Skyline Trail, in **Anthony Chabot Regional Park**, one of the Bay Area's best-stocked fishing reservoirs winds placidly back through steep hills studded with oak, gum, and bay trees. Every pleasant morning brings out scores of anglers to Lake Chabot's piers and rowboats in quest of elusive bass and trout, as well as less-elusive bluegill, catfish and crappie. Chabot Park attracts crowds of campers, target shooters, and picnickers on weekends, but there's still plenty of space to lose yourself in. For those in need of even more elbow room, a vast expanse of East Bay watershed land sprawls beyond where Chabot Park ends, closed to the public, except for the horseman or hiker armed with a permit obtained from the water company offices. For more information, call (510) 835-3000.

Green in winter, yellow in summer, the East Bay hills offer year-round hiking.

Closer to civilization is a site above Oakland's Montclair district first settled by the poet Cincinnatus Hiner Miller, better known as Joaquin Miller. The poet's modest home and much more ambitiously planted property are now preserved by the city of Oakland as **Joaquin Miller Park.** In his day, Miller claimed to have been a farmer, miner, Indian fighter, and Pony Express rider, but in truth, it's hard to separate his real accomplishments from his own embellishments. What is known is that Miller fancied himself a great poet, and he was by every account a charmingly colorful character.

Miller showed up in San Francisco in the 1850s, presenting his poetry to Bret Harte, then editor of the *Overland Monthly*, who rejected it as doggerel. On Ina Coolbrith's advice, Miller then departed for England, where his eccentric manners, sombrero, and red shirt won him a following in fashionable society. His galloping verses were praised as primitive but genuinely spirited Americana; in short, they sold, and Miller became a celebrity.

When he returned to the Bay Area in the 1880s, he found the as-yet uncivilized San Franciscan magazines still disinclined to idolize humbuggery. Miller retired to the more receptive wilds of the Oakland Hills, which he called **The Hights** [*sic*]. There, he built a house called The Abbey and started receiving his curious admirers. One of these was a Japanese poet, Yone Noguchi, who also took up residence. Miller was particularly fond of lady visitors, whom he would impress with a rain dance that he had learned from the Indians. (Noguchi worked the sprinkler atop the Abbey.) The Abbey still stands amidst the forests that Miller planted. **Woodminster Theater,** an outdoor venue used for plays in summer, occupies the hill above. Trails connect Joaquin Miller Park with Redwood Regional Park.

Nearby Knowland State Park contains a small zoo with tigers, lions, elephants, monkeys and other mammals and birds, as well as a children's petting zoo. Because of its compact size and intimacy, Knowland Zoo is a favorite among children.

If it is wilderness that you seek, you can find it pocketed in the East Bay hills. Most is not true wilderness in the sense of land unchanged by human beings, for almost all is ranch land that has been turned over to the park department. Nevertheless, if it is extensive, empty of human habitation, and wild enough for beasts to call it home, it is wilderness enough to keep most city dwellers from discovering it. **Las Trampas Regional Park** is one of these spectacular places, straddling the rugged ridges west of San Ramon Valley. The land falls and rises grandly in steep hills and sandstone cliffs, occasionally cut by wind caves, and softened with chaparral and woodland.

The brave young city by the Balboa seas
Lies compassed about by the hosts of night—
Lies humming, low, like a hive of bees;
And the day lies dead. And its spirit's flight
Is far to the west; while the golden bars
That bound it are broken to a dust of stars.
Come under my oaks, oh, drowsy dusk!
The world and the dog; dear incense hour
When Mother earth hath a smell of musk,
And things of the spirit assert their power—
When candles are set to burn in the west—
Set head and foot to the day at rest.

—Joaquin Miller, "Twilight at the Hights."

The greatest wilderness challenge so far enshrined in the East Bay Regional Park system is the **Ohlone Trail**, which starts in **Mission Peak Regional Preserve** in Fremont (near the old Mission San Jose de Guadeloupe), and straggles some 30 miles (50 km) through three regional parks—**Sunol, Ohlone,** and **Del Valle**. The trail traverses canyon and mountain, forest and glen, opening wide on the ridge tops to grand vistas of earth and sky, yet thoroughly secluded from the noisy distractions of civilization. This country is only seen on foot or horseback. Designated campgrounds have hand-pumped water, a superlatively cool refreshment in the hot days of summer, when the Ohlone Trail is a real test of stamina. In spring and on clear winter days, the hills glow a bright shade of winter-green, a treat for the eyes. It is along the Ohlone Trail where you are most likely to see a mountain lion, coyote, eagle, or bobcat. There's no need to fear; they are all deathly afraid of human beings.

■ SOUTHERN ALAMEDA COUNTY

Most San Franciscans think it nothing but a sprawling bedroom community, but southern Alameda County's link with Bay Area history is fascinating and tangible. A car will be handy to reach these far-flung sites.

The Ohlones lived for centuries in what is now **Coyote Hills Regional Park**, west of Fremont. The hills themselves are peculiar, rising abruptly from the surrounding marshes and mud flats of San Francisco Bay. The Ohlones established one of their villages in the lee, near the mouth of Alameda Creek. Mounds of their castoff shells and debris are now being excavated by archaeologists, who have resurrected some of the village ways in park seminars open to the public. Kids of all ages enjoy learning how to make acorn mush, chip obsidian arrowheads, weave cord and netting, build tule boats and kindle fires by the ancient Ohlone methods. The small visitor center is not nearly so interesting as wandering out on the living marshes, on boardwalks, amongst the marsh rodents and migratory flocks. The adjacent **San Francisco National Wildlife Refuge** extends the protected acreage of Coyote Hills by over 20 times. Here, visitors can glean some idea of what life was like here before the arrival of the Spaniards.

After founding Mission Dolores in San Francisco, the Spanish set out to develop the more fertile and heavily populated regions of what is now Fremont. Established in June 1797, **Mission San Jose de Guadeloupe** grew famous for its music. Examples of Ohlone instruments and handicrafts are displayed in the old living quarters of the mission, one of the most absorbing small museums of the Bay Area. The graveyard, olive groves, and detached church, painstakingly reconstructed in the 1980s, exude a strong feeling for the vanished era. Perhaps that is because the hills behind the mission are preserved by Mission Peak Regional Preserve, in much the same state that the Ohlones would have known. For those who wish to experience it for themselves, the Ohlone Trail starts at the end of Stanford Avenue, about two miles south on Mission Boulevard from Mission San Jose.

Yankee-era history is preserved at nearby **Ardenwood Historical Farm**. The fields and barnyards are still worked as they were between the 1870s and 1920s. The land is plowed by horse-power and the crop harvested in the neighborly fashion of the threshing bee, where all comers can lend a hand. Get a feel for bygone country life by learning how to milk a cow or crank-wring the laundry, and by watching the blacksmith, farrier, and quilters at work. On special occasions, you can even taste Victorian recipes, or play Victorian games on the mansion house lawn.

The Discovery Zone is a new, high-tech playground of tubular mazes, climbing bars, and "swimming pools" filled with small balls, dedicated to the principle that fitness can be fun. Kids pay the entrance fee; their minders are free. It's on the Fremont Hub at Mowry Avenue.

Niles District, another section of Fremont, was America's first Hollywood. From 1911 to 1916, over 450 westerns and other features were filmed in its still-rustic streets, and in nearby Niles Canyon—including that famous final scene of *The Tramp*, where Charlie Chaplin saunters into the sunset. Strong on atmosphere, the main street of Niles today just moseys along without much attention from anyone.

At the eastern end of Niles Canyon the village of **Sunol** is the only municipality in the United States—perhaps the world—with a dog serving as elected mayor. His election drew strong criticism from the People's Republic of China as a prime example of the shortcomings of American democracy. However, it is only fair to note that Sunol has suffered not one S&L failure, political scandal, budgetary crisis, or stray cat invasion under Mayor Bosco's administration, and he steadfastly refuses to draw a salary. He's not the only altruistic institution in town. The **Niles Canyon Railway**, a group of train hobbyists, transports passengers on wood-burning puffer-bellies through a stretch of the canyon on the first and third Sundays of every month, for free; but donations are appreciated.

■ THE EASTERN VALLEYS

Though development is now threatening even the farthest reaches of the East Bay, enough ranchers and vintners are still around to make a cowboy feel at home in the Livermore Valley. The **Alameda County Fair** in neighboring Pleasanton has a

Mission San Jose was rebuilt in the 1980s to its original design.

strong country atmosphere that would feel right at home in the rural Central Valley. The fair is short—just two weeks centered on the Fourth of July—but it packs in a fun schedule of fireworks, carnival rides, tent shows, horse-racing, live country-and-western music and, best of all, the judging of the county's best farm animals, and homemade jams, pickles, and pies.

Livermore's wine industry is small compared with Napa's or Sonoma's, but its venerable history and excellent wines still demand attention. **Wente Brothers Cellars** has been run by the same family since 1883. In 1937, their Sauvignon Blanc won the Grand Prix at the Paris World's Fair and Exposition, setting a precedent that Napa and Sonoma have followed. They have two facilities for visitors. Wente Brothers Sparkling Wine Cellars & Restaurant, at 5050 Arroyo Road, is perhaps the more interesting by virtue of the sandstone caves, where wine is stored. The Wentes produce still wines at their Estate Winery, 5565 Tesla Road. Just up the street, **Concannon Winery**, which dates from 1883, supplements its wine-tasting room with a shady picnic area amidst the vineyards, a delightful place to sample a chilled bottle of wine on a hot summer's day. Before you go, get a map of these and other wineries at the Chamber of Commerce, 2157 First Street, Livermore.

The **Lawrence Livermore National Laboratory** is so well known as a major weapons developer that its other projects go unnoticed. You can see for yourself what it's all about at the modest visitor center, featuring a couple of holograms, a diorama of an atomic testing site, laser displays, computer quizzes, and a slick multimedia presentation. Take the Greenville Road exit from Interstate 580 in Livermore, and drive two miles south (3.2 km) to the gate. The visitor center is open daily on weekdays, and on weekend afternoons. Group tours of some of the internal facilities can be arranged in advance.

Mount Diablo, the 3,849-foot (1,173-m) summit of the East Bay hills, dominates the back end of the East Bay, and is usually seen above the horizon from San Francisco. Monte de Diablo—the devil's mountain—was named after a frightening encounter on its slopes with an Ohlone shaman, whom the Spaniards mistook for Satan himself. At least that's one story. Bret Harte told another—of a Spanish cleric who was treated by the devil to a mountaintop vision of Yankee hordes storming into California, seizing the land from Spain. Today, the mountain is protected as part of Mount Diablo State Park, which you can reach in a car by way either of Danville or Walnut Creek. A two-lane road winds clear to the top for a view that sweeps east on clear days across the Central Valley to the lofty Sierra Nevada range, and 300 miles north (480 km) to Mount Shasta—the widest view that can be seen from any point in the United States. Kids love to climb on the sandstone formations at Rock City, on the mountain.

The suburban town of Danville has a claim to fame unbeknownst even to most local residents. Arguably the greatest dramas of the American stage were written here by its foremost playwright, Eugene O'Neill. On a visit in 1936 (the same year that he won the Nobel Prize for literature), O'Neill fell in love with the beautiful views of Mount Diablo. He and his wife, Carlotta, bought 157 acres (388 ha) on the slopes of Las Trampas Ridge, west of Danville, and built **Tao House**. Between 1937 and 1944, he wrote his last five plays there, including *The Iceman Cometh, A Moon for the Misbegotten,* and *Long Day's Journey into Night.* Now protected as a national historic site, Tao House is still relatively remote, and can be visited only on scheduled free tours that meet in downtown Danville. Make an appointment with the National Park Service by calling (510) 838-0249. The house is being refurnished as O'Neill knew it, right down to the books on his writing room shelves.

Blackhawk is one of the Bay Area's most exclusive communities. Sightseers will be turned away at the gate, but they can come for a gawk at **Blackhawk Plaza**, the dazzling neighborhood shopping mall. It's something like Rodeo Drive with a concerted theme of pink Mediterranean, built around luxuriant fountains and a spectacular, ever-flowing artificial stream. Everything is done to a tasteful excess. The restaurants and boutiques are very smart, as one would expect, and even the grocery store carts are a suave shade of black and gold.

Blackhawk Plaza has two excellent museums. The **Behring Auto Museum** is an absolutely scintillating collection of vintage roadsters, polished to a splendid sheen and enchantingly arranged about a darkened hall. The jazz age models put to shame anything on the road today for style and pure up-your-nose snob appeal, not to mention comfort. These are the most beautiful machines in the world, and the Behring Museum is an ideal setting.

The University of California at Berkeley Museum opened somewhat curiously at Blackhawk in 1991. No matter that Blackhawk is a long way from Berkeley, both in miles and in temperament; the building is architecturally striking and glittering with treasures from 5,000 years of all the world's cultures. Rotated regularly from the university's Kroeber collection, each piece is a work of art as well as a cultural touchstone. Traveling science exhibitions, lectures and stories, seminars, and children's craft workshops round out the museum's program.

A more earthy experience can be had at the **Lindsay Museum** in Walnut Creek, where handling snakes and petting rabbits is part of the guidelines. This small

wildlife museum is designed with kids in mind. Note the stuffed California Grizzly, an extinct species, standing by the back door.

■ CARQUINEZ STRAITS

Martinez is an old town by California standards, built on the Carquinez Straits where San Francisco Bay squeezes down to its narrowest point between San Pablo and Suisun bays. Legend says that the martini was named after this town when a San Francisco bartender invented it as fortification against the chilly trans-bay ferry crossing to Martinez. (If this story be true, however, why wasn't the drink called a martinez?)

John Muir, known around the world as the prime mover of the conservation movement, lived for 25 years, and died, in Martinez. His farm is now a national historic site. You can wander at will through the 1882 white frame house. Notice especially the cluttered study where he wrote while managing his fruit orchards. Photographs from his life hang on the walls, and some of the period furnishings are originals. On the grounds, you can also see the two-story Martinez adobe, built by the town's namesake, Don Vicente Martínez, in 1849. Muir's books are on sale in the park office at the gate, where you can also see a short film on his life. Muir was buried nearby on what is still private property; ask directions from the park office. The house, at 4202 Alhambra Avenue, is open daily for a small admissions fee.

Another era of Bay Area history is recalled at **Black Diamond Mines Regional Preserve**; drive 21 miles (35 km) east to Antioch on State Highway 4, then south on the Sommersville Road to park headquarters. The discovery of valuable coal deposits in the 1860s brought a mineral rush to the north side of Mount Diablo. Sommersville, Nortonville, and three other boomtowns sprang up, flourished for a half century, and died. A second boom hit the area in the 1920s, when miners tunneled for industrial-quality sand used for glass and casting molds. Today, the old towns have fallen to pieces, except for a few relics culled from archaeological digs and a moody old pioneer cemetery. Thirty-four miles (55 km) of trails lead to mining sites in the dry hills, and a sand mine near the picnic area has been converted to a fascinating Underground Mining Museum. Tours are led by rangers. Reservations are necessary; call (510) 757-2620.

Sunrise over the wetlands of the San Francisco National Wildlife Refuge.

The hamlet of **Port Costa**, about five miles (eight km) west of Martinez on the Carquinez Scenic Road, hangs on to a history much larger than itself. When the first transcontinental railway train chugged down from Sacramento, no bridge crossed the Carquinez Straits, as two do today at Martinez and Vallejo. The tracks ended at Benicia, on the north side of the Straits, where the cars were loaded on waiting ferries and floated across to Port Costa. The largest train ferries in the world, the *Solano* and *Contra Costa*, operated on these waters until the completion of the rail bridge at Martinez in 1930. Port Costa today has changed little from the last century. It's a pleasant little side trip, perhaps with dinner at the Bull Valley Inn on its main street.

The historic town of **Benicia**, seen across the straits from Port Costa, can be reached from Martinez by the Benicia-Martinez bridge. Looking east from the high span, you can see the remnants of Liberty Ships from World War II for which the Navy no longer has any use. Anchored in the straits, they are known as the Mothball Fleet. Arriving on the north shore of the Carquinez Straits, you are now in Solano County.

Benicia, a small, quiet town, has had a fascinating role in California history. Its low-key appearance does not exactly dazzle the eye, but for those who make an effort to learn the stories behind it, Benicia is an unspoiled beauty. It was founded on land owned by General Mariano Vallejo, who was egged on in the venture by two Yankee leaders of the Bear Flag revolt, Robert Semple and Thomas Larkin. They named it after Mrs. Vallejo. Benicia was an early rival to Yerba Buena, and was almost certainly the better situated of the two for trade, sitting midway between the Central Valley hinterland and San Francisco Bay. Competition between the two villages prompted the citizens of Yerba Buena to rename their burg after the famous bay of San Francisco, a shrewd move that brought recognition from strangers around the world. As noted already, the first transcontinental railroad passed through here, reinforcing Benicia's *natural* superiority over peninsular San Francisco; but by then, the city by the Golden Gate was already fixed as the economic capital of California.

When Concepcion Arguello joined a Dominican monastery to forget the unhappy promises of Nikolai Rezanof, she retired to Benicia. She died in 1857, and was buried in Saint Dominic's Cemetery, on Hillcrest Avenue between East Fifth and Sixth streets. Her gravestone, carved with the name of Sister Mary Dominica, is at the end of the second row, on the left. A larger monument stands beside it.

Benicia's main stem, First Street, hosts a few antique shops, cafés, restaurants, and historical houses. For a self-guided tour of the town, pick up a map and brochure from the **old State Capitol** on the corner of First and G streets. This handsome Greek Revival building dates from 1852, and served as California's capital house in 1853 and 1854. For a small admission fee, you may visit the Assembly and Senate chambers, set up as they were during the 1853 session. Note the interior pillars: they were masts from ships abandoned off Benicia during the gold rush.

The U.S. Army established a barracks in Benicia in 1849, adding an arsenal in 1852. Remnants of the base, which closed in 1964, still stand around the east side of town, including the formidable sandstone powder magazine built in 1857, the Clock Tower Fortress, the post hospital and cemetery, the 1860 Commandant'ss house, and the old guardhouse. Actually, this is the third guardhouse on the site.

A little-known story is connected with the first one, built in 1852. A young soldier named Hiram Grant, passing through San Francisco en route from the Mexican War to Humboldt County, California, was tried and briefly imprisoned here in 1852 for getting roaring drunk in public. This hardly gives Benicia a pivotal role in American history, but it does have an interesting twist in that Grant went on to become the supreme commander of the Union army in the Civil War, and eventually, president of the United States. How many other towns can boast of having locked a future president in their cooler for being drunk and disorderly? (Quite in character with his unpretentious manner, Hiram Ulysses Grant never bothered to change the name that West Point erringly recorded on his admission papers as Ulysses S. Grant.)

Another military site worth visiting is the **Camel Barns**, on Camel Road north of Highway 780. The camels came to Benicia after a failed experiment by then-Secretary of War Jefferson Davis, who imported them for use in the American deserts. Actually, the camels performed well under arid conditions, but weren't to the liking of American handlers, who failed to understand their impertinent manners. The camels were stabled in the Benicia Camel Barns in 1863, and auctioned off in 1864. Today, the barns are part of the Benicia Historical Museum.

West of Benicia, and just across the Carquinez Bridge from western Contra Costa County, is the city of Vallejo. Its greatest tourist draw is **Marine World Africa USA**, a combination of aquarium, zoo, marine circus, and water-ski show. For a single entrance fee, you have the run of the park, choosing from among several daily shows by trained dolphins, sea lions, killer whales, birds, elephants, chimps, tigers, lions, and folks on water skis. A playground for kids is built with ropes, nets, bridges and tunnels. At the aquarium, visitors handle sea animals under supervision of park biologists. Marine World is entertaining, especially for kids and out-of-staters who have never seen a dolphin or killer whale up close. You can get to Vallejo by ferryboat from Fisherman's Wharf in San Francisco. (See "Practicalities" for information.)

■ NORTH SOLANO

Heading north toward Sacramento from either Benicia or Vallejo, Interstate 80 passes through the towns of Fairfield and Vacaville. Fairfield is about 45 miles (72 km) from San Francisco, and Vacaville about 10 miles (16 km) farther. Urban sprawl is rapidly changing the lifestyle of these communities from farming to bedroom, but you can still find fruit orchards in Suisun Valley, an exquisite sight when the blossoms are out in spring. Travis Air Force Base, home of the **Air Force Museum**, is east of Fairfield on East Texas Street. The guard at the main gate can direct you to the museum. The most impressive sights here are the actual aircraft, which you may walk through if the duty officer has them open (usually on weekends). Among the giants are a B-52 bomber and a huge C-124 cargo transport plane, built in 1952. Several other planes and helicopters are parked alongside, including some fighters. There's even some talk of a MIG coming soon.

Inside the museum, be sure to see the pioneer airplane built and flown by the Bay Area's Gonzales brothers, and the scale model of a Mercury capsule. The museum shop sells pictures, pins, badges, and aircraft models. Interestingly enough, you can also buy astronaut ice cream. The museum is free.

Once upon a time, when Vacaville was still open countryside, an entrepreneur opened a fruit stand and restaurant called **The Nut Tree**. The place is still operating, but is now much more than a place to eat. The Nut Tree is something of an institution for families taking a break on the drive between Sacramento and the Bay Area. Besides the restaurant, there are curiosity shops, a fancy playground, a miniature train, and a small airport. The large bookstore specializes in aircraft books and maps. To get there, follow the signs from Interstate 80.

A newer attraction in Vacaville is called **the Wooz**. It is, quite simply, a walk-through maze. People pay to go in and find their way out again. There are three outdoor mazes: a small one for kids, a big one for adults, and a more difficult one called the Superwooz. The Superwooz is a reward for people who find their way through the big maze within 40 minutes. Apparently, mazes are the latest craze in Japan, and this is one of the pioneering efforts in the United States. The Wooz, on Orange Drive near Interstate 80, is open seven days a week.

■ THE DELTA

The Delta is that 1,200-square-mile (3,100-sq-km) triangle of land where the Sacramento and San Joaquin (and half a dozen smaller rivers) flow together before crashing San Francisco Bay. The Sacramento River ship channel is navigable by large vessels as far as Sacramento, and the San Joaquin River as far as Stockton. The rest is island and slough, slough and island.

The Delta's 50-odd islands were created by over a thousand miles (1,600 km) of levees, many of them originally built by Chinese laborers. These islands have some of the richest agricultural land in the United States, ideal for fruit and rice, among

Locke is the only existing rural settlement in America founded by Chinese.

other things. Land behind the dikes is mostly lower than the river level; it's a startling sight to stand in a pear orchard and see the bow of a ship drift past above the trees. More than one major flood has covered an island in this century. A glance at the map shows at least one still drowned—Frank's Tract.

The Delta is a fisherman's paradise. Salmon, catfish, striped bass, steelhead, sturgeon, and other catch thrive in season. You can fish from slough banks or rent boats from towns throughout the Delta. For longer vacations, you can also rent houseboats. Cars can visit most of the islands, scooting along the levee roads, hopping from island to island on small ferries and singing drawbridges. Hunters come here to bag waterfowl, and bird-watchers are always guaranteed a binocular full. You can camp on Brannan Island, across the river from Rio Vista, where you also find a number of marinas and fishing resorts.

Rio Vista, 22 miles (35 km) east of Fairfield, is the main "city" of the Delta. Once a thriving port on the riverboat run between San Francisco and Sacramento, the city's boom times passed on with the great boats themselves. Millionaires' Row seems a bit down at the heel now, but still makes an attractive riverside walk.

Cross the Sacramento River from Rio Vista, and drive north, keeping to the right bank. You will pass through interesting little river towns, like Isleton and Walnut Grove, but none more fascinating than **Locke**. One of the few American rural towns built by Chinese settlers, Locke was founded in 1915 by a man named Tin San-chan. At the height of its population—about 2,000 people—Locke supported a post office, theater, dentist, poolroom, church, shoe repair shop, bakery, five boarding houses, six restaurants, five grocery stores, two saloons, two cigar stands, and some gambling parlors. Almost all are gone today.

A few residents of Chinese ancestry still live around Locke. One of them, in neighboring Walnut Grove, farms the largest pear orchard in the United States. For the most part, however, Locke just basks in splendid solitude. Its rows of false-front buildings lean unsteadily on ramshackle balcony piers. The dirt side streets give it the feel of an old movie set. The liveliest place in town is Al's, where you can grab a steak and a beer, and speculate on how they got all those dollar bills to stick on that high ceiling.

THE PENINSULA
AND SOUTH BAY

SAN FRANCISCO WAS NOT THE ONLY CITY where William Ralston (the man "who built San Francisco") made his mark. Twenty-odd miles (30-odd km) to the south, he built an 80-room mansion called Belmont, from which he could commute to San Francisco by means of relay horses. Ralston set the tone for San Francisco's rich, who carved out great country estates on the Peninsula. After the catastrophe of 1906, many of them fled the city for such millionaire enclaves as Hillsborough, Woodside, and Belmont.

Today, millions of the rank and file have followed their precedent. Between the bay shore and the hills, the urban sprawl presses down the Peninsula from San Francisco to Silicon Valley. A range of high hills also runs the entire length, dividing the urban strip from a surprisingly pristine, mountainous coastline.

There are many good reasons to spend a day or two exploring this area. Families who enjoy large amusement parks will like Great America in Silicon Valley, and the Boardwalk in Santa Cruz. The Winchester Mystery House and the Egyptian Museum fascinate people of all ages, while the incredible estates of the California gentry, like Villa Montalvo and especially Filoli, will overwhelm anyone with an interest in history, architecture or gardening. Others may want to walk among the redwood giants of the Santa Cruz mountains, or to meet the spectacular sea elephants of Año Nuevo State Beach.

Of the five main roads leading down the Peninsula from San Francisco, the workhorse is Interstate 101, known locally as the Bayshore Freeway, which plows south parallel to the shore through the midst of urban sprawl. If you are driving for pleasure, avoid it. The Junipero Serra Freeway (Highway 280) has been called the most beautiful freeway in the country. Running along a ridge top, with magnificent views of hills and city, it is also a practical freeway for people in a hurry. If possible, use it instead of Highway 101.

El Camino Real is the old road established by the Spaniards to connect their missions; within San Francisco, it is called Mission Boulevard. Today, the road leads through the downtown stretches of several Peninsula cities, a frustrating run of traffic lights for the most part, but a good way to see the town centers.

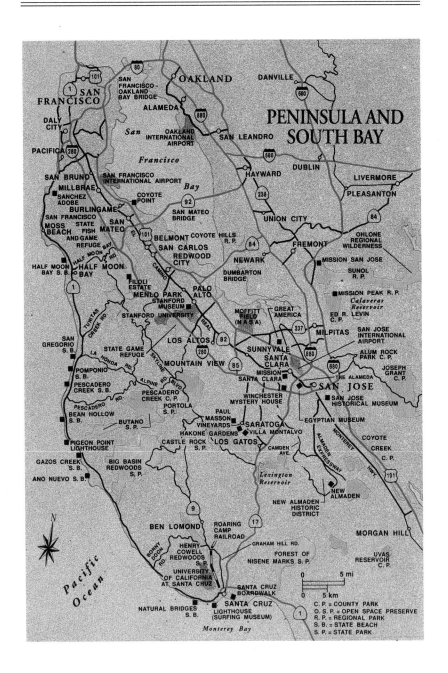

Skyline Boulevard and Highway 1 are scenic alternatives, popular among Bay Area residents for Sunday drives. Skyline winds some 50 miles (80 km) along a high Peninsula ridge overlooking city, bay, and greenbelt, to the Santa Cruz Mountains. Side roads lead down to the bayshore urban areas and the coastal Highway 1, a narrow, winding road that skirts the cliffs and beaches.

■ THE PENINSULA'S BAY-SIDE

With a population of about 1.5 million, **Colma** is easily the largest city of the Bay Area. The only reason you never hear of much stirring in Colma is that only about 500 of its residents actually *live* there.

Colma is San Francisco's necropolis, its City of the Dead. It comprises several cemeteries lining both sides of El Camino Real, just south of Daly City. Some of the cemeteries cater to specific religious or ethnic groups—Italians, Chinese, Japanese, Jews, Serbs, and Greeks. Though each cemetery has its particular character, the most spectacular is Cypress Lawn, which contains hundreds of family crypts scattered like tiny Greek, Roman, and Egyptian temples over the rolling landscape. Other residents of Cypress Lawn rest in an enormous, rambling columbarium, lit during daylight by acres of stained glass. Woodlawn Memorial Park, entered through a massive sandstone chateau-gate, is the cemetery of choice for numerous notable San Franciscans, including Emperor Norton, Ishi, Lillie Hitchcock Coit, James King of William, and Beniamino Bufano. Perhaps the most famous resident of Colma is none other than the celebrated sheriff of Tombstone, Arizona, who fought the shoot-out at the O.K. corral. Wyatt Earp is buried beside his wife in the Hills of Eternity cemetery.

Of livelier interest to children is **Coyote Point Museum**, just south of San Francisco International Airport, off Interstate 101. Ecology is the overriding theme, presented in a fun and colorful way. The museum displays an environmental progression through the Peninsula, from the bay to the Pacific, showing sample habitats and mankind's role in preserving them. Of special interest is the food-chain pyramid, a living colony of squirming termites, and a beehive that invites youngsters to listen in. The museum is open Wednesday through Friday, and on weekend afternoons. The small admission charge is waived on Fridays. Drivers must also pay an entrance fee at the park gate.

Some of the great manor houses of the Peninsula have been converted to public use, with visitors welcome. The Elizabethan-style Kohl Mansion, now a girls' school in the Burlingame hills (2750 Adeline Drive), and Ralston's 1868 mansion in Belmont, now on the grounds of the College of Notre Dame, both offer conducted tours by appointment. Call (415) 343-3631 for the Kohl house, and (415) 593-1601 for the Ralston. If you have time for a tour of only one Peninsula estate, however, skip both and go instead to the Filoli estate, described below.

A few minutes south of San Francisco, Skyline Boulevard and Highway 280 both skirt a long, north-south valley partially submerged under Upper and Lower **Crystal Springs reservoirs.** The San Andreas fault, responsible for the San Francisco earthquake of 1906, runs right up the valley floor, certainly the most visible section of fault line south of San Francisco. Part of the extensive San Francisco State Fish and Game Refuge, the lakes store water, piped from Hetch Hetchy Reservoir in the Sierra Nevada range, for San Francisco's use.

The supposed resemblance of Crystal Springs reservoirs to Ireland's Lakes of Killarney inspired one William Bourn II, in 1915, to build a fabulous 654-acre (265-ha) estate on its southernmost shore. (The fact that he was president of the water company no doubt provided further inspiration.) Bourn, who earned a big hunk of his fortune from his Empire gold mine in Grass Valley, California, named his mansion **Filoli**, an acronym of his motto: *Fi*ght, *Lo*ve, *Li*fe. Television viewers familiar with the Carrington estate on "Dynasty" already know some of its exquisite gardens and buildings.

Designed by Willis Polk, the mansion is a great pseudo-Georgian manor house set amidst ancient California oaks and unobstructed views of the distant hills. Tours visit the ground-floor kitchen, library, office, and dining rooms, dawdling longest in the gardens. These are a virtual Eden of blooms, trees, lawns, formal alleys, fountains, arbors, courts, and special gardens, such as the English knot garden, the Dutch garden, the Chartres garden (planted to resemble the cathedral window pattern), a sunken garden, and an extensive rose garden. Among the special trees are dawn redwoods, pomegranate, and avenues of Irish yew. Every season brings new blooms, though the peak season for color is probably March.

Filoli feels more like a living house than a museum. The busy gardeners in their slouch hats, the helpers in the kitchen, the small tea shop on the patio, and the gift shop in the carriage house fill the estate with life and purpose. Tours of Filoli run on Tuesday through Saturday, February through November; for the special Christmas tour in December, the house is festively decorated. Hikes along a nature trail leading through the estate are also scheduled. Reservations for all tours are essential; call

(415) 364-2880. There is a fee both for the tour and the nature hike. Surrounded by the game refuge, Filoli is on Canada Road, near Woodside.

Incidentally, you can get a bite to eat in the restaurants and coffee shops along Woodside Road in the wealthy community of **Woodside.** At the intersection of Tripp and Kings Mountain roads, the quaint Woodside Store, built in 1854 to serve the logging communities, has been turned into a pioneer museum.

Back down the hill toward the bay, the city of Menlo Park has three low-key stops of specialized interest. Map collectors may want to visit the retail offices of the **United States Geological Survey,** maker of detailed government maps, at 345 Middlefield Road. Nearby is the headquarters for *Sunset,* an innovative publisher of books and magazines specializing in travel, cooking, gardening, and home remodeling for residents of the western states. Their experimental gardens, workshops, and kitchens are open for tours on weekdays at the adobe showroom, on the corner of Middlefield and Willow roads; call (415) 321-3600 for details. A third site in Menlo Park is the **Allied Arts Guild,** a Spanish-style collection of special shops where crafts people display and sell their weaving, candles, pottery, painting, needlepoint, carpentry, and other arts. With attractive gardens and a small restaurant, the guild is at 75 Arbor Road.

Filoli's gardens are among the most ornate and sophisticated in the West.

One of the wealthiest, prettiest, and most stimulating cities of the Bay Area is **Palo Alto**, best known as the home of **Stanford University**. In marked contrast to the manic streets of Stanford's nemesis, Berkeley, the main commercial district of Palo Alto gathers handsomely along a clean, prosperous, charming, and eminently walkable thoroughfare, **University Avenue**. At its head, beyond the Caltrains railroad station, sprawls the Stanford campus—likewise a markedly different scene from Berkeley's, though each is consistently one of the highest-ranked universities in the nation.

The entrance to the campus always surprises first-time visitors with its natural vegetation of sparse, native oak, and wild weeds. Within these dry Elysian fields stands a lonely white **mausoleum**, guarded by sphinxes, encompassed by trees. Leland Stanford Jr., the namesake of the university, lies entombed therein with his parents. After you pass through this almost desolate landscape, the Main Quadrangle and Hoover Tower jump up with sudden, refreshing vigor. You can obtain a map of the grounds from the information desks to the left of the entrance to the Main Quad (as it's called) and at Tressider Union.

The **Main Quad** is the focus of the university, surrounded by symmetrical cloisters and buildings made of peach-colored sandstone, heavy, almost monastic, in feel. In the seat of honor basks **Stanford Memorial Church**, a Romanesque affair with brilliant murals and mosaics. Unfortunately, it was damaged in the Loma Prieta Earthquake, and remains closed.

The grounds are dominated by the 285-foot (87-m) square **Hoover Tower**, named after Herbert Hoover, probably Stanford's most prominent graduate. Visitors may ride to the top for an overview of the South Bay area. The Stanford University Art Gallery, exhibiting contemporary work, stands in front. Not far behind on White Plaza, you'll find the Stanford Bookstore, a gargantuan and lively emporium. On the western edge of the vast campus, you can take a tour of the Stanford Linear Accelerator—it's on Sand Hill Road in Menlo Park. Doll lovers will enjoy the extensive collection housed in the lobby of the Stanford Children's Hospital. Many of these are from the Shirley Temple Black collection, sent to the child film star by fans around the world.

Stanford University Museum of Art, the oldest museum in the American West, was built around a nucleus of curiosities collected by the younger Leland Stanford, who showed great promise as a budding antiquarian and archaeologist. One of his curious contraptions was a Megalethoscope, made in 1866. When you peek into the box and push a button, you can watch a cycle of day and night pass over Saint Mark's Square in Venice. Of great historical interest is the Golden Spike, kept under glass in a safe, and a shovel used to turn the first earth for the transcontinental railway. Note that it is stamped with the name of Mark Hopkins, who was a Sacramento hardware dealer (and shovel retailer) before he found his true calling as the Big Four's bean-counter. Take the time to inspect the Stanford family portraits, as well as collections of nineteenth- and twentieth-century European paintings and other works of art from Asia, the Pacific, Africa, the Americas, and classical Europe. One wing of the building and the outdoor Cantor Sculpture Garden are devoted to the work of Auguste Rodin, and particularly to details of his *Gates of Hell.* The museum was damaged in the Loma Prieta earthquake and has not yet opened.

While in Palo Alto, you might want to take in the **Barbie Hall of Fame,** a world-renowned collection of the best-selling Mattel doll. According to the museum proprietress, the museum is 99.8 percent complete. Here you can witness not only the evolution of Barbie, but the evolution of American style and social conscious since the fifties, from the original, girl-next-door, hand-painted, 1959 model, through rising and falling hemlines and hairdos, through the hippie and mod squad eras and the Jackie Kennedy-look, to the present post-Gulf War model in military fatigues. Here also you can contemplate the transfigurations of Barbie and her friends, including Ken, in all their professional, multi-racial, international, chrono-progressive, and socio-economic identities. Even if you've never played with Barbie, there's plenty here for an intriguing sociology thesis or two. This small, surprisingly captivating museum is just off University Avenue, at 460 Waverley.

Immediately south of Palo Alto, **Mountain View** nurtures one of the most strollable downtowns of any Bay Area city. Its new City Hall and Center for the Performing Arts, at Castro and Mercy streets, sets the elegant tone, which it carries down Castro Street by means of classy street-lamps and broad, clean, well-manicured sidewalks. Castro Street is noted for its score or more of excellent Mandarin (Beijing, Shanghai, and other northern cuisines) restaurants, making it a sure-fire winner for a cheap bowl of noodles or a banquet, without reservations. One of the Bay Area's glorious bookstores, Printer's Ink, attracts the crowds in for coffee, music and, of course, books till late at night. Find it at 301 Castro.

■ SILICON VALLEY

Less than one generation ago, the South Bay was a fertile land of walnut, apricot, and prune orchards. Now San Jose is the largest city in the Bay Area—yes, larger than San Francisco. Santa Clara, Sunnyvale, Cupertino, and other towns have

joined in a massive and complex grid of freeways, sprawling city blocks, parking lots, and malls that remind San Franciscans somewhat disconcertingly of Los Angeles. The metropolis is loosely linked under the name of Silicon Valley, in reference to the semiconductor and computer-chip industries that were largely pioneered here in the 1960s. Those were the days when the likes of Steve Jobs, Steve Wozniak (the dual behind Apple Computers), Bill Hewlett, and Dave Packard were working in garages, while John Warnock and Chuck Geschke created the first program for what was to become Adobe Systems in a home bedroom. Hewlett-Packard, Apple Computer, and Lockheed keep their headquarters in Silicon Valley.

Where Silicon Valley actually starts and ends is anybody's guess, but you can recognize it by its general modernity, the monolithic high-tech electronics plants, wide highways, and new business hotels and restaurants. Silicon Valley rides a wave of economic prosperity, but as far as tourism is concerned, points of interest tend to be few and far between. This is not to say that the South Bay lacks charm. Saratoga, for one, is an elegant, tree-shaded city. San Jose, which was California's state capital from 1849 to 1851, is a venerable Spanish-era city, linked by the tree-lined Alameda to the mission of Santa Clara de Asis.

A good warm-up for Silicon Valley is a visit to Foothill College in Los Altos Hills, which can be reached by following signs from Highway 280. Foothill is a pretty campus, noted for its Japanese Culture Center, where traditional arts of Japan (including the tea ceremony) are faithfully practiced. The **Electronics Museum** here dwells on an age of invention before the computer chip, when television tubes were state-of-the-art. Vintage broadcasting equipment, TVs, radios, and telephones on display will make old-timers wax nostalgic, and may give youngsters a new perspective on what people did before video games were invented. The museum charges a small entrance fee, and is open Thursdays and Fridays, and on weekend afternoons.

With some planning, you can also see what's cooking at the NASA (National Aeronautics and Space Administration) **Ames Research Center** at Moffett Field near Mountain View. As might be expected, the theme here is the mechanics of flight. Scientists employ a score of wind tunnels (including the world's largest) and computers to test new aircraft designs. Visitors are welcome on free, escorted tours, but reservations are mandatory and should be made two to three weeks in advance. There are two tours per week; call (415) 604-5000. Children under nine years old are not allowed. Don't forget to visit the gift shop before you leave.

Stanford Memorial Church reflects both Californian and Byzantine influences.

Visitors may experience the sensation of flying at northern California's answer to Disneyland: **Great America**. People come here for many reasons, and none more compelling than to challenge some of the country's most stomach-wrenching roller coasters, like the double-corkscrew Demon, the Tidal Wave (which does a full loop forwards and backwards), the Vortex (where you ride *standing up*), and the guaranteed-to-get-you-wet Rip Roaring Rapids. Grandma, toddlers, and wimps, meanwhile, can play on the gentler rides, visit the theme sections, watch a movie on the country's largest theater screen, and chat with the likes of Bugs Bunny and Fred Flintstone. A single admission ticket lets you do it all. You'll find the park at 1 Great America Parkway, Santa Clara.

South Bay summers, far removed from Frisco's fogs, are hot enough to make a hit of another theme park called **Raging Waters**, at 2333 South White Road in San Jose. Bring your swim suit to try the water slides.

Reconstructed **Mission Santa Clara de Asis** now stands on the campus of the University of Santa Clara. This mission was noted for having the largest population of any in old California. Founded in 1851, the university is the oldest in the state. Its flower gardens, trees, and the old adobe wall behind the church retain a charming, old mission flavor, though no doubt its bucolic days were hardly so immaculate. See for yourself at the campus **de Saisset Museum**, principally an art gallery with a history section downstairs.

Of spookier interest is the **Winchester Mystery House**, a legacy of the superstitious heiress of the Winchester Repeating Rifle fortune. Sarah Winchester commenced building the house in response to a fortuneteller's prophecy that she would live only while the house remained unfinished. The clincher was that this revenge would be meted out by the spirits of people gunned down by the Winchester rifle, who would . . . well, we're not quite sure *what*, but something *terrible*. The bottom line is that Mrs. Winchester made sure her carpenters kept busy 24 hours a day for 38 years, until she died. The result is something really weird: a 160-room monstrosity with some 2,000 doors and 10,000 windows, stairs that lead nowhere, secret passages, and sealed doorways. The tour guides milk the story for all it's worth—and who can blame them? The house is intriguing and, naturally, is said to be haunted. Go to 525 South Winchester Boulevard, in San Jose. Tours are given daily. A firearms museum is adjacent.

Far fewer tourists ever find their way to the **Rosicrucian Egyptian Museum**, the largest collection of Egyptian antiquities in the western United States. Aside from a large collection of mummies (including a cat, bird, snake, fish, and of course, people), dioramas of pyramids and ancient cities, and displays of Egyptian, Sumerian, Babylonian, Assyrian, and Persian artifacts, the museum houses the only full-sized reproduction of an Egyptian rock tomb in the Western Hemisphere. Winding your way down the dark, narrow passages to a ransacked burial chamber is exciting and a little eerie. The Rosicrucian Science Museum and Planetarium is next door. The Egyptian Museum is open daily from Tuesday to Friday, and during the afternoon on weekends and Mondays. A moderate admission fee is charged. It is located in Rosicrucian Park on Park Avenue at Naglee.

Downtown San Jose is a gracious blend of old-time and high-tech styles. The opera, museums, theater, restaurants, main library, hotels, offices, parks, and convention center all congregate within the few downtown blocks between Almaden and Second streets, and from San Carlos to Santa Clara. The campus of the California State University at San Jose starts two blocks east, on Fourth Street. Downtown San Jose's clean, handsome streets and plazas invite walkers; pick up a map and directions at the San Jose Metropolitan Chamber of Commerce, at 180 South Market Street. If you don't feel like walking, ride one of the airy cars on the new light rail system.

Among the congenial surprises in the Spanish mode is the brick-paved El Paseo Court, with its fountain and tiles and colorful South American handicrafts hanging from the balcony of the Machu Picchu Gallery. Around the corner on San Fernando Street, the patio restaurant of the Gordon Biersch Brewing Company always attracts a crowd on typically balmy South Bay days. The shiny, new, open-air mall called **The Pavilion**, on Park between First and Second, provides alfresco tables.

Two landmarks of old San Jose stand on opposite corners of San Fernando and Market streets. The graceful copper domes and stately pillars of **St. Joseph's Cathedral** were raised in 1877 and renovated in 1991. The handsome, sandstone Post Office Building, a historical landmark from 1892, now houses the **San Jose Museum of Art**. Expanding into a new wing in 1991, the gallery hosts world-class traveling exhibits and a well-stocked gallery store.

The **Children's Discovery Museum**, a mere stroll from downtown San Jose at the corner of West San Carlos and Woz Way, is a walloping adventure for kids, who can explore the structure of a city by sliding down a sewer pipe, commandeering the stoplights, sending messages by pneumatic tube, and taking over the dentist's office, theater dressing room, fire engine, and waterworks. As wonderful as it is for kids, however, adult interests generally start flagging here faster than they do at the Exploratorium, the Lawrence Hall of Science, and The Garage, all of which are geared for older attention spans.

Fortunately, **The Garage** is only just up the street at 145 West San Carlos. You know you've arrived at an enthralling spot even before walking in the door. One glance at the kinetic sculpture *Imaginative Chip* and you're caught for at least 30 minutes watching billiard balls bounce and coil and fly through a maze of track, chiming gongs as they pass.

It only gets better. Inside you can maneuver a spacecraft through a simulated exploration of Mars, run experiments on new materials, command a robot to pour coffee or clean up a kitchen mess, see how a silicon chip is made, and design an aerodynamically improved bicycle. The museum, which is being temporarily housed here while a larger building can be built, showcases the history of Silicon Valley technology.

History of a different era is preserved at the **San Jose Historical Museum**, on the south side of Kelly Park. Many historic buildings from old San Jose have been removed to this site (or built from original plans) to give a feeling of the earlier days. You can poke through Gianinni's first Bank of Italy (Gianinni was born in San Jose), sip a soda at O'Brien's Soda Fountain, or inspect the equipment at the livery stable and old firehouse. The post office houses the first radio station in the United States—KQW—which was licensed in San Jose in 1912. A number of furnished farmhouses capture the rare scent of Victorian times. The park also preserves a vintage gas

The rugged San Mateo coast contains many wild beaches and coves.

station, smithy, dentist parlor, and—soon—a temple from San Jose's Chinatown. There is an excellent bookstore behind the soda fountain, specializing in history and regional travel. Pay an entrance fee at the park gate.

Another exciting destination, especially for older children, is the observatory atop the 4,209-foot (1,283-m) summit of Mount Hamilton, east of San Jose. **Lick Observatory** was built with funds from San Francisco millionaire, James Lick, who is buried beneath the largest telescope. At its founding, it was the world's first permanently staffed observatory, and its 36-inch (91-cm) refracting telescope had no peer. It still works fine, but the smog and bright lights of the city below interfere with viewing. The visitors' gallery is open daily, but it is more interesting to come for the Friday evening summer programs, between mid-July and mid-September, when some telescopes are open for public viewing.

You confront a less benevolent face of high technology at the Wall of Garbage, the centerpiece of **The Recyclery**, at 1601 Dixon Landing Road, in Milpitas. The Wall represents the amount of garbage an average person throws away in six years. The theme of this small museum, built on the edge of the Newby Island landfill, is the virtue of recycling. Exhibits show what happens to garbage when it is recycled—a real eye-opener for anyone who wonders just what they do with all those used plastic soda bottles. In another demonstration, kids aim a laser at different pieces of garbage on the wall, and zap them to find out which are recyclable.

Saratoga, nestled against the Santa Cruz Mountains, is a wealthy, genteel town. Its main street, Big Basin Way, is a delightful place to dine or shop for sweet nothings. San Francisco's ex-Mayor James Phelan, a devoted patron of the arts, chose the hills behind town to build his estate, which he called **Villa Montalvo**. When he died, his will directed that Villa Montalvo be used henceforth to promote the arts and artists. He would be happy today to see what his trustees have done with the beautiful Italian country house. It's now a retreat for artists, musicians, and writers with work in progress. The Mediterranean gardens and pavilions are used to stage plays, poetry readings and concerts. The gardens are open daily and have no admission fee. The art gallery charges a nominal entrance fee, and is open on weekends and on Thursday and Friday afternoons. Villa Montalvo is at 15400 Montalvo Road, in Saratoga; call (408) 741-3421 for events.

Another variation on the sylvan mood is struck in **Hakone Japanese Garden**, one of the most authentic ever created outside Japan. Built on a steep hill where a small artificial creek cascades into the pond, the garden draws visitors in quietly, soothing their senses with gentle sound and beauty. Secluded pavilions invite guests to sit and relax, or to have tea. The garden was designed in 1917 by a master Japanese gardener, Mr. Shintani, on principles of design popular in seventeenth-century Japan. The garden, at 21000 Big Basin Way, is open daily.

In addition to its fruit orchards, Santa Clara Valley was also once a major wine-producing region. Today, development has put much of the vineyard acreage to retreat, but some historic wineries continue to do business. One of the oldest is **Mirassou winery**, still run by the Mirassou family, as it has since Pierre Mirassou became a vintner in 1881. The winery is at 3000 Aborn Road, on the eastern side of San Jose.

■ THE SAN MATEO COAST

The western side of the Peninsula is one of the Bay Area's richest treasures. Though developers keep pecking away at Half Moon Bay, the fact that so much of these coastal ranges remain rural and wild is truly a wonderful benefit of their ruggedness.

Sweeney Ridge, which climbs out of Pacifica on the coast south of San Francisco, is the southernmost outpost of the Golden Gate National Recreation Area. A trail leads up to the site where Portola's men first saw San Francisco Bay, a sight today much changed but no less spectacular. While in the Linda Mar section of Pacifica, you may want to see the two-story adobe built by San Francisco's *alcade* (mayor), Francisco Sanchez, in the early 1840s, as the headquarters of his huge cattle ranch. The house, now set in a park at 1000 Linda Mar Boulevard, is open Tuesday through Thursday, and on weekend afternoons.

Montara Mountain falls abruptly into the sea at **Devil's Slide**, a very unstable and narrow bit of Highway 1 south of Pacifica. From there, Highway 1 pushes south above the crawling Pacific, past a continuous string of beaches and coves under state park protection. Swimming at any of these is never warm, and almost always dangerous, until you get to Santa Cruz. Aside from a few daring surfers in wet suits, most locals come here for the scenery, sunbathing, and picnicking.

Gray Whale Cove State Beach, reached by a stairway from Highway 1, is popular among nude sunbathers. Next door, long Montara State Beach is crowded on hot weekends. Beyond the 1875 **Montara Lighthouse** (site of a 35-bed youth hostel), the tide pools of Moss Beach stretch down the coast to Pillar Point. The pools are great places for kids to study crabs, starfish, anemones, and other sea creatures at low tide—but remind your explorers not to remove anything. Nature walks are arranged for those who care to join.

Half Moon Bay curves gracefully beyond Pillar Point, providing several popular beaches for picnickers and a working fishing harbor on the north end at **Princeton-by-the-Sea**. When the fishing fleet comes in, you can watch them unloading salmon, flounder, rockfish, and sole at the Princeton pier.

The town of **Half Moon Bay**, settled mostly by Portuguese and Italian farmers and fishermen, still has the salty flavor of a seacoast village along its main street. The saltiness has been somewhat sweetened in recent years with bed-and-breakfasts, restaurants, and galleries. The town is famed for its pumpkins, celebrated in the October Pumpkin Festival, when visitors carve jack-o'-lanterns, inspect the heftiest monsters, and eat whatever it is that one makes out of pumpkin, including pie. Local stables rent horses, and some of the beaches have campgrounds.

The country grows leaner south of town, giving way to windswept hamlets, farm roads, empty beaches (on the typically foggy days of summer), and the ever-present crash of breakers. Winding roads crawl up the canyons and through fog-nurtured woods to the ridge at Skyline Boulevard. Mountain creeks dash down to the coast through secluded valleys and across the beaches. San Gregorio, Pomponio, Pescadero, Bean Hollow, and Gazos Creek state beaches are always beautiful to look at, but usually too brisk for anything less than long pants and sweaters.

Several mountain parks climb the canyons and crown the hills. Up La Honda Road (and also reached from Skyline Boulevard), **Portola State Park** and the county parks of Pescadero Creek, Sam McDonald, and San Mateo Memorial welcome hikers through bosky forests of redwood, Douglas fir, oak, and huckleberries. The rustic village of **La Honda**, a favorite hangout of Ken Kesey and the Merry Pranksters during the sixties, still keeps an alternative air about it. Another redwood preserve with camping, **Butano State Park**, is hidden on the Cloverdale Road, near Pescadero.

A tiny town settled largely by Portuguese farmers, **Pescadero** is noted for its artichokes. You can—in fact, you *should*—try the fried artichoke hearts at Dinelli's (which serves Greek, not Portuguese, food). The artichoke soup at Duarte's Tavern is reported to be excellent, too.

Pigeon Point lighthouse, 15 miles (25 km) south of Half Moon Bay, is one of the tallest in the country, and a sight to soothe sore New England eyes. Its 115-foot (35-m) tower is open to visitors on Sundays, and the buildings at its foot serve as a youth hostel. The lighthouse took its name from the nearby wreck of the *Carrier Pigeon* in 1853.

Easily the most astounding sight along the San Mateo coast is the elephant seals of **Año Nuevo State Reserve**. Lest you think these creatures are the sleek black mammals you see tossing beach balls with their noses on TV, dispel the notion. The adult males, with their bulbous noses that give them their name, can grow as long as 20 feet (6 m) and weigh as much as 6,000 pounds (2,700 kg). (Just take a look at the life-size model in the wild California Hall at the Academy of Sciences in Golden Gate Park!) But just because they are big, don't think they can't move with amazing speed and agility if they don't take a liking to you.

Visitors are truly in sea elephant territory at Año Nuevo. They have to walk a mile and a half (2.5 km), much of it over shifting sand dunes, just to get to the shore. Rangers are on hand to answer questions and keep you from straying too close. The sight of these primordial giants hauled up on the beach, fighting, mating, or even just sleeping, is astounding.

The sea elephants are not present all year round. Females start arriving in December, and stay till May; males are found here between June and September. Human impact on the scene is controlled by permits. Reservations are advisable during mating season, from December through March; call (415) 879-0595, or buy permits in advance from Ticketron. The rest of the year, you can simply pick up a permit from the park ranger station between 8 a.m. and 4 p.m., on a first-come, first-served basis. At the interpretation center on the grounds, the ranger will answer your questions and prepare you for the outing.

■ SANTA CRUZ COUNTY

Heading south from Año Nuevo, you soon cross the Santa Cruz County line. The county seat and namesake, **Santa Cruz**, about 35 miles (56 km) south of the park, was once the summer resort capital of northern California.

Santa Cruz sustained major damage in the earthquake of 1989, but even before that, it was suffering from sprawl, traffic, and an excess of motels and fast-food restaurants. Still, it is well worth visiting for its mile-long (1.6-km) beach and Boardwalk. The swimming at this beach is about the safest in northern California.

The **Boardwalk** is a piece of Americana, one of the last of its kind, where you still can chew on saltwater taffy, dance at the Coconut Grove ballroom, play the penny arcades, and ride the bumper cars and carousel. Best of all is The Giant Dipper, a vintage roller coaster. This wooden behemoth has been blowing lunches since 1923, and is ranked by aficionados as one of the best in the country. The Boardwalk is open daily in summer, and weekends in winter, from 11 a.m.; call (408) 426-7433 for the latest.

The **Santa Cruz Municipal Pier** anchors down the northern end of the Boardwalk. Reaching a half mile (.8 km) into the bay, it attracts hordes of hopeful fishermen. In case you strike out, there are plenty of fish in the restaurants that line the side.

Another Santa Cruz attraction is the **Surfing Museum** in the lighthouse at Lighthouse Point. The museum overlooks a favored surfing spot called Steamer Lane. The legend is that the sport was brought to Santa Cruz around 1885 by two Hawaiian princes. The locals learned the art aboard 100-pound (45-kg), handmade, redwood surfboards. The boards are on display in the museum.

The Santa Cruz branch of the **University of California** is sequestered in a redwood forest on a hill above the city. The secluded campus feels more like a convention retreat than a high-powered university. Take a stroll around, with a stop for coffee or lunch in one of the many woodsy dining rooms.

Arching between Silicon Valley and Santa Cruz, the Santa Cruz Mountains give shady respite from the summery lowlands. They are not so high as to escape the heat, but even on the hottest days, the redwood forests and creeks impart a coolness of the mind.

The most direct route through the mountains is Highway 17 from San Jose and Los Gatos, but it's fast and no fun at all. From Saratoga, Highway 9 leads past Hakone Gardens and into the redwoods. A more leisurely route down the Peninsula is by Skyline Boulevard, turning right (southwest) at the intersection of Highway 9.

The largest redwood preserve in the mountains, and one of the oldest and most beloved of all Bay Area state parks, is **Big Basin**. Its huge, cool forests invite strollers and more serious hikers through the mountains to waterfalls and ferny valleys. You can also bicycle the 14-mile (23-km) dirt road through the park to the sea; bikes and guides are available for rent. The giant groves near the entrance shade picnic tables and campgrounds. Deer like to graze in the nearby meadows during the evening.

Another wonderful redwood forest is preserved in **Henry Cowell Redwoods State Park.** Broad sections of it reach through the mountains clear to the University of California at Santa Cruz, but the main grove is just south of Felton on Highway 9. Lacking the crowds of Muir Woods, it is one of the best places in the Bay Area to sense the majesty of the coastal redwood forests. As in most redwood parks, visitors tend to be most impressed by the oddities of nature, like the walkthrough Clothespin Tree and the Grizzly Giant. The most amazing tree of all is the John C. Frémont Tree, named after the ambitious soldier who camped here in 1846, and whose presence forced the American seizure of California from Mexico. The tree is hollow. After crouching through the low entrance, allow a couple of minutes to adjust your eyes to the dark. You will see then that the room inside this living tree is large enough to shelter several people standing up.

In 1875, a freight railroad line was built up the San Lorenzo River from Santa Cruz to Felton. The tracks still pass through Henry Cowell's redwood forests, but today the **Roaring Camp Railway** hauls passengers, who have a choice between chugging up the steepest railroad grade in North America to the top of Bear Mountain, or down through the forested San Lorenzo River canyon to the Boardwalk in Santa Cruz. The trains make the spectacular round-trip journey to Santa Cruz twice a day during summer, and several trips daily up the shorter, steeper line to Bear Mountain. Trains also run on weekends and holidays the rest of the year, except from November to March. The depot is only a short stroll from Henry Cowell park headquarters, but the main entrance and parking lot is on Graham Hill Road, east of Felton. You can buy sweets, rail books, snacks, and souvenirs from the general store near the depot, or join the organized barbecues held in the picnic grounds on weekends from May through October. With the redwoods, the steam trains, and the Santa Cruz Boardwalk, this day trip is hard to beat for families with kids.

One of the odder tourist destinations in the Santa Cruz Mountains is the **Mystery Spot,** three miles (five km) north of Santa Cruz, at 1953 Branciforte Drive. Here, according to guides and your own perceptions, a mysterious force distorts the laws of gravity. Water flows uphill; optical illusions play havoc with your senses. Children and gullible adults will marvel at it, and even the hardheaded should enjoy figuring out how it's done. (If you need a hint, take a look at the optical illusion display at the Exploratorium.)

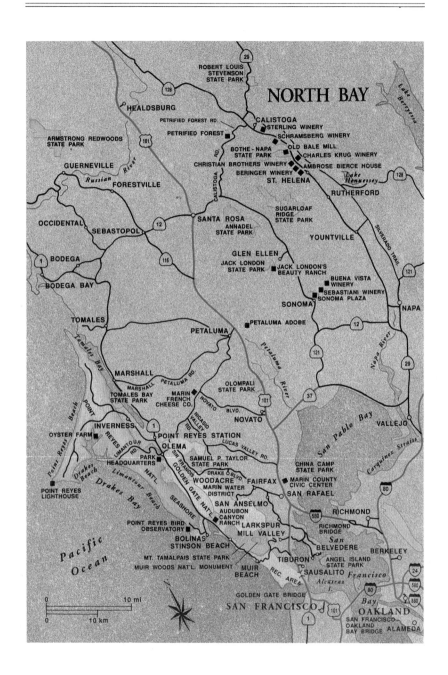

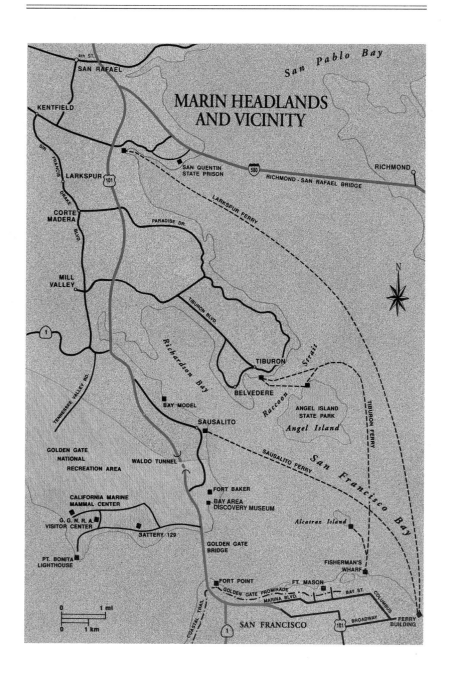

THE NORTH BAY

AMONG SAN FRANCISCO'S MANY RARE ENDOWMENTS, there's none more wonderful than the ease with which you can leave the town. The perfect escape is north, across the Golden Gate or on the splendid little ferries. Whether your tastes run to seascape or mountain scenery, backpack trails or tea in a cultivated setting, sensational shopping or oyster shucking, gargantuan feasting or wine and cheese sampling, you can start your vacation within minutes of leaving San Francisco.

■ MARIN HEADLANDS

The dramatic cliffs of Marin County, rising above the northern shore of the Golden Gate, are known as the Marin Headlands. The military early on commandeered these strategic heights, closing them to the public, and thus preserving them from development. When modern technology rendered their gun batteries obsolete, the army retreated gracefully, leaving the land most fortunately in the hands of the Golden Gate National Recreation Area.

Stark, windy and rugged, the Marin Headlands offer ravishing views, solitude, seasonal wildflowers, and a handful of interesting military sites to explore. There are hike-in campgrounds, wildlife tours, and guided walks through the bunkers and garrisons. The headlands fall into two sections, divided by Highway 101. Fort Baker is on the east, on low ground hemmed between the Bay and the Golden Gate Bridge. Forts Barry and Cronkhite, a considerable chunk of land, roll clear from the highway to the Pacific breakers. For information about park events, inquire at the visitor center in Fort Cronkhite's converted chapel on Field Road, or at park headquarters in Fort Mason, San Francisco. You can also check the quarterly newspaper, *Park Events*, or call (415) 556-0560.

Though lacking the wild splendor of Cronkhite and Barry, **Fort Baker** has its quiet charms. Military buffs might well imagine the thrumming chords of the cavalry march, by gazing upon the old, white-frame officers' housing built around the parade ground, now grown weedy. The gun batteries on the shore are fun to explore, and you can walk out to the Lime Point lighthouse for an ungentlemanly view of the underside of the Golden Gate Bridge. To reach Fort Baker, drive north on the bridge, past the vista point, and exit at Alexander Avenue. Turn left at the second intersection, and then right, down the hill toward the bay.

Some of the old Fort Baker buildings have been converted to the **Bay Area Discovery Museum**, an educational romp for children. They can, for instance, climb over a make-shift fishing boat, crawl through an "undersea tunnel," investigate glassed-in, working models of plumbing fixtures, and sketch on a drafting table. There's a science store and cafeteria. This museum, absorbing for kids, is as yet much smaller than the San Jose version.

The scenery in the headlands west of Highway 1 is more exciting. The only way into the western headlands at present is by **Conzelman Road**. To get there, exit Highway 101 at Alexander, cut under the freeway at the first intersection, and swing right up Conzelman. This is a perfectly good, two-lane road, but it twists and turns so high above the sea that flatland drivers may find it disconcerting. Park in one of the several turnouts for stunning views of the great bridge looming offshore, beneath the cliffs, and San Francisco framed between its towers. When the fog comes in, this is, quite simply, the most sublime cityscape this side of Jupiter. For rarer views, a footpath winds down to Kirby Cove.

These hills beyond Conzelman are peppered with gun emplacements. Two of the most interesting batteries are right ahead by the side of the road. The largest is **Construction 129**, which was built in World War II to accommodate two massive million-pound, 16-inch guns (ca. 450 MT, 410 mm). Park on the turnout and walk through the tunnel to the empty carriage well, overlooking the Pacific. The guns intended to fit this battery were designed to lob 2,100-pound (950-kg) shells 27 miles (43 km) out to sea. For better or worse, the rapid advance of aircraft technology during the war rendered them obsolete, and they were abandoned before they were finished.

Rodeo Beach (or Cronkhite Beach, as some call it) is washed by seas too rough for all but expert swimmers. Trails lead out from here over the hills to the north and south, and around Rodeo Lagoon, a favorite of bird-watchers. Guano-covered Bird Rock glowers offshore like a great white whale. On the rise above the lagoon, the **California Marine Mammal Center** operates a hospital for sick and orphaned seals and sea lions. Staffed largely by volunteers, the center runs a small nature store, and is open to the public daily, when visitors can view the patients inside their recovery pens.

The most exhilarating short walk in the Marin Headlands leads to **Point Bonita Lighthouse**, the last lighthouse in California that was tended by a human keeper.

This half-mile (.8-km) trail starts at the marked parking area on Field Road, a short drive beyond the visitor center. Descending a good path on the rocky cape, stupendous views of the sea and the Gate fall away on either side. Passing through a tunnel chiseled by hand in 1877, you emerge on the ocean side of the rocks, then cross to Point Bonita on a shaky wooden suspension bridge built in 1954, after waves washed away the original path. The bridge is open to only five people at a time. Waves breaking on the rocks below add to the excitement.

The present lighthouse was built in 1877 on a rocky ledge above rough seas at the mouth of the Golden Gate. It is now controlled automatically. The lens, built in France by Frensel in 1855, weighs 300 tons (272 MT), and was considered a technological marvel in its day. The light, visible from 18.5 miles (30 km) out to sea, is now bolstered by an automatic foghorn. When it was first built, the lighthouse keeper had to fire a cannon every 30 minutes in foggy weather. The *Point Bonita Times*, a newspaper published by the GGNRA, records the stories of some actual shipwrecks in these waters, and describes the lonely life of the lighthouse keeper in times past; pick up a copy at the visitor center. The GGNRA trail guide to the Marin Headlands notes that a Coast Guard officer reported 130-foot (40-m) waves breaking over the stubby lighthouse in 1967.

Houseboats at Sausalito

During weekdays, the path is closed to the general public at the tunnel. Rangers open the tunnel gate from 12:30 to 4:30 p.m. on weekends, March through October. Because of rough weather during the rest of the year, guides lead the tours, starting at the tunnel on weekends at 1 p.m. Rangers also organize occasional sunset and full moon tours; phone (415) 331-1540 for information.

Not all the GGNRA trails start in the south. One popular trail begins at the end of Tennessee Valley Road (which starts near Tamalpais Valley Junction) and runs two miles (3.2 km) to splendidly isolated **Tennessee Beach**, named for the ship that ran aground here in 1853. Other trails fan out over the ridges to more remote parts of the park, with connections to Mount Tamalpais and Point Reyes.

■ SAUSALITO

Tourist promoters like to compare Sausalito to the Riviera. A certain visual similarity exists, but don't expect warm beaches and bikinis. Built on a steep, wooded hillside tumbling straight into the deep, blue bay, Sausalito *is* a pretty sight. Yachts and houseboats crowd its harbors, and a carefree air of leisure plays about its shops and restaurants.

Sausalito has not always been thought a pretty face. During the Second World War, it was a major shipyard. In the Depression, the town was a haven for bootleggers. At the turn of the century, it was full of rough-and-ready waterfront bars and gambling parlors. Today, Sausalito has become a little precious. The colorful old buildings remain, but too many of them are in the T-shirt and knickknack business. Though by no means as rampant as Fisherman's Wharf, it is awfully crowded with tourists on weekends.

Still, Sausalito has managed to keep its charm. If you come on a weekday morning, especially, you can enjoy the town with room to breathe. But even if you can only come on a weekend, the ferry ride alone is worth the trip.

Sausalito can be reached by car from Highway 101, but parking will likely be troublesome. Certainly the prettiest arrivals and departures are by regular ferry from the San Francisco Ferry Building at the foot of Market Street. Seasoned commuters on board wind down at the bar, but the view from the top deck, with a bracing wind, is much more exhilarating. Pick up a schedule at the pier.

The main street of Sausalito is **Bridgeway**, which runs parallel to the shore, intersected by stairs and steep residential streets from on high. The old town center gathers near the ferry pier. Across the parking lot stands Plaza Vina del Mar, a small park dedicated to Sausalito's Chilean sister city. The twin elephants holding up the lampposts were salvaged from San Francisco's 1915 Panama Pacific Exhibition.

Cross Bridgeway to Village Fair, a large old garage converted into a mall of boutiques, toy stores, housewares, and other shops. Interior stairs lead to pretty little patios and overlooks. El Monte Lane climbs up the side to Bulkley Avenue and the Alta Mira Hotel, a rambling weekend resort for San Franciscans (and anyone else) in need of a change of pace. Nearby, the Casa Madrona Hotel cushions guests in Victorian rooms with romantic views over the bay.

Walking south on Bridgeway from the Plaza, you can wander for hours through the shops and galleries, admire the classy views of San Francisco across the Bay, and partake of the restaurants and watering holes. Bridgeway opens to the sea at **Yee Tock Chee Park**, named for a beloved Sausalitan grocer who steadfastly honored his customers' credit through the cash-poor years of the Great Depression, saving many from going hungry. Bridgeway hugs the shore beyond, a delightful walk past scuttling crabs and a bronze, rock-bound seal, within constant view of the spires and towers of San Francisco.

Sausalito's most absorbing sight is the **Bay Model**, at 2100 Bridgeway, at the northern end of town. Built by the Army Corps of Engineers to study the effects of engineering projects in the bay and local river systems, the model is a gigantic working map of the Bay Area. You won't see all the familiar *land*marks, but the shape and dynamics of the bay and its tributaries are produced accurately, right down to the tides, currents, salinity, and sedimentation. (The only compromise in accuracy is that the Delta and the Sacramento and San Joaquin rivers had to be bent above the Carquinez Straits to fit into the building.)

The Bay Model is a fascinating piece of engineering. Its scale and complexity are downright amazing. As the rivers and streams flow at one-tenth their actual velocity, the tide rolls through an entire cycle in 15 minutes, a month of tides in 7.2 hours. You can watch the salt collecting on the mud flats of the South Bay, or inspect the prevailing flow of water through the bay's shipping channels and submarine canyons. A look at the sunken islands of the delta will show in an instant the disastrous effects of a broken dike. The Army Corps of Engineers has done a magnificent job of presenting the model to the public, with interpretive displays, elevated walkways and recorded explanations. The few other exhibits on display pale in comparison to the model itself. The model is open Tuesday through Saturday. Entrance is free.

The *Wapama*, last of the Pacific coast steam schooners, sits outside the Bay Model visitor center. She looks the part of a tough tramp steamer, reflecting a hard life in the lumber trade at the turn of the century. Now part of the National Maritime Museum, the Wapama is dry-docked indefinitely until funds for repairs can be raised, allowing her to rejoin the other ships at San Francisco's Hyde Street pier. In the meantime, there are weekend tours and work parties for volunteers who want to help with the restoration.

At the north end of Bridgeway, drivers can rejoin Highway 101; cut under the highway to Mill Valley, Muir Woods, and Mount Tamalpais, or branch off to the scenic, two-lane coastal byway, Highway 1.

■ MOUNT TAMALPAIS

Mill Valley started life as a lumber camp on the slopes of Mount Tamalpais. When the first-growth redwoods had been felled, the loggers moved on, while city people built summer homes among the new growth trees. Today, the trees have grown tall again, and summer people now live here all year round. And who can blame them? Mill Valley is one of the nicest little towns in the state, as pretty for walkers as Sausalito, but catering more to community than tourists.

The center of town, where Miller and Throckmorton streets meet, is a redwood-shaded widening in the road called Lytton Square. Homey shops and restaurants stand comfortably about, like small-town gents genially swapping stories at the general store. The streets wander with the contours, hardly ever keeping a straight line, ambling over a creek here, a wooded gulch there, disappearing up a stairway into the forest. Mill Valley has a woodsy, yet bustling atmosphere—a prosperous mountain town. Local artists and backpackers pass on the sidewalks. Coffeehouses like the Book Depot, which doubles as a bookstore, do a thriving business.

The 6.8-mile (11-km) **Dipsea Trail**, darting over the shoulder of Mount Tamalpais to Stinson Beach, starts at Lytton Square. Its famous climb of almost 700 steps out of Mill Valley, between Cascade Way and Edgewood Avenue, has

knocked the wind, if not the will, out of generations of hikers. The Chamber of Commerce next to the Book Depot on Lytton Square can point you in the right direction.

You can reach both **Mount Tam** (as the locals call Mount Tamalpais) and Muir Woods from Mill Valley via Montford, Molino, Edgewood, and Sequoia roads, but the route is not easy to find without a good map. Ask for directions at the Chamber of Commerce, and if it looks intimidating, backtrack to Tamalpais Junction and take Highway 1, turning off on the Panoramic Highway three miles (4.8 km) from the junction. The road to Muir Woods National Monument swings south (left) a mile (1.6 km) farther; just follow the signs.

Muir Woods is a mossy treasure, a grove of ancient redwoods untouched by lumberjacks. Being the closest grove to San Francisco, it receives a huge number of visitors throughout the year. Trail guides are printed in several languages, and parking is formidable. Though in some ways prettier than the Santa Cruz mountain groves at Henry Cowell and Big Basin state parks—for one thing, there are fewer grotesques—the crowds distract from the peaceful contemplation of some of nature's greatest handiworks. But if you come early on a weekday, or on a rainy day, or if you take some of the longer trails, Muir Woods is an enchanting place.

Coast redwoods are the tallest living things, but the loftiest tree in Muir Woods—a paltry 252 feet (76.8 m)—is a good hundred feet (30 m) shorter than the noblest specimens growing in Redwood National Park, up the California coast. Still, it is impressive to keep in mind that if this same 252-foot tree were growing on the surface of San Francisco Bay, it would poke about 32 feet (10 m) higher than the roadway of the Golden Gate Bridge. Redwoods can live beyond a thousand years, but few of the trees in Muir Woods are a day over 800.

Muir Woods National Monument has a small visitors' center, gift shop and cafeteria. The park has no entrance fee. The short, gentle walks through the groves along the valley floor are easy for just about everyone. More strenuous hikes connect the park with Mount Tamalpais State Park and the GGNRA.

Mount Tamalpais is San Francisco's Mount Olympus—a sylvan backdrop to countless cityscapes, an inspiration to writers and artists, an almost pagan symbol of nature worship for generations of city hikers. For the latter are some 250 miles of trails through peaks and meadows, along mountain creeks, down redwood canyons and to the sea. The park also offers camping and picnicking, and is popular with mountain-bike riders.

A road winds up to a point near the 2,571-foot (784-m) summit of East Peak. At the Pantoll junction, you can get a trail map from the ranger station. For the summit, continue right (north) up Pantoll Road to East Ridgecrest Boulevard, and thence to the top. The view, over the Pacific and the bay, down canyons to Point Reyes and south to San Francisco and beyond, is extraordinary.

A classic half-day hike meanders some 6.5 soothing miles (10.5 km) from the **Mountain Theater** parking lot, above the Pantoll junction, to the West Point Inn, and back. En route, you pass through the great stone amphitheater, lyrically ensconced like an ancient Greek ruin on slopes of oak and madrone. In the best old world mountaineering traditions, **West Point Inn** offers tea (and lemonade) to hikers on its wooden porch. Floating far off to the southeast, the inconsequential towers of San Francisco fade before the more demanding flurry of a blue jay, begging for your sandwich. Rustic accommodations are available to those who reserve them at least 10 days in advance; call (415) 388-9955.

■ Highway 1 to Point Reyes

Highway 1 is California's coastal highway. Except for a few sections, it is a two-lane affair that follows the integrity of the land—it winds and dips pretty much as the hills and coastline dictate. Between San Francisco and Eureka on Highway 1, there are no cities. Small towns, plunked down every few miles, have food and lodging, frequently in a beautiful setting. There is something redolent of New England in their simple white-frame farmhouses and churches, yet something also distinctively Californian in the sheltering cypress trees, the orderly rows of eucalyptus, and the stark hills of yellow grass in summer, green in winter.

Many artists are drawn to these coastal towns—not only painters, but furniture makers, potters, weavers, writers, and photographers. A brochure listing galleries along Highway 1, "Marin Coastal Arts Trail," is available from the West Marin Chamber of Commerce in the Creamery Building, Point Reyes Station; call (415) 663-9232. Another handy source of travelers' information is a free newspaper, *Coastal Traveler*, which lists campgrounds, bed-and-breakfast inns, stables, festivals, and restaurants, and publishes articles on the history and culture of West Marin. Keep an eye out for it in hotels and visitor centers.

Muir Beach, the first coastal settlement north of San Francisco, is more a village than a town. Pocketed at the mouth of Redwood Canyon, where the creek from Muir Woods makes its entry into the sea, Muir Beach is a nice place for a picnic. The most remarkable thing about the village itself is the **Pelican Inn**, a replica of a sixteenth-century English public house. Though it is of recent vintage, the Pelican is nothing like the thousands of other "olde English pubs" with mock-Tudor beams and bottle glass; there is something extremely convincing about it. Built largely of old timbers and bricks, and hosted by an English publican, the Pelican has the look, feel, and even the *smell* of an old English roadhouse. A garlic wreath hanging near the front door keeps witches at bay, though to be sure, courage is bolstered by the inscription carved above the fireplace: "Fear Knocked at the Door; Faith Answered; No One Was There." Wooden tables, an inglenook with priest's hole, an English lawn, and even bricked-up windows (to avoid the window tax) add to the atmosphere. Rooms are available for the night, and hearty English fare is offered at breakfast, lunch and dinner. The pub serves London's Pride, Watney's, Harp, Bass, and Guinness for those long Marin winter nights.. Local stables rent horses for exploring the nearby trails. If thou desireth, thine host can arrange an evening gallop along the beach, perhaps by the light of a smuggler's moon.

Stinson Beach is the most popular swimming spot in the Bay Area north of Santa Cruz, and one of the few where the water is reasonably protected from riptide currents. The beach, which stretches for about three miles (4.8 kilometers), fizzles out in a beautiful sandy spit across the mouth of Bolinas Lagoon. The quiet town of Stinson Beach has a great bookshop, Stinson Beach Books, as well as stores where you can buy picnic provisions.

The rich, protected waters of **Bolinas Lagoon** attract great flocks of feeding and roosting birds. **Audubon Canyon Ranch**, north of Stinson Beach on Highway 1, preserves some of the favorite nesting canyons of egrets and great blue herons, which return from their migrations to breed in spring and early summer. A half-mile (.8-km) trail to Henderson Overlook permits nosy birdwatchers to spy on nests without disturbing domestic affairs. The ranch is open on weekends and holidays from mid-March through mid-July. It is free, though donations are encouraged. A bookstore sells birding books and binoculars; call (415) 868-9244.

You probably won't find signs directing you to the town of **Bolinas**. However often the county puts one up, Bolinas residents take it down. It's not that they dislike tourists per se; they simply don't want to encourage tourist development.

Should a friendly visitor happen to stumble upon Bolinas (by following the road west, and then south, around Bolinas Lagoon), he or she would undoubtedly find an amenable reception.

Once a booming fishing and lumber town, Bolinas today is a quiet enclave of creative people who derive their happiness from the joys of nature, homemade bread, and small community pleasures. It's an easy-going, shabby-looking sort of place, comfortable like an old pair of shoes. If you seek to know where San Francisco's Bohemians have gone, you could do worse than look in Bolinas. But don't tell them I sent you.

Off the southwest shore of Bolinas is **Duxbury Reef**, one of the richest reefs in temperate American waters. Stretching some 1,000 yards (900 m) into the sea at low tide, the reef is protected as a marine preserve for starfish, mussels, seaweed, sea urchins, clams, anemones, and other creatures. You can look all you like, but don't disturb or collect them.

Sitting at the bottom of the Point Reyes peninsula, Bolinas is a good base of operations for exploring the wild southern sector of Point Reyes National Seashore. Accommodation is available in Bolinas inns. Mesa Road, leading to the Palomarin

A local dog makes himself at home in Bolinas.

trailhead, first passes the **Point Reyes Bird Observatory**, where visitors can get some background on the 361 species that make their home here at least part of the year. Trails from Palomarin lead into the Phillip Burton Wilderness Area. A short, steep path drops down the cliffs to tide pools.

■ POINT REYES

Olema, Point Reyes Station, and Inverness are three more "gateway" towns to Point Reyes National Seashore. All are good places to buy groceries, eat in a restaurant, or find lodging, most fortuitously in one of the many bed-and-breakfast houses. Like Bolinas, they provide civilized, peaceful, and attractive bases for exploring the surrounding parklands. Hikers can also stay at the Point Reyes Youth Hostel, on Limantour Road, in the park itself. Call Coastal Access at (415) 663-1315 for information on lodging in West Marin.

Olema is a crossroads village. Sir Francis Drake Boulevard meets Highway 1 here after a 17-mile (27-km) journey from San Rafael, on the bay side of Marin County. Three miles (4.8 km) before Olema, it passes through Samuel P. Taylor State Park, where campers and hikers enjoy the redwood forests. Olema has a nice country store, some bed-and-breakfast inns, and a popular restaurant, Jerry's Farm House, serving seafood and steaks. Trails to Point Reyes skirt the western edge of Olema, convenient for hikers staying in the local inns.

Two miles up the road is the larger town of **Point Reyes Station**. This is cattle country, as you will sense from the old false-front buildings, saddle shop, and feed store. But Point Reyes Station is a cow town of great distinction, where oysters joust with beef on the menus, and the local newspaper, the *Point Reyes Light*, won the Pulitzer Prize in 1979.

Some four miles (6.4 km) west and north of Point Reyes Station, on the western shore of **Tomales Bay**, lies **Inverness**, a backwoods settlement of great beauty and refinement. Here you can find a general store, post office, wonderful library, some of the most enchanting bed-and-breakfast inns in the country, and a handful of excellent restaurants (two of them Czechoslovakian!).

So much for the gateways . . . To get at the heart of Point Reyes is another matter.

Point Reyes is an enchanting mystery, a world quite removed from the rest of the Bay Area. It moves to a different rhythm; the natural cycles of bird migrations, rising and falling tides, the crash of waves, the passing of storms, and quiet stretches

Point Bonita Lighthouse stands at the entrance to the Golden Gate.

of utter solitude. The human side also lives in conscious respect of nature—the ranchers tending dairy herds, the fishermen following the shoals, the tourists who migrate in summer and on weekends, and who disappear back down the coast when the big Pacific storms blow in.

Point Reyes has an air of big things that happened long ago, mysterious things —of vanished tribes and Elizabethan privateers, sunken Spanish galleons, an English ghost-fort, Russian pelt-hunters, traces of Ming China washed up on the beach. It is the most thoughtful and thought-provoking of landscapes, hauntingly beautiful, often stark, humbling to city people used to bullying around seasons to fit their busy schedules.

Part of Point Reyes' feeling of separateness from the rest of the world is that it *is*, literally, from someplace else. The peninsula is separated from the "mainland" by the San Andreas Fault, which runs up the rift of Bolinas Lagoon, the Olema Valley (under Highway 1) and Tomales Bay, making it the most clearly visible section of the fault in the Bay Area. The peninsula, on the western plate, is moving north at a good clip. Its origins have been traced to some 300 miles (480 km) south of its present location. During the 1906 earthquake, the Point Reyes peninsula lurched north by some 20 feet (six m) in one movement, displacing roads and fences, and destroying buildings. The Earthquake Trail near the park visitor center at Bear Valley makes a short loop past one of these displaced fences, while interpretive displays point out other signs of the earthquake's impact.

The barn-like **Bear Valley Visitor Center** displays dioramas of Point Reyes animals, plants, and birds. This is the place to collect maps, books, postcards, and park information, including tide tables. (The last is extremely important if you intend to hike the beaches, because most of Point Reyes' beaches are backed by cliffs and can be covered at high tide.) The center provides a good introduction to the natural world of Point Reyes' forest, heath, lagoon, and maritime provinces. Parts of the park are designated wilderness, and others are working ranches.

Outside the visitor center, a short path leads to **Kule Loklo**, a replica of a native Miwok village. The Miwok, who lived north of the Golden Gate, hunted elk, fished, and gathered acorns for their sustenance. Both Sir Francis Drake and the Russians who settled north of here some 250 years later, reported that the Miwok treated them with great kindness. Some local Miwoks apparently thought their pale visitors were ancestors returning from the place of the dead, to the west. Like the Ohlone tribes south of the Golden Gate, however, they were soon overwhelmed by disease and cultural upheaval during the Spanish and American eras.

On the other side of the visitor center, you can follow the signs to the **Morgan Horse Ranch**, where patrol horses are bred for use by rangers in other national parks. The powerful, good-spirited Morgan, as you learn from displays, is the first American breed of horse, descended from a stallion acquired by a Vermont choirmaster, Justin Morgan, in 1795. You can watch the horses being put through their paces.

Point Reyes has many excellent hiking trails and roads through pristine forest and marsh land, to long, seldom-visited beaches. To find these hard-to-find beaches and coves, many accessible only by scrambling through sea caves at low tide, buy one of the many detailed park hiking guides. Riders can rent horses at Five Brooks and Bear Valley stables. Bicyclists will enjoy the relatively flat, slow-paced roads. Backpackers, day-hikers, and even car-bound visitors can watch for birds, elk and migrating whales. Swimmers, however, should know that Point Reyes has some of the most punishing surf on the coast. Drakes Beach is the most protected for waders. The park also offers walk-in and group camping, seminars and environmental education programs. Call (415) 663-9029 for weather and information.

A good cross section of the park is visible along **Limantour Road**, which runs from the Bear Valley Road through Douglas fir forests and rolling coastal meadow to Limantour Beach. From there, you can see the white cliffs fronting Drake's Bay where, according to historians, the English privateer Sir Francis Drake probably anchored for repairs in the sixteenth century. Drake stayed a month and claimed the land for England. He christened it Nova Albion. (Albion was a poetical name for England derived from the Latin word for "white," probably in reference to the white cliffs of Dover—which the Point Reyes coast resembles.)

Another two-lane country highway, **Sir Francis Drake Boulevard**, goes from Inverness through the partly wooded, moor-like ranch lands of the northern Point Reyes peninsula, to the tip of the point itself. If you are an oyster fancier, stop by **Johnson's Drakes Bay Oyster Farm**, on a bumpy turnoff just before crossing the arm of Drake's Estero. The "farm" is a ramshackle camp of trailers, piers, and huts, one of which has an oyster counter. You can take home or eat them raw on the spot with (or without) Johnson's special oyster sauce.

Farther on, spur roads lead off Sir Francis Drake Boulevard to north and south sections of long Point Reyes Beach, where wild breakers roll in the Pacific, mile after mile. Other small roads lead to sheltered Drakes Beach, where you will find a small café and a plaque commemorating Drake's purported visit, and to the Chimney Rock trailhead.

Sir Francis Drake Boulevard ends at the mountainous headland of Point Reyes itself. Many ships have run aground here. **Point Reyes lighthouse**, some 20 miles (32 km) from the Bear Valley Visitor Center, was built in 1870 to warn ships off this most treacherous headland on the Pacific coast. The lighthouse sits 160 feet (49 m) above the sea, and some 300 steps down an exposed spine of rock from the parking area. Waves crash and sea lions roar on the rocks below. From mid-December through March, you can watch migrating whales swim past Point Reyes. On clear days, you can see San Francisco, but when the fogs come in, they are thick enough to chew. The lighthouse is open Tuesdays through Sundays, except in stormy weather.

Pierce Point Road, which branches off Sir Francis Drake Boulevard about two miles (three km) north of Inverness, opens up yet another section of the park. At the end of the road is rugged McClure's Beach and a tule elk refuge. Along the way, signs point out the road to Tomales Bay State Park, where high, forested hills fall sharply into the blue bay. Protected from the pounding surf, Tomales Bay is safer for swimmers than the other beaches.

North of Point Reyes, the number of visitors along Highway 1 diminishes. The north coast is full of beautiful places to see for travelers with more time on their hands. Some of the highlights are Occidental (acclaimed for its Italian restaurants), Bodega Bay, the Sonoma Coast beaches, the Russian River, and Fort Ross, a stockade built and held by the Russians in the early nineteenth century.

■ OTHER SIGHTS OF MARIN

In addition to Sausalito, San Francisco ferry boats zip to three other Marin County destinations.

Tiburon is an attractive harbor town with much of the quaint feel of Sausalito. Ferries run from Fisherman's Wharf, though not very frequently, so check the schedule before going. Browsers wandering Main Street's refurbished old shops and galleries, or along the new waterfront parade, can make a day of it without spending a dime. The rustic string of shops continues around the corner to Ark Row. Anchor down a bench in one of the bay-side restaurants, like Sam's Anchor Café or the Conditori Sweden House—the latter especially for breakfast. Views across Raccoon Straits to Angel Island, and the tang of the salt sea air, will make you want to grab the next ferry.

No problem. **Angel Island State Park** ferries leave from Tiburon's Main Street pier on the hour, daily, in summer and on weekends and holidays. The last ferry leaves Angel Island at 4:30 p.m. Angel Island ferries also leave directly from Fisherman's Wharf during summer. Call (415) 435-2131 for schedules, and to reserve space for your bike.

Far removed from the commotion of the bay around it, Angel Island is a peaceful natural preserve. Hiking trails ring the island and ascend the low peak, linking several nineteenth-century military garrisons (abandoned) and the immigration station, in use between 1910 and 1940. During summer, there is a round-island tram tour. The views of San Francisco from Angel Island are beguiling, especially at night for a few fortunate campers.

Larkspur is not a tourist town, but riding the commuter ferry offers a lovely ride right up the middle of the bay past Angel Island and the swaybacked Richmond-San Rafael Bridge. The sight of San Quentin Prison looming off the anchorage, huge and forbidding, is enthralling. The Larkspur terminal is not near the center of town, but there are some modern shops and restaurants within easy walking distance.

San Rafael, largest city in the county, was built around the Spanish mission of San Rafael de Archangel. The present church on Fifth Avenue and A Street is a replica. The town worthies erected their houses around the corner on B Street, now known as Mansion Row. The gingerbread Gate House at the corner of Mission and B, once merely a Comstock millionaire's guest cottage, is now a county historical museum. Fans of *American Graffiti* will be gratified to know that it was filmed in downtown San Rafael, which has the comfortable, bustling appeal of an archetypal Main Street USA. Director George Lucas's studio, Industrial Light and Magic, is on nearby Lucas Road.

If you've never been shocked by a work of art, you've never seen the **Marin County Civic Center**. Marching through the hills just east of Highway 101 in San Rafael, it was Frank Lloyd Wright's last commission before he died in 1959. How to describe it? Well . . . it's huge, pink, and blue, with a dome and a spire, and will probably be called futuristic until well into the next century. By all means, enter to see the indoor gardens thriving along the space-age corridor. You can lunch at the public cafeteria.

China Camp State Park, five miles (eight km) east of Civic Center, is the last of some 30 Chinese fishing villages that once ringed San Francisco Bay. The Chinese, pioneers of the California fishing industry, were in time legislated out of business by discriminatory laws that stacked the deck against them. China Camp once supported hundreds of people. Today it is just a dock, a handful of buildings, and a vintage diner that serves fresh crab and other seafood on weekends. The visitor center illustrates the history of the town with old photographs and interpretive displays.

The small **Marin Museum of the American Indian** stands in Miwok Park, at 2200 Novato Boulevard, in Novato. Though contemporary exhibitions include arrowheads, tools, beads, and artwork from different tribes, the main displays concentrate on the culture of the native Miwoks. Of great interest is the garden of native California plants that the Miwok used in their daily lives. A small shop sells Native American books and crafts.

Cheese lovers will not begrudge the extra effort required to visit the remote **Marin French Cheese company**. Drive nine miles (14 km) west of Novato on Novato Boulevard to Petaluma-Point Reyes Road, then south (left) for a quarter mile (.4 km). The factory produces four excellent cheeses under the Rouge et Noir label: Camembert, Schloss, Brie, and Breakfast, a mild white cheese that goes well with jams and fruits. After the tour, you can buy all the fixings for a picnic lunch, and enjoy it right on the grounds. Tours and tastings are offered daily, except on holidays.

The **Renaissance Pleasure Faire** is one of Marin County's merriest festivals. It'ss a grand Elizabethan hippie romp, when visitors show up in costume to join the artists, craftsmen, puppet shows, jousting knights, musicians and play actors who gather in late summer at Black Point, east of Novato on Highway 37, just before the picturesque Petaluma River. There is an entrance fee to enter the grounds. Costumes are not mandatory, but they are more fun. Good Queen Bess or Sir Francis Drake himself may be on hand to bless the revelers, nor is there likely to be a more fun-loving pair. A good time is had by all.

■ SONOMA COUNTY

The Petaluma River divides Marin County from Sonoma County. It was once the third busiest river in California, linking San Francisco with the Sonoma County breadbasket of **Petaluma**. Known as "the egg capital of the world," Petaluma also raised hay, grain, and produce, and shipped them from the crowded Petaluma River turning basin at the center of town. Today, the old paddle-wheel steamers and scows are museum pieces, like the river itself.

Petaluma's Old Town, where Petaluma Boulevard and Kentucky Street intersectt Washington Street and Western Avenue, is a pleasant place for strolling. You can pick up free maps and walking guides from the excellent visitor center on the corner of Baywood Drive and Lakeville. Old Town has the atmosphere of an American country town of brick, wood, and iron facades; some buildings date as far back as the 1870s and 1880s. Among the buildings still standing, though given over to other purposes, are old hotels, the blacksmith, feed and flour mills, the Odd Fellows Hall, and the library at Fourth and B streets, now converted to the city museum. The greatest gathering of shops is at the Great Petaluma Mill at 6 North Petaluma Boulevard, overlooking the turning basin of the Petaluma River.

Petaluma was built on one of the largest ranchos in California, established by General Mariano Vallejo. His two-story **adobe hacienda** stands on a rise southeast of town. Surrounded by fields and built around a courtyard, it is still an impressive sight. Wander around the rooms and verandas to get an idea of the rustic prosperity enjoyed by feudal landholders of the Mexican era. The tallow hall (where candles were made), kitchen, store house, the General's quarters, overseer's room, and visitors' rooms are furnished. There is an admission fee.

Sonoma County's largest city, **Santa Rosa**, was built on some of the finest agricultural land in the country. Such was the opinion of America's most famous horticulturist, Luther Burbank, who selected the spot for his home and experimental farm. Here, he scientifically bred and developed over 800 new varieties of fruits, flowers, vegetables, and other plants now common through the United States, including the Santa Rosa and satsuma plums, the Shasta daisy, rainbow corn, the plumcot, the Royal walnut, the spineless cactus, the Black Giant cherry, and new strains of prunes, nectarines, berries, tomatoes, and apples. His old gardens and house stand in downtown Santa Rosa, at the corner of Santa Rosa and Sonoma avenues. The **Luther Burbank Gardens** and modest house, now a museum of Burbank's life, are open daily. Burbank himself is buried near his dog under the large Cedars of Lebanon tree on the grounds.

Across Sonoma Avenue and down half a block is a curiosity that's hard to believe—though maybe not. It's the **church built from one tree**, a Russian River redwood that stood 275 feet (84 m) tall and 18 feet (5.5 m) in diameter. Appropriately,

the church now preserves the memorabilia of Santa Rosa's most famous native son, Robert L. Ripley, creator of Ripley's Believe It or Not. Aside from being a curiosity itself, the building houses a collection of Ripley's cartoons and personal effects, some rotating county history displays, and a handful of Ripleyesque oddities. (If you are intrigued primarily by the oddities, you're better off at the Ripley's museum at Fisherman's Wharf.) The church is open daily from May through August; the rest of the year, Thursday through Monday.

Downtown Santa Rosa, centered north of Sonoma Avenue around Santa Rosa Avenue and Fourth Street, is a handsome, sparkling, unabashedly modern district of plazas, malls, and spruced-up historical buildings. To see the latter, start at the **Sonoma County Museum**, on Seventh Street, and finish at Railroad Square Historic District. The museum is open Wednesdays through Sundays. Pick up a walker's map at the Burbank House or the visitor's bureau on Third Street.

Sonoma County's two main vineyard regions are the Sonoma Valley and the Russian River Valley, including the Alexander and Dry Creek valleys near Healdsburg. Russian River wineries, of which more than 50 welcome tours, are listed in a free brochure called "The Russian River Wine Road" from Sonoma County tourist offices; call (707) 433-6935. Many of the wineries have picnic grounds, encouraging you to buy a bottle and enjoy the lovely setting.

The mustard blooms between dormant vines in Napa (opposite)

Sonoma Valley wine directory.

The Sonoma Valley has the distinction of being the cradle of the California fine wine industry. Though the mission fathers were first to plant the grape, the Buena Vista Winery, founded in 1857 by a Hungarian count, Agoston Haraszthy, was first to grow imported European vine stock on a commercial scale. **Buena Vista Winery** is still in operation northeast of the town of Sonoma, on Old Winery Road. It is one of Sonoma's most delightful winery tours. Visitors can picnic on the tree-shaded grounds, and guide themselves on a walk through the foliage-covered stone buildings that front rough-hewn, cask-filled wine caves. Closer to town, the vast **Sebastiani Vineyards**, on Fourth Street, offers more comprehensive tours. Beyond the handsome tasting rooms, dark and richly decorated with wood carving, rows of enormous redwood tanks and oak barrels march with pungent gusto through the aging cellars.

The town of **Sonoma** was founded in 1823, over the hills east of Santa Rosa. General Mariano Vallejo, the richest and most powerful man in Mexican California, moved here to manage his huge rancho, and to lead occasional raids against hostile Indian tribes to the north. The **Sonoma Plaza**, largest in California, still retains some of the color and history from those early days.

It was in Sonoma Plaza that Robert Semple and his American compatriots raised the Bear Flag and declared California a republic, after first seizing General Vallejo at his house across the street (where he calmly treated them to a glass of brandy). A heroic statue stands in the square, but historians disagree on the heroism of the rebels. Imprisoning the statesmanlike Vallejo as a prisoner of war was theatrical, but unjust. When Vallejo was set free, he found that his ranch had been ransacked by the state's "founding fathers," his livestock and tools carried off. Vallejo accepted the Yankee conquest philosophically, and even joined in the new government as one of California's first state senators.

Mission San Francisco Solano de Sonoma, last to be founded in California, occupies the corner northeast of the plaza. Especially impressive is the enormous cactus growing in the back. Across Spain Street, Vallejo built a hotel called The Blue Wing. Among his guests were the likes of Kit Carson, Ulysses S. Grant, William Tecumseh Sherman and, by tradition, the bandit Joaquin Murietta.

The barracks, the servants' wing of Vallejo's home, and the 1850-era Toscano Hotel, originally known as The Eureka, are on the north side of the plaza. The two-story barracks is now a museum of early California history, with emphasis on the Bear Flag Revolt. Like the mission, all are administered as part of the Sonoma

State Historic Park, covered by a single entrance fee also good for visiting General Vallejo's nearby home, Lachryma Montis.

Other points of interest on the plaza are the Sonoma Cheese Factory, and The Sonoma Hotel, on the corner of First West and Spain. The hotel has a venerable western saloon, still in perfect working order.

After retiring from state politics, General Vallejo built a new house on the grounds west of Sonoma, where it stands today. **Lachryma Montis** is an elaborate gingerbread structure, furnished as it was when the general and his family (there were 16 children) knew it.

The town of **Glen Ellen** lies a few miles north of Sonoma. This section of the Sonoma Valley is also called Valley of the Moon, a name made famous by Jack London, who spent the last years of his life at the Beauty Ranch, in the hills above town. The ranch is preserved as **Jack London State Park**. In his day, London sold more books than any other writer in the world, and he remains today probably the best-known American writer outside the country. He used his income to buy the Beauty Ranch, which he developed without heed to cost. His last big project was Wolf House, an immense mansion, which mysteriously burned on the eve of completion. You can see the magnificent ruins after a half-mile (.8-km) walk through the woods from the parking lot. London's ashes, placed in an urn and covered with a boulder, can be visited nearby.

The ranch house where London lived and died (of an apparently suicidal drug overdose in 1916) is also on the property, surrounded by barns and a distillery. Most interesting of all, however, is the House of Happy Walls, built by London's widow after the writer's death, and now a museum of London artifacts, photos, and books.

The pretty Glen Ellen Winery lies next door to the London property. In the town of Glen Ellen, the Jack London Bookstore at 14300 Arnold Drive carries a good stock of used books with an emphasis on Jack London.

■ NAPA COUNTY

The Napa Valley, America's most famous wine-producing region, draws so many tourists these days that local wine makers have taken measures to thwart them. Two and a half million visitors annually come to Napa not only to tour wineries, but to dine in gourmet restaurants, shop in smart boutiques, and tootle through

The lore of wine at Sterling (left), Sebastiani (top), and Christian Brothers (above).

and over the valley by wine train, balloon, or glider. In response, Napa vintners have voted for zoning laws to restrict tourist-oriented "boutique wineries." Some wineries have even adopted the drastic measure of charging for tours and glasses of wine—on weekends, at any rate.

The glamor of the Napa grape is rooted firmly in the rare beauty of the Napa Valley, especially the section north from Yountville. Here the valley closes in between high, forested ridges, sometimes sharpening to cliffs. The rolling vineyards are dotted with oak trees and old stone buildings, some the scale and shape of French chateaux, others of Rhineland estates. The wine mystique thrives in the old, musty cellars and wine caves in the hills, and the music and food that accompany it. And no doubt, too, it is bolstered by the romantic aura of exclusive quality that surrounds the mysterious art of making, and drinking, wine. Certainly, nobody makes much of a fuss over San Joaquin Valley vintages, which by far outweigh the Napa Valley's. The beauty, the quality, the *mystique* of a Fresno wine grape just can't compete with one from Napa.

Visitors can savor the Napa Valley better if they go on a weekday to beat traffic jams and extra charges. They will enjoy tours and tastings more, too, if they join an organized coach tour of the wine country. The most famous wineries are along Highway 29, on the west side of the valley; the Silverado Trail (on the east side) is the more bucolic and less traveled route.

As with Sonoma, choosing which to visit from the more than 130 wineries in Napa Valley is a task beyond the scope of this guidebook. Detailed discussions of the wineries can be found in Sunset's *Wine Country California*, and, more succinctly, in the *Wine Spectator's Wine Country Guide to California*.

Napa, the town at the south end of the valley, is quickly growing into just another California suburban town. The old town center has some interesting shops and buildings, but if you have only a day for the Napa Valley, skip it, and head north.

Yountville is smaller, with more polish and less urban sprawl. The net result is a tourist attraction. Vintage 1870, an old brick winery building fashioned into a collection of boutiques, is certainly picturesque. The Keith Rosenthal Theatre has a 15-minute music and slide show of the Napa Valley, which runs several times a day. It's a good introduction to the Napa mystique. There is a moderate entrance charge.

Saint Helena is a beautiful small town with a traditional Main Street. Two of the most famous winery buildings in the Napa Valley stand on the north side of town. **Beringer Brothers**, with their half-timbered mansion, is famous for its wine caves, dug by Chinese laborers in the 1870s. Next door, the spectacular chateau of **Christian Brothers**, behind the tunnel of elm trees along Highway 29, is prettier than a picture. Both wineries offer first-rate tours.

Robert Louis Stevenson visited the Napa Valley on his honeymoon in 1880, camping on Mount Saint Helena (now part of the undeveloped Robert Louis Stevenson State Park) and visiting many of the other sights. He described his stay in a short book called *The Silverado Squatters*. In Saint Helena, next to the library on the eastern side of town, a small museum is dedicated to the beloved Scot. The **Silverado Museum** houses some 8,000 pieces of memorabilia, including several first editions by the author, a lock of hair, pictures, and the actual toy soldiers described in his poem "Land of Counterpane" from *A Child's Garden of Verses*. The free museum is open afternoons Tuesday through Sunday, except holidays.

One of California's most original and well-known block-print artists built his studio at 1124 Pine Street, in Saint Helena. Henry Evans, who died in 1990, specialized in California wildflowers.

Ambrose Bierce used to live in a house around the corner from the Evans Studio, at 1515 Main Street. One of the most intriguing and disturbing figures of American literature, Bierce was infamous for his cynical commentary on the state of mankind. His most famous work is the brilliantly misanthropic *Devils Dictionary*, but he was better known in his own day for his supernatural short stories. Bierce worked as a columnist for the *San Francisco Examiner*, and made it his business to improve the literature of California by attacking what he deemed was bad, and praising what he deemed was good. His fame today stems partly from his mysterious disappearance in Mexico in 1913.

Bierce actually spent most of his time in San Francisco. When he arrived in Saint Helena on occasional weekends, he would entertain friends like the eccentric Lillie Coit, the photographer Eadweard Muybridge, and the actress Lillie Langtry, who was then living in Lake County. The house is now a bed-and-breakfast inn. Bierce's wife and two sons—both of whom died under tragic circumstances—are buried in the verdant, old-world burial grounds west of town on Spring Street.

When the Napa Valley was first cultivated, wheat, not grapes, was the main cash crop. The farmers gathered to have their grain ground at a mill owned by an English brother-in-law of General Vallejo, Edwin Bale. The old **Bale Grist Mill** still stands in a park north of Saint Helena. It has recently been refurbished to give visitors an idea of how the job was done using a 36-foot (11-m) waterwheel and two one-ton millstones. The mill is open daily, and there is an admission fee. It is surrounded by the Bothe-Napa Valley State Park, which offers camping and hiking.

Two wineries between Saint Helena and Calistoga exemplify the long and distinguished career of wine-making in this region: Schramsberg and Sterling.

Schramsberg Vineyards still retains the isolated feel that it had when Robert Louis Stevenson described his visit in *The Silverado Squatters*. "Mr. Schram's . . . is the oldest vineyard in the valley," he wrote. (The German had founded it in 1862.) "Now, his place is the picture of prosperity: stuffed birds in the veranda, cellars far dug into the hillside, and resting on pillars like a bandit's cave: all trimness, varnish, flowers and sunshine, among the tangled wildwood." Stevenson tasted every variety on the premises, and expressed his approval of the setting, which "made a pleasant music for the mind." Those who would like to know that music today require an appointment, for the Schramsberg champagnes are of far too limited vintage to allow the large-scale tours and tastings common at some Napa wineries. Call (707) 942-4558. Schramsberg is in the hills at 1400 Schramsberg Lane, which is off Petersen Lane. Petersen is about two miles (three km) north of the Old Bale Mill, on the west side of Highway 128.

A balloon launches near Calistoga on a calm winter morning.

A splendid example of a new winery that has made its mark, graciously, upon this special valley is **Sterling Vineyards**. It resembles a great white Greek monastery on a high knoll overlooking the vineyards, accessible to the public only by cable car. Self-guided tours take visitors step by step on elevated platforms through the wine-making process, ending in an airy tasting room—a fascinating and elegant experience. Sterling is in the middle of Dunaweal Lane, which runs east (right) off Highway 128 about two and a half miles (4 kilometers) north of Saint Helena. You pay an entrance fee when you board the cable car.

Calistoga is the town at the northern end of the Napa Valley, 27 miles (43 km) from Napa. Sam Brannan founded it as a hot-spring resort, with hopes that it would become the California version of Saratoga; hence the name. The venture did not work out for Brannan, and indeed, Californians' enthusiasm for Calistoga has been rather lukewarm over the decades. Today, however, Calistoga is back in favor. The surging interest in Napa wine has made Calistoga, and its spas, very fashionable indeed.

Calistoga retains its comfortable, old-West feel in the false-front buildings and the bracing air of the surrounding mountains. Most businesses, restaurants, and spas are concentrated around Lincoln Avenue, including the old Calistoga Inn (1250 Lincoln), which brews its own beer above a leafy beer garden. Many of the beautiful old houses in Calistoga's tree-shaded residential neighborhoods have been converted to bed-and-breakfast inns that really strive to impart the slower pace and grace of another century. In fact, you can even stay in one of Brannan's original cabins, the Brannan Cottage Inn.

Calistoga's **hot baths** are today enjoying the business that Brannan hoped to reap. The little industry offers a whole gamut of treatments—saunas, mud baths, facials, herbal wraps, hot-spring soaks, Swedish and shiatsu massage, steam baths, mineral jacuzzi, body wraps, foot reflexology—with, and even more blissfully without, the twentieth-century version of a snake-oil seller's claims. The volcanic mud feels great, but it sure looks ugly.

For timid souls who balk at climbing into mud, there are two other ways to appreciate Calistoga's thermal blessings. First, you can drink a Calistoga Mineral Water. Second, you can visit the **Old Faithful Geyser**, at 1299 Tubbs Lane, about three miles (five km) north of Lincoln Avenue. Not to be confused with the Old Faithful of Yellowstone fame, the Calistoga version is privately owned. Sixty-foot (18-meter) blastoffs occur roughly every 40 minutes. There is an admission fee.

There's more to Calistoga than what comes from the ground. The town is also famed as a center of gliding and ballooning adventures. The scenery from the air is superb, and the amenities for enjoying it surprisingly plentiful. See "Backmatter" for some names.

History buffs will enjoy browsing through the **Sharpsteen Museum**, at 1311 Washington Street, in the center of town. Aside from a lively diorama of the Calistoga of Brannan's dreams, you can see odds and ends of Brannan memorabilia, pioneer guns, and a good deal of displays on animation. The latter was the special interest of museum founder Ben Sharpsteen, an Oscar-winning animator with Walt Disney Studios. Among his movie credits are *Pinochio, Fantasia,* and *Dumbo.* The museum is open daily; phone (707) 942-5911.

Beyond Calistoga, all roads lead out of the Napa Valley. To the north, Highway 29 climbs Mount Saint Helena to Clear Lake. To the west lies Sonoma County.. Heading toward Santa Rosa on Petrified Forest Road, you will encounter that marvel of nature just across the county line. Stevenson visited the **petrified forest** and came away disappointed, but a lot more of the fossil trees have been uncovered since those early days. The largest of the stone giants is 60 feet (18 m) long and six feet (1.8 m) thick. There is a fee to enter the park. A store on the premises sells pieces of petrified wood and other fossils.

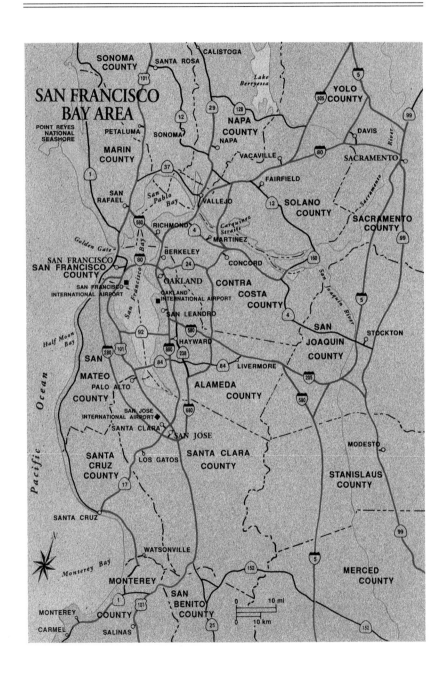

PRACTICALITIES

ORIENTATION

San Francisco lies at roughly the same latitude as Seoul, Athens, Seville, Wichita, and Richmond, Virginia. It is a small, densely populated city of 740,000 people crammed into only about 49 square miles (127 sq km). San Francisco's population is considerably swelled every year by some eight million tourists.

The San Francisco Bay metropolitan area—or the Bay Area as it's commonly known—embraces some 90 miles (145 km) north to south, and 60 miles (100 km) east to west, with about six million people. The Bay Area is the fourth largest metropolitan area in the United States, after New York, Los Angeles, and Chicago.

The Bay Area is divided into nine counties, but locals habitually abbreviate them as five geographical entities:

- ❧ the city (San Francisco County);
- ❧ the peninsula (San Mateo County);
    - ❧ the South Bay (Santa Clara County);
    - ❧ the East Bay (Alameda and Contra Costa counties, and from a San Franciscan's point of view, Solano County); and
    - ❧ the North Bay (Marin, Sonoma, and Napa counties).

The grape-rich valleys of Napa and Sonoma counties are known as the Wine Country, while Santa Clara Valley is called Silicon Valley by outsiders.

THE PEOPLE

The Bay Area, and San Francisco in particular, is one of the most ethnically diverse regions of the United States. Eight of the 15 most ethnically varied municipalities in the country are Bay Area cities.

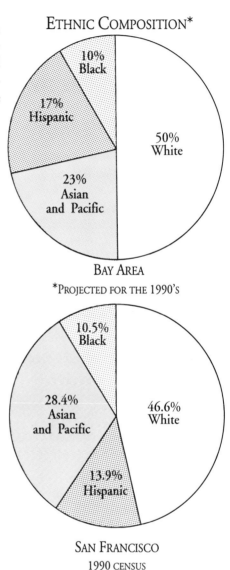

ETHNIC COMPOSITION*

10%
Black

17%
Hispanic

50%
White

23%
Asian
and Pacific

BAY AREA

*PROJECTED FOR THE 1990'S

10.5%
Black

28.4%
Asian
and Pacific

46.6%
White

13.9%
Hispanic

SAN FRANCISCO
1990 CENSUS

WHEN TO GO

San Francisco has no unpleasant season per se, but it does have cold days, as well as clusters of bright, clear days, in every season. Come prepared at any time of year with a sweater or coat.

Winter, from November to March, is when the most rain falls, sometimes quite heavily and for days at a time. Late spring and summer are famous for their thick, knife-edge afternoon-to-morning fogs, much chronicled by photographers. September and October are the warmest months.

Summer temperatures in the North, South, and East Bay are commonly several degrees warmer than in San Francisco. Temperatures of 100°F (38°C) and hotter are not rare in the Central Valley during July and August.

TEMPERATURE AND RAINFALL					
Temperature				Rainfall	
Average Daily Temperature °F		Average Daily Temperature °C		Average Monthly Rainfall	
MINIMUM	MAXIMUM	MINIMUM	MAXIMUM	INCHES	MILLIMETERS
(J) 45	55	7	13	4.7	119
(F) 47	59	8	15	3.8	97
(M) 48	61	9	16	3.1	79
(A) 49	62	9	17	1.5	38
(M) 51	63	11	17	0.7	18
(J) 52	66	11	19	0.1	3
(J) 53	65	12	18	0	0
(A) 53	65	12	18	0	0
(S) 55	69	13	21	0.3	8
(O) 54	68	12	20	1.0	25
(N) 51	63	11	17	2.5	64
(D) 47	57	8	14	4.4	112

Jaunty sailboats test the winds just inside the Golden Gate (overleaf).

ARRIVING BY AIR

San Francisco International Airport (SFO) is about 14 miles (23 km) south of downtown San Francisco, in San Mateo County. The terminals are built in a partial circle around a parking garage, making it easy to find your way around once you understand the layout. (Unfortunately, most people don't master the layout until after two or three trips.) For the benefit of travelers caught between flights, SFO maintains a hall in the north terminal for art and museum exhibits. Call (415) 761-0800 for airport information.

Buses run frequently to the city from dawn till after midnight. The downtown airport bus terminal is located in the Tenderloin, one of the rougher sections of town, but only two blocks from the major hotel district near Union Square. Taxis and door-to-door shuttle service are also available. Check the telephone book yellow pages under "Airport Transport" for companies.

Oakland International (OAK) and San Jose International (SJC) airports offer less stressful alternatives, since each operates at about 50 percent capacity. Oakland is handy for passengers using BART to San Francisco. San Jose is convenient for visiting Silicon Valley. Train connections from SJC to San Francisco's railroad depot aree available on Caltrain. Check the telephone book yellow pages under "Airport Transport" for details of airport shuttles and buses. For airport information, call Oakland at (415) 577-4000, and San Jose at (408) 277-4759.

ARRIVING BY SEA

Ship is still the most romantic way to arrive in San Francisco, though not the obvious choice it once was. Passenger and cruise ships dock at Pier 35, near Fisherman's Wharf. The Yorktown Clipper, with cruise packages to Alaska and up the Sacramento River with stops at Sausalito, Rio Vista, Napa, and Sacramento, home ports on the Peninsula in Redwood City. For information, contact the cruise companies listed in "Backmatter."

ARRIVING BY LAND

The commercial coach terminal is south of Market in the Transbay Terminal, on Mission between First and Fremont.

Caltrain, a commuter rail line, connects San Francisco's Townsend Street station (at Fourth) with San Jose; call (800) 558-8661. AMTRAK pulls into Oakland Station (corner of 17th and Wood streets), and runs passengers across the bay by bus; call (800) 872-7245.

GETTING AROUND BY CAR

San Francisco gives up its best to people willing to explore its hills and neighborhoods on foot. But to explore farther-flung city neighborhoods, or to reach destinations beyond San Francisco where distances are considerable and public transport not uniformly developed, you may need wheels. Whether it's best to go by tour, public transport, or private car depends on where you are going and your own whims.

In San Francisco a car can be a handicap. The infamously steep hills play havoc with greenhorns, especially those who are driving a manual shift. When parking on a hill, *curb your wheels and use your hand brake*. Forgetting to do so will cost you a fine and maybe your car—or somebody else's.

Parking is horrific in San Francisco. Statistics suggest that the city has the highest density of cars of any city in the world. Think about it: about 500,000 cars are registered in San Francisco, and another 250,000 commute into it each day, but there are only about 250,000 *legal* parking spots. Residents routinely park illegally and justify the fine as part of the cost of owning a car here.

San Franciscans can be very helpful to confused strangers when met on foot. Met behind a wheel, however, they give no quarter to hesitant drivers. Let the driver beware.

GETTING AROUND BY PUBLIC TRANSPORT

San Francisco's public bus and streetcar system is called MUNI. It's cheap, convenient, and relatively safe (relative to New York, for example). Exact fares are required, and passes are available. A transport map with all routes costs $1. Call (415) 673-6864 for information.

BART (Bay Area Rapid Transit) is San Francisco's version of the Paris Metro or New York's subway system, though smaller and cleaner than either, by far. In fact, a lot of tourists like to ride BART just for the *fun* of it! BART whisks commuters to Daly City on San Francisco's southern border, and under the bay to Concord, Richmond, and Fremont in the East Bay. If your destination lies near a BART station, you are better off riding BART than driving. All stations have detailed neighborhood street maps posted. Call (415) 788-2278 for information.

MUNI streetcars share four downtown stations with BART, making Embarcadero, Montgomery, Powell, and Civic Center stations the four key transfer points between intra-city and inter-city transport systems. The streetcar is a particularly interesting and easy way to ride to Golden Gate Park (the N-Judah to Ninth Avenue) or the San Francisco Zoo (the L-Taraval to the end of the line).

MUNI sells "Passports" to ride all streetcars, buses, and cable cars. Passports also entitle you to discounts at the zoo and city museums. Buy them from cable car terminals at Fisherman's Wharf, Ghirardelli Square, and Hallidie Plaza; the Cable Car Barn; and the Visitor Information Bureau at Hallidie Plaza.

Ferries, a most civilized means of transport, are limited to a few commuter routes. Golden Gate Transit ferries run to Larkspur and Sausalito in Marin County from the downtown Ferry Building. Red and White Ferries go to Angel Island, Sausalito, and Vallejo from Fisherman's Wharf. Ferry service also connects Oakland's Jack London Square and Alameda with the Ferry Building. (These East Bay routes were set up as an emergency measure following the October 1989 earthquake. Insufficient ridership keeps their future uncertain.) For schedules and information, call Golden Gate Transit at (415) 332-6600, Red and White at (415) 546-2815, and the Oakland-Alameda ferry at (510) 522-3300.

For a coordinated, comprehensive explanation of all the transport systems of the Bay Area, buy a copy of the *San Francisco Bay Area Regional Transit Guide*, published by the Metropolitan Transportation Commission. The book is available in downtown BART stations, among other places.

CABLE CARS

When Andrew Hallidie set the first cable car trundling down Clay Street hill on August 2, 1873, he breached the hill barrier once and for all. The rich flocked to Nob Hill, and in time, six cable car lines spread through the city on more than a hundred miles of track. London, Sydney, and several American cities adopted the ingenious device.

To the sound of fog horns, an early cable car climbs Nob Hill.

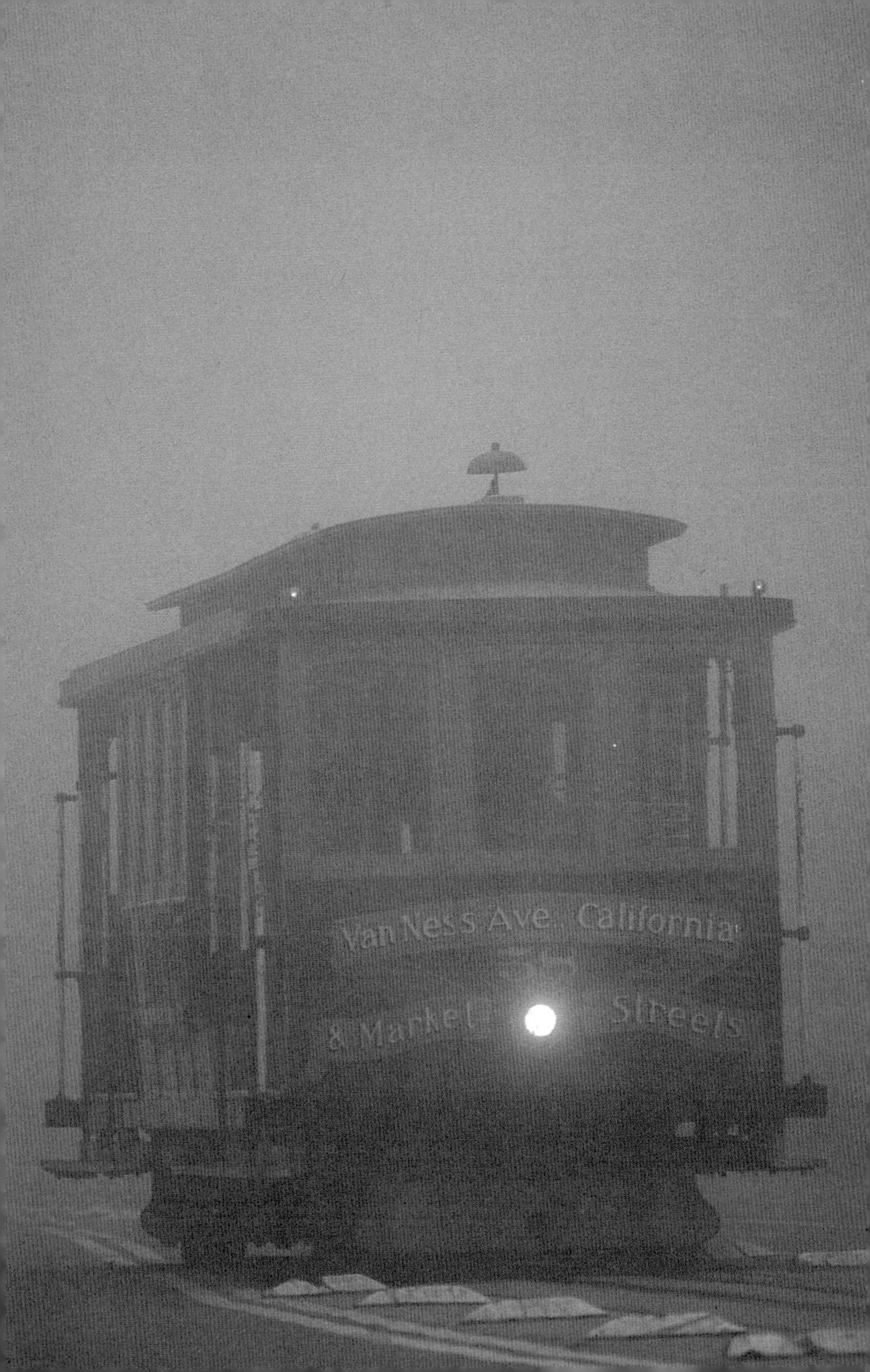
Van Ness Ave. California
& Market Streets

When the bus, streetcar and automobile rendered them obsolete, cable cars disappeared all over the globe, except in sentimental San Francisco. Today, the cable cars are the nation's only moving National Historical Monument. Despite their expense and questionable safety record, they are a much-loved symbol of the city.

Cable car fare is $2 per person. To avoid long lines boarding at any terminus, catch a car somewhere along its route, if there's room. Three lines are operational:

The Powell-Mason line runs between Hallidie Plaza and Bay Street, near Fisherman's Wharf.

The Powell-Hyde line runs from Hallidie Plaza to Ghirardelli Square, via the thrilling 21.3 percent Hyde Street grade.

The California Street Line runs 17 blocks in a straight line along California Street from Embarcadero Center (Frost Plaza) to Van Ness Avenue.

TOURIST INFORMATION

The San Francisco Convention & Visitors Bureau dispenses maps and tons of valuable information on hotels, restaurants, sights, tours, and current events. The bureau's main office is located at the Lower Level of Hallidie Plaza, near the corner of Powell and Market. Write them at Box 6977, San Francisco, California 94101. You can also call their Daily Events Information Line: (415) 391-2001.

The Community Access Pages of the telephone book yellow pages (also called the "Smart Yellow Pages") has listings of theaters, sporting venues, clubs, kids' programs, weekend getaways, recreational activities, transport information and maps, services, radio stations, and a calendar of annual events.

KEEPING UP WITH WHAT'S GOING ON

The *San Francisco Chronicle*, a morning edition, has the largest circulation of any Bay Area newspaper. Its "Datebook" section of the Sunday *Chronicle*, known as the pink sheet for the color of its newsprint, is the last word on what's going on, culturally, around the Bay Area. Herb Caen, San Francisco's best-read columnist, is a *Chronicle* institution.

The *San Francisco Examiner* is the main afternoon paper; the Friday edition lists a mix of weekend happenings. The free *Bay Guardian* is another excellent source

Brazilian carnivals are the most flamboyant of festivals.

FESTIVALS AND EVENTS

With such a broad spectrum of cultures and causes to celebrate, something is always happening in San Francisco. Some of the bigger celebrations are listed below. Keep in mind that the dates may change from year to year, so check schedules in advance.

Chinese New Year (late January to March, depending on lunar calendar)—firecrackers, the Miss Chinatown pageant, and the famous Chinatown parade.

Saint Patrick's Day (March 17)—when anyone who wants to can be Irish for a day, join the big parade, or hoist a few with the merrymakers at the bars.

Cherry Blossom Festival (April)—Japantown celebrates the new blooms with a fair featuring traditional arts and crafts.

San Francisco International Film Festival (March-April)—the City's biggest cinematic event, based at the Palace of Fine Arts.

Carnival (spring, depending on Easter)—San Francisco's version of Mardi Gras, celebrated in the streets of the Mission District.

Easter—An Easter Sunday sunrise service is held at dawn on Mount Davidson. Russian Orthodox Easter is colorfully celebrated at the Cathedral of the Holy Virgin, in the Richmond District.

Cinco de Mayo (May 5)—Mexican Independence Day, celebrated in the Mission District with a colorful parade and festivities.

Gay Freedom Day (June)—marked by a parade up Market from Castro Street to Civic Center.

Haight Street Fair (June)—neighborhood celebration with booths, arts and crafts.

Noe Valley Street Fair (June)—ditto.

Union Street Spring Fair (June)—ditto.

Upper Grant Avenue Street Fair (June)—ditto.

Fourth of July—usually celebrated with fireworks over the bay, though the fog layer is often too low to see much.

San Francisco Flower Show (July)—held in Hall of Flowers at Strybing Arboretum, Golden Gate Park.

Renaissance Pleasure Faire (August-September)—Elizabethan theme fair held in Marin County.

Aki Matsuri (September)—Japantown festival, with taiko drummers, arts and crafts.

Opera Season Opening (September)—the city's premier gala event, with the opera glitterati at center stage.

Castro Street Fair (October)—neighborhood celebration with booths, arts and crafts.

Columbus Day (October 12)—a city holiday, especially honored in the Italian community. Festivities (occurring on different days) include the blessing of the fleet, Columbus landing pageant, and parade.

Exotic-Erotic Ball (October 30)—the annual costume party where anything goes.

Halloween (October 31)—celebrated with wild costumes and parties on Castro Street.

Day of the Dead (November 2)—a Hispanic festival to honor dead ancestors, marked by special foods, dances, costumes, and a parade in the Mission District.

Dickens Christmas Fair (November)—a Victorian Christmas theme fair.

Christmas (December)—Stores and homes around town decorate for the holidays.

Not a week goes by without San Franciscans finding something to celebrate.

of information on current events. The *San Jose Mercury* is an outstanding South Bay alternative to city papers, while the *Oakland Tribune* is the main East Bay version. Out-of-town newspapers, including foreign-language press, are available in many places; but if you happen to be downtown, try Harold's Hometown Newsstand, at the corner of Post and Taylor. Oakland's counterpart is DeLauer News Agency, att 1310 Broadway.

San Francisco Focus, a monthly magazine, lists restaurants and events of cultural interest alongside articles by some of the Bay Area's literary lights.

BOOKSTORES

San Francisco Bay Area is one of the largest book marts in the world. The greatest concentration of walk-in bookstores is not in San Francisco, however, but in Berkeley along Bancroft and Telegraph avenues, near the university. Palo Alto and downtown Oakland are also happy hunting grounds for bibliophiles.

Book-hunting is good in San Francisco's North Beach, Richmond District (especially Clement Street), Noe Valley, the northeast corner of the Sunset, and around Union Square. Among the many city stores that keep late hours, City Lights and Columbus bookstores in North Beach, and Green Apple in the Richmond, are favorite nighttime haunts.

San Francisco is renowned for its antiquarian stores. Many are concentrated within a few blocks of Union Square. A small directory of second-hand and antiquarian dealers, called *Book Finder*, is sold at the counter of most secondhand bookstores. The Bay Area has a fascinating array of specialty bookshops. Check "Backmatter" for an abbreviated list.

TOURS

Countless tours are available from hotels, Fisherman's Wharf, the Transbay Terminal, and travel agents. Choose from a bag of city, helicopter, ski, boat, mountain, seashore, whale-watching, or Wine Country tours, gamblers' specials to Reno or Lake Tahoe, even excursions to the Colma cemeteries. Some of the best city tours are led afoot through far-flung neighborhoods, most with a special emphasis on architecture, history, and food. See "Backmatter" for lists.

LODGING

San Francisco's main hotel district lies west of Union Square, a good place for shopping, theater, and nightlife. Some of the cheapest hotels in the city are in the neighboring Tenderloin, and though the hotels themselves may be quite good, the neighborhood usually is not. Nob Hill is famed for its luxury hotels, while the large hotels in the Financial District cater to executives on business accounts. A handful of family-style motels congregate on Lombard Street in the Marina District, along Van Ness Avenue, and around Fisherman's Wharf.

The bed-and-breakfast idea has taken hold in California. San Francisco and environs have some of the most charming ones, many occupying older Victorian buildings in interesting neighborhoods. Many Spartan, European-style pensions for budget-minded travelers exist in areas like North Beach and Chinatown. A few youth hostels and campgrounds lie within striking distance of the city.

A partial listing of accommodations appears in "Backmatter."

MUSEUMS

The four big fine arts museums of San Francisco are the Museum of Modern Art, the M.H. de Young Museum, the Asian Art Museum, and the California Palace of the Legion of Honor. The city also has two large science museums: the Exploratorium and the California Academy of Sciences. (The latter houses an aquarium and a planetarium.) In addition, San Francisco supports a zoo, botanical gardens, the National Maritime Museum, and a surprising number of small, sometimes eccentric museums.

Entry fees range from free to expensive. Budget travelers should note that most large museums in San Francisco grant *free* entry on the first Wednesday of every month.

Many other museums and historical sites lie beyond San Francisco. Among the more extensive and spectacular are the Oakland Museum (with some of the best natural history and California history displays in the state), the Lawrence Hall of Science and the University Art Museum in Berkeley, the Leland Stanford Jr. Museum in Palo Alto, and the Egyptian Museum in San Jose.

ART GALLERIES

The area around Union Square, particularly along Sutter and Grant, contains the greatest number of established galleries in the city. Many newer artists keep studios south of Market, in the Mission, at Hunters Point, and elsewhere. Once a year, the Open Studio offers a peek into artists' studios around town.

You can pick up a free quarterly pamphlet called "Bay Area Gallery Guide" at many galleries around town, with a map and artist listings.

Artweek, a weekly newspaper (biweekly in summer) sold in art galleries, museums, and some bookstores, keeps track of the local art scene. If you cannot find one, call the circulation department at (415) 763-0422.

SHOPPING

One of the premier retail districts of the country, the vicinity of Union Square harbors scores of major department stores, galleries, sporting goods stores, and famous apparel outlets. Well-heeled shoppers are also drawn to the boutiques and specialty stores of charming Union Street in Cow Hollow, and high-toned Sacramento and upper Fillmore streets on the edges of Pacific Heights. Embarcadero Center caters to the Financial District crowds. Grant Avenue is Chinatown's premier tourist shopping street. Ghirardelli Square and The Canary, built in old brick factory buildings near Fisherman's Wharf, provide atmospheric browsing through unique shops. Two handy, detailed guides to interesting neighborhood and downtown shops are Richard Wurman's *San Francisco Access* and Judith Maas Rheingold's *Shopwalks* map.

Some of the Bay Area's most outstanding gift shopping, especially for older children, can be found at the science museum shops. Dinosaur books and models, star constellation maps, science experiments, New Age music tapes, off-beat games and toys, collectors' kits, natural history and outdoor recreation books, binoculars, magnifying glasses, microscopes, crystals, high-tech measuring devices, bird whistles, and much more are on display. Some of the offerings can be found at the Exploratorium, the Lawrence Hall of Science, the Garage, the Bay Area Discovery Museum, the Children's Discovery Museum, the Oakland Museum, the Academy of Sciences in Golden Gate Park, and any of The Nature Company stores.

Art museum stores also furnish excellent gifts, particularly cards, artsy T-shirts, lusciously-printed art tomes, and reproductions of world masterworks. Among the best are the Museum of Modern Art, the M.H. de Young, and the California Palace of the Legion of Honor in San Francisco, and the San Jose Museum of Art.

Some of the best bargains in the city are found at the many brand-name apparel factory outlets, many of which congregate in the South of Market district. More than 50 outlets are listed and mapped in a pamphlet, "San Francisco South of Market Factory Outlets." Pick one up at any outlet, or phone (415) 896-0988 or (415) 648-9240.

ENTERTAINMENT AND NIGHTLIFE

So much of San Francisco's nightlife takes place in the neighborhoods that it is hard to pinpoint one main "nightlife district." Broadway, so long the action strip for clubs and sex shows, has lost a good deal of steam lately. Certainly, the Theater District has a lot going on till the wee hours. The Nob Hill hotel scene, with its elegant view bars, draws a mix of tourists and loyal regulars. If you want to talk Proust or protest till dawn, the North Beach coffeehouses might be your scene. Gay nightlife centers on lower Castro Street and south of Market, singles bars dot Union Street, the punk crowds meet on Broadway and SoMa, and everybody shows up sooner or later on "Restaurant Row" in the Richmond District. If salsa's your thing, the Mission District Latin clubs might be your place. The Haight, upper Fillmore, and Union Street neighborhoods support a number of popular evening rendezvous. Across the bay, Berkeley always hosts lively student crowds, offering everything from coffeehouses and beer halls to symphonies and art films. Lectures, poetry readings, seminars, club meetings, exhibitions, and craft shows fill up the far-flung nooks and crannies of the metropolis. At the bottom end of the scale, the Tenderloin, a rough neighborhood after dark, is the dive *du jour* for porn and peep shows.

The Bay Area is a big center of the performing arts. Some, like the San Francisco Opera, ACT (American Conservatory Theater), and the Berkeley Repertory, have national reputations, but there are scores of innovative smaller companies, like the Eureka Theater, the Magic Theater, the Asian American Theater, the Young Performer's Theater, and the San Francisco Mime Troupe, scattered throughout the city and beyond. *Beach Blanket Babylon,* a whacky, long-running musical revue, continues to play to packed houses in Club Fugazi, North Beach.

Dance, like theater, is dominated by famous names—in this case the San Francisco Ballet and the Margaret Jenkins Dance Company. The San Francisco Bay Area Dance Coalition operates an information service for the scores of other lesser-known companies; call (415) 252-6240.

From chamber orchestras to the Grateful Dead, somebody's always setting up to make music here. The San Francisco Symphony season runs from September through May. The California Palace of the Legion of Honor arranges regular concerts of classical music, including demonstrations of antique forms and instruments, as well as lectures. The Asian Art Museum hosts an annual Asian American Jazz Festival. Blues, jazz, folk, country and ethnic music, including Irish bands and Cantonese opera, spice the mix. For the current word on concerts, clubs, and music festivals, call the KKSF Bay Line at (415) 982-4636. If it's jazz you're after, try the KJAZ Jazzline: (415) 769-4818.

San Francisco is famed for its comedy clubs, which nursed such national figures as Mort Sahl, Lenny Bruce, Bill Cosby, the Smothers Brothers, Shields and Yarnell, and Robin Williams.

New releases and seldom seen classic films play nightly in the city's cinemas, but film lovers should keep an eye on the universities, especially Berkeley, where the Pacific Film Archives serves as the Bay Area's film gallery. The San Francisco International Film Festival, based in the Palace of Fine Arts, but showing in cinemas all over town, brings works from around the world to San Francisco every spring.

Complete listings of cinema, dance, music, clubs, and other happenings appear weekly in the Sunday *Chronicle Datebook* section, along with some restaurants. Alternatively, you can call the Convention & Visitors Bureau Daily Events Information Line at (415) 391-2001, or the even more extensive BASS Tickets information number at (415) 676-2222, to find out what's on.

SPORTING EVENTS

San Francisco sports fans cheer the Forty-Niners in football and the Giants in baseball. Both teams play at Candlestick Park. The Oakland Athletics play baseball in the Coliseum across the bay. The Golden State Warriors basketball team also bangs the boards in Oakland, but draws support from both sides of the bay.

Collegiate sports have a moderate following here, growing to crescendo during the annual Big Game between the Berkeley and Stanford football teams.

BUYING TICKETS

You can, of course, buy tickets straight from the theater or stadium box office, but it is often easier and surely more certain to go through a ticket agency. These are listed in the telephone yellow pages under "Ticket Sales—Entertainment and Sports." You can charge tickets over the phone by calling the BASS Tickets number at (415) 762-2277.

If you happen to be near Union Square, the Hotel Saint Francis Theater Ticket Agency, right in the lobby arcade, is handy: call (415) 362-2325.

EATING

Dining out is San Francisco's most consuming passion. The planet's most finicky critics quibble endlessly about the city's place in the culinary firmament, but people who simply *enjoy* eating know that San Francisco is tops. At last count, there were over 4,200 restaurants, roughly one for every 176 residents. Expand your sights to the whole Bay Area, and your choices expand exponentially.

Along with their sophisticated palates, San Franciscans cultivate the habit of seeking out new cuisines while discovering the regional distinctions of old favorites. Gourmets don't simply eat Chinese food in San Francisco; they run a gauntlet of Mandarin, Shanghai, Hunan, Shandong, Sichuan, Mongolian, Cantonese, *dim sum* (a Cantonese delicacy), Chaozhou, Hakka, Straits Chinese, Burmese Chinese, Indo-Chinese, American Chinese, Chinese vegetarian, and the ubiquitous noodle and *juk* house. The same might pertain to San Francisco's abundant Italian restaurants, if most did not serve dishes from a mix of provinces. Within living memory, Japanese, Mexican, Greek, Korean, Vietnamese, and Thai cuisines have each enjoyed discovery and subsequent elevation to restaurant-goers' Favored Nation Status. American cookery, both regional (e.g., Creole, Tex-Mex, Southwest, California) and institutional (e.g., diner, ice cream parlor, pizzeria, greasy spoon), maintains its host of apologists and shrines, while Czech, Swiss, Scandinavian, German, Indonesian, and Polish are all represented somewhat more

THE EAST BAY FIRE OF 1991

Two years to the week after the Bay Area was rent by the Loma Prieta Earthquake, it was visited by yet another disaster so vast and devastating that it captured the nation's headlines. The disaster this time wasn't an earthquake but a wildfire that roared for 69 hours through the heart of Oakland's hilly neighborhoods, and at the height of its intensity was so powerful that it was destroying a city block every five minutes.

It all began innocuously enough on a Saturday afternoon when a conventional brush fire broke out in the dry grass high on the hills which separate California's hot inland valleys from the cool coastal areas about San Francisco Bay. The brush fire was brought under control by the fire department, but early on the morning of October 20 it was still smouldering when the sun rose on an unseasonably hot Sunday (92 degrees) and extremely rare "Santa Anna" type winds, which began racing across the hot Central Valley of California toward the Oakland hills at a velocity of 50 miles an hour.

It was then that an ember from the previous day's brush fire, finding ready fuel in a landscape parched dry by five years of drought, burst into a wall of yellow flame, and began roaring up trees, and racing across meadows until, within 15 minutes 100 acres were engulfed in a rampaging fire.

Down below these dry hills, on Highway 24, casually curious Sunday drivers passing by on the freeway, noted flames on the ridgetops, but none knew of the confusion and panic that had suddenly overwhelmed these steep curving streets. One resident, leaping into her car, gunned it straight through a wall of flame and came out on the other side unscathed. Others, terrified and disoriented, were engulfed by fire. Fire trucks raced toward the hills, but their own effectiveness was hindered by streets so narrow and curving that fire trucks were unable to maneuver properly. Water pressure in the fire hydrants was low, and among the residents, general confusion reigned.

Traffic on the freeway below began to slow. Fire and police vehicles had begun to arrive, then, almost inexplicably, flames leapt over the freeway and began racing up the hills of two more hillside neighborhoods. By mid-afternoon one thousand firefighters, drawn from all over Northern California were fighting the blaze, desperately trying to draw lines some distance from the fire, and maintain them. One of these lines was behind the landmark Claremont Hotel, a rallying point not only because of the building's charm and historical value, but because if that vast and rambling, dry-as-kindling wooden palace had indeed burned, it might well have taken much of Berkeley with it.

In the meantime, in those neighborhoods still threatened but not yet engulfed by the fire, police loudspeakers were ordering residents to evacuate. Some did. Others, dragging their lawn hoses up onto their roofs, stayed behind. Some saved their homes, and sometimes with great heroism, saved the homes and lives of their neighbors. Not until Monday afternoon had the army of firefighters, aided by dying winds managed to bring the blaze under control. Among the people uprooted by the fire were a county supervisor, a state senator, judges, professors, novelist Maxine Hong Kingston (who lost a work in progress), and baseball great Reggie Jackson. Among the famous structures destroyed were irreplaceable architectural gems by Bernard Maybeck and Julia Morgan.

In the end the human cost was terrible: 26 dead, 150 injured, 5,000 homeless, 3,350 homes destroyed. The toll on pets, wildlife, gardens, and natural beauty was similarly devastating. Where before there had been shady roads, streams, birds, deer, and fine homes, there were now great piles of white ashes, burned chassis of over 2,000 cars, and lines of charred telephone poles, their broken, and curled live wires moving slightly in the wind. The total cost of the fire was estimated at between $1.5 and 2 billion, making it one of the costliest disasters in American history.

PHOTO BY RON DELANY

tentatively. French, oblivious to public whim and frugal budget, dwells eternal in the bosom of established grace. Curiously, the rich and wondrous cuisine of India, despite some excellent in-town restaurants, seems planted more firmly in Berkeley.

Such a legacy might yet be matched by a dozen other metropolitan areas, but which others also offer Laotian, Caribbean, Argentine, Moroccan, Basque, Salvadoran, Russian, Brazilian, Cambodian, Ethiopian, Armenian, Afghani, Nicaraguan, Persian, Filipino, Danish, Lebanese, Polynesian, Burmese, Hungarian, and Peruvian restaurants? And these categories fail to take into account the subtle *blending* of cuisines, both unconscious and self-conscious, that is evolving in California.

No single neighborhood has a monopoly on good restaurants. They are where you find them, scattered all over the city. There are, of course, some general rules of thumb. North Beach is weighted toward Italian, while the fare in Nihonmachi (Japantown) is, not surprisingly, mostly Japanese. Chinatown's traditional restaurants serve up home-style Cantonese and American-Chinese dishes, while new-style Chinese restaurants (found all over the Bay Area) tend to balance their menus with favorite dishes (according to American palates) from all over China. The up-and-coming "Southeast Asia Town" along Ellis Street in the Tenderloin District iss a center of the *phö*, a small café-like institution specializing in hearty soup noodles. The Mission District, though no slouch for Continental and Asian restaurants, has a decidedly Latin-American flavor, of which most are devoted to Mexican and the rest to Cuban, Nicaraguan, Salvadoran, Argentine, and others. The Richmond District, especially along Clement and Geary streets, is justly famed for its multi-ethnic restaurants, with a strong emphasis on Asian. A short listing of restaurants appears in "Backmatter."

Another explanation for San Francisco's fecundity of gastronomic pleasures is its geographic placement between a teeming sea and the most productive farming region in the United States.

The bay, though crippled by pollution, still breeds a harvest of sea life, including the Dungeness crab, San Francisco's answer to the Maine lobster. Crab season is from mid-November through June, during which time you can buy them fresh at Fisherman's Wharf and Chinatown. The waters outside the Golden Gate and up to Bolinas and Tomales bays yield a good variety of fish. Most tourists head to Fisherman's Wharf for seafood, but many locals swear that the best seafood restaurants are not even on the water, but downtown. The Italians, Chinese, Japanese, Cajun, French, and others have their own recipes.

Northern California grows some of the most beautiful produce in the world. Unfortunately, American consumers all too often buy their fruit and vegetables solely for their beauty and girth, unlike the Chinese, who believe that small fruit is sweeter and juicier than large ones, and the Europeans (and Asians), who know that ugly fruit sometimes tastes the best. San Franciscans, fortunately, are more savvy than most Americans about what's good to eat, and you will find many excellent produce stalls, particularly in the Chinatown, Richmond, North Beach, and Mission districts. The Farmers Market at 100 Alemany Boulevard, on the south side of Bernal Heights, sells the surplus of California farms from Tuesday to Saturday; phone (415) 647-9423. Closer to downtown, the Civic Center Market spills over United Nations Plaza between Leavenworth and Hyde on Wednesdays and Sundays. Oakland and Marin County both support their own farmers' markets. And lest you think that San Francisco can't grow its own, some 70 community gardens in the city raise vegetables and herbs for neighborhood tables.

Some culinary inventions have been claimed by San Francisco as her very own. No doubt the most famous is the Chinese fortune cookie—invented, ironically, in the Japanese Tea Garden. Cioppino, an Italian fish stew, is another dish that has been called a native. San Franciscans like to spar with New Yorkers for the honor of inventing chop suey. San Francisco *may* have been first to see it on a menu, but come on now! Chinese home cooking has known the dish—which is essentially chopped up odds and ends—for centuries.

Probably the favorite San Franciscan specialty is sourdough French bread—and it really does have a magnificent history. The bread started, according to legend, in the days before shortenings or yeasts were widely available, when gold miners used to raise their breads through fermentation induced by a *starter*. The starter, a fermented mix of flour and water that was added to the bread batter, caused the dough to rise. Before the loaf was baked, a section was pinched off and preserved for use in "starting" the next batch of bread. It is this starter that gives the bread its characteristic sourness, which connoisseurs swear improves with age. The most highly cherished part of any sourdough bakery is its starter. When San Francisco burned in 1906, heroic bakers braved the flames to save their venerable starters, which survived to consecrate countless generations of new loaves to this day. Thus, when we eat sourdough bread, we eat a bit of history descended from gold rush bacteria. Long may they live!

Some of the best shows in San Francisco are free to the public.

Drinking

San Francisco is distinguished for the invention of the only indigenous American method of brewing beer. It is called steam beer—though it has nothing at all to do with steam.

What, then, is unique about steam beer?

Steam beer is made without ice. To make a lager, the temperature must be lowered to freezing. Unfortunately, in the early days of the gold rush, San Francisco's mild climate produced no ice, and the unslackable thirst for beer could not be quenched by imported stock. San Francisco brewers devised a brewing method that used air cooling instead of ice. As the idea caught on, other steam-beer breweries started up, but all disappeared with the advent of refrigeration, except San Francisco's own Anchor Steam brewery.

Anchor Steam traces its roots back to 1851, when the founding family started brewing in San Francisco. (The name of Anchor was not used until 1896.) The modern plant, located at the northern foot of Potrero Hill, now brews three ales, two lagers, and a delicious wheat beer by their special method. They also partake of the old brewers' custom of making a special Christmas vintage, a rare and valuable limited edition. Beloved by San Franciscans, Anchor Steam has won a devoted and partisan cult following. Beer fanciers who want a taste of the gold rush should seek it out.

San Francisco is the capital of another alcoholic mystique: California wine. Despite what the French (and their greatest customers, the English) say about wine, California needn't apologize. The Napa Valley produces the most sought-after vintages, followed by those from Sonoma County. Alameda, Mendocino, Lake, Santa Clara, Solano, Santa Cruz, Monterey, and counties farther afield also produce good and plentiful wines. Still, Napa and Sonoma have the greatest number of famous wineries, and get the lion's share of publicity. Visiting wineries is one of the most pleasant day trips that you can make from San Francisco.

For those who want to know about wine, the local network embraces hundreds of books, newsletters, winery and vineyard tours, wine stewards, and specialty purveyors that can answer your questions and recommend vintages. Unfortunately, many San Franciscans take their wines a little too seriously. If all the superfluous air expelled in talking about wine were put to use in making Anchor Steam Beer, the world would be a much happier place.

The Great Outdoors

San Francisco's greatest asset is its close proximity to the countryside. Immediately to the north a semi-wilderness of national, state, and regional parklands stretches more than 40 miles (64 kilometers) from the Golden Gate, including Muir Woods, Point Reyes, and Mount Tamalpais. The regional parks of the East Bay Peninsula, and South Bay embrace still more acreage, with forests, beaches, wildlife, and hundreds of miles of trails. If that's not enough room for you, San Francisco is only four hours from the Sierra Nevada, and deep-sea fishing on the wide Pacific or San Francisco Bay starts as close as Fisherman's Wharf.

Within San Francisco's own narrow boundaries, the parks and Presidio preserve a large percentage of the city for public use. Among the more popular outdoor activities available are golf, horseback riding, hiking, picnicking, bicycling, skateboarding, swimming, fly-casting, rowing, horseshoe pitching, ball games, camping, lawn bowling, sailing, and hang gliding. Keep up to date with the Recreation and Park Department's newsletter, "What's Doing in the Parks," available at Golden Gate Park's McLaren Lodge, or call (415) 666-7201.

Recommended Reading

Thousands of books have been written about San Francisco. For background, start with Tom Cole's entertaining *A Short History of San Francisco* (Lexikos), which is widely available in the museums and bookstores. Track down Herbert Ashbury's *The Barbary Coast* for an entertaining jaunt through some of San Francisco's shadier byways. The history and culture of pre-European Bay Area residents are treated in Malcolm Margolin's *The Ohlone Way* and *The Way We Lived: California Indian Reminiscences, Stories, and Songs* (Heyday Books). The tong wars are the subject of Richard Dillon's somewhat lurid, if entertaining, *The Hatchet Men* (Comstock Editions, Inc.). Thomas Chinn's history of Chinatown, *Bridging the Pacific* (Chinese Historical Society), is the most complete on the subject. *San Francisco Chinatown—A Walking Tour*, by Shirley Fong-Torres (China Books & Periodicals), is the most intimate guide to the city's most populous quarter.

Among the many fun and informative walking companions are the works of *Chronicle* writer Margot Patterson Doss. Her *San Francisco at Your Feet* (Grove Press) gives the same selective, personal treatment to San Francisco's neighborhoods as her *Golden Gate Park at Your Feet* (Chronicle Books) does for the park,

There, There (Presidio Press) for the East Bay, and *Paths of Gold* (Chronicle Books) for the Golden Gate National Recreation Area.

Adah Bakalinsky's illustrated *Stairway Walks in San Francisco* (Lexikos) pokes around some of the city's most enchanting stairways and obscure neighborhoods, territory unknown even to most natives. Another good walking companion, who sketches as he goes, is Earl Thollander, whose *San Francisco—30 Walking Tours from the Embarcadero to the Golden Gate* is published by Clarkson N. Potter.

San Francisco Access (AccessPress), by Richard Saul Wurman, describes city shops, restaurants, hotels, and sights, street by street, with attention to architectural detail. Sally and John Woodbridge's *San Francisco—the Guide* (American Institute of Architects) is even more thorough in its treatment of architecture. My personal favorite, however, is Randolph Delehanty's *The Ultimate Guide: San Francisco* (Chronicle Books). Delehanty's pleasant style, excellent maps, and rich observation of architecture, history, and city planning is a self-contained education in the humanities.

The Literary World of San Francisco & Environs, by Don Herron (City Lights), is geared for literary tours of specific neighborhoods, and is written by the man who gives the Dashiell Hammett walking tours. *Literary San Francisco* by Lawrence

The Marina District basks by the bay like a Mediterranean seaport.

Ferlinghetti and Nancy J. Peters (City Lights Books and Harper & Row) covers similar territory with terrific portrait and group photos. Herbert Gold makes his own literary history in *Travels in San Francisco* (Arcade).

For independent travelers who like structured itineraries, Jack Shelton's *How to Spend 1 to 10 Perfect Days in San Francisco* (Shelton Publishing) might prove handy. The *AM/PM Guide* runs slickly through restaurants, clubs, sightseeing, trendy night-spots, etc.

When it comes to dedicated restaurant guides, you are really on your own. There are so many, and they are so specialized and timely, that you are best to go with what strikes your fancy at the moment.

Sally Socolich presents the definitive shopping guide, arranged by item, in *Bargain Hunting in the Bay Area* (Wingbow Press). An easy-to-carry map to San Francisco's favorite shopping streets, *Shopwalks*, was compiled by Judith Maas Rheingold.

Beyond the city, car travelers will enjoy discovering out-of-the-way destinations with *Bay Area Backroads* (Harper & Row), by Jerry and Catherine Graham. The authority on Berkeley, and an entertaining read in its own right, is Don Pitcher's *Berkeley Inside/Out* (Heyday Books). Malcolm Margolin wrote the history chapter. *Across the Golden Gate* (Harper & Row), by Alan Magary and Kerstin Fraser Magary, and *Making the Most of Sonoma* (Presidio Press), by Don Edwards, give thorough treatment of the North Bay. If you are visiting wineries, the Sunset guide *Wine Country* lists them all, virtually, with maps.

The natural side of the Bay Area is thoroughly explored in a mighty host of volumes. The Sierra Club publishes many of them, including *To Walk with a Quiet Mind*, a good companion on the Point Reyes and Mount Tamalpais trails by Nancy Olmsted. *An Outside Guide to the San Francisco Bay Area* (Wilderness Press), by Dorothy L. Whitnah, ventures to yet other outdoor areas.

Two out-of-print guidebooks are worth grabbing if you happen to find them in the secondhand bookstores. One is *The Other Guide to San Francisco* (Chronicle Books), by Jim Hansen. Written with humor, it is particularly informative for persons tracking down such fading memories as Haight-Ashbury hippie haunts and North Beach beatnik rendezvous. *The Native's Guidebook—San Francisco Free & Easy* was edited by William Ristow and published in 1980 by Downwind Books under sponsorship of *The Bay Guardian*. Though extremely dated now, it's still a good eye-opener for residents.

B A C K M A T T E R

Shirley Fong-Torres contributed extensively to the following lists:

ACCOMMODATIONS

B = Budget; under $50   M = Median; $50-150   L = Luxury; over $150

H O T E L S ,   M O T E L S ,   I N N S

Archbishop's Mansion (B & B); 1000 Fulton St., S.F. (Alamo Square); (415) 563-7872; M-L

Bed and Breakfast Inn (B & B); 4 Charlton Ct., S.F. (Cow Hollow); (415) 921-9784; M

Campton Place; 340 Stockton St., S.F. (near Union Square); (415) 781-5555; L

Holiday Inn; 750 Kearny St., S.F. (Chinatown/Financial District); (415) 433-6600; M

Claremont Resort; 41 Tunnel Road, Oakland; (510) 843-3000; M-L

Donatello; Post at Mason, S.F. (Theater District); (415) 441-7100; L

Fairmont Hotel; 950 Mason, S.F. (Nob Hill); (415) 772-5000; L

Four Seasons Clift Hotel; Geary at Taylor (Theater District); (415) 775-4700; M-L

Garden Court Hotel; 520 Cowper St., Palo Alto; (415) 322-9000; M-L

Grant Plaza Hotel; 465 Grant Ave., S.F. (Chinatown); (415) 434-3883; B

Grosvenor House; 899 Pine St., S.F. (Nob Hill); (415) 421-1899; M
(long- and short-term suites)

Huntington Hotel; 1075 California St., S.F. (Nob Hill); (415) 474-5400; L

Hyatt Regency; 5 Embarcadero Center, S.F. (Financial District); (510) 788-1234; L

Hyatt Regency Oakland; 1001 Broadway, Oakland, (510) 893-1234; M-L

Inn at Union Square; 440 Post St., S.F.; (415) 397-3510; M-L

Jackson Court Bed and Breakfast Inn; 2198 Jackson St., S.F. (Pacific Heights);
(415) 929-7670; M

Juliana Hotel; 590 Bush St., S.F. (near Union Square); (415) 392-2540; M

Mandarin Oriental; 222 Sansome St., S.F. (Financial District);
(415) 885-0999 or (800) 622-0404; L

Mansion Hotel (B & B); 2220 Sacramento St., S.F. (Pacific Heights); (415) 929-9444; M

Mark Hopkins Inter-Continental Hotel; Number One Nob Hill; (415) 392-3434; L

Marriott; 777 Market St., S.F. (South of Market); (415) 896-1600; L

Miyako Hotel; 1625 Post St., S.F. (Japantown); (415) 922-3200; M-L
(Western and tatami rooms)

Monticello Inn; 127 Ellis St., S.F. (Theater District); (415) 392-8800; M

Nikko Hotel, 222 Mason St., S.F. (near Union Square); (415) 394-1111

Obrero Hotel and Basque Restaurant; 1208 Stockton St., S.F. (Chinatown);
(415) 989-3960; B

Pan Pacific Hotel; 500 Post St., S.F. (Theater District); (415) 771-8600; L

Park Hyatt; 333 Battery St., S.F. (Financial District); (415) 392-1234; L

Phoenix Inn; 601 Eddy St., S.F. (near Civic Center); (415) 776-1380; B-M
Queen Anne Hotel; 1590 Sutter St., S.F. (Cathedral Hill, Western Addition);
   (415) 441-2828; M
Ritz-Carlton; 600 Stockton, S.F. (Nob Hill); (415) 296-7465; L
San Francisco Airport Hilton; S.F. International Airport; (415) 589-0770
   or 1-800-HILTONS; M
San Remo Hotel; 2237 Mason Street, S.F. (North Beach); (415) 776-8688; B-M
Sheraton Palace Hotel; Market at New Montgomery, S.F. (Financial District);
   (415) 392-8600; L
Stanford Court Hotel; 905 California St., S.F. (Nob Hill); (415) 989-3500; L
Stanyan Park Hotel; 750 Stanyan St. (in Buena Vista); (415) 751-1000; M
Union Street Inn (B & B); 2229 Union St., S.F. (Cow Hollow); (415) 346-0424; M
Victorian Inn on the Park (B & B); 301 Lyon St., S.F. (Haight-Ashbury);
   (415) 931-1830; M-L
Vintage Court Hotel; 650 Bush St., S.F. (near Union Square); (415) 392-4666; M
Washington Inn; 495 10th St., Oakland; (510) 452-1776; M
Washington Square Inn; 1660 Stockton St., S.F. (North Beach); (415) 981-4220; M
Westin St. Francis; 335 Powell St., S.F. (Union Square); (415) 397-7000; M-L

CAMPING

Note: For reservations in any state park, call (800) 444-7275.
Angel Island State Park; backpack camping
Anthony Chabot Regional Park Family Camp; off Marciel Gate on Redwood Road,
   about five miles (eight km) from Castro Valley, in the East Bay;
   (510) 538-6470
Big Basin State Park; Big Basin Way, off Highway 9 in the Santa Cruz Mountains
Del Valle Regional Park; Del Valle Road off Mines Road south of Livermore,
   in the East Bay; (510) 636-1684
Golden Gate National Recreation Area; group and backpack camping; (415) 556-0560
Half Moon Bay State Beach; at Francis Beach, along Highway 1 in San Mateo County
Henry Cowell State Park; Graham Hill Road between Felton and Santa Cruz,
   in the Santa Cruz Mountains
Mount Tamalpais State Park; family and backpack camping
Ohlone Wilderness backpack camps; on Ohlone Trail between Sunol and Del Valle
   regional parks in the hills south of Livermore, in the East Bay; (510) 636-1684
Point Reyes National Seashore; backpack camping, in Marin County; (415) 663-1092
Portola State Park; family and backpack camping, in San Mateo County
San Mateo County Park; on Pescadero Road near La Honda, on the Peninsula;
   (415) 879-0212
Sunol Regional Wilderness Family Camp; Geary Road, off Calaveras Road, six miles
   (10 km) south of Interstate 680 between Pleasanton and Fremont, in the East Bay;
   (510) 636-1684

YOUTH HOSTELS

Fort Mason (see S.F. International Hostel)

Golden Gate Hostel (on western side of Marin Headlands in Golden Gate National Recreation Area); Building 941, Fort Barry (near Sausalito); (415) 331-2777

Hidden Villa Hostel; 26807 Moody Road, Los Altos Hills (San Mateo County); (415) 941-6407

Montara Lighthouse Hostel; 16th St. (Highway One), Montara (San Mateo coast); (415) 728-7177

Pigeon Point Lighthouse Hostel; Pigeon Point Road (Highway One), Pescadero (San Mateo Coast); (415) 879-0633

Point Reyes Hostel; near Limantour Beach in Point Reyes National Seashore (Marin County); (415) 663-8811

San Francisco International Hostel; Building 240, Fort Mason, S.F.; (415) 771-7277; (while there, pick up information on other northern Californian hostels)

RESTAURANTS

B = Budget; under $10 per person, excluding drinks
M = Median; $10-25 per person, excluding drinks
L = Luxury; over $25 per person, excluding drinks

AFRICAN

Blue Nile; 2525 Telegraph Ave., Berkeley; (510) 540-6777; B

Nyala; 39 Grove St., S.F. (Civic Center); (415) 861-0788; B

Rasselas; 1690 Market, S.F. (Civic Center); (415) 621-8601; M

AMERICAN/CALIFORNIA CUISINE

Alcatraz Bar and Grill; Pier 39, S.F. (near Fisherman's Wharf); (415) 434-1818; B

Auberge du Soleil; 1860 Rutherford Hill Rd., Rutherford (Napa Valley); (707) 963-1211; L

Big Four, The; in the Huntington Hotel, S.F. (Nob Hill); (415) 474-5400; M-L

Bix; 56 Gold St., S.F. (Jackson Square); (415) 433-6300; L

California Culinary Academy and The Academy Grill; 625 Polk St., S.F. (near Civic Center); (415) 771-3500; B-M

Campton Place; 340 Stockton, S.F. (Union Square); (415) 781-5155; L

Chez Panisse; 1517 Shattuck Ave., Berkeley; (510) 548-5049; L

Cypress Club; 500 Jackson St., S.F. (Jackson Square); (415) 296-8555;M

Fat Lady, The; 201 Washington St., Oakland; (510) 465-4996; M

Fog City Diner; 1300 Battery St., S.F. (Financial District); (415) 982-2000; M

Fourth Street Grill; 1820 Fourth St., Berkeley; (510) 849-0526; L

Gingerbread House, The; 741 5th St., Oakland; (510) 444-7373; L (Cajun and Creole)

Greens; Fort Mason Center, Building A, S.F. (Marina); (415) 771-6222; B-M (Vegetarian)

Harris'; 2100 Van Ness, S.F. (Pacific Heights); (415) 673-1888; L

Hayes Street Grill; 324 Hayes St., S.F. (near Civic Center); (415) 863-5545; L

Izzy's Steak and Chop House; 3345 Steiner St., S.F. (Marina); (415) 771-6222; M

Julie's Supper Club; 1123 Folsom St., S.F. (South of Market); (415) 861-0707; M

Lark Creek Inn; 234 Magnolia, Larkspur; (415) 924-7766; L

Leon's Bar-B-Q; 1911 Fillmore St., S.F. (near Japantown); (415) 922-2436; 2800 Sloat Blvd., S.F. (near the zoo); (415) 681-3071; B-M

McArthur Park; 607 Front St., S.F. (Financial District); (415) 389-5700; M

Mel's Drive-In; 3355 Geary Blvd., S.F. (Richmond District); (415) 387-2244; or 2165 Lombard St., S.F. (Marina District); (415) 921-3039; B

Milly's; 1613-4th St., San Rafael; (415) 459-1601; M (Vegetarian)

Mustard's Grill; 7399 Highway 29, Yountville (Napa Valley); (707) 944-2424; M

Postrio; 545 Post St., S.F. (Union Square); (415) 776-7825; L

Ruth's Chris Steak House; 1700 California St., S.F. (Pacific Heights); (415) 673-0557; M

South Park Café; 108 South Park, S.F. (South of Market); (415) 495-7275; B-M

Stars; 150 Redwood Alley, S.F. (near Civic Center); (415) 861-7827; L

Tommy's Joynt; Geary at Van Ness, S.F.; (415) 775-4216; B-M

Val's Burgers; 2115 Kelly St., Hayward (East Bay); (510) 899-8257; B

Zola's; 395 Hayes St., S.F. (near Civic Center); (415) 864-4824; M-L

Zuni Café; 1658 Market St., S.F.; (415) 552-2522; M-L

BASQUE

Des Alpes; 732 Broadway, S.F. (North Beach);(415) 788-9900

Obrero Hotel and Basque Restaurant; 1208 Stockton St., S.F. (Chinatown); (415) 989-3960; B (set meal at set time nightly)

BRAZILIAN

Bahia Brazilian Restaurant; 41 Franklin St., S.F. (near Civic Center); (415) 626-3306; M

Brazil Restaurant; 2114 Fillmore St., S.F. (Western Addition/Pacific Heights); (415) 346-9888; M

Eunice's Restaurant; 3392 24th St., S.F. (Mission District); (415) 821-4600; M

CAMBODIAN

Angkor Wat; 4217 Geary Blvd., S.F. (Richmond District); (415) 221-7887; M

Phnom Pehn; 631 Larkin St., S.F. (Tenderloin); (415) 775-5979; M

CARIBBEAN

El Nuevo Frutilandia; 3077 24th St., S.F. (Mission District); (415) 648-2958; B-M

Miss Pearl's; 601 Eddy, S.F. (near Civic Center); (415) 775-5267; M

CHINESE

Cafe Pacifica; 333 Bush St., S.F. (Financial District); (415) 296-8203; M (dim sum)

Chef Jia's; 925 Kearny St., S.F. (Chinatown); (415) 398-1626; B

China Moon; 639 Post, S.F. (near Union Square); (415) 775-4789; M (dim sum)

China Station; 700 University Ave., Berkeley; (510) 548-7880; M

Dol Ho; 808 Pacific Ave., S.F. (Chinatown); (415) 392-2828; B (dim sum)
East Ocean; 3199 Powell St., Emeryville (at Emeryville Marina, in the East Bay); (510) 655-4456; M (dim sum)
Golden Dynasty; 10140 San Pablo Ave., El Cerrito (East Bay); (510) 524-7851; M
Happy Immortal; 4401 Cabrillo, S.F. (Richmond District); (415) 386-7538; B
Harbor Village; Four Embarcadero Center, S.F. (Financial District); (415) 781-8833; M (dim sum)
Honey Court; 760-778 Clay St., S.F. (Chinatown); (415) 788-6100; B (dim sum)
Hong Kong Flower Lounge; 5322 Geary Blvd., S.F. (Richmond District); (415) 668-8998; 1671 El Camino Real, Millbrae (San Mateo County); (415) 588-9972; 51 Millbrae Ave., Millbrae; (415) 692-6666; M (dim sum)
Hunan Restaurant; 396 11th St., Oakland; (510) 444-1155; M
Hunan Restaurant; 924 Sansome St., S.F. (Chinatown); (415) 956-7727; B
Imperial Palace; 919 Grant Ave., S.F. (Chinatown); (415) 982-4440; M-L
J & J; 615 Jackson St., S.F. (Chinatown); (415) 981-7308; B
Kowloon Vegetarian; 909 Grant Ave., S.F. (Chinatown); (415) 362-9888; B
Lucky Creation; 854 Washington St., S.F. (Chinatown); (415) 989-0818; B (vegetarian)
Mandarin, The; 900 North Point, S.F. (Ghirardelli Square, near Fisherman's Wharf); (415) 673-8812; M-L
Monsoon; 601 Van Ness Ave., S.F. (Civic Center); (415) 441-3232; M
New Asia; 772 Pacific Ave., S.F. (Chinatown); (415) 391-6666; B-M (dim sum)
North Sea Village; 300 Turney, Sausalito (Marin County); (415) 331-3300; M (dim sum)
Royal Kitchen; 2353 Mission St., S.F. (Mission District); (415) 824-4219; B
Silver Restaurant; 737 Washington St., S.F.; (415) 433-8888; B
Tai Chi; 2031 Polk St., S.F. (Polk Gulch); (415) 441-6758; B
Tommy Toy's Haute Cuisine Chinoise; 655 Montgomery, S.F. (Financial District); (415) 397-4888; M-L
Vallejo Café; 750 Vallejo St., S.F. (Chinatown); (415) 433-2229; B
Wu Kong; 101 Spear St., S.F. (Financial District); (415) 957-9300; B-M (dim sum)
Yank Sing; 427 Battery St., S.F. (Financial District); (415) 362-1640; M (dim sum)
Yuet Lee; S.F.; 1300 Stockton St., S.F. (Chinatown); (415) 982-6020; B

CONTINENTAL

Cafe Majestic; 1500 Sutter, S.F. (Pacific Heights); (415) 776-6400; M
Julius'Castle; 1541 Montgomery St., S.F. (Telegraph Hill); (415) 362-3042; L
L'Avenue; 3854 Geary Blvd., S.F. (Richmond District); (415) 386-1555; L
Maltese Grill; 20 Annie St., S.F. (South of Market); (415) 777-1955; M
1001 Nob Hill; 1001 Nob Hill, S.F. (Nob Hill); (415) 441-1001; L
Splendido's; Embarcadero 4, Podium Level, S.F. (Financial District); (415) 986-3222; M
Square One; 190 Pacific Ave., S.F. (Financial District); (415) 788-1110; L

CUBAN (SEE CARIBBEAN)

ENGLISH
Lisa's Tea Treasures; 1203 Lincoln Ave., San Jose; (408) 8327; high tea; M

ETHIOPIAN
Fana Ethiopian Restaurant; 464 Eighth St., Oakland; (510) 271-0696; M
Nyala; 39 Grove St., S.F. (Civic Center); (415) 861-0788; M

FRENCH
Amelio's; 1630 Powell St., S.F. (North Beach); (415) 397-4339; L
Dining Room, The; 600 Stockton St., S.F. (Financial District); (415) 296-7465; L
Fleur de Lys; 777 Sutter St., S.F. (Downtown); (415) 673-7779; L
Masa's; 648 Bush, S.F. (near Union Square); (415) 989-7154; L
Pacific Grill; 500 Post St., S.F. (near Union Square); (415) 771-8600; M-L

GERMAN
Shroeder's; 240 Front St., S.F. (Financial District); (415) 421-4778; M

GREEK
Stoyanof's Cafe and Restaurant; 1240 Ninth Ave., S.F. (Sunset); (415) 664-3664; M

INDIAN
Gaylord's; Ghirardelli Square, S.F. (near Fisherman's Wharf); (415) 771-8822; L
Maharani; 1122 Post St. (Downtown); (415) 775-1988; M
North India; 3131 Webster, S.F. (Marina); (415) 931-1556; M
Viceroy India House; 22532 Mission Blvd., Hayward (East Bay); (510) 886-9411; B

ITALIAN
Buca Giovanni; 800 Greenwich St., S.F.; (415) 776-7766; M-L
Cafe Macaroni; 59 Jackson, S.F. (North Beach); (415) 956-9737; M
Cafferata's Ravioli Factory; Columbus at Filbert, S.F. (North Beach);
 (415) 392-7544; B-M
Caesar's; Bay at Powell, S.F. (near Fisherman's Wharf); (415) 989-6000; M
Donatello; 501 Post, S.F. (near Union Square); (415) 441-7182; L
Etrusca; 121 Spear St., S.F. (South of Financial District); (415) 777-0330; L
Gold Spike; 527 Columbus, S.F. (North Beach); (415) 421-4591; M
Green Valley; 510 Green St., S.F. (North Beach); (415) 788-9384; B-M
Kuleto's; 221 Powell St., S.F. (Union Square); (415) 397-7720; M-L
Palio D'Asti; 640 Sacramento St., S.F. (Financial District); (415) 395-9800; M
Tra Vigne; 1050 Charter Oak Ave., St. Helena (Napa Valley); (707) 967-4444; M
U.S. Restaurant; 431 Columbus, S.F. (North Beach); (415) 362-6251; B
Vanessi's; 1177 California St., S.F. (Nob Hill); (415) 771-2422; M
Vicolo; 201 Ivy, S.F. (Civic Center); (415) 863-2382; M
Zachary's Chicago Pizza; 1853 Solano Ave., Berkeley; (510) 525-5950; or
 2801 College Ave., Oakland; (510) 655-3042; M-L

JAPANESE
Dai Ten; 1830 Webster St., Oakland; (510) 836-3021; M
Kabuto; 5116 55th Ave., S.F. (Richmond District); (415) 752-5652; L
Osome; 1923 Filmore, S.F. (Richmond District); (415) 346-2311; or 3145 Filmore, S.F.
Sanppo Restaurant; 1702 Post Street, S.F. (Japantown); (415) 346-3486; B
Yoshi's; 6030 Claremont Ave., Oakland; (510) 652-9200; (famous for its live jazz) L
Yoshida-Ya; 2909 Webster, S.F. (Japantown); (415) 346-3431; M-L

KOREAN
Sorabol Korean Restaurant; 372 Grand Ave., Oakland; (510) 839-2288; M

MEXICAN
Cadillac Club; 325 Minna St., S.F. (South of Market); (415) 543-8226; M
Chevy's; 150 Fourth St. S.F.(Financial District); (415) 543-8060; M
Corona Bar and Grill; 88 Cyril Magnin, S.F. (Union Square); (415) 392-5500; M
Guaymas; 5 Main Street, Tiburon; (415) 435-6399; B-M
La Cumbre; 515 Valencia, S.F. (Mission District); (415) 863-8205; B
La Imperial; 948 C St., Hayward (East Bay); (510) 537-6227; B
La Taqueria; 2889 Mission, S.F. (Mission District); (415) 285-7117; B

MOROCCAN
Mamounia; 4411 Balboa, S.F. (Outer Richmond); (415) 752-6566; or 200 Merrydale
Road, San Rafael; (415) 472-1372; M

NICARAGUAN
El Trebol; 3324 24th St., S.F. (Mission District); (415) 285-6298; B
Nicaragua Restaurant; 3015 Mission St., S.F. (Mission District); (415) 826-3672; B

PERUVIAN
Fina Estampa; 2374 Mission St., S.F. (Mission District); (415) 824-4437; (also Spanish
food) B

RUSSIAN
Petrouchka; 2930 College Ave., Berkeley; (510) 848-7860; M
Russian Renaissance; 5241 Geary Blvd., S.F.; (415) 752-8558; M

SEAFOOD (WESTERN STYLE)
Alioto's #8; 8 Fisherman's Wharf, S.F.; (415) 673-0183; M
Bentley's Seafood Grill; 185 Sutter St., S.F.; (415) 989-6895; M
Blue Dolphin; San Leandro Marina (East Bay); (510) 483-5900; M
Pacific Green; 2424 Van Ness Ave., S.F. (near Marina District); (415) 771-3388; L
Pacific Heights Bar and Grill; 2001 Filmore St., S.F. (Lower Pacific Heights);
  (415) 567-3337; M
Sabella's; 2766 Taylor St., S.F. (Fisherman's Wharf); (415) 771-6775; M-L
Scott's Seafood Grill & Bar; Jack London Square, Oakland; (510) 444-3456; L
Scott's; 2400 Lombard St., S.F. (Marina); (415) 563-8988; M-L

Spenger's Fish Grotto; 1919 4th St., Berkeley; (510) 845-7771; B
Tadich Grill; 240 California St., S.F. (Financial District); (415) 391-2373; M

S P A N I S H
Alejandro's; 1840 Clement, S.F. (Richmond); (415) 668-1184; M

T H A I
Khan Toke; 5937 Geary Blvd., S.F. (Richmond); (415) 668-6654; M-L
Plearn Thai; 2050 University Ave., Berkeley; (510) 841-2148; B-M
Royal Thai; 951 Clement St., S.F. (Sunset); (415) 386-1795; B-M
Swatdee; 4166 24th Street, S.F. (Noe Valley); (415) 824-8070; M

V I E T N A M E S E
Golden Turtle; 308 Fifth Ave., S.F. (Richmond); (415) 221-5285; M
Le Cheval; 1414 Jefferson St., Oakland; (510) 763-8495; B
Thanh Long; 4101 Judah St., S.F. (Sunset); (415) 665-1146; B-M

TOURS

C R U I S E   L I N E S   S E R V I N G   S A N   F R A N C I S C O
Admiral Cruises Inc.; 1220 Biscayne Blvd., Miami, Florida 33132; (305) 374-1611
Clipper Cruise Line of Saint Louis; (314) 727-2929 (serving Redwood City)
Cunard; 555 Fifth Ave., New York, New York 10017; (800) 221-4770
Holland American Line Westours Inc.; 300 Elliott Ave. W., Seattle, Washington 98119;
    (206) 281-3535
Princess Cruises; 2029 Century Park East, Los Angeles; (213) 553-1770
Regency Cruises; 260 Madison Ave., New York, New York 10016; (800) 457-5566
Royal Viking; 750 Battery Street, S.F.; (415) 398-8000
Sitmar; 10100 Santa Monica Blvd., Los Angeles; (213) 553-1666

B U S   T O U R S
Gray Line Tours; (415) 558-9400; Bay Area tours
MUNI **Tours**; (415) 673-MUNI; public transport tours available on request
Near Escapes; (415) 386-8687; behind-the-scenes tour of San Francisco Zoo and the U.S.
    Naval Weapons Station, shopping tours of SoMa, backstage theater tours, cemetery
    tours, etc.
Starlane Tours; (415) 982-2223; bay cruises, nightclub tours, Chinatown dinner tour, etc.

W A T E R   T O U R S
Blue and Gold Fleet; (415) 781-7890; bay cruises
Dolphin Charters; (415) 527-9622; marine tours, whale watching
Golden Gate Ferry Service; (415) 332-6600; scheduled ferry service to Sausalito and
    Larkspur

M.V. Questuary; (510) 836-3230; tours from Jack London Square
Red and White Fleet; (415) 546-2896; bay tours and scheduled service to Sausalito, Alcatraz, Wine Country, Tiburon, Marine World, Angel Island
Starlane Tours; (415) 982-2223; bay cruises by day or night
Whale Watching Tours; (415) 474-3385; boats leave S.F. and Half Moon Bay for several hours outside the Golden Gate during whale migration season (January to April)

WALKING TOURS

Chinatown Adventure Tours with the Wok Wiz; (415) 355-9657; culinary and historical strolls with cookbook author and television chef Shirley Fong-Torres, with lunch or dinner
Chinese Culture Foundation; (415) 986-1822; culinary tour and heritage walk
City Guides; (415) 557-4266; architectural, cultural, and historical walking tours of City Hall, Civic Center, Coit Tower, Market Street, North Beach, Pacific Heights, fire houses, Mission District murals, Cathedral Hill, Japantown, Presidio, Gold Rush city (Jackson Square), Golden Gate Bridge, etc.
East Bay Regional Parks; (510) 531-9300; ranger-led tours and activities in most of the parks are geared for children and adults
Frisco Tours; (415) 681-5555; film, fiction, and witty crime tours by bus or on foot with author Mark Gordon
Golden Gate National Recreation Area; (415) 556-0560; ranger-led interpretive walks throughout the park, including Sutro Baths, Marin Headlands, Muir Woods, the Maritime Museum ships, Sutro Heights, photography walks, gun battery walks, tide pool walks, Tennessee Valley, Indian folklore walks, sunset walks, etc.
Helen's Walk Tours; (510) 524-4544; San Francisco neighborhood tours in English, French, Spanish, or Arabic
Heritage Walks; (415) 441-3000; architectural tours of Pacific Heights, Telegraph Hill, North Beach, Gold Rush S.F. and the Financial District
Landscape Architecture Tours; (415) 974-5430; annual tours of Downtown districts by the American Society of Landscape Architects
Literary Tours; (707) 939-1214; Don Herron leads a tour of Dashiell Hammett's haunts in S.F., sometimes in period costume; other literary tours (e.g., Russian Hill) can be arranged
Mexican Museum; (415) 441-0404; docent-led tours to S.F.'s Diego Rivera murals, self-guided Mission District mural tours
National Cemetery of San Francisco; (415) 561-2986; tours of the Presidio's National Cemetery are offered on Armed Forces Day and Memorial Day
Oakland Heritage Alliance; (510) 763-9218; architectural and historical tours of Oakland's neighborhoods and Mountain View Cemetery
Wing It!; (510) 235-5659 Oakland Chinatown tours

T O U R S   B Y   A I R
Commodore Helicopters; (415) 332-4482; sightseeing tours by helicopter
Helicopters Unlimited; (510) 632-9422; helicopter tours and shuttle service to and
  around the Golden Gate Bridge, Monterey and Carmel, the Wine Country

T O U R S   B Y   H O R S E
Sonoma Cattle Company; (707) 996-8566

BOOKSTORES

A Clean, Well Lighted Place for Books; 601 Van Ness Ave., S.F. (near Civic Center);
  (415) 441-6670; Larkspur Landing; (415) 461-0171; general
Acorn Books; 740 Polk St., S.F. (near Civic Center); (415) 563-1736; general, used
Albatross Bookstores; 166 Eddy Street, S.F. (Tenderloin); (415) 885-6501; general, used
Albatross III Book Shop; 143 Clement, S.F. (Richmond); (415) 752-8611; general, used
Argonaut Book Shop; 786 Sutter St., S.F. (near Union Square); (415) 474-9067;
  antiquarian
Arkadyan Books and Prints; 926 Irving St., S.F. (Sunset); (415) 664-6212; antiquarian
Asian Art Museum; Golden Gate Park, S.F.; (415) 668-8921; art
Avenue Books; 2904 College Ave., Berkeley; (510) 549-3532; general
Beard's Books; 637 Irving St., S.F. (Sunset); (415) 566-0507; general, used
Bell's Book Store; 536 Emerson St., Palo Alto; (415) 323-7822; general, antiquarian
Black Oak Books; 1491 Shattuck Ave., Berkeley; (510) 835-5845; general
Book Depot; 87 Throckmorton, Mill Valley; (415) 383-2665; general
Book Passage; 51 Tamal Vista, Corte Madera (Marin County); (415) 927-0960
Bookbuyers, The; 504 Emerson, Palo Alto; (415) 322-1993; general, records
Bookfriends; 3610A Sacramento St., S.F. (Pacific Heights); (415) 928-3610; general,
  children's; 633 Vallejo St., S.F. (North Beach); (415) 781-3329; China and Asian-
  American
Bookstall, The; 708 Sutter St., S.F. (near Union Square); (415) 673-5446; antiquarian
Brick Row Book Shop; third floor, 278 Post Street, S.F. (near Union Square);
  (415) 398-0414; antiquarian
Builder's Bookstore; 1817 4th, Berkeley; (510) 845 6874; architecture, landscape design
Campus Textbook Exchange; 2470 Bancroft Way, Berkeley; (510) 848-7700; general,
  used
City Lights; 261 Columbus, S.F. (North Beach); (415) 362-8193; general, small press,
  poetry
Cody's; 2454 Telegraph, Berkeley; (510) 845-7852; general
Complete Traveler, The; 3207 Fillmore, S.F.; (415) 923-1511

Cover to Cover Booksellers; 3910 24th St., S.F. (Noe Valley); (415) 282-8080; children's
Diesel, A Bookstore; 5820 Shellmound, Emeryville Marketplace, Emeryville (East Bay);
(510) 653-9965; general
Drama Books; 134 Ninth St., S.F. (South of Market, near Civic Center); (415) 255-0604;
theater
East West Bookshop; 1170 El Camino Real, Menlo Park (Peninsula); (415) 325-5709;
metaphysical
Eastwind Books and Arts, Inc.; 633 Vallejo St. and 1435-A Stockton St., S.F. (China-
town); (510) 781-3331; 1986 Shattuck Ave., Berkeley; (415) 548-2350; Chinese lan-
guage and culture
Easy Going; 1400 Shattuck, Berkeley; (510) 843-3533; 1617 Locust, Walnut Creek;
(510) 947-6660; travel, maps
Elsewhere Books; 260 Judah, S.F. (Sunset); (415) 661-2535; science fiction
European Book Company; 925 Larkin, S.F. (near Civic Center); (415) 474-0626;
European-language books
Fantasy; 808 Larkin, S.F. (edge of Tenderloin, near Polk Street); (415) 441-7617; fantasy
Green Apple; 506 Clement, S.F. (Richmond); (415) 387-2272; general, used
Gull Book & Print Gallery; 1551 San Pablo Ave., Oakland; (510) 836-9142; antiquarian,
general, used
Holmes Book Co.; 274 14th St., Oakland; (510) 893-6860; general, used
In and Out of Print Books; 401-A Judah, S.F. (Sunset); (415) 665-1116; general, used
Jack London; Glen Ellen; (707) 996-2888; antiquarian, Jack London
Jeremy Norman & Co. Inc.; 720 Market St., S.F. (near Union Square); (415) 781-6402;
antiquarian
John Scopazzi; 278 Post St., S.F. (near Union Square); (415) 362-5708; antiquarian
Jordan's Village Books; 3324 Village Drive, Castro Valley (East Bay); (510) 538-2249
Kepler's; 1010 El Camino Real, Menlo Park (Peninsula); (415) 324-4321; general
Kinokuniya; 1581 Webster St., S.F. (Japan Center); (415) 567-7625; Japanese language
and culture
M.H. de Young Museum; Golden Gate Park, S.F.; (415) 750-3600; art
Map Center/Wilderness Press; 2440 Bancroft Way, Berkeley; (510) 841-6277; maps,
travel, outdoors
Marcus Bookstore; 1712 Fillmore St., S.F. (Western Addition); (415) 346-4222; African-
American
Maritime Store, The; Hyde Street Pier, S.F. (near Fisherman's Wharf); (415) 775-2665;
nautical
Moe's; 2476 Telegraph, Berkeley; (510) 849-2087; general, used
Museum of Modern Art; Van Ness at McAllister, S.F. (Civic Center); (415) 863-8800; art
Natural Instincts; 600 Sycamore Valley Rd. West, Danville (East Bay); (510) 820-8654;
nature

Nature Company, The; 4 Embarcadero Center, S.F. (Financial District); (415) 956-4911; Fourth and Hearst, Berkeley; (510) 524-9052; Ghirardelli Square, S.F. (near Fisherman's Wharf); (415) 776-0724; nature

Ninth Avenue Book Store; 1348 9th Ave., S.F. (Sunset); (415) 665-2938; general, used

Owl Books; Blackhawk Plaza, Danville; (510) 736-2462; general

Pendragon New and Used Books; 5560 College Ave., Oakland; (510) 652-6259; general, used

Phileas Fogg; 87 Stanford Shopping Center, Palo Alto; (415) 327-1754; travel

Printer's Ink; 310 California Ave., Palo Alto; (415) 327-6500; 301 Castro St., Mountain View; (415) 961-8500; general

Rand McNally; 595 Market St., S.F. (Financial District); (415) 777-3131; travel, maps

Russian Books; 332 Balboa, S.F. (Richmond); (415) 668-4723; Russian language and culture

San Francisco Mystery Bookstore; 746 Diamond St., S.F. (Noe Valley); (415) 282-7444; mystery

San Francisco Opera Shop; 199 Grove St., S.F. (near Civic Center); (415) 565-6414; opera

Shakespeare and Co.; 2499 Telegraph, Berkeley; (510) 841-8916; general, used

Shambala; 2482 Telegraph, Berkeley; (510) 848-8443; metaphysics, religion

Sierra Club Bookstore; 730 Polk St., S.F. (near Civic Center); (415) 923-5600; 6014 College Ave., Oakland; (510) 658-7470; nature, ecology, travel

Stacey's Bookstore; 581 Market St., S.F. (Downtown); (415) 421-4687; 219 University Ave., Palo Alto; (415) 326-0681; general

Stanford Bookstore; 135 University Ave., Palo Alto; (415) 327-3680; medical, business

Stanford University Bookstore; White Plaza, Stanford University, Palo Alto; (415) 329-1217; general

Sunset Bookstore; 2161 Irving Street, S.F. (Sunset); (415) 664-3644; general, used

Thomas Brothers Maps; 550 Jackson St., S.F. (Jackson Square); (415) 981-7520; maps

University Press Books; 2430 Bancroft Way, Berkeley; (510) 548-0585; university press publications

US Geological Survey; 555 Battery St., S.F. (Financial District); (415) 705-1010; 345 Middlefield Rd., Menlo Park (San Mateo County); (415) 329-4390; topographical maps

US Government Printing Office and GPO Bookstore; 450 Golden Gate Ave., S.F. (near Civic Center); (415) 556-6657; government publications

Whales & Friends; 550 2nd St., Oakland; (510) 763-0585; Blackhawk Plaza, Danville; (510) 736-1161; nature, science

William Stout Architectural Books; 804 Montgomery, S.F. (Jackson Square); (415) 391-6757; architecture

Yerba Buena Books; 882 Bush St., S.F. (near Union Square); (415) 474-2788; antiquarian

Znanie Bookstore; 5237 Geary Blvd., S.F. (Richmond District); (415) 752-7555; Russian language and culture

MUSEUMS, AMUSEMENTS, AND CULTURAL CENTERS

African-American Historical and Cultural Society; Building C, Fort Mason, S.F.; (415) 441-0640

Air Force Museum; Travis Air Force Base, Fairfield; (707) 424-5000

Alcatraz; ferry leaves from Pier 41, near Fisherman's Wharf; (415) 546-2896

American Indian Contemporary Arts; 685 Market St., S.F.; (415) 495-7600

Ansel Adams Center; 250 Fourth St., S.F. (South of Market); (415) 495-7000

Ardenwood Historic Farm; Neward Blvd., Fremont (East Bay); (510) 796-0663

Asian Art Museum; Music Concourse, Golden Gate Park, S.F.; (415) 668-8921

Balclutha (See National Maritime Museum)

Bancroft Library; east side Doe Library, University of California, Berkeley; (510) 642-3781

Bank of American History Room; mezzanine, Bank of America, Montgomery at California; (415) 622-4997

Barbi Hall of Fame; 460 Waverley St., Palo Alto; (415) 326-5841

Bay Area Discovery Museum; 557 East Fort Baker (GGNRA, near Sausalito); (415) 332-9646

Bay Model; 2100 Bridgeway, Sausalito; (415) 332-3870

Behring Auto Museum; 3750 Blackhawk Plaza Circle, Danville; (510) 736-2277

Benicia Camel Barns; 2024 Camel Rd., Benicia; (707) 745-3385

Benicia Old State Capital Building; First at G streets, Benicia; (707) 745-3385

Black Diamond Mines Regional Preserve; Sommersville Rd., Contra Costa County (East Bay); (510) 757-2620

Boxing Museum; third floor Civic Auditorium, S.F. (Civic Center)

Cable Car Barn; Mason at Washington, S.F. (near Chinatown and Nob Hill); (415) 474-1887

California Academy of Sciences; Music Concourse, Golden Gate Park, S.F.; (415) 750-7145

California Marine Mammal Center; near Rodeo Beach, Golden Gate National Recreation Area; (415) 331-0161

California Palace of the Legion of Honor; Lincoln Park, S.F.; (415) 750-3600

Camron-Stanford House; 1418 Lakeside Drive, Oakland; (510) 836-1976

Cartoon Art Museum; 665 Third St., S.F. (South of Market); (415) 546-3922

Chevron Oil Museum; 557 Market St., S.F. (Financial District); (415) 894-4895

Children's Discovery Museum; corner of West San Carlos St. and Woz Way, San Jose; (408) 298-5437

China Camp State Park; five miles east of Marin County Civic Center; (415) 456-0766

Chinese Cultural Center; third floor, Chinatown Holiday Inn, 750 Kearny St., S.F. (Chinatown); (415) 433-6600

Chinese Historical Society; 650 Commercial St., S.F. (Financial District/Chinatown); (415) 391-1188

Coit Tower; Telegraph Hill; (415) 274-0203

Coyote Point Museum; Coyote Point, San Mateo; (415) 342-7755

Craft and Folk Art Museum; Building A, Fort Mason, S.F.; (415) 775-0990

de Saisset Museum; Santa Clara University, Santa Clara; (408) 554-4528

De Young Museum; see M.H. de Young Museum

Diego Rivera Gallery, San Francisco Art Institute; 800 Chestnut St., S.F. (Russian Hill); (415) 771-7020

Discovery Zone; 39103 Fremont Hub (at Mowry Ave.), Fremont; (510) 791-8900

Egyptian Museum (see Rosicrucian Egyptian Museum)

Electronics Museum (see Foothill College Electronics Museum)

Eugene O'Neill House (see Tao House)

Eureka (see National Maritime Museum)

Exploratorium; 3601 Lyon St., S.F. (Marina District); (415) 561-0360

Federal Reserve Bank; 101 Market St., S.F. (Financial District); (415) 882-9798

Filoli Estate; Canada Rd., near Woodside (San Mateo County); (415)364-2880

Fire Department Museum (See San Francisco Fire Department Museum)

Foothill College Electronics Museum; Foothill College, Los Altos Hills; (415) 949-7777

Fort Point; end of Marine Drive, S.F. (under the Golden Gate Bridge); (415) 921-8193

Garage, The; 145 W. San Carlos, San Jose; (408) 279-7150

Guinness Museum of World Records; 235 Jefferson St., S.F. (Fisherman's Wharf); (415) 771-9890

Haas-Lilienthal House; 2007 Franklin St., S.F. (Pacific Heights); (415) 441-3004

Hyde Street Pier (See National Maritime Museum)

Jack London State Park; Glen Ellen; (707) 938-5216

Jewish Community Museum; 121 Steuart St., S.F.; (415) 543-8880

John Muir House; 4202 Alhambra Ave., Martinez (East Bay); (510) 228-8860

Joseph D. Randall Junior Museum; 199 Museum Way (near Corona Heights Park), S.F.; (415) 863-1399

Judah L. Magnes Memorial Museum; 2911 Russell St., Berkeley; (510) 849-2710

Lachryma Montis; Third St. West, Sonoma; (707) 938-1519

Laserium; in Morrison Planetarium, Golden Gate Park; (415) 750-7138

Lawrence Hall of Science; Stadium Rim Road, University of California, Berkeley; (510) 642-5133

Lawrence Livermore Laboratory; Livermore; (510) 422-1100

Lazer Maze; 107 Jefferson St., San Francisco (Fisherman's Wharf); (415) 885-4975

Lick Observatory; Mount Hamilton, east of San Jose; (408) 274-5061

Lindsay Museum; 1901 First Ave., Walnut Creek (East Bay); (510) 935-1978

Lowie Museum of Anthropology; Kroeber Hall, University of California, Berkeley; (510) 643-7648

Luther Burbank Home and Gardens; 204 Santa Rosa Ave., Santa Rosa; (707) 576-5115

M.H. de Young Museum; Music Concourse, Golden Gate Park, S.F.; (415) 750-3600

Main Library History Room; third floor Main Library, S.F. (Civic Center); (415) 558-3949

Marin County Historical Museum; The Gatehouse, Mission at B streets, San Rafael; (415) 454-8538

Marin Museum of the American Indian; 2200 Novato Blvd., Novato; (415) 894-4064

Marine World Africa USA; 1000 Fairgrounds Ave., Vallejo; (707) 643-6722

Mexican Museum; Building D, Fort Mason, S.F.; (415) 441-0404

Mission Dolores; Dolores at 16th, S.F. (Mission District); (415) 621-8203

Mission San Jose; Mission at Washington boulevards, Fremont (East Bay); (510) 657-1797

Morrison Planetarium; Music Concourse, Golden Gate Park, S.F.; (415) 750-7141

Museo Italo Americano; Building C, Fort Mason, S.F.; (415) 673-2200

Musée Mechanique; Cliff House, S.F.; (415) 386-1170

Museum of Modern Art; Veterans Memorial Building, Van Ness Ave., S.F. (Civic Center); (415) 863-8800

Museum of Ophthalmology; 555 Beach St., S.F. (Fisherman's Wharf); (415) 561-8500

Museum of Photography; third floor, 45 Kearny at Maiden Lane, S.F. (shopping district); (415) 392-1900

Museum of Russian Culture; 2450 Sutter, S.F.; (415) 921-4082

Museum of the History of San Francisco; 3rd floor, The Cannery, S.F. (near Fisherman's Wharf)

Museum of the Money of the American West; basement, Bank of California, 400 California St., S.F. (Financial District); (415) 765-0400

NASA/Ames Research Center; Moffett Field, Mountain View; (415) 604-5000

National Maritime Museum; Beach at Polk, S.F. (near Fisherman's Wharf); (415) 556-8177

Navy, Marine Corps, Coast Guard Museum; Treasure Island Naval Base; (415) 765-6182

Niles Canyon Railway; Main Street Foothill Rd., Sunol (East Bay); (510) 462-4557

North Beach Museum; 1435 Stockton St., S.F. (North Beach)

Oakland Museum; 1000 Oak St., Oakland; (510) 273-3401

Octagon House; 2645 Gough at Union, Cow Hollow, S.F.; (415) 441-7512

Old U.S. Mint; Fifth at Mission, S.F. (South of Market); (415) 974-0788

Pacific Heritage Museum; 608 Commercial St., S.F. (Financial District)

Paleontology Museum; Earth Sciences Bldg., University of California, Berkeley; (510) 642-1821

Petaluma Adobe; 3325 Adobe Rd., Petaluma; (707) 762-4871

Petrified Forest; Petrified Forest Rd., Calistoga (Napa County); (707) 942-6667

Point Reyes Visitors' Center; Bear Valley, Point Reyes National Seashore; (415) 663-1092

Police Museum; fourth floor Civic Auditorium, S.F. (Civic Center); no phone

Precita Eyes Mural Arts Center; 534 Precita Ave., S.F. (Mission District); (415) 285-2287

Presidio Army Museum; Funston at Lincoln, S.F. (the Presidio); (415) 561-4115

Recyclery, The; 1601 Dixon Landing Rd., Milpitas (South Bay); (408) 262-1401

Ripley Museum; 492 Sonoma Ave., Santa Rosa; (707) 576-5233
Ripley's Believe It or Not Museum; 175 Jefferson St., S.F. (Fisherman's Wharf);
(415) 771-6188
Rosicrucian Egyptian Museum; Park Ave. at Naglee, San Jose; (408) 287-9171
SS *Jeremiah O'Brien*; Fort Mason, S.F. (see National Maritime Museum)
San Francisco Archives for the Performing Arts; 399 Grove at Gough, Civic Center, S.F.;
(415)255-4800
San Francisco Bay Model (see Bay Model)
San Francisco Craft and Folk Art Museum; Building A, Fort Mason, S.F.; (415) 775-
0990
San Francisco Fire Department Museum; 655 Presidio Ave., S.F. (Western Addition);
(415) 861-8000
San Francisco History Room; Main Library, Civic Center; (415) 558-3949
San Francisco International Toy Museum; The Cannery, S.F. (near Fisherman's Wharf);
(415) 441-8697
San Francisco Museum of Modern Art; Van Ness at McAllister, S.F. (Civic Center);
(415) 863-8800
San Francisco Performing Arts Library and Museum; Grove at Gough, S.F. (near
Civic Center); (415) 255-4800
San Francisco Zoo; Sloat Blvd. at 45th Ave., S.F. (Sunset District); (415) 661-2023
San Jose Museum of Art; 110 South Market St., San Jose; (408) 294-2787
Sharpsteen Museum; 1311 Washington St., St. Helena (Napa County); (707) 942-5916
Silverado Museum; 1490 Library Dr., St. Helena (Napa County); (707) 963-3757
Society of California Pioneers; 456 McAllister, S.F. (Civic Center); (415) 861-5278
Sonoma State Historical Park; Sonoma Plaza, Sonoma; (707) 938-1519
Stanford University Museum of Art; Museum Way, Stanford University, Palo Alto;
(415) 723-4177
Steinhart Aquarium; Music Concourse, Golden Gate Park, S.F.; (415) 750-7145
Surfing Museum; Lighthouse Point, Santa Cruz; (408) 429-3429
Tao House; Danville (East Bay); (510) 838-0249
Tattoo Art Museum; 837 Columbus, S.F. (North Beach); (415) 775-1262
Telephone Pioneer Communications Museum; 180 New Montgomery at Natoma, S.F.
(South of Market); (415) 542-7053
Treasure Island Museum (see Navy, Marine Corps, Coast Guard Museum)
USS *Pampanito* (see National Maritime Museum)
Underground Mining Museum (see Black Diamond Mines Regional Park)
University Art Museum; 2626 Bancroft Way, Berkeley; (510) 642-1207
University Botanical Gardens; Stadium Rim Road, University of California, Berkeley;
(510) 642-3343
University of California at Berkeley Museum, The; Blackhawk Plaza, Danville; (510)
736-2277

Vallejo's House (see **Lachryma Montis**)

Villa Montalvo; 15400 Montalvo Rd., Saratoga; (408) 741-3421

Wax Museum at Fisherman's Wharf; 145 Jefferson St., S.F. (Fisherman's Wharf); (415) 885-4975

Wells Fargo History Room; 420 Montgomery St., S.F. (Financial District); (415) 396-2619

Winchester Mystery House; 525 South Winchester Blvd., San Jose; (408) 247-2101

I N D E X

DISCOVER AMERICA
WITH COMPASS AMERICAN GUIDES

WRITTEN FOR THE "LITERATE TRAVELER," this series of guides conjures up the images, explores the myths and legends, and reveals the spirit of the cities and states of the Great American West and Canada. Each title gives voice to the place in such a way that these books are less destination guides than guides to the people, landscape, communities, and cultures that shape the character of North America.

Superb color photography commissioned from internationally acclaimed photographers captures what is contemporary, while archival illustrations bring the past alive.

Meticulous maps and extensive indexes provide an easy-to-use reference guide. An informative back section in each guide covers accommodations, dining, tours, and other tips essential for the traveler.

Compass American Guides are available in general and travel bookstores, or may be ordered directly from the publisher by sending a check or money order, including the cost of shipping and handling, payable to: Compass American Guides, Inc., 6051 Margarido Dr., Oakland, CA 94618. Tel. (510) 547-7233. Or ask your bookseller to order for you.

Shipping & Handling Charges: Domestic UPS or USPS 1st Class (allow 10 working days for delivery): $3.50 for the 1st book, 50¢ for each additional book. California residents should include 6% sales tax.

Booksellers: Compass American Guides are distributed to the trade by Publishers Group West, and are also available from Ingram, Baker & Taylor, Gordon's, Pacific Pipeline, and other regional wholesalers.

Prices: All prices are subject to change.

CITIES

San Francisco and the Bay Area San Francisco has something for everyone, whether your taste runs to cappuccino or dim sum, to downtown honky tonk or Davies Symphony Hall. Special emphasis on the surrounding Bay Area, from the wine country of the Napa Valley to the markets of the East Bay.
Author: Barry Parr—Photographer: Michael Yamashita
ISBN 1-878867-16-4; 396pp.; Price $14.95

Las Vegas Deke Castleman's rollicking introduction to the capital of glitz, with a tale of fifty hotels, a celebration of tacky museums, a guide to quick weddings and sign language, and, of course, a system for playing slots, craps, blackjack, poker, and other games of chance.
Author: Deke Castleman—Photographer: Michael Yamashita
ISBN 1-878867-01-6; 302pp.; $12.95

WESTERN STATES

Wyoming High, wide and handsome, a land where tales of Indians, pioneers, gun slingers, cattle barons, cowboys and other characters of the Old West still cling to life. Nat Burt, son of pioneering dude ranchers, roams the state where the myth of the cowboy was born.
Author: Nathaniel Burt—Photographer: Don Pitcher
ISBN 1-878867-04-0; 396pp.; Price $14.95

Utah Unspoiled as the day Brigham Young proclaimed "this is the right place," this land of red-rock canyons and snow-capped mountains offers glorious scenery and a glimpse of the magnificent cliff-dwellings of the ancient Anasazi Indians. Special emphasis on outdoor recreation.
Authors: Tom & Gayen Wharton—Photographer: Tom Till
ISBN 1-878867-09-1; 364pp.; Price $14.95

Arizona From hidden canyons to museums of archaeology, from the civilized pleasures of Phoenix to jagged wildlands, author Larry Cheek reveals Arizona's scenic, cultural, and historical attractions and colorful eccentricities.
Author: Larry Cheek—Photographer: Michael Freeman
ISBN 1-878867-08-3; 320pp.; Price $14.95

Montana Love of land and sky runs deep in Montana. Mountain ranges with names like the Crazies, Snowies, and Sapphires. Legendary rivers—the Madison, Big Hole, Yellowstone, and Missouri. Curiouser creeks—Froze-to-Death, Stinking Water, and Hellroaring. High plains, once home to herds of buffalo, still offer wide vistas to the eye and soul. This Land of the Big Sky may well be the last best place.
Author: Norma Tirrell—Photographer: John Reddy
ISBN 1-878867-10-5; 304pp.; Price $14.95

New Mexico Space, light, purity—New Mexico has cast a magical spell of mystery over its inhabitants for centuries. Native Americans expressed their reverential relationship with the land through their art. In more recent times, artist Georgia O'Keeffe and writer D.H. Lawrence settled here hoping to capture the seemingly indescribable. In spite of their efforts, and those of many others, there is only one way to appreciate New Mexico—by experiencing it.
Author: Nancy Harbert—Photographer: Michael Freeman
ISBN 1-878867-06-7; 288pp.; Price $14.95

C A N A D A

Canada Veteran journalist Garry Marchant approaches the second largest country in the world as not one, but six different nations. Special sections on the Inuits, Canadian sports, rail hotels, 'Newfies,' Quebecois culture and the Calgary Stampede.
Author: Garry Marchant—Photographer: Ken Straiton
ISBN 1-878867-12-1; 320pp.; $14.95

"Books can make thoughtful (and sometimes even thought-provoking) gifts for incentive travel winners or convention attendees. A new series of guidebooks published by Compass American Guides is right on the mark."
—SUCCESSFUL MEETINGS *magazine*

Consider Compass American Guides as gifts or incentives for VIP's, employees, clients, customers, convention and meeting attendees, friends and others. Quantity discounts and customized editions are available. For catalog and further information please write to Marketing Director, Compass American Guides, 6051 Margarido Drive, Oakland, CA 94618, or call (510) 547-7233.

■ ABOUT THE AUTHOR

Born and raised in the San Francisco Bay Area, writer and editor Barry Parr brings to this guide both a native's first-hand knowledge of the city and the perspective of a world traveler. Mr. Parr earned degrees in English literature from the University of California at Berkeley and from Cambridge University in England. He has lived for several years in England and Hong Kong, where he worked as a magazine editor and writer. He has contributed articles to *Travel and Leisure, Discovery, Mandarin, Asiaweek, PATA Travel News,* and other publications. Once again residing in the Bay Area, he enjoys spending his free time with his wife and two children and partaking of the urban and rustic pleasures of life in Northern California.

■ ABOUT THE PHOTOGRAPHER

San Francisco-born photographer, Michael S. Yamashita, has been shooting pictures for National Geographic Society magazines and books since 1979. He is a frequent contributor to *Travel and Leisure* and *Portfolio,* and his many corporate clients include the Mexican Tourist Board, Singapore Airlines, and Nikon Cameras. While on assignment for these clients and other publications, he has covered locations worldwide.

Mr. Yamashita's work has been exhibited at the Smithsonian Institution's Museum of American History, the National Gallery in Washington, and Kodak's Professional Photographer's Showcase at EPCOT Center in Florida. His work has received citations from the Pacific Area Travel Association, and the Asian-American Journalists Association.